W9-AXE-104

Churchill & His Generals

MODERN WAR STUDIES

Theodore A. Wilson
General Editor

Raymond Callahan
J. Garry Clifford
Jacob W. Kipp
Jay Luvaas
Allan R. Millett
Carol Reardon
Dennis Showalter
David R. Stone
Series Editors

Churchill & His Generals

Raymond Callahan

University Press of Kansas

© 2007 by the University Press of Kansas
All rights reserved

Published by the University Press of Kansas (Lawrence, Kansas 66045), which was organized by the Kansas Board of Regents and is operated and funded by Emporia State University, Fort Hays State University, Kansas State University, Pittsburg State University, the University of Kansas, and Wichita State University

Library of Congress Cataloging-in-Publication Data

Callahan, Raymond.
Churchill & his generals / Raymond Callahan.
p. cm. — (Modern war studies)
Includes bibliographical references and index.
ISBN 978-0-7006-1512-4 (cloth : alk. paper)
1. Great Britain. Army—History—World War, 1939–1945. 2. Great Britain. Army—Drill and tactics—History. 3. World War, 1939–1945—Great Britain. I. Title.
II. Title: Churchill and his generals.

D759.C256 2007
940.54′1241—dc22
2007006194

Printed in the United States of America

10 9 8 7 6 5 4 3 2 1

The paper used in this publication meets the minimum requirements of the American National Standard for Permanence of Paper for Printed Library Materials Z39.48-1992.

To Mary Helen, who never let me forget . . .
and to Aidan and Shaun, who may someday read this.

Contents

Acknowledgments

I began thinking about the issues explored in this book while researching and writing studies of the fall of Singapore and the Burma campaign some thirty years ago. Three individuals who greatly helped me then and so got the present book started are sadly no longer alive to receive my thanks in person: Bill Reader, a Fourteenth Army veteran and a fine historian of organizational success and failure; Lieutenant General Sir Ian Jacob; and Ronald Lewin.

I decided to write the book while spending a memorable year as John F. Morrison Professor at the Combat Studies Institute of the U.S. Army's Command and General Staff College, where the company and conversation of Ed Drea and Roger Cirillo were extremely stimulating. Lectures at the U.S. Marine Corps Staff College gave me a chance to field-test some ideas, as did papers presented at conferences in Cambridge, England, and Singapore. I thank all those who listened carefully and offered criticisms and suggestions.

I had begun drafting the book when my career moved into academic administration. Mike Briggs of the University Press of Kansas and Professor Theodore Wilson, general editor of its Modern War Studies, were very understanding while I tried to move the project forward amid the many distractions of my new life. Students in the graduate seminar I was still able to teach were most patient as I tried ideas out on them.

Dean Mark Huddleston of the University of Delaware (UD) College of Arts and Sciences was immensely helpful in allowing me to carve out the time necessary to get the manuscript resurrected and advance it to completion, and a UD retirement sabbatical did the rest. A tricky problem in retrieving early drafts from cyberspace was solved by Timothy Miller, also of the University of Delaware. Allen Packwood and his dedicated staff at the Churchill Archive Centre at Churchill College, Cambridge, were most supportive as I did the final bits of research, and Hal Winton made very helpful suggestions for final revisions. My greatest debt is recorded in the dedication.

Prelude:
An Evening at Chequers

On the evening of Sunday, April 27, 1941, Winston Churchill broadcast a message to the nation from Chequers, the official country residence of British prime ministers since 1917. He had arrived there from a whirlwind tour of Manchester, Liverpool, and the Merseyside, all vital industrial areas that had been heavily blitzed (up to that weekend, the Luftwaffe had launched sixteen major night attacks in April). As he left London to begin his tour, the evacuation of British forces from Greece was getting under way, a setback balanced by the extension of the American "security zone" 2,000 miles into the Atlantic. This latter action, symbolic of American support and promising some relief from the strains of the war against the U-boats, came in a month when 195 ships totaling some 700,000 tons were lost. But even the Blitz, Greece, and the Battle of the Atlantic were not the sum total of Churchill's concerns. Confrontation with Japan was a real possibility. A pro-Axis revolt in Iraq imperiled Britain's control of a key position in its vast Middle Eastern base area. And a hitherto unknown German general, Erwin Rommel, had erased in a week all the gains that had been made in the successful British desert offensive against the Italians the previous winter (from December 1940 to February 1941). Hustled back to the frontier of Egypt, the British had left behind an Australian division, isolated and besieged in the port town of Tobruk.

Churchill had to put the best face he could on all this when he broadcast that evening. He did so in his own incomparable fashion, grimly reciting the defeats and retreats but balancing them by reference to growing American help and reiterating his conviction that ultimate victory was assured: "No prudent and far-seeing man can doubt that the eventual and total defeat of Hitler and Mussolini is certain, in view of the respective declared resolves of the British and American democracies." He concluded by reading a poem, redolent of exertion and hope, by the Victorian poet Arthur

Hugh Clough. Its final, and most apposite, line was "But westward, look, the land is bright."

Pausing only to telephone an old friend, Lady Violet Bonham Carter, to remind her that she had introduced him to Clough's poem thirty-five years before, Churchill went in to dinner with his guests, among them Major General John Kennedy, the director of military operations at the War Office, and General Sir Alan Brooke, the commander-in-chief, Home Forces. During the meal, Kennedy began discussing contingency planning with Churchill. Expressing the War Office view that an invasion of Britain was still a possibility, Kennedy argued that the retention of Egypt was not as important as making secure both the home islands and Singapore, the bastion of Britain's position in the Far East. It was not the right moment to argue that losing Egypt to Rommel would not necessarily be fatal. "Wavell has 400,000 men," Churchill declared. "If they lose Egypt, blood will flow. I will have firing parties to shoot the generals."[1] Kennedy made a bad situation worse by pointing out that Wavell already had contingency plans covering the possible loss of Egypt. "I never heard such ideas," the prime minister replied. "War is a contest of wills. It is pure defeatism to speak as you have done." The party rose from the table at midnight, but the argument rumbled on in Chequers's Great Hall until 3:00 A.M. Churchill repeatedly came up to Kennedy and reiterated the Napoleonic dictum about the role of willpower in war, alternately reminding him of the example of Ferdinand Foch, the great French apostle of offensive determination during World War I. At some point in the course of the evening, according to Brooke's postwar recollections, the prime minister denounced generals who were "only too ready to surrender, and who should be made examples of, like Admiral Byng."[2] Finally, after a concluding sally—"The German advance in Cyrenaica was the quintessence of generalship. It is generalship we need in Egypt"—Churchill retired to bed.

General Sir John Dill, the chief of the Imperial General Staff (CIGS) and Kennedy's boss, attended a meeting with the prime minister the following day and discovered how blazingly angry Churchill still was. Alerted by Dill, Kennedy hastily wrote a placatory note, seeking to clear himself of any imputation of defeatism: "I have never believed, and never will, that we can lose this war. No one under your leadership can believe such a thing." One of Churchill's most emotional directives, however, was already on its way to the War Office: "It is to be impressed on all ranks, especially the highest, that the life and honor of Great Britain depends on the successful defense of Egypt. No surrenders by officers and men will be considered tolerable unless at least 50 percent casualties are sustained by the unit or force in question . . . Generals and Staff Officers surprised by the enemy are to use their pistols in self-defense."[3] This out of his system, Churchill replied on Tuesday to Kennedy's letter. "My dear General, our conversation was purely personal and private," he wrote. "I do not agree with your views but you were perfectly entitled to express them."[4]

Wartime tensions between military and political leaders are inevitable. There is no easy formula for resolving these disagreements. The mantras "civilian supremacy" and "military professionalism" shed no light upon how, in any specific case, disputes are best resolved. A careful study of episodes for which we have full information can, however, provide some sense of how complex these issues truly are—and a warning against believing that simplistic solutions are ever available. Winston Churchill's relations with the British Army form exactly such a case. Admirals, air marshals, civil servants, and political colleagues all felt the lash of his tongue, but nothing he said about the other services or any government department came near to the depth of concern he displayed over the leadership and fighting spirit of the British Army. During the war, Churchill's minutes, cables, and conversations were full of criticism of British generalship. That criticism, although more carefully phrased, was repeated in his memoirs, a work that still shapes the popular history of the war in the English-speaking world.

Churchill was a person of vast experience, formidable energy, and clear ideas about what the British Army should do and how it should set about doing it. The generals with whom he dealt were also experienced, courageous, and (despite much mythology to the contrary) for the most part professionally able. But they had different views—sometimes very different—of what was wise or even possible. Lurking behind these differences was the issue of what the British Army was in fact trained and equipped or could be retrained and reequipped (in today's jargon, transformed) to do. Such a military transformation, if it was to be undertaken at all, would be enormously complicated because it needed to be achieved under wartime conditions. All in all, there was a lot to quarrel about.

In defense of Churchill's position, it should be noted that his wartime complaints and postwar commentary about British generalship were echoed within the British Army. When selections from Brooke's wartime diaries were first published between 1957 and 1959, embedded in Sir Arthur Bryant's florid prose, it became clear not only that Brooke's relations with the prime minister after he became CIGS in late 1941 were often fraught but also that Brooke himself was concerned with the quality of his generals.[5] Further support for the view that there were problems with the way the British Army was commanded came in 1958 when the best known—and, by some British and most American officers, the least liked—British general of the war, Bernard Montgomery, published his notorious *Memoirs*.[6] "Monty" was very critical, directly or by implication, of most of his colleagues and superiors, with the important exception of his patron, Brooke. If Brooke (who was no pushover, even for Churchill) and Monty both criticized British generalship, perhaps Churchill's concerns were soundly based?

But if views during the twenty years after the war were shaped by the memoirs and biographies (authorized and otherwise) of participants, the moment inevitably came when those participants had passed from the scene and the records began to open. More objective assessments then began to appear, and the picture began to change. After 1918, the British Army had never been given a clear mission that would in turn have helped shape doctrine, training, and equipment. It went to war in 1939 with no settled doctrine, in the midst of trying to modernize its equipment and with its junior officers and soldiers trained in a way that discouraged initiative. Then came three years of defeat followed by retreat and evacuation (for the fortunate) or surrender. The British Army was playing catch-up in all areas while trying to fight a major war—and from 1942 on, doing so with an uneasy awareness of its steadily dwindling manpower reserves. Given its relatively small population, upon which multiple pressing demands were made, Britain fielded the smallest army of any major combatant. And from 1943 on, even that army could not be kept up to strength. Wellington's observation that he had to take good care of his army because it was Britain's last applied with even greater force to the British Army of World War II, a fact not lost on its senior commanders. For a nation that still aspired to Great-Power status, full participation in the defeat of Germany was essential. But demography counseled prudence, and unreadiness in many spheres made the cost of imprudence unusually high.

Looked at from this perspective, the British Army's story is one of institutional transformation under extreme stress, with impressive results. New commanders came to the fore, and new techniques were developed. Some deeply embedded problems and characteristics remained to the end, but by 1943, new skills were in evidence as well. The British Army, even as it inexorably shrank, gave some impressive battlefield performances, while also showing how hard it is to wean institutions from deeply ingrained habits and patterns of behavior. Churchill's criticisms had some validity, as did Brooke's and Monty's, but they were far from the whole story. Indeed, one aspect of Britain's war—the long Burma campaign waged largely by the Indian Army—was one of the most dramatic examples World War II afforded of the rebuilding of a badly beaten army into a tactically and operationally sophisticated fighting force, comparable in some ways to the Russian military renaissance from 1943 to 1945. It was also a campaign that threw up the best British military commander since Wellington, "Bill" Slim. Readers of Churchill and Brooke catch only a faint echo of this, however, since the war that mattered most to the prime minister, the CIGS, and most of the British public was the war against Germany.

The story of why the British Army fought as it did is not very well known (except by specialist historians) in the United States, where the British contribution to the defeat of the Wehrmacht is all too often reduced to a discussion of how wrong Monty was, and the Burma campaign has never been part of American popular consciousness of the war. The relationship of political leaders' aims and their armies' capabilities is, however, again a matter of intense discussion, and Churchill, "the greatest war statesman of the century," is once again invoked to validate the assumption by civilian leaders of authority over the details of military engagement.[7] The time seems ripe, therefore, to revisit the issue of Churchill's expectations and the military's performance in the last great war imperial Britain would fight. Military transformations are, after all, a subject of continuing interest, and politicians and generals still disagree about how best to fight wars, what is meant by victory, and how to reconcile the tensions that arise when two very different sets of responsibilities and skills must coexist in the most stressful of environments.

1

Legacies

"I thought I knew a great deal about it all," Winston Churchill wrote, describing (nearly a decade after the event) his feelings on becoming prime minister. There is no reason to doubt that these words accurately summarized his assessment of his own capacities to direct Britain's war. Fifty years on, dissenting opinions have been entered against Churchill's summary judgment—one of the first, and still among the most powerful, by his wartime collaborator Field Marshal Lord Alanbrooke, in diaries partially published shortly after Churchill's final retirement. What in Churchill's past made him so sure in 1940 that he could function effectively not only as prime minister but, in his newly created office of minister of defense, also as general manager of Britain's war effort?

Churchill's personality is perhaps the starting point. As a young man, he was aggressive, frighteningly ambitious, and boundlessly self-confident. He was also brilliant, voluble, witty, and often charming. He antagonized many—perhaps as many as he enthralled. Over the years, some of the sharper edges of Churchill's personality may have become rounded, but the young cavalry officer–cum–war correspondent of the late 1890s was still visible in the national leader of 1940, and those who had to work with or for him still found themselves captivated, inspired, infuriated, and frightened by Churchill.[1] The observable continuities in his personality can lead to the assumption that his ideas, in particular his ideas about war, were also firmly rooted in the Victorian years of his youth.[2] This would be a mistake.

Churchill's formal military training began and ended at Sandhurst. In his four years with the 4th Hussars, he contrived to see a great deal of action in the empire's frontier wars; he certainly knew combat, but it was of a type already then fading into history. After leaving the regular army for politics, he kept what today would be called a reserve commission in the Oxfordshire Hussars, but his principal contacts and activities with the armed forces prior to 1914 were with the navy (whose civilian head, or First Lord, he became in 1911) rather than the army and had as much to do with questions of organization, administration, and matériel as with strategy and tactics—the latter being the areas where his mentor, Admiral Sir John Fisher, was weakest. Prior to 1914, Churchill's military background was that of a field-grade reserve officer with a great deal of obsolete subaltern combat experience and a taste for military history. At the level at which a national war leader operates, he knew far more that was useful about the navy than he did about the army. It was not his subaltern experiences as a 4th Hussar, however, but World War I that stamped itself on his views of land warfare.

Churchill's World War I career is so well known that it requires no recapitulation here, but certain aspects are worth highlighting. Until May 1915, he was responsible for the Admiralty (where he was deeply and controversially involved in operational detail), and in addition, as a key member of Herbert Henry "H. H." Asquith's cabinet, he took part in the formulation of national and alliance strategy. He saw firsthand not only the terrible pressures and dilemmas of total war but also how hard it was to formulate and execute national—or even theater—strategy with a flawed instrument of central command and control. Even after he left the Admiralty in May 1915, an impotent and increasingly bitter observer, he retained for six months a seat on the policymaking Dardanelles Committee, Asquith's inchoate War Cabinet. When Churchill got a chance to rebuild his political career in 1917, it was as minister of munitions, the position in which the mobilization of manpower, industrial effort, and technological innovation to support total war was coordinated.

However vivid Churchill's memories of war on the North-West Frontier of India, in the Sudan, or in South Africa may have been, they paled before the terrible reality of the Western Front. Present at the siege of Antwerp in the war's opening weeks, he later commanded an infantry battalion in the trenches for five months (thus acquiring more frontline combat experience than some U.S. Army officers who would rise to senior positions in World War II). As minister of munitions, he interpreted the need to stay in touch with the users of his ministry's products as requiring him to visit the front in France on a frequent basis, and he happened to be at a divisional command post shortly before the great German offensive of March 1918 fell on the British front lines. Realizing at an early date that the stalemate on the Western Front would not be quickly or easily broken, Churchill became one of a number of searchers for a new technological solution to the impasse technology had created. His drive—and his position at the

Admiralty—made him one of the godfathers of the tank, a weapon he later had the satisfaction of mass-producing as minister of munitions. Out of the searing experience between 1914 and 1918, Churchill learned much about the formulation and execution of strategy; about the mechanism for central direction of a national war effort; and about concentrating the manpower, production, and ingenuity of a nation in support of a total war effort. He learned as well how formidable an opponent the German army could be, how terrible were the costs of ill-considered plans, and what industrialized total war was like at the "sharp end." If the years from 1914 to 1918 conditioned British thinking, civil and military, about war, they conditioned Churchill's as well.

Churchill's multivolume memoir on the war, *The World Crisis*—part apologia, part analysis, part money earner—is not read nearly as widely as his massive *Second World War.*[3] This is unfortunate. Written by a brilliant controversialist in his prime, it tells the reader what Churchill felt had been well—or poorly—done in World War I. That assessment would shape and color much that he would do from 1940 to 1945. His reflections on the experience of total war in *The World Crisis* were reinforced a decade later when, out of office and in need of money as always, he began a long meditated study of his great ancestor, John Churchill, the first Duke of Marlborough.[4] The resulting volumes, as has often been pointed out, have serious defects as both history and biography, but they are fascinating when looked at as Churchill's thoughts on coalition war. The War of the Spanish Succession (1703–1713), like the two twentieth-century world wars, was fought by an alliance created to contain a would-be European hegemon. Marlborough's role, if not exactly comparable to that of his illustrious descendant in World War II, was certainly similar in some ways to General Dwight D. Eisenhower's in that struggle. When Churchill approached both the conduct of total war and the difficulties of coalition war, he did so against a unique background of experience and reflection. This background is probably more important in assessing his relations with the British Army's leadership than his contacts with that group in the 1920s and 1930s.

In 1919, the prime minister, David Lloyd George, gave Churchill the responsibility for both the army and the fledgling Royal Air Force (RAF). The problems of demobilization, insurgency in Ireland, intervention in Russia, the reestablishment of the army on a peacetime basis, and the future of the infant RAF were all-consuming. How the British Army would fight the next war was a marginal concern to Churchill at that moment. After he left the War Office in 1921, his contact with the army was not very significant. As chancellor of the exchequer (from 1925 to 1929), he shaped the budgets of all three services, but the great defense issue of those years was the Royal Navy's cruiser strength, not the army's future configuration. When Churchill left office in 1929 and two years later consigned himself to the "wilderness" by resigning from the Conservative shadow cabinet over India, another major land war in Europe still seemed remote.

During the ensuing decade, while Churchill wrote his Marlborough books and the first draft of what became *The History of the English-Speaking Peoples* and spoke against appeasement (as well as for continued British control of India and the cause of Edward VIII), a great argument raged in the British Army over mechanization and mobility. This contest, which involved both reformers within the army and "defense intellectuals" such as B. H. Liddell Hart, revolved around not only the shape of a future European war but also Britain's likely contribution to that war, not only what was possible but also what Britain could—or ought to—afford. Clearly, Churchill was aware of all this: he knew Liddell Hart, and common opposition to appeasement drew them together in the late 1930s. His interests where defense matters were concerned, however, lay elsewhere—the organization of a ministry of defense (which, coincidentally, he might occupy) and, above all, in the face of a growing Luftwaffe, the adequacy of Britain's air defenses. Moreover, Churchill's numerous contacts in the French army, which he clearly regarded as the premier European military force, would not have focused his attention on mechanization and mobile warfare, since most French generals were conservative in their approach to the latter-day "military revolution" wrought by the internal combustion engine. Churchill was being substantially accurate when he admitted, in the second volume of his war memoirs, "I did not comprehend the violence of the revolution effected since the last war by the incursion of a mass of fast moving heavy armor. I knew about it but it had not altered my inward convictions as it should have done. There was nothing I could have done if it had."[5] It was perhaps his greatest initial deficiency as minister of defense that, cavalryman though he had once been, the full meaning of the impact of mechanization on war was, at least initially, something he missed. Of course, the same could be said of many British and French generals.

Much, then, that he would need to function as a national war leader Churchill did in fact know, even if there were gaps and misperceptions. Above all, he understood the link that Carl von Clausewitz's oft-quoted sentence posits between policy and strategy. He understood that the goals of British policy—national survival, a restored European balance, and continued British membership in the small club of Great Powers—would have to shape national strategy. He grasped as well the Clausewitzian dictum that war is violence carried to its logical extreme. Translated into his own idiom, that became the Churchillian dictum that "in war, armies must fight." He was, of course, pugnacious by nature, but his desire to see the British Army succeed on the battlefield was not simply displaced personal aggression, memories of the Malakand Field Force, or false analogies with Marlborough's wars. It was, rather, the clear sense that policy required victorious campaigning, since victory was the currency used in alliance politics. It was his generals' failure to supply that currency, when and where needed, that lay at the root of Churchill's frustration with the British Army. Could it win? More ominously, did it even know how to?

But if Churchill did indeed know "a great deal about it all," there were nonetheless important gaps in his knowledge. These gaps produced some of his sharpest clashes with British (as well as American) generals during the war. He was impatient with the logistic problems whose solution is the foundation of strategy, and this impatience produced the endless arguments over the ratio between "teeth and tail" (that is, combat versus support formations). Curiously, in his Marlborough volumes, he had noted and commended the duke's great care for his logistics. Yet it is important to remember that even if Churchill did not have the staff college education that might have given him a more balanced view of this and other issues, he did have three superb staff officers—Hastings Ismay, Ian Jacob, and Leslie Hollis—supporting him in his capacity as minister of defense. He had as well Professor Frederick Lindeman's statistical section to give him an independent assessment of the data used by service departments and theater commanders. (It is also useful to remember that the legacy of its past had left the British Army with a bias toward logistic caution.)

But if Churchill's understanding of the links between operations and logistics was weaker than his grasp of the dynamics of strategy and alliance politics, perhaps his greatest weakness was not intellectual but emotional. He was a confrontational and aggressive person who obviously had struggled in his youth with concerns about his own physical toughness and courage. All his life, he tended not only to admire bravery but also to assume that well-attested courage was proof that an individual had as well those other traits of mind and character that would qualify him for high-level political and military responsibilities. He deeply admired holders of the Victoria Cross; he felt decorated ex-officers would make appealing Conservative candidates in 1945. This impulse to equate courage with abilities of a very different sort accounts in part for his support for Admiral of the Fleet Sir Roger Keyes, VC, the first director of Combined Operations, as well as his admiration for Bernard Freyberg, VC, and the gallant, much-decorated Harold Alexander. If courage was twinned with a romance long gone from large-scale industrialized war—as in the cases of T. E. Lawrence and Orde Wingate—Churchill tended to be far less critical in evaluating their concepts and activities than he was when he turned his mind to less charismatic, if more conventional and professional, soldiers.[6]

Churchill's strengths and weaknesses, not to mention his restless activism, would have made for a complex and fraught pattern of relationships with the British Army in any case, but the final touch was added by his sense of what was at stake, how narrow Britain's margins were, the daily cost of the war effort to the nation—and the fear that incapacity or irresolution was squandering opportunities and resources that might never come again.

It is impossible to assess Britain's generals—or Churchill's relationship to them—without first looking briefly at the army they commanded. Generals' tools are, after all, the units they control. Those units in turn are more than the sum of the official doctrine added to the soldiers and equipment on organization charts. Morale, leadership, training—all the intangibles that are so hard to quantify but that, time and again, decide battles and wars—have to be considered as well. Finally, there is the inescapable fact that societies differ. Attitudes and values brought into armies from the larger society survive, muted perhaps, as a factor even more difficult to measure but nonetheless crucial to the way a given army functions. So any analysis of British generalship has to begin with a brief look at the weapon the generals sought to wield and the forces that had shaped it.

The first of those forces was the fact that Britain was a small country waging a very big war. Ruthless use of its own assets (especially after Churchill took over) and the ability to draw on American factories allowed it to mount a war effort well in excess of its intrinsic strength. Churchill openly acknowledged this fact in the first chapter of *Their Finest Hour*, published in 1948, but it is often overlooked. Although American lend-lease aid could provide goods, however, it could not cure the most basic problem of all: the lack of men. From their own population (which they mobilized with great thoroughness, including very large numbers of women), the British had to maintain the maximum possible industrial and agricultural output, staff the Royal and merchant navies and the Royal Air Force (whose heavy bombers were at one point seen as a lonely Britain's one real hope of victory), and provide an army. In the course of World War II, the British Army raised forty-six divisions—some of which were disbanded at later stages of the war—and by 1944, British manpower was insufficient to keep even a thirty-five-division army up to strength. The basic fact with which all British generals had to contend was that if Napoleon was correct about God's partiality for big battalions, they did not have enough men to ensure his constant goodwill.[7]

Demographics held the British Army to a size that made it the smallest of the major combatants' forces. In addition, its generals had to deal with the legacies of Britain's military past, its social structure, and its industrial deficiencies. These factors together ensured that Britain would have not only a small army but also one unready for the war to which it was committed in 1939.

From the early eighteenth century, when Britain emerged as a Great Power, until 1914, the Royal Navy had been the key element in national strategy. When British armies fought on the Continent, as they did under Marlborough, again during the Seven Years' War (1756–1763), and yet again in the long wars against Napoleon, they did so as part of a coalition. Often called into being by British diplomacy and invariably financed by British subsidies, these coalitions were the natural response of a wealthy maritime and commercial power with limited military resources to the problem of how to confront a powerful continental state. The troops sent to Flanders or Germany or Spain (usually relatively small expeditionary forces, swelled by hired German troops) were a gauge of Britain's commitment to the defeat of a common enemy. They were not, by themselves, expected to be the decisive force, nor were they. This all began to change early in the twentieth century. The German threat to the European balance of power drew Britain inexorably toward a coalition with France and later Russia. Army reformers in England were simultaneously working to remedy the multitudinous weaknesses exposed by the Boer War. They also argued for a national strategy that would put the army on an equal footing with the navy. Circumstances favored them. The Royal Navy had no impressive spokesperson for its strategic vision, such as it was, and the French certainly wanted a visible British commitment in the form of British soldiers on the ground in France. Out of all this, the "continental commitment" was born.

Between 1914 and 1918, the British fielded the largest mass army in their history, eighty-four divisions (nearly double the 1939–1945 total). Over 22 percent of the male population of the United Kingdom served in the army. In World War I, the British Expeditionary Force (BEF) played a central role on the most crucial front (for, unlike the situation in World War II, the Russian army could collapse without assuring German victory). After the grinding attrition of Verdun in 1916 and General Robert Nivelle's disastrous 1917 offensive had temporarily wrecked the French army, the British Expeditionary Force carried the burden of the war on the Western Front, absorbed the hardest blows in the last great German drive in the spring of 1918, and drove relentlessly forward in attack from August until the armistice. The price for all this was very heavy. In numbers, nearly half of the 4.9 million wartime enlistments became casualties—700,000 dead and 1.6 million wounded or sick. The trauma inflicted by the war on the larger society from which those 2.3 million men came is such a historical commonplace as to need no underlining.

This experience—atypical in terms of the British Army's history—forms the backdrop to that army's performance in World War II. In the first place, all the army's senior commanders from 1939 to 1945, all three incumbents of the office of the chief of the Imperial General Staff (CIGS), and all those who became theater, army group, army, and corps commanders were veterans of World War I, as were most of the divisional commanders and brigadiers and many battalion commanders. Most had served on the Western Front; most had been wounded. Not a few had multiple decorations attesting to great personal courage. If the British Army remembered World War I with pride as well as anguish, there was good reason. Furthermore, there were institutional as well as personal reasons for remembering it well. In 1917 and 1918, the British Army had found a technique for advancing against the hitherto unbreakable German defenses on the Western Front. Careful planning, methodical and controlled attacks, lavish use of artillery employing carefully orchestrated fire plans, and support from the new air arm—all these kept the British relentlessly moving forward from August 1918 to the war's end. Those months tend to be overshadowed in memory by the dreadful carnage of the Somme (1916) and Passchendaele (1917). They were nonetheless a period of considerable achievement and one on which the British Army could ponder in the lean interwar years. It pondered something else as well. The casualties of World War I were never thereafter absent from the army's calculations. The military counterpart to the spread of achingly poignant war memorials across the British landscape, a constant reminder of the cost of victory, was the evolution of a doctrine that stressed technology and firepower over infantrymen's blood. After 1918, senior officers in the British Army knew that a blank check on the nation's manpower would never again be proffered to them.

The quest for a formula that would produce victory with low casualties began immediately after the armistice and continued throughout the interwar years—even though an official study of the war's lessons was commissioned only in 1931. The army's official mission was laid down by the government in 1919 as "imperial policing," but the army actually spent a lot of time and energy on how it would fight a "first-class" opponent. The answer was mobility and firepower applied through combined arms tactics. If it had been able to field formations in 1939 that were trained, equipped, and structured to do this, it would have been, unit for unit, more competitive with the Germans. The army's structure, however, got in the way of applying doctrine, and financial concerns dominated both. Its top-down command system inhibited initiative by subordinate commanders, and this, coupled with an emphasis on carefully consolidating gains, meant that fleeting opportunities for exploiting success went ungrasped. Moreover, the desire to increase mobility meant that many choices in weapons and equipment would turn out to lack battlefield punch. Finally, the ingrained belief that senior commanders had the right to interpret doctrine meant that, however perceptive the army's General Staff might have been about the lessons of World War I and the likely shape of future battles, the army did not in practice have a common doctrine until the autocratic Bernard Montgomery, with Brooke's backing, began to try to impose one after 1943 (and even Monty's doctrinal answer was far from completely successful).[8]

There was another problem with British interwar doctrine as well, and that had to do with the future role of the tank, the weapon the British had led the way in developing. This particular issue has spawned an enormous literature. It has been claimed that a backward-looking army leadership, blinkered by tradition and besotted with horsed cavalry, squandered Britain's early lead in armored warfare, thus placing the country at a grave disadvantage. This argument, developed at great length over several decades by Liddell Hart, a World War I infantry officer turned journalist and popular writer on defense issues, is much more colorful than accurate.[9] No one really questioned the tank's importance after 1918—an army that had become sensitive about casualties and was thinking about mobility and firepower was unlikely to make that mistake. Moreover, the necessity of using tanks in cooperation with infantry and artillery—combined arms tactics, the holy grail of military doctrine during and since World War II—was

Montgomery at the Canadian War Memorial at Vimy Ridge, September 1944. Taking Vimy Ridge in 1917 cost 11,000 British and Canadian casualties. Memories and lessons from such battles shaped much British generalship in World War II. (Courtesy Imperial War Museum, image no. BU 763)

apparent by the 1920s.[10] The problem was that the equipment necessary to make it possible, particularly to give cross-country mobility to the infantry, simply did not yet exist. The result was an acceptance of the idea that infantry and tanks would not be combined in all arms formations but would be separate units whose cooperation, when necessary, would be the responsibility of senior commanders. That in turn opened the way for a further deformation of doctrine by the "apostles of mobility."[11] The believers in victory through armored mobility generally saw the future of war as dominated by the clash of rival tank formations. The conviction that tank-heavy units would dominate the battlefield, marginalizing the infantry, eventually led the British Army into producing two different sorts of armored units. Heavily armed "infantry" tanks would work with the foot soldiers, much as in 1918. Swift "cruiser" tank formations would seek out and destroy enemy armor—after which the opposing infantry would be dealt with at leisure. Thus developed two different doctrines: the official one, unimplemented for lack of proper equipment (especially cross-country transport for the infantry), and the tank enthusiasts' variant. This erosion of a combined arms concept would haunt the British Army until well into World War II.[12]

Another aspect of British defense planning cast a long shadow over the British Army's ability to prepare itself doctrinally and in other ways for another major European role. Historically, the defense of the empire had been one of its primary responsibilities. World War I was the aberration, and the 1919 cabinet ruling that "imperial policing" would be the army's principal role was merely a reassertion of a deeply embedded view of the army's roles and missions. That, however, reinvigorated the so-called Cardwell system, named for Edward Cardwell (secretary of state for war from 1868 to 1874), who restructured the army around the needs of imperial security. Units in the United Kingdom were to train soldiers for comparable units stationed abroad and prepare to rotate with those units, usually at long intervals. The new armored units fit poorly into this system, as they were of little use in many imperial policing situations. When added to financial constraint and doctrinal controversy, the British Army's imperial role became yet another drag on its ability to focus on what became a steadily more likely renewal of the continental commitment.[13]

Any consideration of the development of British military planning and doctrine directs attention to the sort of equipment the army actually had in 1939. Two problems stand out. Some of the army's equipment, acquired with mobility in mind, proved too light for optimal battlefield effectiveness: the Royal Artillery's standard 25-pounder field gun and the 2-pounder adopted as both the standard tank and antitank weapon. The firepower of British infantry platoons was adversely affected throughout the war by the decision taken in the 1920s not to develop a new generation of automatic weapons because of the huge surplus stocks of .303 Lee-Enfield bolt-action rifles, originally introduced in 1903. This decision was actually not the army's but the Treasury's, and in support of it, the Treasury could cite the army's official imperial policing role—a task in which the General Staff agreed that the more accurate, controlled fire of the Lee-Enfield was actually preferable. This was another example of the distorting effect of the army's imperial role.

Above all, of course, mobility meant tanks and motor vehicles. Here, problems abounded. Tank design and development was constrained by arguments over what kind of tanks were needed and by steadily shrinking budgets. Work on a new generation of medium tanks stopped during the depths of the Depression. When it recommenced in the mid-1930s—and even after rearmament began, the army got only about a fifth of the funds made available—the British were already behind the Germans. New tanks that were rushed into service before "teething troubles" could be overcome would perform poorly on the battlefield, with predictable results in terms of crew confidence. Yet another problem arose from the interwar requirement that tanks be movable by rail, which restricted size and turret configuration, and that in turn drove the decision to use the inadequate 2-pounder gun. None of this could be fixed until well into the war. Similarly, the trucks, on which army logistics were heavily dependent, had to be based on what British industry could mass-produce. For reasons grounded in the British tax code, British manufacturers had concentrated on relatively small trucks. The British Army's heavy dependence on American tanks and trucks was not due simply to horse-loving officers and inept manufacturers, as has sometimes been alleged, but to a combination of army doctrine, Treasury restraint on spending, the nature of the British motor industry, and the gauge of British railways.[14]

Of course, doctrine and equipment are far from the sum total of factors to be considered. Equipment-poor but well-led, well-trained, and highly motivated armies have beaten lavishly equipped forces inferior in all three categories. The human element has always been a key variable in the military effectiveness equation. What kind of officers and "other ranks" made up the army that Churchill's generals commanded?

There is an extraordinarily durable myth about the officer corps of the British Army. Born out of Victorian episodes, reinforced by World War I poets as well as memoir writers such as Robert Graves and apparently authoritative commentators such as Liddell Hart, and kept burnished by theater, film, and television, it goes something like this: the officers were often titled, almost invariably from the landed classes, graduates of "public" (that is, exclusive private) schools that stressed character and sports over intelligence, conventional, dim, horse-loving, and conditioned to treat their troops with patronizing paternalism at best and callous indifference at worst. Their one redeeming feature was their personal courage. Like most stereotypes, there are shards of truth here and there in this depiction. Two British Army officers, writing about World War II, referred to the favored persona of many British officers as "self-deprecation combined with an ineffable sense of superiority"; a very distinguished British general would recall from his staff college experience that the commandant was overly impressed by students who participated in the college "drag hunt" (a foxhunt with a scent trail substituting for a live quarry).[15] The complete picture is, however, considerably more complex.

The dominance of the titled and landed classes over the army had faded before World War I, although they were still well represented in the Guards and the cavalry. Most officers of the interwar army came from middle-class and professional backgrounds, and many were themselves the sons of army officers. Public school backgrounds were certainly the norm. The army believed that these institutions inculcated highly desirable qualities, and in some ways, they did. Public school conditioning did other things as well, however. It probably had much to do with the cult of gentlemanly amateurism that could be certainly found among army officers, as it could be found in so much of interwar British society. (A young platoon leader who fought in the British Second Army from D day to VE day would put it more forcibly: "The damnably casual attitude we British, including many regular soldiers, brought to most of our enterprises was unforgiveable."[16]) The "style" affected by officers, noted earlier (and a rich source of bemusement to outsiders), almost certainly had public school roots. Indeed, there were a few expressions of concern before the war about the intellectual torpor that the social and educational base of the officer corps was producing. General Sir Phillip Chetwode (who had been a corps commander under General Sir Edmund Allenby during the latter's brilliant Megiddo battle in 1918) was brutally frank in addressing a gathering of British officers at the Indian Army Staff College at Quetta in October 1934 at the conclusion of his tour of duty as commander-in-chief, India. He criticized "a supercilious narrowness of outlook in every direction," adding that "it would almost seem that it is a crime . . . to be one inch out 'sealed pattern' and regulations." He then posed a question to his audience that still hangs over the history of the British officer corps during these years: "Am I altogether wrong in thinking that, to many Englishmen, to be independent in thought, to have imagination, to go outside the obvious, to be different to others, is to be almost un-English, or even that more frightful crime 'not sound'?"[17]

Despite the recognition that widening the basis of officer recruitment, particularly allowing rankers to achieve commissions, would be valuable, this did not begin to happen to any appreciable degree until the vast expansion of the army after 1940—and the presence of the Labour Party in Churchill's coalition government—changed the dynamics of the system. Yet the background of the 1939 officer corps cannot fully explain how the army was led during the war, unless to it is added some consideration of the way those officers, whatever their backgrounds, were trained.

The British Army's command system was a top-down one that stressed obedience to orders rather than initiative. (When coupled with the doctrinal emphasis on consolidation of gains rather than their exploitation, this would have the effect of producing an army that one thoughtful veteran of it pronounced "over-deliberate, slow, reactive."[18]) The failure, until well into the war, to begin imposing a common tactical doctrine on the army did nothing to improve matters. Nor did one of the few aspects of the British Army generally admired by foreign observers, the regimental system. Embedded deeply in the army's history and psyche, regimental loyalties undoubtedly fostered unit cohesion and that redoubtable endurance for which the British soldier was justly famed. It promoted other things as well, however. Brigadier Bernard Fergusson, whose career began in the early 1930s, remarked in his memoirs that he felt far more a part of his regiment, the Black Watch, than he did of the British Army. Regimental parochialism helped to foster the tendency for different arms to fight separate wars, a trait seen at its worst in the Western Desert Force/Eighth Army in 1941 and 1942. Combined arms tactics, at which the Germans excelled, were harder to inculcate in an army that had not been trained for them before the war and whose officers had an almost subconscious attitude that they were part of a federation of quasi-autonomous groups rather than a unitary service.[19]

The power of the regimental system may explain something else about the British Army in World War II. What differentiated one regiment from another was not merely the date when it had been raised or the names of the engagements on its battle flags but the tiny minutiae of dress and custom. All these were very useful in bonding men to the extended family of their unit, but they accustomed the British Army as well to cherishing individual quirks and oddities. This may explain the otherwise hard to account for fact that the British spawned more unorthodox and irregular formations than any other combatant power. Neither the allegedly revolutionary Soviets nor the American champions of individualism could begin to match the British for numbers and variety of special-purpose units. There were the Commandos, the Long Range Desert Group, the Long Range Penetration formations, the Special Air Service Regiment, and many more. It remains an open question whether the proliferation of these units, usually sold by their champions as force multipliers, was a fruitful use of Britain's limited and shrinking pool of high-class military manpower. (Of course, the eagerness of many officers to serve in these units may also have something to do with the grim memory of what conventional soldiering had meant in World War I.)

Officers, of course, are not the whole of an army. What an army is and does is determined as well by what sort of soldiers those officers command. Just as the public schools and the cult of gentlemanly amateurism pervading those classes from which Britain drew its leadership affected the type of leader the army had, so the nature and culture of the British working class determined what that army's other ranks were like—and were capable of doing.

The gap that had yawned between officers and other ranks before 1914 may have narrowed slightly by 1939 but not by very much. The British officer corps came almost literally from a different nation than the other ranks. The latter were overwhelmingly drawn from the British industrial working class. That class, shaped in culture and attitudes by the experience of Britain's Industrial Revolution, lived in a remarkably homogeneous and self-contained world, one in which solidarity and pride kept company with poor education, housing, and health care. The working class had little social mobility. The picture, although less bleak than before 1914 thanks to a generation of cautious social legislation that had mitigated (but not eliminated) many of the harsher features of working-class life, was still a depressing one. One angry British historian, surveying the condition to which a century and more of laissez-faire had reduced the British working class by 1939, characterized the result as the creation of a body of "coolies."[20] He also pointed out that these individuals were more poorly trained for work in an advanced technological society than either German or American workers. (And war, as waged by Western industrial nations, is very much an advanced technological activity.) In particular, it has been claimed that the British working class lacked the initiative that education and self-confidence can foster. Curiously, the British Army also worried that urban-bred soldiers would be neither as enduring nor as dependable as those from a rural background—a remarkable example of the durability of myths about the English countryside.

Here also, however, one must be cautious about correlating social history with battlefield performance. The British Army, with its belief that technology and firepower won wars, put its better-educated soldiers into its more technical units, and the infantry took the residue. (The U.S. Army did the same; the Germans, by contrast, always directed a proportion of their high-quality recruits into the infantry.) British infantrymen were trained—as were the officers who led them—in a system that prized obedience and offered little, if any, incentive to show initiative. The army in fact believed that its other ranks would not perform to acceptable standards unless closely supervised. Furthermore, as the army expanded from 1939 to 1942, many of the new junior officers and noncommissioned officers (NCOs) had little experience upon which to draw as they were training and leading their men. The rapid expansion of the army (about a hundredfold) was bound to lead to a drastic dilution of cadre and at least a temporary loss of quality, quite apart from the deficiencies in doctrine, equipment, and training regime. Finally, over all the soldiers and junior officers of the British Army hung the shadow of their fathers' war. The popular memory of the Western Front, as it had taken shape in Britain in the 1930s, did not dispose anyone to assume that aggressive tactics were the way to anything but an early grave. All this said, however, it is important to note that between 1944 and 1945—by which time equipment, training, and junior leadership had improved—British infantrymen in northwest Europe were taking casualties at about the same rate as the 1914–1918 average (100 per battalion per month), and some units in Normandy had sustained Passchendaele-level losses. Neither Churchill nor his generals, as it turned out, needed to worry about the fundamental soundness of the British soldier.[21]

This, then, was the instrument that Churchill had at hand when he took over as prime minister in May 1940—one with multiple flaws that it would try to correct or work around while it simultaneously grew exponentially, rearmed itself (often with defective weapons), and undertook a series of doomed campaigns that seemed always to end with the Royal Navy plucking remnants off beaches.

2

Retreats and Evacuations

The British Army's encounters with the Wehrmacht in 1940 and 1941 were brief and unsuccessful, ending either with the Royal Navy at great cost collecting soldiers, minus their heavy equipment, off open beaches or in disorganized retreat or surrender. This pattern, depressing to British public morale and to the neutrals that Britain was desperately trying to impress, was the background to Churchill's growing disenchantment with the army, which climaxed with the military debacles of 1942.

Churchill described the Norway venture as a "ramshackle campaign." It is a description that would be hard to improve upon. The forces hastily landed in central and northern Norway, he added, "lacked aircraft, anti-tank guns, tanks, transport and training."[1] The Germans had both the initiative and air superiority. The whole venture was poorly coordinated from London and, in the end, swallowed up by the much greater defeat in France. Only two officers, Lieutenant General Claude Auchinleck and Major General Bernard Paget, made a positive impression on Churchill.[2] The hesitations of Major General P. J. Mackesy, the first commander of the force rushed to the Narvik area, however reasonable in the circumstances, adversely impressed Churchill and ended Mackesy's career. Churchill's retrospective summary—"In this Norwegian encounter, our finest troops, the Scots and Irish Guards, were baffled by the vigour, enterprise and training of Hitler's young men"[3]—was echoed years later by General Sir David Fraser. "German tactical ability, at every level and particularly the most junior . . . here experienced for the first time . . . shocked the British Army . . . the German soldier seemed a natural winner. Compared to the enemy, British training appeared, even at its best, to have produced an army over-deliberate, slow, reactive."[4] This unease, a sense that something was fundamentally wrong, would steadily deepen over the next two years.

Norway was the final straw for the large body of anti-Chamberlainites in Parliament. The Labour Party, the Liberals, and dissident Conservatives, in one of the most dramatic parliamentary episodes of the twentieth century, forced Neville Chamberlain's resignation. Out of forty-eight hours of swirling political crisis, Winston Churchill emerged as prime minister at the head of a national coalition government. It has often been pointed out that Churchill bore more direct responsibility for the campaign in Norway than did Chamberlain. It was not, however, solely the Norwegian debacle that brought Chamberlain down. Norway was the proximate cause, but the hostility to Chamberlain had begun to mount well before the outbreak of war. It is, in any case, hard to regret the disappearance of someone as manifestly ill suited to the task of leading Britain in a total war as was Neville Chamberlain. As Churchill recalled the moment, "I felt as if I were walking with Destiny. . . . I was sure I should not fail."[5] That may well have been how he felt at the time, and it certainly read splendidly after the war. But the first month of his premiership saw a concerted effort by the Chamberlainite members of his War Cabinet (Chamberlain himself and Lord Halifax) to explore a negotiated peace with Hitler while simultaneously the British Expeditionary Force, comprising nearly all of Britain's regular army, was fighting in Belgium and northern France and was threatened with encirclement and annihilation. If the BEF had not avoided destruction, the political crisis over whether Britain should fight on could well have ended differently. The British Army may have done Churchill its greatest wartime service by surviving, barely a fortnight after he became prime minister, to fight another day.

Churchill, of course, had long believed in the fighting qualities of the French army. Impressed by its performance in World War I and bolstered by interwar contacts with French generals, he failed to appreciate that, like the British Army, it had a top-down command structure and slow reaction times.[6] The shock administered by his first visit to Paris as prime minister on May 16, when the confusion and despondency of the French high command were all too plain, began to disabuse him. Even then, however, Churchill felt he had no choice but to concur with France's plans, since it was so clearly the senior partner in the land war. On May 22, he returned to Paris, where a new French commander-in-chief, Maxime Weygand, had replaced Maurice Gamelin, whose defeatism had so struck Churchill on his earlier visit. Weygand proposed an Anglo-French counterattack in which the BEF and the French First Army, isolated north of the "panzer corridor" to the sea, would in effect turn around and strike south, while another French army drove north to meet them. If successful, this maneuver would sever the panzer corridor and restore a continuous Allied front. Churchill sent the BEF commander, General Lord Gort, VC, a telegram on the evening of May 22, instructing him that "the British Army and the French First Army should attack southwest at the earliest moment certainly tomorrow."[7] Churchill may have thought that the "Weygand plan" offered a chance to retrieve the situation, or he may merely have accepted that it had to be tried. It is hard not to believe that he had serious doubts. "This would be most important if it came true" was his postwar recollection of his assessment at the time.[8] In fact, Weygand's plan was stillborn. An attack to the south by the heavily engaged French First Army was not possible; the attack north from the Somme was equally chimerical. That left the BEF.

General the Viscount Gort, VC, is a virtually forgotten man today, even in Britain. But on a May evening in 1940, at the chateau of Premesques in Belgium, he took a lonely decision that may have been the most important any British general made during the war, a decision as critical as that which confronted the British fleet commander at Jutland in 1916: as Churchill wrote of that commander, "Sir John Jellicoe was the only man on either side who could lose the war in an afternoon."[9] Gort, a Guardsman whose personal valor had been legendary in World War I, had stepped down as CIGS in 1939 in order to take command of the British Expeditionary Force. At that moment, his quarter-million soldiers faced catastrophe. South of him, German armor, which had already reached the sea four days earlier, severing his lines of communication, was now swinging north, and his only remaining links with England (the channel ports of Boulogne, Calais, and Dunkirk) were in danger. On his other flank, the Belgian army was crumbling. The French chain of command through which he received his orders—and which was supposed to coordinate Weygand's fantasy offensive—was disintegrating. So rapidly was the situation changing that orders from London were irrelevant to Gort's situation; equally, he had no time to refer his problems there. On that afternoon, all those problems boiled down to this: he was under orders to attack south, in conjunction with French units, to restore the contact with the rest of the French armies and his own bases that had been severed four days before. Simultaneously, however, the imminent collapse of the Belgians on his left exposed his communications with Dunkirk. With Boulogne and Calais endangered, it was the one remaining port through which resupply or withdrawal could take place. Gort rightly had little faith in the French plan for a counterattack to close the gap. The two British divisions earmarked to participate in it were his only reserve. His choices were stark: he could obey orders, he could ask London to revise them (and lose precious

General Lord Gort and his chief of staff, Lieutenant General Henry Pownall, during the "Phony War." Gort saved the BEF in May 1940. After a series of staff appointments in nearly every theater, after the war Pownall became a key member of Churchill's "syndicate" of assistants on his war memoirs. (Courtesy Imperial War Museum, image no. O 357)

time), or he could ignore them and use the two divisions to safeguard the withdrawal route to Dunkirk.

A piece of fortuitously acquired intelligence helped clarify matters. A German staff car had driven into a British patrol; its driver was shot, and his passenger fled, leaving his briefcase. The patrol commander, a sergeant, retrieved it. Its contents told Gort that the Germans were mounting an attack by two army corps aimed at the gap the Belgian collapse was opening (the staff officer had been the liaison between the German army commander-in-chief and one of the army commanders controlling operations in Belgium). Gort hesitated no longer. Ignoring his orders, at 6:30 in the evening on May 25, he moved his two divisions to plug the gap, saving the route to Dunkirk and much more: "He saved the British Expeditionary Force," wrote the official historian.[10] It was a classic example of clear thinking, decisiveness, and moral courage. Later that night in London, Churchill and the British Chiefs of Staff, independently, came to the conclusion that the Weygand plan was hopeless and instructed Gort to do what he was already doing—retire on Dunkirk.[11]

The ensuing "deliverance of Dunkirk" inspired the British nation at a critical moment. Churchill, determined to fight on, was wrestling with powerful figures in his cabinet who were deeply pessimistic about the prospects of survival, much less victory, and correspondingly anxious to explore the possibility of a negotiated peace.[12] Moreover, the basic machinery for defense and counterattack, a trained army, was at risk in Belgium. So were nearly all the men who would be key figures in the next five years of the British Army's war against Germany. Brooke (CIGS from 1941 to 1946) and Ronald Adam (adjutant general from 1941 to 1946) were corps commanders; Montgomery and Alexander were division commanders. Many of their future corps, division, brigade, and battalion commanders were also serving under Gort.[13] On that spring evening, Gort may have helped preserve Britain's will to fight on in circumstances most observers regarded as hopeless. He certainly saved the regular core on which Britain could build the 2-million-strong army it fielded by 1945.[14]

On the evening of May 25, after the Defence Committee of the War Cabinet had directed Gort to march to the channel, a conversation in Churchill's room at Admiralty House shaped the prime minister's relationship with the army for the next fifteen months.[15] Gort saved the army for Britain; the resignation that evening of the chief of the Imperial General Staff, General Sir Edmund "Tiny" Ironside, put at its head General Sir John Dill, with whom the prime minister would never find it easy to work.

Ironside had never been tipped to be CIGS. The youngest brigadier in the army in 1918, the large, bluff Ironside was far more a field commander than a staff officer and was never comfortable in the Whitehall setting in which the CIGS operated. At the war's outbreak, Ironside was inspector general of Overseas Forces and the BEF's commander designate. However, Gort, the incumbent CIGS, had come to dislike Whitehall and especially the secretary of state for war, Leslie Hore-Belisha, intensely. Although Gort was a capable chief of staff (he was a former staff college commandant), his heart was also in the field. He therefore proposed to take the BEF to France, while Ironside became CIGS. It was a fateful decision. It positioned Gort to play an absolutely critical role in May 1940 but left the army with a relatively weak CIGS. Churchill, who had known Ironside and thought highly of him before the war, found working with him during the chaotic Norway campaign somewhat disillusioning. So did others. Perhaps for that reason, the War Office team was strengthened on April 23 by bringing Lieutenant General Sir John Dill back from a corps command in the BEF to become vice chief of the Imperial General Staff. Dill had long been regarded as a likely future CIGS—indeed, some thought him the logical successor to Gort in September 1939. As the Norway campaign drew to its dismal conclusion and then was swallowed by the catastrophe unfolding in France, Ironside's already dim star waned rapidly. That May evening at Admiralty House, Ironside suggested that he stand aside in favor of Dill as CIGS, becoming instead commander-in-chief, Home Forces. The offer was accepted with alacrity. "No one could doubt," Churchill wrote later, "that [Dill's] professional standing was in many ways superior to that of Ironside."[16] Although relieved, Churchill remained grateful that Tiny had jumped before it became necessary to push him. A field marshal's baton accompanied Ironside to Home Forces, and the following year, by which time he had been edged out of Home Forces and into retirement, he became Lord Ironside. Churchill later wrote, "The high dignities and honours which were later conferred upon him arose from my appreciation of his bearing at this moment in our affairs."[17]

Sir John Dill, who become CIGS officially on May 27, remains an enigma. Long considered one of the army's rising stars, he was the obvious candidate, as Ironside's unsuitability became clear, for the newly created position of vice CIGS. When Churchill flew to Paris on May 16 and again on May 22, it was Dill, not Ironside, who accompanied him. (Was this the hint that decided Ironside to offer his resignation on May 25?) But although he was a superb staff officer (he, too, had been a staff college commandant), he had other weaknesses that, in the long run, would undermine him as much as lack of Whitehall and War Office skills undercut Ironside. For one thing, Dill—at least in the estimation of Alexander, who commanded a division in Dill's I Corps—lacked decisiveness and was burdened with a streak of pessimism. The latter may be related to the bleak circumstances of his private life—his wife, paralyzed by a stroke, was slowly dying. Dill's professional skills made him an obvious choice for his job; his temperament, however, did not augur well for his success in it.[18]

Moreover, Dill became CIGS at a moment when the whole machinery for war direction was being recast, and that reconfiguration would put him into far more intimate contact with the prime minister than his World War I predecessors had had to endure with Lloyd George. This change had actually begun before Churchill became prime minister, when the obvious deficiencies in the handling of the Norwegian campaign led to the creation of the Vice Chiefs of Staff Committee to take some of the burden off the Chiefs of Staff, allowing them to focus on key issues. Then, more fundamentally, in Chamberlain's last reorganization of his machinery for war direction, Churchill was made responsible on May 1 not only for chairing the War Cabinet's Military Coordination Committee—made up of the three service ministers and their Chiefs of Staff—but also for providing "guidance" to the Chiefs of Staff. In addition, he was empowered to summon them "for personal consultation." Most important of all, he was to be given a "suitable central staff" to assist him, headed by Major General Hastings Ismay. Thus, on the eve of becoming prime minister, Churchill was already virtually minister of defense, although still subject to the prime minister and the full War Cabinet. How well this arrangement would have worked in practice is impossible to say, but it provided the template for the structure and machinery Churchill would create less than two weeks later.

On becoming prime minister, Churchill immediately named himself minister of defense. His powers were undefined—something he was comfortable with because he could range over the entire military landscape, from strategy to operations and tactics, supply, and appointments. Senior officers were considerably less comfortable with this arrangement. The Military Coordination Committee morphed into the War Cabinet Defence Committee. The service ministers disappeared; they would be confined henceforth to administering their departments. The Defence Committee was Churchill, the Chiefs of Staff, whoever else Churchill decided to include—and Ismay. Of all the generals with whom Churchill was to work during the ensuing five years, none, not even Brooke or Montgomery, was more important to his success than Ismay.

Hastings Lionel Ismay was an officer of the Indian Army, a cavalryman whose regiment, the 21st Prince Albert Victor's Own Cavalry (originally known as Daly's Horse after the East India Company officer who raised it in 1849), was a Frontier Force unit, one of the famed "Piffers" who guarded the North-West Frontier and dealt with its turbulent and formidable tribes. Ismay's career, however, had been very different from that of other Indian Army officers, such as Auchinleck and William Slim, who rose to the top during World War II. After regimental service on the North-West Frontier, Ismay spent the World War I years, when so many of his public school and Sandhurst contemporaries died on the Western Front, in British Somaliland; there, a simmering, low-level insurgency led by a Muslim cleric dubbed by the British the Mad Mullah required the presence of some regular forces to back up the locally recruited, British-officered levies endeavoring to suppress it. In July 1914, Ismay had secured a place in the Indian Army contingent detailed to Somaliland and thereby changed the course of his career. Somaliland was controlled by the Colonial Office, and so were the troops serving there. From 1914 to 1918, the Colonial Office adamantly refused to release Ismay to return to regular soldiering, a bit of bureaucratic turf defense that may have saved his life. Professionally sidelined during the war, Ismay thereafter was given only staff appointments. Here, he found his true métier. Intelligent, adaptable, and emollient but recognized also for discretion and integrity, he moved steadily upward. In 1938, Ismay's rise culminated in his taking over as secretary to the Committee of Imperial Defence (CID) from the legendary Sir Maurice Hankey, the Royal Marine officer who had created Lloyd George's War Cabinet secretariat and built the CID into the key element in interwar British defense planning. A major general in 1939, Ismay became deputy secretary (military) to Chamberlain's War Cabinet. Then came the additional assignment to head the small staff created for Churchill in early May, an assignment that carried with it a seat on the Chiefs of Staff Committee. When Churchill named himself minister of defense, Ismay became his chief staff officer, a position he held for the remainder of the war. Assisted by a small team of able staff officers, whose prominent members were Ian Jacob, a Royal Engineer, and Leslie Hollis, a Royal Marine, Ismay and his "Defence Secretariat" gave Churchill a purchase on the vast, ponderous, but remarkably effective machine of British government. Many feared in May 1940 that Churchill's temperament would

General Sir Hastings Ismay at a reception in London. Ismay's ability to work smoothly with military men, politicians, and senior civil servants made him invaluable to Churchill—and to many of those who had to work with Winston. (Courtesy Imperial War Museum, image no. A 30046)

make him a rogue elephant, incapable of working that machine. That he succeeded brilliantly was due to two things: the fact that he was far better at being number one than at holding any other position and the effectiveness of Ismay, Hollis, and Jacob in translating Churchill's constant stream of ideas, admonitions, inquiries, and exhortations into bureaucratically effective action.[19]

In the aftermath of Dunkirk and the fall of France, the British Army's first priorities were reorganization, reequipment, and preparation to face an invasion. The scope of the reequipment needed was massive. Nearly the entire regular army plus five Territorial Army divisions fought in France; they left behind eight to ten divisions' worth of equipment. In early June 1940, there was only enough equipment in reserve to fully outfit one division. The ammunition supply available would have sustained one day of hard fighting, and there were only fifty modern tanks.[20] To reequip and simultaneously enlarge the army, there was no choice but to order the maximum production of existing models of equipment in all categories: better an inadequate weapon than no weapon at all. The Defence Committee took this decision in early June. It was inevitable, but its consequences would dog the army until 1942. Weapons known to be obsolescent—the 2-pounder antitank gun and the lumbering infantry tank—continued in service because quantity temporarily had to take priority over quality. The state of the British Army post-Dunkirk makes it abundantly clear that the decision to fight on was a gamble on the ability of the Royal Air Force and the Royal Navy to prevent invasion, since the army was months away from readiness for even limited operations. It also makes it the more remarkable that at precisely this time a decision was made that would commit the army to a campaign in a distant and difficult theater. Churchill was at the center of the decisions to fight on, to both expand the army and equip it with whatever could be produced quickly, and to defend Britain's position in the Middle East. All three decisions were correct in the circumstances, but they meant the British Army was committed to a campaign that brought Churchill's relations with it to a crisis point by 1942, not least because its repeated failures had left him on the brink of a major political crisis.

The British had never intended to make the Middle East the focus of their war effort against the European Axis. That the region nonetheless came to be so important by August 1942 that Churchill's political fate was tied to an Eighth Army victory is a demonstration of war's ability to generate its own momentum. Britain became the dominant European power in the Middle East after World War I. This fact, together with the area's oil and its crucial role in imperial communications with India, ensured that the Middle East would thereafter rank high on London's list of interests to be preserved. The growing German threat and Britain's estrangement from Italy after 1936 sharpened British leaders' concerns about their grip on their Mediterranean lifeline to the East. They responded with a slow but unacknowledged shift of strategic emphasis from the retention of Singapore as the empire's ranking defense priority (after the security of Britain itself) to a concentration on the Mediterranean and Middle East—with ultimately disastrous consequences in the Far East. By the time war came in 1939, the British, with a powerful fleet based on Malta and Alexandria and dominant from Egypt to Iraq (even though both of those countries were nominally independent), could feel reasonably secure. With their French allies, they heavily outweighed the Italians at sea and held Italian Libya in a vise between Egypt and French-controlled Tunisia. Greece was a semi–client state and Turkey a benevolent neutral. Appeasement of Arab nationalist emotions, centering on Palestine, and the presence of client rulers in Baghdad, Amman, and Cairo seemed to promise internal security. The Italians appeared to confirm the relative strength of the British position by remaining neutral. The five weeks that began on May 10, 1940, however, altered everything.

With France falling out of the war and Italy rushing in, Britain's whole strategic calculus changed. From a position of assured dominance in the Mediterranean, the British found themselves asking whether they could even retain a foothold there. As France staggered toward surrender, planners in London suggested pulling the ships of the Mediterranean Fleet out through the Suez Canal and blocking it behind them. Gibraltar would be held, and the Mediterranean would thus be sealed at both ends. The Mediterranean Fleet commander, Admiral Sir Andrew Browne Cunningham, vehemently rejected the proposal, forcefully pointing out that a "landslide in territory and prestige" would be the result of adopting it. Certainly, given the slender physical resources available to the British in the Middle East at the time, accumulated prestige and the aura of invincibility inherited from the past were among the empire's most significant assets in the area, and the Royal Navy embodied these qualities as did nothing else. An even more important figure than Cunningham was also opposed to any suggestion of withdrawal. Winston Churchill had not yet completed a full month in office—had not in fact yet moved into 10 Downing Street—but was already faced with a situation several orders of magnitude worse than the most pessimistic imaginings of any prewar planner. Trying simultaneously to persuade the French government, or some fragment of it, to stay in the war and to convince the Americans that Britain, all too likely soon to be alone, could survive an attack by a military machine that had just crumpled Europe's reputedly finest army like wastepaper, Churchill could not afford to cede anything further anywhere. Never formally discussed by the War Cabinet, the decision to hold on in the Middle East was nonetheless one of the most crucial of the war. It shaped the course of Britain's land war against the European Axis.[21] It also made the war in the Mediterranean theater very much an imperial war.

The bulk of the regular British Army, substantially intact but nearly weaponless after the withdrawal from France, was rearming, retraining, absorbing floods of new conscripts, and preparing to defend Britain itself. The easiest way to build up the forces in the Middle East was to draw on the Indian Army, which was told to tear up its prewar plans for gradual expansion and grow as rapidly as possible, and on the citizen-soldiers of Australia and New Zealand. To these, South African units were soon added. Ultimately, only the Canadians were missing from the ranks of the desert warriors (and they arrived to join Eighth Army when it landed in Sicily in July 1943). In addition, various European exile governments and organizations—Polish, Greek, Free French—furnished contingents large and small. Thus, it is apparent that, from the beginning, British commanders dealt with a heterogeneous and polyglot army and that, although the Union Jack flew over it all, the complexities of coalition war were decidedly present.

Geography and local politics added another unique set of characteristics. The British position in the Middle East was vulnerable to external assault from two directions, as well as to enemies within. To the west, in Libya, the Italians had a numerically overwhelming army (some 200,000 men, including nine regular divisions) whose fundamental structural weaknesses were not yet fully apparent. To the north, Lebanon and Syria were controlled by the Vichy regime, whose anti-British sentiments were only too obvious from the beginning. Turkey and the various Balkan states might fear Germany and wish Britain well, but could they interpose any sort of effective barrier to the southeastward march of Hitler's armies? Finally, what of Britain's Arab subjects? Technically, Britain did not directly rule very much—only the troubled Palestine Mandate and Aden. The reality, however, was that Britain exercised a real, if indirect, suzerainty everywhere in the area. Arab nationalists disliked both the British and their local client rulers, and some of those nationalists were in touch with Germany and Italy. During the course of the desert war, the British would have to suppress a rebellion in Iraq and stage a virtual coup against the Egyptian king to keep him in line. In a moment of exasperation, Churchill told his Middle East commander-in-chief that the best way to handle Arab nationalism was to win a few battles, since what the Arabs really respected was strength and success. But during the long period when victory proved elusive, no British theater commander could ever forget that his base was not completely secure.

Two generals in succession tried to cope with this baffling mix of problems between June 1940 and August 1942. Both were relieved by Churchill. Each of them might have been chosen as the embodiment of the service from which he came: General Sir Archibald Percival Wavell of the British Army and General Sir Claude John Eyre Auchinleck of the Indian Army. Wavell's war, which began on June 10, 1940, the day Italy entered the conflict, ironically opened with a success so sweeping that it would remain unique in Britain's struggle against the European Axis—Lieutenant General Richard O'Connor's virtually total destruction of the Italian Tenth Army by a vastly outnumbered British force, a classic campaign of annihilation.[22]

Archibald Percival Wavell was the son of an army family. His grandfather had served in the East India Company's Bengal Army, as well as in those of Spain and Mexico (in the latter, he held the rank of general). His father was a more conventional British Army regular. Wavell went to Winchester, a public school with a reputation for the intellectual acuity of its graduates, and then to Sandhurst, thereafter joining the premier Highland regiment, the Black Watch, which had been his father's regiment (although the Wavells had no Scottish connections). He lost an eye and was decorated for outstanding valor as a young infantry captain in 1915. Three years later, he was a temporary brigadier general and chief of staff to a corps in Palestine when General Sir Edmund Allenby won the great victory at Megiddo, the most brilliant feat of British generalship during World War I. Over the next twenty years, Wavell's reputation mounted.[23] Fifty-seven years old in 1939 and one of the most senior generals in the army, he was tough, self-confident, and given to long and intimidating silences. Wavell was outwardly a stolid and conventional, if highly capable, professional soldier, but there were other currents running deep in his character. He had a gambler's streak, a penchant for believing that things would work out, a tendency to give the unorthodox and unconventional a chance, and a fondness for poetry that led him to take time during the war to publish an anthology of it (a diversion Churchill found baffling). Perhaps, at some level, Wavell had always wanted to be something else.[24] Despite his silences, he was an inspirational figure to those officers who served under him. He would show himself at his best in balancing, at theater level, his slender resources against multiple demands. The closer he came to operational, or tactical, decisions, the less certain his touch became. But in the desert in 1940, these were not Wavell's concern. Those problems were O'Connor's.

O'Connor was summoned from Palestine, where he was a divisional commander, to take over the newly created Western Desert Force in June 1940. A small, wiry, intense man, O'Connor, an infantryman, had not been a major figure in the prewar disputes about the role of armor. He was now, however, taking command of a force whose key component, the 7th Armoured Division, had been created by one of the most ardent of the apostles of mobility, Major General P. C. Hobart. O'Connor would, moreover, operate in an arena that might have been designed as a laboratory of mobile warfare. Hobart had put his armored division together in 1938 from units stationed in Egypt and trained it thoroughly between 1938 and 1939. A strong believer in independent operations by armored divisions that were tank heavy, Hobart left an important legacy to future British desert commanders: the conviction that the tank operates best alone. Although he was the creator of Britain's first armored division, Hobart would not lead it into battle. His burning professional zeal brought him into collision with his immediate superior, the commander of British troops in Egypt, Lieutenant General Sir Henry Maitland "Jumbo" Wilson, and in November 1939, Hobart was retired.[25] The division was taken over by a cavalryman, Major General Michael O'Moore Creagh. O'Connor's other formation was the 4th Indian Division, commanded by Major General Noel de la Poer Beresford-Peirse. The 4th was an elite formation made up of long-service, prewar regular soldiers. Dilution to provide cadre for new units being raised in India (known as milking) had not yet affected its quality.[26] Never again would a British commander in the desert take into battle a formation whose units were all as professional and well officered as O'Connor's. This made the contrast with his opponents particularly sharp.

The Italian army was the victim of the gap that yawned between Benito Mussolini's rhetoric and the reality represented by training, equipment, leadership, and doctrine. Mussolini's boast of "eight million bayonets" was inadvertently all too accurate about his army's suitability for modern war. The Italian army's equipment was obsolete—its basic infantry rifle dated from 1891, its artillery from World War I, and its tanks were dismissed by a German armored specialist as "moving coffins." Training had been neglected, morale was uneven, and Italian doctrine had not advanced much beyond 1918. Italy's industrial base, although considerable, had been inadequately organized to support a major war. This and a total lack of domestic supplies of oil and rubber meant that Italy committed an unmotorized army to the desert war. In reality, the Italian army was quite incapable of much beyond the colonial-style campaigning it had done in Libya and Ethiopia in the 1920s and 1930s. And no one knew this better than some of its senior officers. Ordered to attack Egypt, Marshal Rudolfo Graziani hesitated. (Well he might, for he was a former army chief of staff and had told Mussolini that the Italian army was as modern as the Macedonian phalanx. Il Duce replied that he need not worry, the army was largely for show.)

Threatened with removal if he did not invade Egypt, Graziani had his Tenth Army move gingerly across the border in early September, after which it advanced some 60 miles and halted. His troops then dug themselves into a series of widely separated camps stretching south from the coast. The southern end of the line hung in the empty desert, vulnerable to a wide outflanking movement. The light British screening forces, which had raided across the frontier from the moment Italy entered the war and then slowly fallen back before Graziani's lumbering phalanx, had already established a moral ascendancy over the Italians that boded ill for the Tenth Army.[27]

By the time the Italian advance into Egypt halted, Churchill had deeply involved himself in the operational and tactical issues of the theater. This was not merely because of the restless activism that was one of his most salient characteristics; it was also because the area of the Mediterranean and Middle East was the only one in which Britain could contemplate offensive operations. Thoroughly conscious of the belief widespread outside Britain that Germany would soon knock Britain out of the war, Churchill was clear that no chance could be lost to impress upon both British and neutral opinion (especially opinion in the most important neutral of all across the Atlantic) that his country could and would strike back hard at every opportunity.[28] This had been made manifest in June, when, at Churchill's insistence, the Royal Navy had struck preemptively at the French fleet. "In July 1940," he wrote later, "I began to concern myself increasingly about the Middle East."[29]

Wavell, whom Churchill had never met, was summoned home for consultations. The ensuing week of discussions set the tone for one of the most fraught relationships Churchill would have with any senior British officer during the war. Twice, Churchill would remove Wavell—and then twice reemploy him, the second time as viceroy of India with a peerage. The incompatibility between the two men was essentially temperamental. Churchill respected articulate individuals who could hold their own with him (Brooke is the most famous example), and Wavell's trademark silences quickly led the prime minister to assume there was little to him. He told intimates dismissively that Wavell reminded him of a suburban golf club chairman. Churchill cross-examined him relentlessly, not only on theater strategy but also on the disposition of his troops as well as tactical and logistic detail. It was in the course of these discussions that, at Dill's initiative, the decision was taken to send to the Middle East an armored brigade, which at that point represented about half of the organized armored force available in Britain. Characteristically, Churchill endorsed the decision and then pushed to have the units rushed directly through the Mediterranean rather than being sent by the slower route around the Cape. Caution prevailed on this point, but Churchill's commitment to early offensive action by Wavell's force was clear—as were his doubts about whether Wavell was really the right man for the job, although he would later note, "I thought it best to leave him in command. I admired his fine qualities, and was impressed with the confidence so many people had in him."[30] As if to underline the doubts his "severe" discussions with Wavell had aroused, Churchill drafted the "General Directive for Commander-in-Chief, Middle East" that, after minutely detailing the forces available, went on for six more paragraphs headed "Tactical employment of above forces" and ended peremptorily "Pray let the above be implemented." Churchill was so underwhelmed by Wavell that he toyed with replacing him with the comparatively junior Major General Bernard Freyberg, VC, a Guardsman who was currently commander of the New Zealand Expeditionary Force.[31]

The Churchill-Wavell relationship thus started poorly. It worsened almost immediately because of the loss of British Somaliland to the Italians. In 1939, there were no plans to defend this isolated and strategically irrelevant British colony. Wavell, however, felt that British prestige required that it not be tamely given up, and London concurred. A scratch British force (mostly Indian and African troops) was assembled, and when the Italians invaded in overwhelming numbers while Wavell was in London, it conducted a creditable fighting withdrawal to the port of Berbera and the waiting ships of the Royal Navy. Churchill questioned how determinedly the local commander (Major General A. R. Godwin-Austen) had fought, noting that British casualties had been light. Wavell, doubtless completely exasperated at the micromanagement from London, fired off a barbed reply: "A big butcher's bill is not necessarily evidence of good tactics."[32] The shaft went home—Dill later remarked that he had never seen Churchill so angry. In some ways, Wavell's shot was unfair, for Churchill had been one of the most outspoken critics between 1914 and 1918 of tactics that produced massive casualties for slender results. His support for the Dardanelles venture that nearly ruined him was based on the belief that it would, by shortening the war, save British lives. Nevertheless, it is easy to see how Wavell, more articulate on paper than face to face, might have finally decided to make the point that he was the competent judge of battlefield performance in his command. From this point on, however, the relationship between the prime minister and the commander of the army's only active theater of operations went steadily downhill.

Ironically, the rift between Churchill and Wavell widened just as planning began for the British's Army's first major offensive of the war. Wavell's decision to launch a counterattack, christened Operation Compass, was taken shortly after Graziani halted. On September 21, 1940, he issued the orders that began Compass. O'Connor and his extremely talented chief of staff, Brigadier John Harding, did the operational planning.[33] Wavell's original intention was a "spoiling attack" to disrupt Italian preparations for further advance. O'Connor and Harding felt that a larger victory might well be possible, but Wavell's concept reflected the multiple pressures to which he was subject. The Italians had invaded Greece in October, and some of the scanty RAF resources available in the Middle East had already been diverted to support the Greeks—and more might have to follow. Wavell was also planning a campaign to conquer Italy's East African empire. If successful, it would eliminate any danger to Kenya and the Sudan, and most important, by eliminating an Italian foothold on the Red Sea, it would remove any threat to the shipping that supplied the whole theater.

That Wavell should feel the need to set limits to O'Connor's offensive is understandable. What is not is his decision to exclude the prime minister from his confidence. Churchill was not told about Compass until very late in the planning process—not until, in fact, Wavell could no longer avoid doing so. Anthony Eden, secretary of state for war, visited the Middle East in mid-October and was briefed on Compass. Only just before Eden returned to England, barely a month prior to the operation, did Churchill learn that the British Army was about to launch its first major offensive since 1918. Why Wavell behaved as he did is not entirely certain. He may, as his biographer claimed, long have mistrusted Churchill, or perhaps he simply decided to evade further micromanagement from London.[34] To be sure, when they conferred in London in August 1940, there was no real meeting of minds, and that experience was followed by the sharp exchange over the loss of British Somililand. Wavell would afterward claim that Churchill had always disliked him. But whatever the lack of personal chemistry, it is astounding that the preparation for Britain's first land offensive of the war—one that, if successful, would have ramifications far beyond the desert—was kept from Churchill until the last minute. No British general would ever again interpret "need to know" so as to exclude the prime minister.[35] It is difficult not to conclude that Churchill had as much trouble respecting Wavell's professional skills and therefore his ability to carry out his responsibilities as Wavell had in understanding that the prime minister's responsibilities were so great (and his bundle of skills so considerable) that working with him was the only viable option in the unprecedented situation Britain faced. Dill begged Wavell to try to create a personal link with Churchill; Wavell could never bring himself to try.

Through October and into November, O'Connor planned, aided by excellent intelligence. British cryptanalysts at Bletchley Park, north of London, were reading about 80 percent of the Italian air force's high-grade cipher traffic and much of the Italian army's as well. German air force traffic provided an important piece of negative information: no German units were destined for North Africa.[36] But the critical piece of tactical intelligence came from air reconnaissance, confirmed by an infantry patrol: an opening had been left for supply vehicles in the minefield defenses of the Italian camp selected for the initial British assault.

Penetrating the gap between two of the camps, O'Connor attacked from an unexpected (and undefended) direction early on December 9, 1940. The attack itself was a 1918-style set piece with heavily armored I (or infantry) tanks, known as Matildas, leading forward Cameron Highlanders and Rajputs of the 4th Indian Division. Surprised and disoriented, some of the Italian troops tried to rally, and their gunners, who were probably the best of the Italian army's combat arms, fought their obsolescent pieces to the end. The weight and unexpectedness of the British attack, however, made O'Connor's men masters of the camp in a few hours. Meanwhile, the 7th Armoured Division, screened by the armored cars of the 11th Hussars, swept wide into the desert, turned north, and cut the coastal highway, the Italians' lifeline. The 7th's lightly armored and mechanically cranky cruiser tanks met little opposition: according to its doctrine, the Italian army distributed its tanks, World War I–style, among the infantry. Concentrated, even the mediocre Italian tanks might have checked 7th Armoured Division's sweep. Dispersed, they were mopped up along with the camps by the British over the next few days. Some 38,000 Italians were captured, including 4 generals, together with 73 tanks, 237 guns, and mountains of stores. British casualties—killed, wounded, and missing—totaled 624.

This was the pattern for the remainder of the campaign. After the initial victory at Sidi Barrani, Wavell allowed O'Connor to pursue the Italians into Libya. The 4th Indian Division was pulled out to take part in the East African campaign, but in its place, O'Connor got Major General I. G. Mackay's 6th Australian Division, which made up in ferocity and determination what it lacked in professional polish. The Sidi Barrani maneuver was repeated twice in January, with the 7th Armoured cutting off and the Matildas and Australians breaching the defenses of the fortresses of Bardia and Tobruk in turn. Again, the 7th had little fighting to do, and the tank-infantry assaults on the fixed Italian defenses were set pieces of a type well suited to both the Australians' training and the technical characteristics of the Matildas. The whole operation was being run on a logistic shoestring: a characteristic gamble by Wavell and a remarkable feat of improvisation by O'Connor's staff.

The climax came early in February. The remnants of the Italian Tenth Army were retreating by the coastal road. O'Connor ordered a cross-country advance by the 7th to cut them off.[37] By this time, the division was, logistically, on its last gasp, and the treads and engines of its tanks were both on borrowed time.[38] Nonetheless, a small force of guns, armored cars, and motorized infantry, followed by a few tanks, cut the road at Beda Fromm, ahead of the Italians and with a few hours to spare. For the disorganized and demoralized Tenth Army, it was the end. In two months, O'Connor had wiped ten divisions off the Italian army's order of battle, taking 130,000 prisoners, 380 tanks, and 845 guns. His own casualties had amounted to 2,000, with only one-quarter of them fatalities.

The two-month drive from Sidi Barrani to Beda Fromm reinforced the compartmentalized approach to war inherent in the prewar training of the 7th Armoured Division. It operated on its own, while the Matildas and infantry fought a quite separate series of engagements. The Italians exacted no penalties for this; the Germans soon would. Furthermore, the British had gotten an exaggerated idea of what light "columns" could accomplish. But if O'Connor's campaign taught some of the wrong lessons, it was undeniably a remarkable feat of arms, the first British military victory of the war. O'Connor's westward progress ended, however, at Beda Fromm. He later came to believe that he could have pushed on, taking Tripoli and foreclosing German entry into the desert war. But Harding, in retrospect, felt that further advance was simply impossible logistically. Moreover, Wavell now had other concerns. Since early January, he had known that Churchill and the War Cabinet gave priority to aiding Greece. Political imperatives were at work on the other side as well. Hitler could not allow the Italian position in North Africa to collapse totally without risking the destabilization of Mussolini's regime. In January, he had decided to send a "blocking detachment." Five days after Beda Fromm, on February 12, 1941, the force commander, Major General Erwin Johannes Rommel, arrived at the Castel Benito airfield near Tripoli.

Up to this point, the history of the desert war is a fairly uncontroversial one, apart from Wavell's decision that Churchill need not be told about

Compass until the last minute. From the point where O'Connor halted and Rommel stepped out of his aircraft into African sunshine, however, controversy swirls thickly. The crux is the priority given to Greece by Churchill and the War Cabinet, which was based on several interlocking factors. Britain had a commitment to Greece, and British efforts to draw the support of other powers would be ill served by abandoning an ally the moment the Germans appeared. Furthermore, if aid to Greece could function as the catalyst for the formation of a "Balkan bloc" of Yugoslavia, Greece, and Turkey, the Germans might be held; in any case, their arrival on the northern flank of Britain's vital and shaky Middle Eastern empire would be delayed. Late in the 1940–1941 winter, it was far from clear in London that Russia was Hitler's target for 1941. A German drive to the southeast and the oil fields of Iraq and Iran would have been a major threat to the British, and measures to halt or delay it made sense. Nationalist unrest in the Middle East, simmering just under the surface, would become more intense the closer the Germans came, for they were perceived as liberators from British dominance. Yet it is curious that no one in London or Cairo properly assessed how little stopping power Balkan or Turkish armies were likely to have in any encounter with the Wehrmacht, courageous though their tough peasant infantry might be.[39] Eden, sent once again to the Middle East (this time in the company of the CIGS, Sir John Dill), was a strong supporter of the expedition to Greece. Wavell maintained to the end of his life that it was the right decision and, moreover, a reasonable military risk—and Dill went along. When Churchill hesitated at the last minute, concerned about the risk to a largely Commonwealth force, it was the convictions of the men on the spot—Eden, Dill, and above all Wavell—that carried the day. The British decision to go to the aid of the Greeks with a force large enough to provide a considerable hostage to fortune but too small to have any hope of making a difference to the result will doubtless remain controversial. It is clear, however, that the policy was not simply one thrust by Churchill on reluctant commanders, nor did it stop a victorious march by O'Connor into Tripoli.[40]

The whole Greek venture was badly misconceived by Wavell, whose gambler's streak was on display. Lustreforce—composed of an Australian division, New Zealand's only division, and a recently formed and completely inexperienced British armored brigade—went to Greece commanded by Jumbo Wilson, plucked from his post as the military governor of recently conquered Italian Cyrenaica. It seems bizarrely fitting that because Greece and Germany were not yet at war, the British disembarkation at Piraeus was monitored by the German military attaché and his staff. Meanwhile, the

Greeks, who (so Wavell, Dill, and Eden believed) had agreed to withdraw from part of northern Greece in order to hold a shorter, more defensible line, had neglected—or found themselves unable—to do so.[41] Wilson's force was therefore committed to an encounter battle, with little prospect of doing much more than imposing some delay on the Germans. At that point, it was hard to find any senior soldier except Wavell who thought that Operation Lustre was anything other than doomed. The senior Australian and New Zealand commanders in the theater, Lieutenant General Sir Thomas Blamey and Major General Bernard Freyberg, were sure that the Greek venture would end badly. In London, Churchill, as noted, was seized by last-minute qualms. However, Lustre moved forward with the inevitability of a force of nature. Why it did remains an intriguing question. Everybody could see advantages that might flow from confronting the Germans in Greece, and almost everybody could see the costs of abandoning the Greeks. The key to the situation was Wavell. A strong negative from him would have affected the wavering Dill, and the combination would have been hard for Churchill to ignore. The Greek campaign was thus as much Wavell's doing as Churchill's.[42]

The campaign opened on April 6, and within a week, Wavell's staff was planning evacuation. Tactically, it was a long retreat, competently conducted by Wilson and his subordinates in extremely difficult circumstances. Wilson had an advantage that other British commanders would enjoy to an ever-greater degree as the war progressed. Ultra intelligence, based on the breaking of high-grade German ciphers, was available to him: "It was during the Greek campaign that comprehensive appreciations based on . . . Enigma decrypts were transmitted to the commanders in the field for the first time in the war . . . [and Wilson's] main decisions concerned the timing of the repeated withdrawals that were forced on him. They appear to have been extremely well-timed as a result of the Enigma appreciations that were being sent to him."[43] Ultra, the cohesion of his troops, and the Royal Navy's usual skill and determination meant that the Greek campaign ended less badly than it might have, but by the time the troops were being lifted from Greek beaches, disaster had struck in the Western Desert.

Wavell's conviction that large-scale aid to Greece was feasible rested primarily on his belief that his desert flank was secure against any serious counterattack for several months, by which time further reinforcements would have arrived. This assessment and the dispositions based on it are another area of controversy. The British had feared the arrival of the Germans in the Mediterranean for some months. By early January 1941, German air force Enigma traffic, decrypted at Bletchley Park, began to hint at the imminent deployment of the Luftwaffe in Italy and Sicily. Then, on January 10, German bombers based in Sicily crippled the carrier HMS *Illustrious*, which was covering a Malta convoy. Thereafter, signs began to accumulate that the German army would soon follow the Luftwaffe (Hitler agreed in mid-January to deploy a light armored division—the "blocking force"—to Libya by February 20). By February 17, Wavell's intelligence branch had decided that German troops would arrive in North Africa soon (they were in fact already there). Five days later, a British armored car of the King's Dragoon Guards exchanged fire with a German armored car near El Agheila, the westernmost limit of O'Connor's advance.[44] Wavell and his intelligence chief, Brigadier John Shearer, had based their assumptions on two factors: what their intelligence told them about Rommel's forces and their rate of arrival and what they knew about the logistics of movement in the desert.[45] On this basis, they decided that they were reasonably secure until at least May from a major German push to retake Cyrenaica.[46] Their assessment of when the Germans would be able to attack matched that of the members of the German high command, who instructed Rommel on March 21 to wait until mid-May before launching a limited offensive to gain a good position for a later, major attack. Neither Wavell nor Colonel General Franz Halder (the German army chief of staff) yet realized that Rommel was a commander for whom orthodox calculations were not terribly persuasive.

Based on his estimate of the likely threat, Wavell had committed to the defense of his desert flank what he could spare, and that was very little. At the end of his campaign, O'Connor had gone back to Egypt and taken over Wilson's job, and Jumbo, as noted earlier, became head of Cyrenaica Command, a static headquarters designed for an occupation force. The veteran but worn 7th Armoured was withdrawn to the Nile Delta, and the 6th Australian likewise returned to Egypt, since it was scheduled to go to Greece. Jumbo Wilson soon followed the Australians, also destined for Greece. In his place, Lieutenant General Phillip Neame, VC, brought from commanding the Palestine garrison, took over in Cyrenaica. His command, like O'Connor's, had two divisions.

The word *division* ought, however, to be placed in quotes where the 2nd Armoured was concerned. That division had arrived in Egypt early in 1941 and promptly lost the commander who had trained it, Major General J. C. Tilley, who died shortly after reaching the Middle East. His replacement,

Major General M. D. Gambier-Parry, had been with the British military mission in Greece, and like Neame, he had no recent battle experience. Then the division was dismembered. One of its two armored brigades and part of its Support Group (its motorized infantry and artillery) were earmarked for Greece. The divisional headquarters, the remainder of the Support Group, and its other armored brigade went to Cyrenaica. That brigade, however, was not a cohesive formation. Only one of its original battalions remained with it, and of the two that had been added, one was equipped with light tanks and the other with captured Italian models. All the division's British tanks badly needed maintenance. Forward reconnaissance was no longer in the hands of the experienced 11th Hussars, who had also gone back to Egypt. In their place were the King's Dragoon Guards, who had exchanged their horses for armored cars only in January 1941. The 6th Australian Division's place had been taken by Major General Leslie Morshead's 9th Australian, which had never been in action—indeed, it had barely completed its training. Throughout Cyrenaica Command, there was a shortage of transport and radios, both, of course, critical items in mobile warfare. Thus, the advantages of mobility and quality, so heavily on the British side under O'Connor, had definitely swung to that of their opponents by March 1941. Even given that risks had to be taken somewhere, that equipment was scarce, and that the desert flank seemed safe for a while, it is an open question whether Wavell need have left it quite bare of experienced leadership as well. O'Connor may have been tired, but later in the war, generals of all nationalities directed active operations for much longer periods of time than the eight weeks of Compass.

By March, with the movement of troops to Greece under way, Wavell himself was beginning to feel some anxiety over the state of Cyrenaica Command. In a signal to Churchill, he admitted that he had taken risks there, but he remained confident that the enemy could attempt nothing serious until May. In view of the shortages of transport, however, he decided that units of the 9th Australian Division, positioned well forward, should be pulled back to the Benghazi area. Now only the ill-equipped, inexperienced, and understrength 2nd Armoured Division remained in the forward area facing a rapidly growing force that included Rommel's (German) 5th Light Division and an Italian armored division. About this time, the RAF commander in Cyrenaica, Group Captain L. O. Brown, sized up the situation and gave instructions to his formations to prepare for a rapid withdrawal, since he felt certain the army would be unable to stop a German-led attempt to cut off the British in the "bulge" of Cyrenaica by striking across the desert—O'Connor's maneuver in reverse. Eight days later, Rommel struck.

There is no indication that Rommel initially planned anything like the operation that developed. But as his World War I record, interwar writings on tactics, and conduct as a panzer division commander in France the previous year all testified, he believed in both commanding from the front and employing aggressive tactics to grasp or create fleeting opportunities. As the 2nd Armoured Division's Support Group fell back before his initial probe, Rommel sensed the hesitancy of the British command, and what had begun as a limited operation blossomed into an all-out, albeit improvised, offensive to sweep the British out of Cyrenaica. Neame's headquarters were not equipped to handle mobile warfare, nor did Neame have any experience of it. Gambier-Parry was equally inexperienced, and his tanks were in such poor mechanical shape that he forecast a breakdown rate of one tank every 10 miles if his sole armored brigade was involved in active operations. Thus, even if the 3rd Armoured Brigade simply maneuvered without firing a shot, it would quickly cease to exist. At a critical moment on April 2 with Gambier-Parry's two brigades in retreat, Wavell, who had a nose for a brewing crisis, arrived at Neame's headquarters, overruled a tactical decision on the handling of 2nd Armoured just taken by Neame, and imposed his own. Then, feeling no confidence in Neame as a battle manager, he sent for O'Connor. Within forty-eight hours of launching his attack, Rommel had claimed his first victim from the ranks of Britain's generals.

By the time O'Connor arrived on April 3, Wavell had changed his mind. Neame would remain, but O'Connor would "advise" him.[47] At this point, the situation was beyond anyone's control. Grabbing forces as they came to hand, Rommel pushed small German-Italian battle groups eastward across the desert, aiming to cut off and destroy the British forces in the Cyrenaican bulge. It was a gamble that horrified his Italian superiors (and enraged Halder), but Rommel had quickly gotten the measure of his opponent's inferior equipment and tactics as well as the slow reaction time of the British command structure. Neame's command disintegrated. The Australians got away eastward from Benghazi to Tobruk; 2nd Armoured was lost in bits and pieces, as much to mechanical breakdown as to Rommel. Neame, O'Connor, and Brigadier J. F. B. Coombe (who had commanded the 11th Hussars brilliantly during Compass and come up from Egypt with O'Connor) were captured during the withdrawal when their unescorted staff car drove into a German patrol.[48] The finishing touch to the debacle was the destruction of the 3rd Indian Motor Brigade at Mechili, where it had been positioned to block any advance across the desert aimed at the coast road and Tobruk.

The state of the 3rd Indian Motor Brigade was a good commentary on the state of the Indian Army in early 1941. The brigade was made up of three recently mechanized Indian cavalry regiments, carried in trucks. It had no armored vehicles, no artillery, and no antitank guns (and only half of its allotted radio sets). It is hard to see how its troops, armed with nothing more than rifles, could have been expected to deal with even Italian tanks, let alone German, despite the quality of these troops. By the evening of April 7, Brigadier E. W. D. Vaughan's force was loosely encircled by a scratch German-Italian force. With Vaughan by that time were some other fragments of Neame's command: Gambier-Parry and his headquarters, a few British field guns, and some Australian antitank guns. On April 8, the Germans, themselves too few, tired, and poorly supplied to attack at that moment, twice demanded the surrender of the Mechili garrison and were twice refused. Gambier-Parry and Vaughan then decided to try a breakout the following morning. When it failed, they surrendered.

Wavell, Harding, and the Australians saved something from the wreckage. Harding, reaching Tobruk on April 7 and hearing nothing from Neame or O'Connor, decided they had been captured. Together with Morshead, he began rehabilitating the derelict Italian defenses and organizing a force to hold Tobruk. Wavell flew up from Cairo the following day, heard Harding's assessment of the situation, and, after one of his famous silences, simply said, "Well, if you think you can hold it, you'd better." Within three days, Rommel had encircled Tobruk, and one of the war's most famous sieges had begun.

In less than two weeks, Rommel had retaken all that Compass had won. He had wiped the equivalent of a full division off the British order of battle and captured three generals and an equal number of brigadiers.[49] Only Wavell's willingness to gamble, Harding's ability, and Australian toughness kept him from taking Tobruk at a rush. The cause of this disaster is in general clear enough: insufficient forces with the right sort of training, equipment, and leadership, itself a commentary on the degree to which Britain was waging war on a shoestring. There were, however, more specific shortcomings, some of them quite familiar. Once again, the British appeared "over-deliberate, slow, reactive." British equipment, admittedly poorly maintained, did as much damage to the hapless 2nd Armoured as German shells. And Wavell's performance was very mixed. A good case can be made for his initial assumption that the desert flank was secure until May. But when that assumption began to appear shaky, it is hard to see what the 3rd Indian Motor Brigade added to the stopping power of Neame's force. Wavell's loss of faith in Neame led not to his replacement but to the installation of O'Connor as a watchdog, far too late to do any good. Only the clear, courageous decision to hold Tobruk shows Wavell at his best. When assessing Churchill's outburst of fury at the army a few weeks later, it must be remembered that Ultra made it clear to the prime minister just how much Rommel had done with scanty (if qualitatively more impressive) forces. Now it would all have to be won back, and the springtime avalanche of defeat would have to be counterbalanced by victory. But victory over Rommel was to prove singularly hard to organize.

The spring of 1941 was a time of great stress for Churchill. He had been prime minister for a year during which the only successes the British had against the Axis, apart from the supremely important victory in the Battle of Britain, were the defeats inflicted on the Italians in Africa. Yet even these successes had been quickly overshadowed by defeat at German hands in Greece and in the Western Desert. Murmurs were beginning to be heard in Parliament about the quality of Britain's war leadership: not, of course, about Churchill's inspirational qualities but about his management of British strategy. However unfair this might have been, it was not something Churchill could ignore. To him, the basic requirement for the successful conduct of the war was the continued unity of public and parliamentary opinion behind his coalition government. Nothing would help that more than to give the British public—blockaded, blacked-out, bombed, and rationed with increasing stringency—a taste of victory. Without that, dogged resolution sustained by rhetorical defiance might no longer be enough.

Moreover, Churchill had to contend with the convolutions of alliance politics. The United States, an unofficial but supremely important ally, was beginning to voice decided opinions about strategy. One of these was that the British commitment in the Middle East was not necessary to final victory. In this, the Americans ignored both the degree to which war generates its own momentum and the dependence of the British on Middle Eastern oil. Thus, for reasons of both domestic morale and alliance politics, the prime minister felt a victory to be essential. In addition, he believed that he had provided, at great risk, the wherewithal for battlefield success, and the Germans had given him what he regarded as indisputable evidence that the moment was ripe for a counterstroke at an overextended Rommel.

Reading the message traffic from Wavell on an April Sunday morning at Chequers, Churchill decided to hasten the replacement of the tank losses in

Greece and the desert by sending a fast convoy through the Mediterranean rather than by the safer but slower route around the Cape. To carry out this resolve, he had to override the reservations of his professional advisers. (The charge that he had done this between 1914 and 1915 when he was First Lord of the Admiralty, although not entirely fair, had done him great damage and was something that he had battled for years.) Since units of the German air force had established themselves in Sicily in January, the central Mediterranean had been deemed an unacceptably hazardous place for convoy operations. If the Tiger convoy and its escort were destroyed or sustained major losses, the responsibility would clearly be the prime minister's alone. One of the ships was indeed lost, but the other four, carrying 43 Hurricane fighters and 238 new Crusader tanks that Churchill christened the Tiger Cubs, would reach Alexandria on May 12.[50]

A week after the decision that launched Tiger, Churchill's mounting frustration with the army exploded at Chequers.[51] That colorful episode was the beginning of a crisis in the prime minister's relations with the army that ended with him sidelining Dill and sacking Wavell. Lurking just behind the defeats in Greece and the Western Desert were two other issues that added to Churchill's irritation with Wavell and Dill. The first was Wavell's handling of the revolt in Britain's client kingdom of Iraq, which broke out on the night of April 1 and threatened access to oil, communications with India, and the stability of the vast Middle Eastern base. Churchill felt it had to be promptly and decisively suppressed. Wavell, overstretched everywhere, was not eager for another campaign, even a minor one, and he urged a political solution. The prime minister had long thought Wavell soft on the Arabs. "General Wavell, like most British Army officers, is strongly pro Arab," he noted in March.[52] During an exchange with Wavell the previous December, Churchill had told him, "Our policy of conciliating [the Arabs] has not borne much fruit so far. What I think would influence them much more would be any kind of British military success."[53] The argument got sharp enough for Wavell to hint at resignation and for Churchill to make it clear that any proffered resignation would be accepted. In the end, Wavell cobbled together a scratch force that crossed the desert from Palestine to Baghdad and helped in the suppression of the revolt in Iraq. The lion's share of the work was done by Indian Army units, whose prompt dispatch to Basra by the commander-in-chief, India, General Sir Claude J. E. Auchinleck, drew Churchill's praise. From that point on, a new star began to rise in the east.

The quarrel with Dill was much more serious because it involved fundamental issues of strategy. Dill's mood in the late winter and spring of 1941 was strange. He had taken the lead in proposing the bold reinforcement of the Middle East the preceding summer, but as combat deepened there, so did his pessimism. He had doubts about the commitment to Greece but deferred to Eden and Wavell—though he remained very dubious about the result. While visiting Morshead's 9th Australian Division before Rommel's attack or the Greek campaign opened, he startled the divisional staff by speaking of "bloody noses" to come in the desert and the Balkans.[54] As late as midsummer, he told Major General John Kennedy, "I suppose you realize we will lose the Middle East?"[55] Some of this clearly was Dill's innate pessimism, but some of it may well have arisen from the belief that Britain was committing scarce resources in the wrong places. Throughout the late winter and early spring, intelligence assessments continued to indicate that the Germans could and would attempt an invasion in 1941, as the only way to bring the war to a successful conclusion. On April 10, the members of the Joint Intelligence Sub-committee of the Chiefs of Staff gave it as their opinion that Germany considered an invasion of Britain a priority. Despite mounting reports to the contrary, they felt a German attack on Russia was unlikely. (Almost simultaneously, Churchill was coming to the opposite conclusion.)[56] Dill, knowing how far from complete the reequipment and training of the British Army was, became more concerned that the Middle East commitment could expose Britain to a fatal blow by siphoning away resources that would be desperately needed should Hitler's postponed invasion finally be mounted. In the aftermath of Kennedy's stormy evening at Chequers, that concern led Dill to raise fundamental strategic issues with Churchill. The ensuing argument exhausted his credit with the prime minister.

On May 6, working from a draft supplied by Kennedy, Dill sent Churchill a long memorandum entitled "The Relation of the Middle East to the Security of Great Britain," which put the matter as bluntly as possible: "I believe we have gone to the limit, if not beyond it, in respect of the security of Great Britain." Dill added that, in any case, Singapore, not the Middle East, ranked second to Britain itself on the empire's strategic priorities list. Giving that sort of opening to a controversialist of Churchill's mettle was a tactical error. "I gather you would be prepared to face the loss of Egypt and the Nile Valley, together with the surrender or ruin of the army of half a million we have concentrated there, rather than lose Singapore," the prime minister riposted, while not engaging directly with Dill's invasion fears. Dill refused to quit, although in his memoirs, Churchill claimed the discussion lapsed at this point. Two days later, again working off a draft by Kennedy, Dill defended himself against the charge that he was prepared to face the ruin of the Middle East theater, argued again for upgrading Singapore's defenses, and concluded on a defiant note: "I certainly intended to imply that if we reach a point when the maintenance of our position in Egypt would endanger either the United Kingdom or Singapore, we should hold fast to the two latter, even if this meant the loss of Egypt. That is my considered opinion." The German attack on Crete was looming, and at this point, the exchange came to an end. Its consequences, however, did not.[57]

In his postwar memoirs, Churchill remarked that many governments would have "wilted" in the face of the CIGS's démarche but that, supported by the War Cabinet and the other two service chiefs, he was able to maintain the focus on the Middle East that had become central to his strategy. He noted, however, that the documents "astonished" him. In fact, they did much more. They led to the final loss of his already diminished confidence in Dill. In his memoirs, he said nothing of this beyond noting that Dill seemed more concerned with Singapore than Cairo. Ismay, however, writing after the war to Wavell's official biographer, John Connell, was more candid: "If you will read the minute Dill sent to Winston in May 1941 you will see what I regard as the most extraordinary document that has ever seen the light of day. Put yourself in the P.M.'s place and ask yourself whether you would have much confidence in the strategic advice of a man who had put his signature to that document."[58] Churchill's faith in both his CIGS and his principal theater commander had been nearly exhausted by mid-May 1941. Five days later, the Germans attacked Crete.

In an operation as bold as their coup in Norway a year before, the Germans took Crete in the world's first (and to date only) airborne invasion. Crete was defended by part of the recently evacuated Greek expeditionary force under the overall command of Major General Bernard Freyberg, VC, of the New Zealand Division, who had handed over command of his own force to his senior brigadier. Freyberg had only a handful of tanks and virtually no air cover. Much of his force, made up of oddments evacuated from Greece and dumped on Crete, represented little in the way of real fighting power, but he had his own New Zealanders and a brigade of Australians. He had as well the same high-quality intelligence that Ultra had provided Wilson. Indeed, if foreknowledge in detail of enemy intentions could guarantee success, Crete would have been a stunning British victory. Knowing one's enemy's intentions, however, is not enough. The German attackers had to seize an airfield rapidly to allow reinforcement and resupply or else perish. In the opening hours of their attempt to do so by capturing Maleme airfield, near Suda Bay, they found themselves in a precarious situation.

The argument has been made that a rapid and determined counterattack would have crushed the scattered, tired German paratroopers and turned the battle in Freyberg's favor.[59] But Freyberg was reluctant to usurp the role of the acting divisional commander, who in turn did not hustle his brigadiers. They fought their isolated battles cautiously. The opportunity, fleeting as all such were when confronting the Germans, passed. Maleme fell; German reinforcements poured in; and after a grim withdrawal south across the island, the remnants of Freyberg's force were plucked from open beaches by the Royal Navy.[60] To have held Crete would not have turned the tide of the war, although denying Cretan airfields to the Germans would have eased the task of resupplying both Malta and Tobruk, if simultaneously adding to the strain on British sea power and airpower. It would most certainly have been a welcome boost to British morale. As it was, the verdict passed on the small-scale British operations in Norway—"an army over-deliberate, slow, reactive"—again seems a fair commentary.

With Greece and Crete lost, Tobruk besieged and Rommel on Egypt's frontier, the Iraqi revolt as yet unsubdued, and the looming necessity of moving against Vichy Syria (whose deeply hostile French authorities had facilitated the passage of German aircraft to Iraq), Churchill understood that victory against the Germans was a clamant necessity. Wavell had to provide that victory. Not only had Churchill rushed critical equipment to him at great risk in the Tiger convoy, he also had evidence from Bletchley Park that Rommel was in difficulty. Annoyed at the degree to which Rommel had exceeded orders, Halder had sent a senior staff officer, Lieutenant General Friedrich Paulus (who would surrender at Stalingrad in February 1943), to rein him in. On May 2, Paulus sent a long signal to Berlin in which he referred to the "thoroughly exhausted" condition of Rommel's forces. Within forty-eight hours, a decrypt of this signal was available in London.[61] If Rommel's troops were tired and his supplies short, a fleeting window of opportunity was surely, it appeared, open to the British. A victory that would solve or alleviate so many problems seemed to beckon.

This was not, however, how matters looked in Cairo. For months, Wavell had been shuttling resources between widely separated campaigns: East Africa, the Western Desert, Greece, and Crete. To this had been added the suppression of the revolt in Iraq and the preparation of a preemptive invasion of Vichy-controlled Syria. Wavell had resisted these last two commitments;

indeed, as noted earlier, it took a direct order from London to get forces moving toward Baghdad. He bore as well both the responsibility for constructing and managing a vast base area in Egypt and the burden of being virtually military viceroy of a huge, volatile area stretching east into Iraq, south to Kenya, and north to Turkey.[62] No other Allied theater commander of the war would have to juggle quite as many disparate responsibilities—or make do with forces as exiguous—as Wavell during the lonely year when he commanded Britain's only active theater.[63] By the late spring of 1941, he was unquestionably tired, something he himself admitted in a letter to Dill. More than fatigue was involved, though. There was a deep temperamental incompatibility between the reserved but immensely self-confident Wavell and the ebullient, demanding prime minister. Apparent after Wavell's brief visit to London during the fraught summer of 1940, it had deepened thereafter into something like mutual mistrust. In the aftermath of the evacuation of Greece, Churchill temporarily silenced criticism at home by demanding a vote of confidence in the House of Commons (which he won by a margin of 477 to 3). Yet he knew that an end to the grumbling would only come with a victory. Wavell, whose replacement Churchill was by now seriously weighing, was the only British general in a position to supply one. His fate was now bound up with the success of his counterstroke against Rommel.

Wavell, himself conscious of how tired he was as well as how precarious his tenure of command had become, prepared the first British offensive against Rommel handicapped by a problem not of his making and beyond quick remedy. That was the quality of his tanks. The Tiger Cubs, fresh from England, were riddled with mechanical defects. Correcting these flaws and making additional modifications for local conditions delayed the offensive for a month. That was particularly unfortunate, since it gave the Germans time to remedy deficiencies in their forward defenses on the frontier between Libya and Egypt. Ironically, these had been exposed by one of Wavell's characteristic gambles, Operation Brevity. Knowing tank reinforcements were on the way and aware from the Paulus report of Rommel's apparently shaky position, Wavell planned Brevity and set it in motion three days after the Tiger convoy reached Alexandria. The reinforced brigade under Brigadier W. H. E. "Strafer" Gott, which was all that was available, would only have made an impact if Rommel's forces were as unready for mobile war as the Italians had been.[64] As it was, Brevity's few gains were quickly erased, and after analyzing the battle, the Germans strengthened the antitank defenses of their positions along the frontier between Egypt and

Libya.[65] Brevity's successor, Battleaxe, thus would face an alerted and more heavily defended German position backed by the 21st Panzer Division, which had arrived to reinforce Rommel's original light division (the two became the heart of the famed Afrika Korps).

Wavell issued his orders for Battleaxe on May 28. The enemy's frontier positions were to be taken, and it was expected that this would precipitate a clash with Rommel's armor. Victory over the panzers would then be exploited to relieve Tobruk and clear Cyrenaica.[66] The assumptions behind Wavell's orders were as optimistic as Battleaxe's objectives were sweeping. On the same day, however, Wavell sent a message to Dill in which he warned the CIGS that he was doubtful about the degree of success that would attend Battleaxe, largely because of the weakness of his armored formations. Under pressure to produce results, Wavell was in fact rather fatalistically gambling. None of this was passed on to the operational commander, Lieutenant General Sir Noel Beresford-Peirse, who was left in no doubt about either the importance of the operation or the boldness and determination with which the commander-in-chief expected it to be conducted.

Beresford-Peirse, who had commanded the 4th Indian Division in the opening stages of Compass, had under him a weak corps, with Western Desert Force having morphed into XIII Corps. His two divisions, the 4th Indian (under Major General Frank Messervy, an Indian Army cavalryman who had made his reputation as an aggressive brigadier in operations against the Italians in East Africa) and the 7th Armoured (still under Creagh), looked like the old Compass team. But appearances were deceiving. Messervy had only one brigade from his own division, plus the 22nd Guards Brigade. The 7th Armoured, which, in one of Wavell's worst decisions, had been virtually disbanded after Compass, had only recently reassembled. Its tank crews barely had time to acquaint themselves with their new and often mechanically unreliable vehicles. There was no time for collective training. Transport of all sorts was in short supply, and there was no tank-recovery organization to retrieve and repair battle-damaged or (and this was all too likely) malfunctioning tanks. Creagh and Beresford-Peirse would have a further handicap as well: the dominance the heavy German armored cars in Rommel's reconnaissance units quickly established over the lighter British models meant that the flow of tactical intelligence the latter vehicles were supposed to provide would be largely cut off. Controlling a complex battle would be difficult enough for Beresford-Peirse, even with adequate tactical intelligence, because he had placed his headquarters 60 miles (a five-hour drive) to the rear. This was as far forward as he could be and still be in effective communication with the RAF, whose headquarters were in turn 100 miles farther back.

Beresford-Peirse's plan was shaped by geography and the capacities of his armor. At varying distances from the coast, the land rises to the vast inland plateau of Libya. This rise, or escarpment, could be negotiated by wheeled vehicles at only a few points. One of them was Halfaya Pass, strongly held by the Germans. Messervy was given the job of taking both Halfaya Pass and Fort Capuzzo to the northwest. To assist him, he was given one of Creagh's brigades, the 4th Armoured under Brigadier Alec Gatehouse (who, as a lieutenant colonel, had been with 7th Armoured Brigade in Compass). Gatehouse's brigade was equipped with Matildas, the slow, heavily armored infantry support tanks that had wreaked havoc among the Italians six months before. Messervy in turn ordered his Indian brigade, supported by a few of Gatehouse's tanks, to attack from both ends of Halfaya Pass (that is, from both above and below the escarpment), while the rest of Gatehouse's brigade and the 22nd Guards Brigade took on Fort Capuzzo. Meanwhile, Creagh, with the remainder of his division (made up of faster cruiser tanks), would swing wide to the west, protecting Messervy's flank and precipitating the armored clash that would be Battleaxe's critical moment (and in which Gatehouse's Matildas, their infantry support role presumably concluded, would join).[67] The plan bore obvious resemblances to Compass. And since Beresford-Peirse's headquarters were so far to the rear, the task of making this complicated design work was left to the two divisional commanders; they were expected, while each was directing his own battle, to consult together about the timing of its phases. XIII Corps in fact went into action as a corps without an effective commander.

Battleaxe began on the morning of June 15. Messervy's attack on Halfaya Pass was stopped cold. Below the escarpment, four of the six supporting Matildas were knocked out; above it, eleven of twelve were lost. Most of this execution was done by the five German 88mm guns dug into the Halfaya defenses.[68] Meanwhile, Messervy's second prong successfully took Capuzzo. On the desert flank, however, the 7th Armoured Brigade came up against German defenses (including four 88s) that stopped it, with heavy losses. The second day of Battleaxe was no better. Messervy again failed to take Halfaya but beat off a German counterattack at Capuzzo. But the 7th Armoured Brigade was being forced back by the tank regiment of Rommel's 5th Light Division, hurriedly brought up from reserve outside Tobruk to reinforce 21st Panzer.[69] By day's end, the brigade had only some twenty-one tanks in running order. June 17 was the day of reckoning for Battleaxe.

Rommel, as always forward coordinating his battle, ordered both his tank regiments to strike at the weakened 7th Armoured. The attacks began at dawn, and by 8:00 A.M., the German armor had pushed Creagh back to a point where Messervy's forces around Capuzzo were in danger of being cut off. At 9:30 A.M., Creagh got through on the radio to Beresford-Peirse and told him that only twenty-one Crusaders and seventeen Matildas were still operational.[70]

Wavell was at XIII Corps headquarters when this news arrived. He had flown up from Cairo the day before, drawn by the same instinct for a crisis that had led him to fly up first to Neame's headquarters and then to Tobruk in April. He immediately set out with Beresford-Peirse in an unescorted light aircraft and landed at Creagh's headquarters, virtually on the battlefield, shortly before noon. By that time, the critical decision had already been taken—by Messervy. Fearing that the Guards Brigade at Capuzzo would be cut off by Rommel's tanks, he had ordered a retirement, which was in any case already under way. Studying the situation, Wavell confirmed Messervy's decision and ordered the whole operation broken off.[71] He then flew back to Cairo (to be told by the new RAF theater commander, Air Marshal Arthur Tedder, that he was guilty of "criminal lunacy" for exposing himself as he had). Tedder's anger was the least of his concerns, for he must have known that his days as commander-in-chief were now numbered.

British losses in Battleaxe were relatively light—less than a thousand men dead, wounded, and missing. Nearly half the 7th Armoured Division's tanks became casualties, however—two-thirds of the Matildas and nearly one-third of the Crusaders. It was not immediately clear to the British that much of this loss was inflicted by Rommel's handful of 88s. In that failure to appreciate what had really happened lay the germ of further disaster.

The failure of Battleaxe was swiftly followed by a nearly clean sweep of the command structure responsible. Churchill had been too keyed up with anticipation to await the results of the operation in London. He spent the day at his beloved country home at Chartwell, which had been mostly closed for the duration of the war. There, he received the news that Wavell had failed. After walking about the grounds "disconsolately" for a while, he returned to London to dismiss Wavell. For several months, Churchill had had his eye on the commander-in-chief in India, General Sir Claude J. E. Auchinleck, who he believed had the aggressive determination Wavell increasingly seemed to lack. He told one of his staffers that he felt like a fisherman with two lines out. On one, he said, was a tired fish and on the other a lively one, and he proposed to switch them over. Dill was not consulted and only learned of Wavell's dismissal when he received a copy of the prime minister's message to Cairo. Dill lugubriously told Kennedy that the Middle East would be lost; he told John Colville (of Churchill's staff) that Wavell had twice Auchinleck's brainpower and added that Wavell could write and would use his pen after the war. When Colville reported this conversation, Churchill replied that he also planned to write after the war and offered to wager that he would outsell Wavell. Despite this lighthearted reaction, Churchill refused Wavell's request to return home on leave. He would not, the prime minister said, have the general sitting in his club grumbling (and, he might have added, providing a focus for the critics of the prime minister's efforts as minister of defense).[72] Wavell, by his own admission as well as Churchill's evaluation burned out, was to go immediately to Delhi to take over Auchinleck's onerous job. Other dismissals followed. Sir Michael O'Moore Creagh was replaced by Gott as 7th Armoured's commander. Beresford-Peirse lingered for a while before being transferred to the backwater of the Sudan command. Of the Battleaxe team, Messervy alone survived.[73] Four months had passed since Rommel had arrived in Africa; his toll of British generals already stood at six.

Battleaxe was barely a skirmish by the standards of the titanic struggle that opened on the Eastern Front the day Churchill sent his signal to Cairo relieving Wavell. Yet it is worth considering because it has been singled out in the most widely read popular account of the desert war as the one premature offensive of the war into which Churchill succeeded in stampeding reluctant generals.[74] Obviously, there is some truth in this assessment, although it is far from the whole truth. Wavell had to attack to save his job, and he was palpably reluctant to do so. But there is more to the story than that. Battleaxe is also a good point at which to take a snapshot of the British Army a year after Dunkirk and nearly two after the war's beginning. At the top, a void was opening. Dill had lost credibility with the prime minister, who had not yet, however, decided to replace him—or perhaps it would be more accurate to say that he had not yet found a replacement. The bulk of the army remained in the United Kingdom, expanding rapidly with all the constant shuffling of personnel and dilution of quality that entailed. There was no common doctrine, junior leadership was inexperienced, and the necessity to reequip the army after Dunkirk had kept obsolescent equipment pouring from the factories. If Dill was obsessed with invasion, it was because the War Office understood that the British Army was far from ready to face the Wehrmacht. And it was, of course, from the army at home that the army in the Middle East drew its reinforcements, such as the ill-fated 2nd Armoured Division.[75]

The army in the Middle East, however, was very different from the army in the United Kingdom. For one thing, its British component was a minority of the force. Wavell's army was actually a multinational (and multiethnic) coalition. Despite the fact that it served under the Union Jack and British senior officers, it was prone to all the stresses and weaknesses of a coalition. The largest single contingent of troops in the theater was drawn from the Indian Army, a long-service regular force with its own officer corps (still overwhelmingly British), history, customs, and traditions—and undergoing an expansion as rapid and frantic as the British Army's, with the same problems of loss of quality and with an even scantier supply of equipment.[76] Then there were the Dominion formations—three Australian divisions and the New Zealand division. Citizen armies made up of volunteers (neither Dominion conscripted men for service overseas), they were built on minuscule regular cadres. The field-grade and general officers had no combat experience more recent than 1918. Despite their formidable fighting qualities, they were not easy formations to handle—British senior officers deplored Australian "indiscipline" but could do little about it. Moreover, the senior Dominion commanders had the right to appeal to their home governments if they received orders that they felt seriously imperiled their formations. Neither Blamey nor Freyberg ever invoked this "charter," even over Greece (about which both had grave doubts), but Wavell was always conscious that they could. Indian and Dominion formations were infantry; British Army units in the theater were either support formations, gunners, or armored units.[77]

If using British formations did not present the political problems that using Dominion units posed, they offered a bewildering variety of their own. The Matildas were slow and, once the 88s appeared, very vulnerable. The Crusaders were mechanically unreliable and undergunned. But the biggest problem was that the doctrine that governed their employment, going back to Hobart's creation of the 7th Armoured Division before the war, was one that spurned combined arms warfare in favor of tank-heavy formations operating independently. Hobart believed that armor, thanks to the radios installed in every tank, had a communications network far superior to that of the infantry and gunners and that tethering tanks to other arms would slow the pace of operations. The successes 7th Armoured Division had in Compass reinforced Hobart's ideas. That division became an exem-

Wavell (right) and "the Auk." Successive Commanders-in-Chief, Middle East, neither could sustain his credit with Churchill in the face of defeat—but Auchinleck would render two great services: he stopped Rommel in July 1942, and he guided the Indian Army in the transition to independence in 1946–1947. (Courtesy Imperial War Museum, image no. E 5448)

plar of an approach to battle that would affect the way British armor was handled for the balance of the desert war. The British would almost invariably have superiority over Rommel in numbers, and courage was never lacking, but deficiencies in equipment and technique meant that, while the Germans maneuvered and fought as all-arms formations, British armor, infantry, and gunners fought separate wars. The fact that infantry was mainly Dominion or Indian whereas the armored units were British would make this compartmentalization all the more awkward when Dominion troops felt "abandoned" by British tanks.

The army that Wavell commanded had real deficiencies in doctrine, training, and equipment, which contact with the Germans revealed. Whether Wavell understood this is questionable. He operated at a level far above the tactical. Indeed, it seems clear that few British or Dominion senior officers grasped in mid-1941 exactly what the problems were and how they could be fixed. It is also clear that Churchill did not understand much of this either. Nonetheless, this was the army that would have to deliver the victory over Rommel that the prime minister needed. To produce victory with an instrument whose flaws were not yet fully appreciated, Churchill summoned, from New Delhi, General Sir Claude Auchinleck.

3

Rommel's Victims

"The Auk," as General Sir Claude Auchinleck came to be known, was a very different type of soldier from his predecessor. Wavell, despite his Black Watch associations, was thoroughly English. Auchinleck's relatives were Irish Protestants; his mother came from an Anglo-Irish landowning family, and his father, a gunner colonel, was a descendant of those tough Scots who were settled in Ulster early in the seventeenth century. Irish Protestants, a governing minority in a restless land, had always been heavily represented in the commissioned ranks of the British and Indian armies.[1] Claude Auchinleck was sent to Wellington, a public school founded as a memorial to the Iron Duke that sent many of its graduates into the army. Weak at mathematics, he could not follow his father through the Royal Military Academy at Woolwich and into the Royal Artillery. Lacking a private income, neither could he aspire to the regular British Army. So it had to be Sandhurst and the Indian Amy, which he joined in 1903. India would thereafter be his real home. In World War I, he served in Mesopotamia in a campaign as unremittingly vicious, if on a smaller scale, as that on the Western Front. Like Wavell in the British Army, Auchinleck was recognized during the interwar years as one of the Indian Army's up-and-coming men. He was one of two Indian Army officers chosen to attend the Imperial Defence College in its inaugural year (1927) and held a key position on the directing staff at the Indian Staff College at Quetta. Then came one of the Indian Army's most coveted commands, the Peshawar Brigade, which he led in one of the Raj's interminable frontier campaigns, during which his troops performed outstandingly. Newly promoted to major general in 1936, he became deputy chief of staff at Army Headquarters, India, and over the next two years, he wrestled with the problems of modernizing the Indian Army for the war that was clearly looming.

Auchinleck was called back to Britain in January 1940 to take over the newly formed IV Corps, destined to move eventually to France as part of the BEF. Instead, however, he found himself caught up in the doomed Norwegian campaign and given command of the force assembled to take Narvik. Auchinleck did this successfully, although it was necessary to demolish the port and evacuate almost immediately because the catastrophe in France overshadowed the relatively minor disasters in Norway. But his competence at Narvik caught Winston Churchill's eye. In England after Dunkirk, Auchinleck was given the job of forming a new corps, V Corps. When a major command shuffle made Alan Brooke commander-in-chief, Home Forces, in July, Auchinleck succeeded him at Southern Command, which covered that part of the coast most exposed to invasion—the only Indian Army officer, apart from Ismay, to hold a major appointment at home. He himself was succeeded at V Corps by one of Brooke's favorite divisional commanders, Bernard Law Montgomery. And thus began one of the stormiest relationships among British generals during the war and one that still reverberates in the war's historiography. Monty usually found superior authority galling (except, perhaps, that of his patron "Brookie"). The fact that he had not graduated high enough from Sandhurst to enter the Indian Army may have exacerbated his feelings about Auchinleck, although Monty could be equally unpleasant to those who called to mind no past failures of his own.[2] In any case, Montgomery did not have to chafe under Auchinleck for long. At the year's end, Auchinleck was named commander-in-chief, India.

Auchinleck's first tenure as commander-in-chief, although brief, was his springboard to the Middle East, although (being as devoid of the capacity for intrigue as Monty was gifted with it) he certainly did not intend it to be. At fifty-four a full general with a knighthood, he had reached the summit of his professional ladder. The Indian Army, expanding much too rapidly under the pressures of Britain's war needs, required a sensitive hand at the helm to keep the inevitable diminution in quality to a minimum.[3] As commander-in-chief, Auchinleck had to preside over the expansion, training, and dispatch overseas of a steady stream of units. He had also to concern himself, as a member of the Viceroy's Executive Council, with the impact of the war on India's volatile politics, something that in turn could easily affect the morale and cohesion of the army. It was an all-consuming job, even if he was not called upon to make major strategic decisions. Yet it was hard to avoid involvement in those decisions when they affected areas in which the government of India had a long-standing interest, such as Iraq. And it was through Iraq that Auchinleck moved from Delhi to Cairo.

Since World War I, when the Indian authorities had begun, and the Indian

Army had borne the brunt of, the Mesopotamian campaign, Iraq (as Mesopotamia became after that war) had been one of India's strategic concerns.[4] When the internal situation there began to deteriorate in the spring of 1941, Wavell saw it as an unwelcome distraction, another claim on his already overstretched forces. He therefore advised delay in dealing with the Iraqi nationalists who seized power in Baghdad. Auchinleck, however, had been planning for the contingency of armed intervention in Iraq for some time. When asked for help, he promptly diverted to Basra a brigade group, already embarked at Karachi for Malaya. He also arranged for troops to be flown into the exposed RAF base at the Shaiba, near Basra. Once again, Churchill noted Auchinleck's aggressive alacrity and contrasted it with Wavell's reluctance. This was not entirely fair to Wavell, who had multiple pressing commitments in April, whereas Auchinleck had no responsibility for active operations anywhere. Nonetheless, from April on as Wavell's star waned, Auchinleck became more fixed in Churchill's mind as the man he wanted in Cairo. June 21, 1940, was Auchinleck's fifty-fifth birthday and the day he learned he was to succeed Wavell. Nine days later, he stepped off a plane in Cairo. So tightly had the news of his appointment been held that there was no one there to meet him.

To assess Auchinleck's fourteen months in the Middle East, it is crucial to grasp just how different from either the British or the Commonwealth armies the Indian Army really was. Originally the private army of the Honourable East India Company, organized by the merchant adventurers who built an empire, the Indian Army remained institutionally separate when the company was finally abolished in 1858. Its officers were entirely British until 1919, when a very gradual policy of "Indianization" was begun. Upon graduation from Sandhurst, Indian Army officers spent a year with a British Army unit in India (a bow to that army's belief that it set the highest standards) and only then joined their Indian Army regiments. Thereafter, their career paths until retirement were separate from those of their Sandhurst classmates who received commissions in the British Army. India had its own staff college at Quetta, established before World War I. The only Indian Army officer to hold a major command outside India as of that date was Frederick Roberts. Field Marshal the Earl Roberts of Kandahar, VC, already a Victorian hero, had taken over after the first disasters of the Boer War and won the conventional war against the Boer republics, thereafter retiring to England and the post of commander-in-chief of the British Army. Roberts, however, was a rule-proving exception. The Indian Army was a thing apart. Its officers and those of the regular British Army knew little of each other, and there were tensions between the two groups. Part of this was professional rivalry, but part was rooted in the impact of the British class structure on Britain's military institutions. Indian Army officers often came from Indian Army families and almost invariably combined their abilities with moderate financial means. Although commissions ceased to be purchased in the British Army after 1870 (they never had been in the Indian Army), private means were still very important. An officer without them could not really hope to join one of the "good" infantry or cavalry regiments that set the tone for—and whose officers were well represented in the higher ranks of—the British Army. Sandhurst graduates of modest circumstances who graduated high enough, however, could go to the Indian Army, where, with a good salary and low expenses, an officer could live on his pay and perhaps save a bit. That Indian and British Army officers were distinct not only professionally but also in more subtle ways is something to be remembered in all that follows.[5]

But what of their professional abilities? Some British officers felt that Indian Army officers were not quite up to date (as well as being a bit infra dig). The way to determine the validity of this assessment is to look at what the Indian Army actually did. That army had two missions: to support the civil authorities if necessary and to defend the North-West Frontier. The defense of the frontier involved two distinct foes—one was only potential but was much feared nevertheless, and the other was a real but limited antagonist. The menace of Russia loomed in the nightmares of British India's rulers from early in the nineteenth century (and as late as the 1920s, it would preoccupy staff officers in New Delhi). If the Russians came, they would come through Afghanistan and the passes that led into the Indus plain, preeminently the fabled Khyber Pass. While staying alert to meet a major invasion from that direction, the Indian Army could keep in fighting trim (on the terrain where it might be called upon to face invasion) by maintaining the ascendancy of British arms in the face of the numerous and ferocious tribal warriors who lived in the no-man's-land that straddled the Indo-Afghan border. Whether these borderlands could ever have been permanently subdued by the British is arguable; that they were not ensured an excellent training ground for generations of Indian Army officers in a type of warfare that was limited but intense. Indian Army officers returned repeatedly to the frontier at various stages of their careers and might easily see much more action than their British Army contemporaries. This was the basis of the Indian Army officers' belief that they were the British Empire's true military professionals. But how relevant was such experience to warfare against modern armies?

The Indian Army fought in France in 1914 and 1915, but its principal theater was the brutal campaign in Mesopotamia (where Auchinleck and William Slim both served). Frontier war had given the Indian Army a good grounding in company and battalion tactics, and its long-service regular core provided a solid basis for expansion. The Indian Army produced good regimental soldiers, but in 1914 and 1915, its senior officers (the product of an archaic seniority-based promotion system that produced elderly generals) did not make a very impressive showing—and the Turks, although their higher headquarters were staffed with German "advisers," were only a semimodern foe, without the industrial base for a fully up-to-date army. After 1918, the Indian Army went back to the frontier (and "aid to the civil") both literally and symbolically. It reverted to its pre-1914 pattern, although political change driven by rising nationalism was reflected in a small but slowly growing number of Indian officers. It retained its horsed cavalry units until 1939.[6] The wall separating the Indian and British armies remained largely intact. A few outstanding Indian Army officers, such as Auchinleck, returned to England to attend the staff college at Camberley or the newly created Imperial Defence College, and the ideas generated in England, especially by the apostles of mobility, found echoes at Quetta. But the Indian Army still prepared to fight in defense of the North-West Frontier, sustained by supplies borne on mules and camels. Meanwhile, it policed the tribesmen. There was, however, a requirement to send troops to the Middle East to defend imperial interests there. In the circumstances of the late 1930s, this would require a radical restructuring of the Indian Army, something that drove the deliberations of the committees with which Auchinleck, as deputy chief of staff, was deeply involved.

The year of Munich was also the year when the need to modernize the Indian Army was finally faced. In the 1938–1939 winter, a committee of inquiry, headed by Admiral of the Fleet Lord Chatfield (and whose Indian Army member was Major General Claude Auchinleck), took evidence in India and then retired to London to write its report. The conclusions were fairly obvious; indeed, the committee might have come to them without even leaving London. If the Indian Army was to be deployed overseas in a major war, it had to be extensively reequipped (which also implied considerable retraining). Much of the funding and all of the equipment would have to come from Britain itself, since neither the budget nor the economy of the Raj could provide for modern armed forces. In the short interval that elapsed before war came, British factories, trying to meet the demands of Britain's own rapidly expanding services, could provide little for India. And after the strategic revolution of May and June 1940, Britain, struggling to reequip its own army and sustain the war in the Middle East, had virtually nothing to spare.

Until very late in the war, the Indian Army was equipment poor. But unlike the British Army, it was manpower rich. The regular Indian Army was relatively small—with slightly under 200,000 officers and enlisted men at the outbreak of war. The rank and file came from the "martial classes" (a category invented by the British in the late Victorian period that in practice meant conservative agricultural peasants and hill tribesmen from northwestern India) or, like the Nepalese Gurkhas, from client states. The army's reserves were small, and its mobilization plans were designed to double its peacetime strength in a slow, controlled growth. At the outbreak of the war, it sent a division to Egypt and a brigade group to Singapore in conformity with prewar plans. Then France fell—and all prewar schemes became obsolete. The crying need of the British Empire was for troops, and India was a potential reservoir of them.[7] Enlistment remained voluntary, but in India, where the prestige of the army was high (at least among some parts of the population) and the economic incentives to enlist considerable, it seemed there would never be a shortage of recruits. Nor was there. By 1941, the Indian armed forces (for there were small naval and air forces as well as the army) numbered over 1 million, by 1944 nearly 2 million. At the end of the war, the Indian Army was over 2 million strong, making it the largest voluntarily enlisted force in history.

The problems for Wavell in 1940 and 1941 had been strategic and operational; for Auchinleck, they had been largely administrative and organizational. The new commander-in-chief would have a steep learning curve in Cairo, compounded by the fact that he came from a decidedly different personal and professional background. Not surprisingly, Auchinleck initially took over much of Wavell's staff. Lieutenant General Arthur Smith remained chief of staff (although one observant staff officer thought that Smith, a Guards officer, was never as close to Auchinleck as he had been to Wavell). Brigadier John Shearer, who Harding thought much too optimistic in his assessments, remained intelligence chief. For deputy chief of staff, Auchinleck selected Major General Neil Ritchie, who had been his brigadier, General Staff (that is, chief of staff, or BGS), at Southern Command.[8] There were other vacancies to be filled besides deputy chief of staff, and in selecting individuals for them, Auchinleck was handicapped by his comparative lack of knowledge, as an Indian Army officer, of the British Army. He had, it is true, just spent a year in England, but he had held so many postings—IV Corps, Narvik, V Corps, Southern Command—in such rapid order (and at a time of expansion and reorganization when many other officers were also moving from job to job very briskly) that the year's experience did little to remedy the remoteness from the officer corps of the British regular army that resulted from his nearly forty years of Indian service.[9] Yet it was the British regular army that would supply most of his key subordinates in the Middle East—despite the fact that there were more Commonwealth and Indian fighting units than British in the theater when Auchinleck arrived. His lack of firsthand knowledge of the personnel of the British Army and his loyalty to his subordinates, once chosen, were to be a continuing source of weakness.

Moreover, he took over in Cairo at a time when fundamental changes were occurring at every level of the British war effort. Hitler's attack on Russia relieved Britain's isolation but made the task of the commander-in-chief, Middle East, even more complicated. Wavell had had to concern himself with the possibility of a German drive to the southeast, through the Balkans to Turkey or (after Crete) possibly via Cyprus to Syria—hence London's pressure on him to move into the latter. This possibility was, in British minds, by no means extinguished by the launching of Operation Barbarossa. Military opinion in London expected the Wehrmacht to crush Russia in a few months, although the prime minister was skeptical of this assessment. If it turned out to be correct, however, not only could the Germans then return to the southeastern thrust that had come to a halt after the capture of Crete, they also might well strike south through the Caucasus into Persia (as it was still called, especially by Churchill, who disliked minor powers changing their names). Auchinleck's tenure of command in the Middle East coincided with the most successful phases of the German campaign in Russia. When he was relieved by Churchill in August 1942, German troops were driving into the Caucasus and events in Stalingrad were months in the future. The war against Rommel was a crucial consideration for him. But so too was the preparation of two armies, the Ninth (based in Syria under Jumbo Wilson) and the Tenth (based in Iraq under Lieutenant General E. P. Quinan of the Indian Army), that would meet any German thrust through Turkey or the Caucasus. Auchinleck did not balance multiple campaigns as Wavell did, but he fought with one eye constantly looking over his shoulder.

The Russo-German war affected Auchinleck in other ways as well. A voracious new claimant for supplies had appeared. As significant was the Russians' demand for a second front, as they defined it, made within weeks of the German attack and reiterated with drumbeat insistence thereafter. The British, of course, could offer nothing that would make any significant difference on the Eastern Front. But desperate to keep Russia in the war, they offered everything they could think of—supplies and the convoys to carry them. Whatever impact these gestures may have had in Russia, they cost the British dearly. The only things the British could point to, however, that actually engaged German forces in combat were Bomber Command's assaults on German cities and the desert war. Both thereby gained additional importance in Churchill's eyes.

If the pressure Wavell felt for launching an early offensive was transferred immediately to Auchinleck and if the German attack on Russia presented the commander-in-chief with a set of additional strategic anxieties, at least some of the administrative changes made simultaneously with his arrival left him more free to concentrate upon his strategic and operational problems. A year before, Wavell had suggested that some resident political guidance, available continuously, would ease the burdens that fell on him. But nothing had been done in this regard, and in April 1941, the other two commanders-in-chief (Admiral Sir Andrew Browne Cunningham and Air Chief Marshal Sir Arthur Longmore) joined Wavell in repeating the suggestion. What seems to have finally persuaded the prime minister was a letter from his own son Randolph (who had gone out to the Middle East as an officer in the Commandos) urging such an appointment. A week after Auchinleck was appointed, Oliver Lyttleton, then president of the Board of Trade, was named minister of state in the Middle East. Lyttleton would bring with him cabinet rank and a brief that gave him considerable power to supervise and coordinate a whole range of agencies and activities that had hitherto fallen on Wavell's shoulders.

At the same time, an attempt was made to grapple with the problems caused (not least in Churchill's mind) by the enormous administrative facility that had come into existence in Egypt. Wavell had begun the construction of this vast complex of bases, depots, and repair shops, essential if the forces of a Western industrial society were to be headquartered in a technologically underdeveloped area and then conduct operations in the wasteland of the desert. The prime minister had always suspected that, however necessary such establishments were, they had a tendency to grow exponentially and absorb far too much of the manpower and supplies assembled at such cost in Egypt. Given the inexorable nature of Parkinson's Law, there was probably more justice in Churchill's complaints than is usually allowed. Nonetheless, since a huge rear-area apparatus was necessary, the best solution was to manage it efficiently. To do this, Churchill appointed an "intendant general," General Sir Robert Haining, who had been vice chief of the Imperial General Staff. Divorcing logistic from operational control did not prove a workable solution, but Haining's appointment was the first step toward giving the commander-in-chief the necessary staff apparatus to control what amounted to an industrial infrastructure created to sustain his operations.

Auchinleck may have been given a more rational and efficient structure within which to work in Cairo, but none of this would matter unless he could defeat Rommel. Bound up with the problem of Rommel was the business of managing his relationship with the prime minister. Wavell had been dismissed, in part at least, because there was no real basis of mutual trust to cushion the series of hammer blows inflicted by the Germans between April and June. As he settled in to his new job, Auchinleck got a long letter from Dill, written as usual with input from Kennedy. The CIGS—who had warned Auchinleck as early as May 2 that Churchill had lost confidence in Wavell ("if he ever had any")—told Auchinleck that his predecessor had been under extremely heavy pressure to launch Battleaxe. "You may say I should have minimized this pressure. . . . I might possibly have done more to help Wavell than I did, but I doubt it," he went on rather defensively, adding that "the Commander in the field will always be subject to great and often undue pressure from his Government." Then he came to his point: "*You* should make it quite clear what risks are involved if a course of action is forced upon you which, from a military point of view, is undesirable. You may even find it necessary, in the extreme case, to disassociate yourself from the consequences."[10] Ismay later described Dill's May 6 note to Churchill as a "most extraordinary document," and if he had seen this private letter, he would doubtless have had an even stronger reaction. Dill basically admitted that he could not prevent military operations with which he disagreed from being undertaken and invited the theater commander to assume this responsibility, using the threat of resignation.[11] Some weeks later, Auchinleck got much more useful advice from Ismay, who sent a long letter in late August urging him to develop a personal rapport with Churchill: "Do write to him long personal chatty letters occasionally. I know that normally you would recoil in your modesty from doing so. But he isn't a normal person (thank God), and these aren't normal times."[12] It was one of Auchinleck's misfortunes that he seems to have taken Dill's advice more to heart that Ismay's.

By the time Ismay sent his letter, Auchinleck had already had the first of his arguments with the prime minister about the date for a renewed offensive against Rommel. Feeling his way in a strange and complex situation with a staff and field commanders who were new to him, Auchinleck moved cautiously. He had inherited an ongoing campaign in Syria, managed by Jumbo Wilson, and he wanted to wrap that up as a priority. This decision and a concern for the security of Cyprus (to whose defense he committed his one complete British infantry division, the newly arrived 50th) were driven by the fear of a German drive into the Middle East from the north. No one knew how long Russia would last—or that Crete would not be followed by another German airborne descent.[13] Auchinleck made it very clear in the exchanges that went back and forth during July that he would not move before he felt he had a reasonable prospect of success, and that would depend on the rebuilding and augmentation of his armor. Some of the argument was over numbers—Churchill's showing what had been sent to the Middle East and Auchinleck's reflecting the realities of time needed to modify the tanks for desert service and then for individual crews and units to train with what was, for most of them, new equipment. The discussion, however, also surfaced Auchinleck's understanding at this point of the tactical demands of the desert war: "It is quite clear to me that infantry divisions however well trained and equipped are no good for offensive operations in this terrain against enemy armoured forces. Infantry divisions are and will be needed to hold defended localities and to capture enemy-defended localities after enemy armoured formations have been neutralized or destroyed, but *the main offensive must be carried out by armoured formations supported by motorized formations.*"[14]

Clearly, the doctrine that went back through Hobart to the interwar apostles of mobility had quickly become the commander-in-chief's own. It may have been his before he got to Cairo. The Indian Army, although committed to raising armored divisions, had neither tanks nor a history of using armor. Middle East doctrine on the subject, fed back to India where all training was focused on preparing units for that theater, became Indian Army thinking as well.

It is interesting that Churchill, reading Wavell's final report on Battleaxe, had come to a somewhat different conclusion. In a note to Dill on July 11, he remarked that "several important instances are given of the effective use of motorized artillery against hostile tanks, and it would seem that a larger proportion of artillery should be used with every armoured brigade group." Although he went on to embrace the idea of armor as an offensive weapon in terms that Hobart would have approved, the prime minister had clearly spotted one of the weaknesses of British armored practice in the desert. It was an insight that would sow the seeds of another doubt—was the army making proper use of the weapons it had? Characteristically, Dill ignored this point, while spending several paragraphs defending Wavell and Neame against what he saw as unwarranted charges.[15]

As the argument dragged on through July—a month that also saw the receipt by Churchill of Joseph Stalin's first demand for a second front—it became clear to the prime minister that it would not be resolved by signals. Auchinleck was ordered home and told to take with him only a skeleton staff, since the prime minister had decided that the staffers in Cairo, all holdovers from Wavell, were infecting their new chief with their own caution. But Auchinleck stood his ground. On August 1, there was a five-hour meeting of the Defence Committee at 10 Downing Street (at which Clement Attlee, a lawyer by training, also pushed Auchinleck very hard). Auchinleck spent the following day, the eve of Churchill's departure for his first meeting with Franklin D. Roosevelt (FDR), with the prime minister at Chequers. Churchill reluctantly accepted the general's argument that he could not attack with any hope of success until November. On a personal level, the prime minister's meeting with Auchinleck was more successful than his encounter with Wavell the previous year. He told both Oliver Lyttleton in Cairo and the South African prime minister, General Jan Smuts (a longtime and much-valued confidant), that he was greatly impressed with Auchinleck and had full confidence in him. In retrospect, he noted that the commander-in-chief "gave me the feeling that he might, after all, be right, and that even if wrong, he was still the best man."[16] Yet even if, for the time being, the prime minister had been persuaded that an early offensive was not possible, his expectations for the November attack clearly would be very high.

Auchinleck also had a long talk with Ismay, the only Indian Army officer serving in the central directing machine in London. Ismay took pains to explain to Auchinleck ("for whom I had both admiration and affection") "the remarkable phenomenon who was now his political chief." In particular, he cautioned him against what he saw as Dill's great failing: "It was a mistake to take lasting umbrage if his criticisms were sometimes unduly harsh or even unjust."[17] What Auchinleck made of this is unknown. A few weeks later when Ismay urged Auchinleck to write unofficially to Churchill in order to forge a personal link that might become crucial, was Ismay prompted to do so by a sense that Churchill's acceptance of a delay until November was quite grudging? Or was it his concern that he had not convinced Auchinleck when he explained Churchill's nature and the best way to cope with it?

As Auchinleck slowly won his argument with Churchill, the Eighth Army was born. The forces available had outgrown the corps structure that had, in theory at least, run Battleaxe. Beresford-Peirse of XIII Corps was replaced by Lieutenant General Alfred Godwin-Austen, an infantryman who had commanded the defense of British Somaliland (and survived Churchill's disapproval of it) and then the 12th East African Division in the reconquest of Ethiopia. Godwin-Austen would have Messervy's 4th Indian Division and Freyberg's New Zealanders, fully recuperated after Greece and Crete. A second corps, XXX Corps, was created to control the armor. Major General Vyvyan Pope, the director of armored fighting vehicles at the War Office (that is, the most senior General Staff officer concerned with tanks), was named corps commander in what seemed an inspired choice. A much-decorated infantryman in World War I, Pope had transferred to the Royal Tank Regiment afterward.[18] He had moved to the War Office after serving as Brooke's BGS in 1940. To an unimpeachable combat record, he thus added specialization in armored warfare and good connections in the army hierarchy. Brigadier H. E. Russell, one of the original desert warriors who had commanded 7th Armoured Brigade in Battleaxe, became Pope's BGS. Both men, however, died in an airplane crash on October 5, 1941, while on their way from Cairo to the desert. To replace Pope, the commander of the 1st Armoured Division (then en route by sea from the United Kingdom), Major General Willoughby Norrie, was plucked from his ship and flown from Capetown to Cairo. Unlike Pope, Norrie was a cavalryman with no real background in armored warfare ("born on a horse" was one Cairo staff officer's verdict).[19] His key subordinate was Major General W. H. E. Gott, the 7th Armoured Division's new commander, one of the desert veterans whose considerable independence was thereby ensured. Thus, in each corps, only one divisional commander had previous desert warfare experience; neither corps commander had any. A great deal would therefore depend on the army commander who would coordinate their efforts.

Churchill strongly suggested Jumbo Wilson to Auchinleck, who, perhaps wisely, demurred. But the commander-in-chief's choice was scarcely more inspired. Lieutenant General Alan Cunningham, an artilleryman (and brother of the Mediterranean Fleet commander), had commanded East Africa Force, whose three divisions made up the southern arm of the vast pincer movement with which Wavell reconquered Ethiopia. Cunningham had managed very well, but his real enemies were distance and climate, not the poorly led and increasingly demoralized Italian colonial forces (one of Cunningham's divisions covered 1,700 miles in fifty-three days, suffering less than 500 casualties). East Africa Force's march was a logistic triumph but not perhaps the strongest of credentials for taking over an army preparing the first major British offensive of the war against the German army.[20] Why did Auchinleck choose Cunningham? When asked after the war, he said, "I was impressed by his rapid and vigorous command in Abyssinia and his obvious leaning to swift mobile action."[21] This might suggest that Auchinleck had not looked closely enough at what East Africa Force had actually done and in what circumstances. The real problem may well have been that his choices in the theater were limited and he did not know the regular British Army well enough to choose from among the lieutenant generals at home. The number of British officers of that seniority who had commanded in the field during the war was tiny, and at least Cunningham's campaign had ended in victory.[22]

As Eighth Army took shape and the date for the autumn offensive, christened Crusader, was set for November, Auchinleck had to deal with several other vexing issues. The brief, intense Syrian campaign ended shortly after his arrival in Cairo; the equally brief campaign to take control of Persia was handled by Indian Army units based in Iraq.[23] But minor campaigns to consolidate British wartime control of the Middle East were accompanied by the less tractable problems caused by the Commonwealth coalition. In the run-up to Crusader, Auchinleck had problems with all its members.

The South Africans were the newest arrivals, their 1st Division scheduled to play an important role in Crusader. In some ways, it posed the most delicate problems because South Africa's prime minister, General Jan Smuts, was one of Churchill's most revered associates. No Commonwealth figure—perhaps no Allied leader save FDR himself—was listened to so intently by Winston Churchill as was Smuts. A onetime Boer guerrilla leader, Smuts had political skills far exceeding his military gifts and had played a leading role in parlaying the Boer defeat of 1902 into a political comeback and self-government within barely a decade. He had become one of the Commonwealth's most distinguished leaders, and in 1943, Churchill would cause him to be made a British field marshal. Nonetheless, he presided over a white South Africa deeply riven by participation in the war. Only at the price of a major political crisis did Smuts bring his country into the war alongside Britain. Broadly speaking, although Anglophone South Africans supported the war, there were deep currents of opposition among Dutch-descended Afrikaners (though some Afrikaners supported Smuts and served). Smuts's government had to imprison a number of die-hard Afrikaner leaders whose supporters harassed the families of serving soldiers. Needless to say, service in the South African forces, as in all Dominion forces, was voluntary. (Black South Africans also served but only as unarmed support troops.) Because the South African divisions had been hastily raised on the basis of a pre-1939 Permanent Force of 350 officers and 5,000 men, they were still very raw formations, their training having been for the sort of "bush warfare" they had engaged in in Ethiopia. They were not trained or equipped for mobile warfare in the desert. Moreover, because they came from a deeply divided white ruling minority, South African commanders were very sensitive about casualties. Given the likely reactions to South African unhappiness, Auchinleck had little choice but to accommodate them. In the end, the start date of Crusader was postponed from early to mid-November to give Major General G. L. Brink's 1st South African Division an opportunity to run a full-scale divisional exercise.

The New Zealand division presented a different sort of problem. Rapidly approaching fighting trim again after its experience in Greece and Crete, the division had problems centered on whether Freyberg should remain in command. In the aftermath of Crete, a court of inquiry sat in Cairo, and two of Freyberg's brigadiers (one of them a political figure of some weight in New Zealand) did their considerable best to shift the blame for the defeat onto their divisional commander. The New Zealand prime minister, Peter Fraser, was in Cairo for the inquiry, and shaken by it (and driven also by concerns about the future handling of New Zealand's only division), he began canvassing British opinion about Freyberg's retention. Dill deferred to Wavell and Auchinleck. Wavell promptly weighed in in support of Freyberg, correctly pointing out that his brigadiers were the problem, and Auchinleck strongly recommended Freyberg's retention. Freyberg remained, to command the New Zealanders—the best Allied fighting force he encountered, according to Rommel—until the war's end.

Churchill was not involved in the questions of Freyberg's retention in command (although he was disappointed by the general's performance on Crete), but he was deeply engaged in Auchinleck's final Commonwealth issue of the summer: an argument with the Australian government over the withdrawal of its 9th Division from Tobruk that provoked a minicrisis between London and Canberra. Australia was making a major contribution to the war in the Middle East—three of its four divisions available for overseas service were there (the fourth was in Malaya). The 6th Australian Division had served in Compass and then in Greece and Crete. The 7th had done most of the hard fighting in Syria, whereas the 9th had been the backbone of the defense of Tobruk since April. In the late summer, the Australian government asked for the relief of the 9th so that all three Australian divisions could be concentrated, rested, and prepared for further operations as an Australian corps under Australian command. Some of this was driven by the personal ambitions of the senior Australian commander in the theater, General Sir Thomas Blamey, who was both general officer commanding, Australian Imperial Force, and Auchinleck's deputy. But much of it was the product of Australian nationalism; a suspicion about the use of Australian troops by British commanders, which dated back to World War I; and the fact that some of the hardest infantry fighting in the theater had fallen to Australians. Churchill had become very conscious that the prominence of Dominion troops in the desert, Greece, Crete, and Syria gave the impression that the war was being fought with Dominion manpower.[24] He had made clear to Auchinleck that the decision to put the British 50th Division into Cyprus, however sound in principle in the aftermath of Crete, reinforced this perception. Therefore, after trying to persuade the Australians to relent, Churchill and Auchinleck had to accept the withdrawal of the 9th Division in a complex series of operations that added to the burdens of the Royal Navy and RAF as well as the general stress of preparing Crusader. For Auchinleck, it was a distraction; for Churchill, it marked the beginning of a process of growing disenchantment with the Australians that would come to a head a few months later.[25]

During the fraught months of waiting for Crusader to begin, the prime minister's mind turned again to the question of how the British Army was fighting its battles. In reviewing Wavell's Battleaxe report, he had noted a lack of cooperation between armor and artillery. In early October, he returned to the question of the army's battle tactics: "Renown awaits the Commander who first in this war restores Artillery to its prime importance upon the battlefield, from which it has been ousted by heavily armoured tanks."[26] *Combined arms tactics* was not a phrase yet in vogue, but it is clear the prime minister sensed that there were flaws in the British "approach to battle"' in the desert. That flawed approach was most strongly held in the armored units, especially the veteran 7th Armoured; to be commanded in Crusader by Strafer Gott, the 7th would play the key role in the opening phase of the operation.

Planning for Crusader had begun in September. Godwin-Austen's infantry divisions (supported by a brigade of Matildas) were to clear the frontier defenses and then join with Norrie's armor to lift the siege of Tobruk (now held by the 70th British Division and a Polish brigade). The crucial role was allotted to XXX Corps, which had to defeat Rommel's armor. The method chosen reveals how relatively primitive British conceptions of armored warfare still were. Gott's 7th Armoured Division (whose three brigades contained 491 tanks, nearly two and a half times as many as the 174 in Rommel's two panzer divisions combined) would advance to a point in the open desert southeast of Tobruk and await Rommel's reaction.[27] Once the German armor was beaten, the way would be open for Godwin-Austen's infantry. However, both Godwin-Austen and Freyberg, whose New Zealanders would thrust toward Tobruk, were worried about the vulnerability of their infantry to German armor, despite the fact that XIII Corps was accompanied by 1st Army Tank Brigade (which had 132 infantry support tanks, more than either of the German panzer divisions could muster, and the heaviest armor in the desert). To meet their concerns, Cunningham agreed to hold one of Norrie's armored brigades in a position to protect XIII Corps's left flank until the German armor had been engaged by Gott's division. Thus, the dispersion of the crushing British numerical advantage in armor began.[28]

Cunningham's plan therefore handed the initiative to Rommel and involved dispersing 7th Armoured Division's strength before the fighting began, and there were other flaws in the structure of his force as well. Norrie, of course, had no experience in handling armor in battle. (Neither did any other British general, except O'Connor.) One of his three brigades, the 22nd—the first brigade of his former division to arrive in Egypt—was made up of completely inexperienced Yeomanry units (Territorial Army cavalry units recently converted to armor and still cherishing their cavalry traditions). British tanks were still mechanically unreliable, and British armored doctrine was still flawed. Much of this, the legacy of the past, could not have been remedied during the Crusader preparations. Other elements and the decisions behind them, however, are harder to explain. The motorized infantry division in XXX Corps was Major General G. L. Brink's 1st South African Division. Completely innocent of serious battle experience—it had been in Cunningham's East Africa Force—it had gotten its transport so late that the opportunity to train for its role was minimal. As noted, Brink was so worried about his troops' readiness for battle that he sought a further postponement of the offensive and only fell in line when Norrie (perhaps playing on South African racial attitudes) threatened to replace 1st

South African with 4th Indian Division in XXX Corps. Actually, it is hard to see why this was not done to begin with. As it was, Messervy's highly professional division, with more desert experience than any other available infantry formation, was given the secondary job of reducing the German-Italian frontier defenses after they had been isolated by Eighth Army's westward drive.

Crusader, the largest British offensive operation since 1918, began on November 18, 1941. Churchill's eve of battle message to Auchinleck expressed the hope that "the Desert Army may add a page to history that will rank with Blenheim and Waterloo."[29] The month-long struggle that followed was really two battles. Eighth Army lost the first—and its first commander. In a rather ragged fashion, it won the second, making it the initial British victory of the war over the German army. Cunningham was beaten in the opening week of Crusader because his flawed plan was made worse, ironically, by Rommel's untypical failure to react quickly to the British offensive. His eyes fixed on Tobruk, which he was about to attack, Rommel initially ignored the reports of a British forward move, assuming it to be a reconnaissance in force or perhaps a diversion in favor of the Tobruk garrison. Rommel's quiescence tempted Cunningham and Norrie to disperse their armor even more. On November 19, 7th Armoured Brigade headed north for Tobruk, while 22nd moved west toward the entrenched Italian Ariete armored division (the 4th was watching Godwin-Austen's flank). Thus, by the evening of the second day, Gott's three brigades were well out of supporting range of each other. His division had ceased to be a coherent formation just at the moment when Rommel belatedly began to react. In the ensuing four days of confused fighting, the British armored brigades were savaged, and Cunningham was on the verge of accepting defeat, ordering Crusader broken off, and retreating into Egypt.

As Norrie's armor spread out and probed for a reaction, the first major clash revealed the weaknesses built into the structure of Eighth Army. The Yeomanry regiments of Brigadier J. Scott-Cockburn's 22nd Armoured Brigade were ordered by Gott, perhaps with memories of Compass, to attack the entire Ariete division on the afternoon of November 19. They swung into their first action with courage and élan, mounting what one observer described as a cavalry charge in tanks. "They had incredible enthusiasm and dash," a Royal Tank Regiment officer later wrote of the recently converted cavalry units, "and sheer exciting courage which was only curbed by the rapidly decreasing stock of dashing officers and tanks."[30] Ariete, somewhat damaged, remained in place. That evening, the 22nd showed another aspect of deficient training when it reported half the brigade's tanks were out of action. This implied a loss of nearly 80 tanks, but in fact the actual battle losses were 25; the balance comprised mechanical breakdowns, most of which could be and were repaired. In the four days of muddled tank engagements that followed, erroneous figures, whether of German losses or of British runners (as the Eighth Army called operational tanks), were to further thicken the confusion that rapidly enveloped Cunningham. The three armored brigades, once dispersed by the initial plan and then by the decision taken on November 19, never again effectively combined. Gott's division, which outnumbered the whole Afrika Korps (indeed, the entire German-Italian armored strength), was repeatedly beaten in a series of engagements in which its brigades, either singly or, occasionally, paired in loose combination, faced whole panzer divisions or the united strength of the Afrika Korps. Rommel's errors were more than offset by the dispersal of British strength, the skill of the German commanders, and the soundness of German tactics.[31] By the morning of Sunday, November 23, Cunningham was faced with the reduction of 7th Armoured Division's strength to perhaps as few as 30 tanks.[32] This led directly to a command crisis that brought Auchinleck up from Cairo and Cunningham's career as Eighth Army commander to a close.

On November 21, when the battle seemed to be going well, Cunningham had already unleashed Godwin-Austen's XIII Corps. Now, as the dimensions of the defeat of XXX Corps became apparent, Cunningham's resolution began to waver. The New Zealand division was in the process of pushing toward Tobruk. Suppose it was attacked by Rommel's armor? The implications of a disaster to a Commonwealth formation were not only military but also political, and Cunningham started to think in terms of breaking off Crusader. Once he began to do so, however, control of his army started to drift out of his hands. Beresford-Peirse had delegated to his two divisional commanders the task of coordinating matters during Battleaxe. Now Cunningham's two corps commanders assumed the same responsibility. At noon on November 23, Cunningham, his BGS, Brigadier Alexander Galloway, Godwin-Austen, and Major Michael Carver (representing Norrie) met to discuss the situation. Cunningham expressed doubts about the wisdom of pursuing the offensive. Godwin-Austen, however, felt strongly that it should continue.[33] Later that afternoon back at his own headquarters, Godwin-Austen was reinforced in his view by a radio conversation with Norrie, who felt, rather surprisingly, that he could handle any counterattack Rommel might launch that day. Although Cunningham's corps commanders were determined to continue the battle, Cunningham himself was less sure. He asked Auchinleck to fly up from Cairo. Galloway, who also wanted to press on, privately contacted Brigadier Jock Whitely of Auchinleck's staff to stress that Auchinleck's presence was urgently needed. There seems little doubt that Galloway played an important role, perhaps the primary role, in trying to keep Cunningham's growing doubts about Crusader from being turned into orders to retreat. That evening, Auchinleck, accompanied by the RAF theater commander, Air Chief Marshal Tedder, arrived at Cunningham's headquarters, where the atmosphere had not been lightened by the news that the Afrika Korps had overrun and wiped out one of Brink's brigades.[34]

Auchinleck immediately ruled out any course of action except pushing on with Crusader. He sensed that the Germans would have sustained heavy losses in mauling XXX Corps and that he could prevail if he pressed on, by attrition if by nothing else. In fact, he was surprisingly accurate in his assessment. By the evening of November 23, Rommel had only 90 of the 249 German and Italian tanks that were available on November 18.[35] But on the following day, even though he was not fully aware of his own tank losses, he sensed, as he had in March, the uncertainty in the British command, and he gathered up the battered Afrika Korps and hurled it toward the Egyptian frontier. His raid was intended to shatter the remnants of the Eighth Army, driving it into the frontier defenses, most of which were still in German-Italian hands. Rommel misconceived the position, exaggerating the extent of British losses and underestimating his own. Nevertheless, his decision to direct his armor at the area where Eighth Army's vital supply dumps lay (not to mention its headquarters) would almost certainly have tipped the balance in Cunningham's mind toward retreat if Auchinleck had not been present.[36] Having made it clear that Crusader was to be pushed ruthlessly, Auchinleck flew back to Cairo the next day, with the question of the Eighth Army command revolving in his mind.

Auchinleck had become convinced that, even though Eighth Army could still win, a new army commander had to be found. Cunningham had evidently lost both his own confidence in victory and his subordinate commanders' confidence in him.[37] In addition, the RAF had little confidence in Cunningham. Tedder, who had long harbored doubts about the Eighth Army commander, made clear to Auchinleck that the RAF would like a change. But who could succeed Cunningham? Auchinleck did not want Wilson (and in any case, he was now commanding Ninth Army on what could quickly become a vital front). Eighth Army's two corps commanders were involved in a complex battle, and Norrie had not shone so far. Auchinleck did not want to wait for someone from Britain to arrive, even if he had known the British Army well enough to make a good choice. Almost by default, he looked at his own staff in Cairo and chose Major General Neil Ritchie, his deputy chief of staff. Ritchie was an infantryman who had served under Brooke in the BEF and under Auchinleck himself at Southern Command, before arriving in Cairo to join Wavell's staff just as Wavell himself was displaced by Auchinleck. A large, bluff, solid-looking man, Ritchie became an acting lieutenant general when he took over Eighth Army, although he was still junior in rank to both his corps commanders. As with Cunningham, Auchinleck made a choice that was questionable from the beginning.

The new command arrangements were buttressed by Auchinleck's presence at Ritchie's side during the remainder of Crusader, which, with Cunningham's removal and the failure of Rommel's spectacular dash to the frontier, entered a new phase. British leadership, if not necessarily any more deft, had suddenly become much firmer. Moreover, the battle turned into the kind of contest where British tenacity and greater resources could prevail. For the next ten days until Rommel, acknowledging defeat, retreated westward, much of the fighting took the form of a slugging match between Freyberg's tough New Zealanders, supported by infantry tanks, and Rommel's dwindling German forces. Grinding infantry fighting was something the Eighth Army could do well, and Godwin-Austen, the corps commander involved, was perfectly able to handle it. (The spirit of independence shown during Battleaxe, however, persisted: Freyberg made at least one important decision without bothering to inform Godwin-Austen.) By contrast, Norrie's armor, as it returned to action after the defeat and disorganization of Crusader's opening stages, accomplished relatively little. Attempts to turn Rommel's desert flank never quite came off, either through poor coordination by the British or because of good antitank defense by the Germans. In some ways, Crusader resembled Eighth Army's infinitely more famous victory at El Alamein. The initial ambitious plan involving the aggressive use of armor came unstuck and was replaced by a battle of attrition that was won by infantry, gunners, and sappers. And as at El Alamein, the pursuit phase saw the battered enemy successfully withdraw.

The pursuit of Rommel was managed by Godwin-Austen's XIII Corps, rather than by Norrie's corps. The performance of British tank formations during Crusader had, it is true, not been impressive, but the real reason XXX Corps remained behind mopping up Rommel's abandoned garrisons at Bardia and on the frontier may have had as much to do with "tribal" feelings as battlefield performance. "My own idea," wrote G. P. B. "Pip" Roberts, then a lieutenant colonel on XXX Corps staff, "is that Ritchie felt he could handle Godwin-Austen of XIII Corps more easily than Norrie; they both had infantry minds. And then there was a sort of club spirit among the armored commanders from Norrie through to the divisional and brigade commanders which Ritchie found difficult to deal with."[38] Godwin-Austen had Messervy's 4th Indian Division and, initially, 7th Armoured. By Christmas, he had followed Rommel almost to the starting point of the first German offensive nine months earlier. But the year closed on an ominous note. The 60 remaining tanks of the Afrika Korps turned on the 90 of 22nd Armoured Brigade, which was leading Godwin-Austen's pursuit and was out of supporting distance of other formations. For a loss of 7 of their own, the Germans knocked out 37 British tanks (again, many losses were due to breakdowns). Two days later, the Germans struck the luckless 22nd again, and this time, the British lost 23 tanks. The Afrika Korps thereafter continued its retreat unmolested, and the 22nd was withdrawn to rebuild.

As Crusader unfolded, Churchill watched anxiously (even arguing with Auchinleck over who would release communiqués on the progress of the operation). This was Britain's first major offensive of the war against the German army, and the prime minister had much riding on its success. During the planning phase, he had conducted a long discussion by signal with Auchinleck over British tank and air strength, pushing for the earliest possible start. The level of detail Auchinleck as well as Dill and his staff at the War Office had to deal with is impressive—Churchill at one point wanted to know why it had taken two weeks to unload 150 vehicles from three ships. This involvement certainly can be seen as micromanaging, and it has been portrayed in that light by many commentators.[39] Several things, however, have to be kept in mind in assessing this long-distance debate.

Churchill's access to Ultra told him of Rommel's continuing supply difficulties. (Auchinleck, of course, had the same intelligence but was also cognizant of his own multiple problems.) As summer wore into autumn, there were indications that German air strength, moved eastward to support Barbarossa, might redeploy to the west. Although Churchill would say in his memoirs that Auchinleck developed a "disproportionate concern" for his northern flank, no one at the time could be certain that the Germans would not succeed in Russia before winter. Certainly, Dill and Kennedy—as well as Alan Brooke at Home Forces—still had invasion concerns, which affected Churchill's thinking. The window of opportunity for a success against Rommel might not remain open for long. Moreover, there were compelling strategic and political reasons for the prime minister's desire to launch an offensive as soon as possible. American doubts about the strategic importance of the Middle East, first voiced in the spring, might be quieted; Russian demands for British action could only be answered by active British engagement with the German army.[40] Parliamentary and public opinion echoed the Russian question: what was the British Army doing? The problem was that, from their different perspectives, both Auchinleck and Churchill had good arguments. Churchill knew how large a proportion of available troops and equipment had been sent to the Middle East, how many problems Rommel faced, and how important a British victory would be for public morale and alliance politics alike. Auchinleck knew that numbers, of men or tanks, did not directly equate to fighting power; that many of his units were untried (such as the South Africans); and that much of his equipment (including the American light tanks) was new to those who would use it. Neither realized yet—although Churchill had shown glimmerings—that British doctrine was badly flawed. Churchill needed more than his army or its generals could yet give him.

Impatient as the prime minister was for Crusader to start, his mind was already leaping ahead to the exploitation of the victory he expected. Two operations—Acrobat, a drive to Tripoli to expel the Axis from North Africa, and Whipcord, an amphibious leap to Sicily—were under discussion in London and between London and Cairo by October. Auchinleck cautiously endorsed the first, subject to logistics, and felt the second to be impractical, as it certainly was. However, the expectation of a desert victory that could be exploited to seize the initiative in the Mediterranean may have been the factor that caused Churchill to decide to restructure the British Army's high command.

Dill's star had been waning since the spring, and his continuing concern with the possibility of invasion cannot have seemed to Churchill the best of credentials for leading the army into a new chapter of the war when Britain would be on the attack. On the eve of Crusader, Alan Brooke was invited to Chequers. There, Churchill told him that Dill would be stepping down, with a field marshal's baton as consolation, and would become governor of Bombay. Offered the leadership of the British Army, Brooke, with some trepidation (and, by his own account, hesitancy), accepted. "I am fully aware my path will not be strewn with rose petals," he told his wife. He cannot have been surprised by the offer—Dill had warned him a few days earlier of his own impending departure and expressed the hope that Brooke would be his successor.[41] But at that point, Dill thought that General Sir Bernard Paget, then commanding South-Eastern Command, and General Sir Frederick "Tim" Pyle, the head of Anti-aircraft Command and a favorite of Churchill's intimate Lord Beaverbrook, were very much in the running. In fact, Churchill was entertaining a much more radical departure—a forty-five-year-old junior major general then serving as director of staff duties at the War Office, Archibald Nye. It was an idea that tells much about Churchill and the British Army at that point.

Nye's background was unusual. The son of a regimental sergeant major, he was educated at a school for soldier's sons and went to war in 1914 as an NCO like his father. Commissioned a year later into the Leinster Regiment (which was also Dill's regiment), he ended the war with several wounds and a Military Cross for valor.[42] He had been a major general for little more than a year when he caught Churchill's eye. Brooke thought well of Nye—"a first class brain, great character, courage in his own convictions, quick worker with great vision."[43] The problem was that Nye was impossibly junior. The prime minister had to settle for making him vice chief of the Imperial General Staff, offering him the job the day before he invited Brooke to succeed Dill. This move abruptly displaced the incumbent, Henry Pownall, who had been Gort's chief of staff in May 1940 (and who would eventually work with Churchill on his war memoirs). Pownall was designated as the successor to the commander-in-chief, Far East, Air Chief Marshal Sir Robert Brooke-Popham.[44] It was an extraordinary episode. Pownall, understandably piqued, confided to his diary that "the P.M. is like that; he exercises his patronage in very peculiar directions and with little regard to the ordinary decencies."[45] But more than capriciousness was at work. On the same day Pownall complained to his diary, Churchill had lunch with a party that included the Fleet Street editor Charles Eade (who would eventually edit five volumes of Churchill's war speeches). Eade noted:

> Another question discussed was the new military changes. . . . Dill . . . is being retired on reaching the age limit of 60. . . . Mr. Churchill made it very clear to me that the retirement of Dill was not entirely due to the questions of age. . . . He also made it very clear that he has the highest opinion of Major-General Nye, who . . . had a very good grasp of affairs and was able to express himself well and clearly, and was a coming man. Nye is the son of a Sergeant-Major and went to a school for the sons of NCOs. He is, therefore, not a representative of

> the old school tie tradition. . . . In the present conditions, there might be a very good reason for the big promotion for a man representative of a more democratic education.[46]

Churchill, himself a product of one of the great public schools, Harrow, and of Sandhurst, was (at least in his own mind) doing more than elevating an officer who had caught his fancy. The dismissal of Dill and the appointment of Nye were to be a message to the War Office and the army that the prime minister's patience was running very thin.[47]

Alan Brooke began his tour as CIGS on December 1. (In the desert, Auchinleck flew up from Cairo to monitor Ritchie's performance. In the Pacific, the Pearl Harbor attack force was already at sea.) Brooke was a much tougher character than Dill, and he would need every bit of that firmness. A gunner by background, he came from an Ulster landed family. His nephew Basil, Viscount Brookeborough, was a major figure in the politics of Northern Ireland. Churchill, as a young army officer and war correspondent, had known Brooke's elder brothers, Victor and Ronnie, both also army officers. Brooke was marked as one of the army's up-and-coming men during the interwar years, although he was not much involved in the contentious discussions about the future role of tanks on which so much subsequent writing has focused. His ideas were shaped by his experiences as a gunner on the Western Front, where the British Army's successes in the offensive of August through November 1918 were due in large part to the development of very sophisticated artillery techniques. Brooke's approach to battle (like that of Montgomery, who had been a divisional commander under him between 1939 and 1940) would remain heavily influenced by the experiences of World War I, especially of the victorious concluding months. These, of course, were the experiences that, together with the massive casualties of the war, had produced a desire to find an alternative to stalemate through mechanized maneuver. When that attempt was frustrated through a combination of inadequate equipment plus training and doctrinal shortfalls, what remained were the caution about casualties and the methodical infantry-artillery tactics of 1918—a combination perfectly represented by Brooke.

In some ways, Brooke's persona resembled that of Dill, whom he much admired. He was somewhat gloomy and pessimistic—on armistice night in 1918, he noted that he felt low, skipped the celebrations, and went to bed. The opening entry in his 1939–1945 war diary could easily have been written by a peace activist: "It is all too ghastly even to be a nightmare. The awful futility of it all, as proved by the last war!"[48] Whether Brooke's pessi-

The CIGS at his desk. Brooke was Churchill's sparring partner, Monty's patron, and the British Army's dominant soldier, 1941–1945. (Courtesy Imperial War Museum, image no. TR 149)

mism was temperamental or the result of his experiences between 1914 and 1918 is now difficult to say. What is clear is that neither his pessimism nor Churchill's ability to batter his opponents would shake him as Dill had been shaken. A quick mind, even quicker speech, and adamantine determination would carry him through the war, not unmarked (as the candid and often angry entries in his diaries demonstrate) but unyielding in his determination that the British Army would fight in circumstances that would make a significant contribution to victory at an acceptable cost. Churchill would respect and value Brooke, but the warmth that marked his relations with Ismay or Alexander would never be present. The full impact of Brooke, on the army and on Churchill, would, however, be felt in the future. Brooke assumed office at a moment when the fortunes of war seemed to finally be moving in Britain's favor. Auchinleck was winning, slowly and clumsily but surely. The Soviets seemed likely to last at least until 1942. It was the last optimistic moment for nearly a year, for this was the point at which the full price of the commitment to the Middle East, shaped by circumstances in 1940 and deepened by the bitter spring of 1941, became starkly apparent.

In the course of his handover briefings to Brooke, Dill told his successor that he had made little provision for the defense of the Far East because, with British resources stretched so terribly thin, there was simply nothing that could be sent. Brooke, glossing his wartime diaries in the 1950s, noted that he agreed with Dill. In view of the argument between Dill and Churchill in the spring over strategic priorities, which both sharply lowered Dill's credit with the prime minister and led to Churchill's ruling decisively in favor of the primacy of the Middle East, this is a very revealing admission. Dill, it will be recalled, had argued at that time that Singapore, not Egypt, ranked second in priority to the United Kingdom itself and was far from adequately defended. It is hard to avoid the conclusion that his invasion anxieties and fear of overcommitment in the Middle East led him to try to trump Egypt with Singapore. It was a bad miscalculation, and that it was merely a ploy seems clear from his subsequent admission to Brooke.

The strategy based on Singapore as the bastion of Britain's Far Eastern defenses had an element of fantasy to it from the beginning and became increasingly surreal from 1936 on. By 1941, Britain was in a position where it was hard-pressed to hold its own in the war it was fighting—attempting simultaneously to prepare for a second major war on the other side of the world would be risking disaster in the war on which Britain's future depended. Churchill understood this. So did Dill and Brooke. (Unfortunately, no one made this clear to the Australians, thereby laying up more trouble for the future.) Dill did, however, do two things that helped shape the campaign in Malaya that began on December 8: he named the wrong person as general officer commanding there, and he failed to correct the worst of Churchill's misconceptions about the situation in the Far East.[49]

Lieutenant General A. E. Percival, forever frozen in history in the act of surrendering Singapore, was Dill's choice. Percival had been Dill's BGS at the British Expeditionary Force's I Corps in 1939 and 1940. (Henry Pownall, who saw a lot of him, wrote him off as "an uninspiring leader and rather gloomy."[50]) Percival followed Dill back to London in the spring of 1940 to become an assistant chief of the Imperial General Staff. Then came divisional command and finally Dill's decision to send him to Malaya. Although superficially a good choice—Percival had held a senior staff position in Malaya in the late 1930s—the essential soundness of Pownall's judgment became apparent as soon as the task of preparing for war, for which Percival's qualities as a staff officer were an asset, was replaced by the demands of conducting a campaign. The roots of the debacle at Singapore went back two decades, but the speed of the defeat owed much to Percival's failure as a commander.

Dill also failed to correct Churchill's worst misunderstanding about Singapore. The prime minister believed that it was a true fortress, capable of all-around defense. But it was not and had never been intended to be. It was certainly described as a fortress publicly both in Britain and Malaya, and in this case, Churchill may have taken optimistic public relations spin as fact. He believed that strongly defended fortresses could powerfully affect the course of a campaign. He was convinced that the defense of Calais (which he had ordered) had made the escape of the BEF from Dunkirk possible and that Tobruk had been a brake on Rommel's progress. His knowledge of military history furnished him with numerous examples, from Marlborough's campaigns through the American Civil War to Verdun. That he therefore believed Singapore to be such a fortress is not, perhaps, surprising. That neither Dill nor anyone else in the War Office or on his own staff corrected him is. Much later, Pownall would admit in a letter to Churchill that during his time at the War Office (1938–1939 and again in 1941), he could not remember the landward defenses of Singapore ever being discussed.[51] The best Ismay could do when drafting his memoirs was to say that "it had been taken for granted that the commanders on the spot would see to local defences against land attack from the north."[52] Ian Jacob (a Royal Engineer by training) wrote to Ismay after the war that he had never imagined Singapore as a true fortress, capable of all-around defense. Perhaps it seemed so clear to him that he never bothered to raise the issue with Ismay at the time.[53] This curious inattention to Churchill's oft-repeated belief in a "Fortress Singapore" was part of a general pattern of neglect of Far Eastern defense matters at the top in London in favor of the multiple, pressing demands of the war in Europe. A very high price was about to be exacted for this neglect.

The plans for the defense of Malaya and Singapore were a patchwork of half measures. Financial weakness and the need to placate the Americans led

Britain to endorse the Washington Naval Agreement of 1922, which made the Royal Navy a one-ocean force. British interests and obligations in the Far East were, however, not commensurately reduced, and a two-ocean navy was therefore still a requirement. The circle was squared, at least on paper, by the promise that should the security of Australia and New Zealand require it, the main British battle fleet would be sent to the Far East to deal with whatever threats had arisen. A massive naval base on Singapore Island was constructed to house the fleet when and if it arrived. (Carefully never addressed was what would happen if trouble arose in the Far East at a time when Britain itself was already in danger—though surely that was the most likely time for Japan to act.) The fading away of "main fleet to Singapore," in fact an unacknowledged prewar development, had left a vacuum even before the strategic revolution of May and June 1940. In the late summer of 1940, it was finally filled by an equally fanciful plan based on airpower—fanciful because the number of aircraft necessary to execute it (and London and the local commanders could never agree on what that number was) were simply not available in the face of the needs of Britain itself and the Middle East and, after June 1941, the aid given to Russia. The RAF in Malaya nonetheless built airfields the length and breadth of the Malay Peninsula, without much consultation with the army that would be expected to defend them. The army and RAF commanders barely spoke to one another, and the civil government cooperated only grudgingly with either. An overall commander-in-chief, Air Chief Marshal Sir Robert Brooke-Popham, who had been sent out in the autumn of 1940 to improve matters, had been recalled from the retired list and given inadequate staff and no authority over either the civil government or the local naval command.

Matters improved only slightly in 1941. The feuding RAF and army commanders were recalled, with Percival replacing the latter. The governor remained in place, however, and became no more cooperative. Troop strength was slowly built up, but although the numbers became respectable, the quality was not: two new, very raw, and also incomplete Indian Army divisions; an Australian division minus one of its three brigades and with no combat experience; and a number of newly raised and totally inexperienced Malay units. Even the increase in troops managed to introduce complications. The size of the force required a corps headquarters—Percival's own was a cross between a theater command and a local war office—and so III Indian Corps came into existence. The corps commander, Lieutenant General Sir Lewis "Piggy" Heath, was an Indian Army officer who was senior to the newly promoted Percival and had recent combat experience on the

North-West Frontier and in East Africa. (Percival, whose World War I record was good and who had served in Ireland during the Anglo-Irish war, had not seen combat since.) Percival did not hold the Indian Army in high esteem, and Heath was clearly unimpressed by his superior. Had anyone in London been paying attention, though the shortfalls in aircraft and equipment might still not have been remedied, at least the snarled and self-defeating chain of command in the Far East might have been unknotted. But no one was. During the bitter argument between Churchill and Dill over the Middle East in April, Churchill, brushing aside the concerns Dill advanced about Singapore, had ruled: "There is no need at the present time to make any further dispositions for the defense of Malaya and Singapore, beyond those modest arrangements which are in progress."[54] This signaled not only his dismissal of Dill's arguments but also a general waning of attention in London to Far Eastern matters. The defenders of Malaya and Singapore can also be numbered among the victims of Rommel's eruption into the desert war.

Evidence of the lack of coordination in the Far East finally compelled some action in midsummer, but it was cosmetic action without real consequences. Alfred Duff Cooper, a prominent antiappeaser (he was the only cabinet minister to resign from Chamberlain's government over Munich), had been made minister of information by Churchill. A failure there, he was made chancellor of the Duchy of Lancaster (a position without clearly defined duties) on July 20 and sent to Singapore on a face-saving mission of inquiry. He added nothing to the clarity of the command structure in the Far East, developing a dislike of Percival, the governor, and Brooke-Popham. Even had Duff Cooper been objective and incisive, however, it probably would have mattered little. In a September note on priorities, Churchill again ruled: "Malaya can wait."[55]

Finally, on the eve of Pearl Harbor, by which time it was clear that war with Japan was imminent, the command situation in the Far East got some attention. Brooke-Popham had done his best, but he was obviously in need of replacement by someone younger and with better links to London. Bernard Paget, at one point thought of as a possible replacement for Dill, was first selected and then held back, since Churchill had him in mind as the commander of a British contingent to be offered to the Russians for the Caucasus front—after the impending victory in the desert. Henry Pownall, whose job Churchill wanted for Nye, was then named, but he reached Singapore only on Christmas Eve.[56]

When Churchill received the news of the attack on Pearl Harbor that so exhilarated him, carrying its promise of complete victory, the stage had already been set for what he himself would label in his memoirs "the worst disaster" in British military history. So complete had been the inattention in London that he would later admit, in a note written during the drafting of his memoirs, that no one there even seemed to be clear about whether Malaya's northeast monsoon season would affect operations: "It is not to our credit in the highest circle at home that we did not know more about the actual climatic conditions in Malaya at this season."[57]

The disaster in Malaya began with the loss of the *Prince of Wales* and *Repulse* (sent to the Far East on Churchill's initiative to deter the Japanese) on December 10, sunk by Japanese naval aircraft—the first time capital ships, at sea and fully prepared, had been lost to air attack. This stunning loss was swiftly followed by the defeat of the 11th Indian Division, positioned near the Thai-Malay border, between December 11 and 13 by a Japanese force that numbered two battalions with a company of tanks. The division commander had wanted to withdraw to a better position. Heath supported the request. Percival turned it down. This set the pattern for the campaign. Heath and his commanders—Indian Army officers with a good sense of the weaknesses of their troops—wanted to buy time with space. Percival distrusted Indian Army competence and was obsessed with the airfields (from which the RAF had been driven in the first forty-eight hours of the campaign) and desperately anxious to keep the Japanese as far from Singapore as possible while reinforcements were arriving. He therefore imposed on III Indian Corps a slow withdrawal that led to its piecemeal defeat.

Churchill was steaming west on the new battleship *Duke of York*, on his way to a conference, known as Arcadia, that he had virtually forced on his newly belligerent and rather shaken American allies while the 11th Indian Division was being mangled. His principal concern was to preserve the "Europe First" orientation of alliance strategy. To support his case, he prepared three extensive papers on global strategy while the *Duke of York* plowed through a succession of gales. He had taken Dill with him, leaving Brooke, barely a fortnight in office, to mind the store in London. In spite of his focus on the future of alliance strategy, he monitored the new campaign in the Far East and, in one of his flashes of insight, warned on December 15: "Beware lest troops required for the ultimate defense Singapore Island and fortress are used up and cut off in Malaya Peninsula."[58]

The Japanese attack also resurrected Wavell. Denied permission to return home on leave in June (although he did return for consultations in September), Wavell, again in a key position at a bad moment, was told on December 12, "You must now look east. . . . You must resist the Japanese advance towards Burma and India and try to cut their communications down the Malaya Peninsula."[59] The 17th Indian Division, scheduled to leave India for the Middle East (and as raw as the 11th in Malaya), was placed at his disposal, as was the 18th British Division, rounding the Cape on its way to the Middle East, and some additional RAF squadrons. Auchinleck, still being urged to push on in exploitation of Crusader's success—"the only thing that matters is to beat the life out of Rommel and Co."[60]—was also told, "I have a hard request to make of you." A brigade equipped with American light tanks and four of the Middle East's Hurricane squadrons were needed for Malaya.[61]

It was all, of course, much too late. With the inevitability of Nemesis in a Greek tragedy, disaster was already unfolding in Malaya. Auchinleck offered to part with more than had been asked of him, and Wavell promptly shook up the command structure in Burma, hitherto a neglected backwater of Brooke-Popham's vast command. Wavell, however, was an older and more tired man than he had been in the Middle East, and he would never be at his best commanding against the Japanese, whom he consistently underestimated over the next two years. But even had he been the man he was in Cairo, there was really nothing he could have done that would have changed the ultimate outcome in Malaya.

As the year drew to an end and Churchill prepared to leave Washington for Ottawa, the full measure of the debacle ahead was still unclear. The Eighth Army was in Benghazi, and its advance forces were once again where they had been before Rommel's spring offensive. Churchill's focus was still on the westward exploitation of Auchinleck's success, complemented by an Anglo-American descent on French North Africa: "The Americans are very ready to come in on a vigorous application of 'Gymnast' so if you can arrive at the frontiers of Tunis we will put such a screw on Vichy or on French North Africa as will give us the best chance of bringing them out on our side . . . some highly trained American divisions may be thrown into the scale."[62] By comparison, the attention paid to events in Malaya was episodic. At one point, Churchill asked Ismay, "Who is now Commander-in-Chief, Far East. Has Pownall got there? If not, where is he?"[63] In fact, Pownall, delayed in Cairo at the outbreak of the war in the Pacific, got to Singapore four days after Churchill's query, taking over from Brooke-Popham, who had supervised the first crucial two weeks of the war while a lame duck.

The year ended for Churchill with two significant command decisions. The American Chiefs of Staff, especially the formidable army chief, General George C. Marshall, proposed a unified command for the Allied forces trying to stem the Japanese onrush in the Far East. Despite doubts—the preferred British model was the commanders-in-chief committee, such as operated in Cairo—Churchill felt it politic to agree. Marshall also had a candidate for the alliance's first supreme Allied commander—Wavell. Churchill was not enthusiastic. Wavell was not one of his preferred commanders, and moreover, it was evident that the new American-British-Dutch-Australian (ABDA) Command had very bleak prospects. Yet he could hardly refuse, nor did he put forward any other British names. Therefore, Wavell, newly grappling with Burma, was now to move to a headquarters in Java, responsible for everything from Burma (with which he was in only intermittent radio contact) to the Philippines and south to Australia. Churchill suggested Pownall as Wavell's chief of staff. Pownall certainly had experience in serving as a chief of staff in grim circumstances, but moving him barely a week after he took over from Brooke-Popham made for further command instability in Malaya.[64]

The other appointment had a happier result. Dill had established a rapport with Marshall at the Atlantic Conference meeting in August. The decision taken during the Arcadia Conference to establish the Anglo-American Combined Chiefs of Staff Committee meant that a very senior British officer was needed to head the British Military Mission in Washington and serve as the daily link between the British and American chiefs, who would only meet face to face at major conferences. Dill, whose friendship with Marshall would steadily deepen and who also had strong ties to Brooke, was the ideal candidate. Saved from rustication to Bombay, he would remain in Washington until his death in 1944, uniformly regarded as a crucial link in the alliance high command.[65] It is nonetheless ironic that two generals replaced by Churchill during 1941, neither possessing his full confidence, ended the year newly installed in critical senior appointments.

4

Debacles

The eight months that separated Rommel's January 1942 counterattack against Eighth Army from Montgomery's first victory at Alam Halfa (August 31 to September 3) represented both the nadir of the British Army's fortunes in World War II and the most precarious moment in Churchill's political life during his five years as prime minister. His achievements during his first visit to Washington had been considerable. The Arcadia Conference reaffirmed the primacy of the war against Germany. The Anglo-American Combined Chiefs of Staff machinery offered the British the opportunity, which they were to utilize skillfully, of having the maximum possible impact on American plans. Churchill had also begun his ultimately successful effort, forecast in the first of the papers he drafted aboard the *Duke of York*, to focus alliance strategy on the Mediterranean. The westward drive of Eighth Army would, in his vision, be complemented by Gymnast, an Anglo-American descent on French North Africa that would have the effect of "rallying" these Vichy-controlled territories to reenter the war, a plan ultimately realized by Operation Torch.

All of this is clear enough in retrospect. At the time, however, what was most obvious to parliamentary and public opinion was that the British Army was once again in full retreat both in the desert and down the Malay Peninsula. Shortly after his return from Washington, Churchill faced his first serious vote of confidence, and his overwhelming victory barely concealed the widespread unease felt over British military performance in the war's third year. Thereafter, as disaster piled on disaster—Singapore, Rangoon, Tobruk—and surrender followed surrender, Churchill began to voice serious doubts about the army's will to fight. In other quarters, doubts began to spread about his management of the war. By late summer, according to his Boswellizing doctor, one of his closest political associates was convinced that Churchill's political life depended upon victory by the Eighth Army over Rommel. Meanwhile, in India, defeat had produced the worst unrest with which the Raj had had to cope since the great Sepoy Mutiny of 1857.

The series of debacles that was to encompass most of 1942 began in the desert, where 1941 had ended on a generally gloomy note for Auchinleck. With the Russians pushing the Germans back, his northern front appeared safe for the moment. However, the Japanese attack on Malaya had pulled army and RAF units, on their way to the Middle East, into the new war. Auchinleck would lose not only promised reinforcements but also some formations of his own. At the same time that he was feeling the impact of a new war, the constriction of Rommel's trans-Mediterranean supply lines began to ease. Ultra could pinpoint the convoys that supplied the Afrika Korps and even the major ships in each. Only effective air and naval striking forces could decimate those convoys, however, and at the end of 1941, British sea power in the Mediterranean was sharply reduced by a series of calamitous losses. Supplies began to flow more freely to Rommel, who desperately needed them to replenish the attrition caused by Crusader.

One of the worst results of the Japanese entry into the war from Auchinleck's point of view may have been its impact on theater strategy. Churchill wanted Crusader's ragged success exploited as rapidly as possible. American commitment to Gymnast would put muscle behind the "Germany first" agreement. Gymnast in turn would be easier to sell if the Eighth Army was pushing victoriously westward. Thus, Auchinleck felt the sort of intense pressure to which Wavell had previously been subjected for an early resumption of the offensive. As Godwin-Austen's pursuit stalled at the end of its logistic tether and as Rommel began to regain his strength, Auchinleck (and Ritchie) were focusing on the next offensive operation, not on the perils of their forward units. The stage was set for Rommel's second unexpected lightning victory over an unready opponent.

There were some eerie similarities between Godwin-Austen's situation in January 1942 and Neame's in March 1941. The post-Crusader British advance had come to an end, as had O'Connor's advance in February 1941, because supply difficulties made it temporarily impossible to go farther. XIII Corps and the RAF required about 1,400 tons of supplies a day and were getting only about 1,150. (Rommel, of course, tended to ignore administrative problems, which could be tactically effective but operationally dangerous. By contrast, a good supply situation tended to be highly valued by the British, with their long tradition of campaigning in undeveloped places.)

Furthermore, the front was again held by a completely inexperienced and understrength division. The 1st Armoured Division had been committed, in hopeless circumstances, in France in June 1940. Rebuilt in England, it had no sooner been issued some modern tanks than it saw them stripped away again for shipment to the Middle East in the Tiger convoy. Their replacements were soon taken back for modifications in light of the complaints from Cairo about the mechanical state of the Tiger Cubs. Then one of the brigades, the 22nd, was given the best of the tanks and sent ahead of the rest of the division to participate in Crusader. On his way to the Middle East, the divisional commander, Norrie, was tapped to replace Pope. The new commander, Major General Herbert Lumsden, a cavalryman like Norrie, was wounded in an air raid as the division moved up to the front in January 1942 and replaced by Major General Frank Messervy from the 4th Indian Division, who had never handled an armored division. The division's only experienced formation, the 22nd Armoured Brigade, had had to be withdrawn to refit after its mauling by the Afrika Korps in late December. Consequently, the 1st Armoured had a new commander, no combat experience, only half its designed tank strength, and a supply situation that kept its one armored brigade well in the rear of the divisional Support Group (a mix of motorized infantry and artillery), which was thus the most advanced British formation. All this might not have mattered so much if Auchinleck and Ritchie had had a more precise picture of Rommel's strength and intentions.

Brigadier Shearer in Cairo had underestimated Rommel's tank strength in late December. Since then, a convoy carrying tanks had reached Tripoli, and by mid-January, those tanks had reached the front. This Shearer did know, but the original December mistake still led to an assumption of German weakness. Rommel, meanwhile, knew a great deal about his opponents. Tactical intelligence—and detail on supply difficulties—came from signals intelligence acquired by his radio-intercept company, and he had just come into a valuable new source of high-level intelligence, his own version of Ultra. Rommel's staff called it "the good source." It was, ironically, the American military attaché in Cairo, Colonel Bonner Fellers, whose cipher messages (in a key known as "Black" from the color of its binding) were being read by the Germans. Fellers had unlimited access in Cairo and reported voluminously to Washington—and unwittingly to Rommel's intelligence chief, Major F. W. von Mellenthin, as well. Rommel knew in mid-January that he had a window of opportunity for a spoiling attack, but it would probably not last beyond the end of the month. As in March 1941, he decided on a local offensive against the Eighth Army's forward units, and as on the previous occasion, he did not bother to inform Rome or Berlin. Ultra was therefore as silent as the so-called good source was loquacious. On the morning of January 21, 1942, Rommel moved.

Messervy had wanted 4th Indian (now commanded by the very capable Major General Francis Tuker) moved forward to within supporting distance of 1st Armoured. He was told the supply situation made this impossible. Thus, Rommel struck first at the Support Group and a motorized infantry brigade group (200th Guards) that had been placed under Messervy's command. Only forty-eight hours later did Messervy's sole armored brigade become involved. The odds were not overwhelmingly against the British. The Afrika Korps was much understrength, with about 12,500 men and 84 tanks. Even without his second armored brigade, Messervy had nearly 150 tanks (72 of them the light but mechanically reliable American Stuart tank, known to the British as the "Honey"). Rommel, however, leading from the front and with the Afrika Korps concentrated, imposed his own pattern on the battle. The British armored division, like its predecessor in March 1941, fought in bits and pieces. By January 23, Rommel, again sensing the hesitancy and lack of coordination among his opponents, was ready to expand his limited offensive into a more ambitious operation to push the British out of the Cyrenaican bulge. As usual, he brushed aside attempts by his nominal Italian superiors to restrain him, remarking that since German troops would do most of the fighting, only Hitler could order him to break off operations. Just at this point, the British command structure began to creak in an alarmingly familiar fashion.

Ritchie's initial reaction had been to tell Godwin-Austen that Rommel's advance presented an excellent opportunity for a counterblow. Godwin-Austen, closer to the realities of the battlefield than to the pressures for a renewed offensive that Ritchie felt, was not so sure. By early on January 24, the corps commander began to feel that a withdrawal to keep formations from being devoured piecemeal was the best option, and on the evening of January 25, he gave orders for it to begin. But that same day, Auchinleck had traveled from Cairo to Eighth Army headquarters, and no sooner had Godwin-Austen ordered a retreat than Ritchie countermanded it and ordered XIII Corps to attack, accepting the "greatest risks." Godwin-Austen, who by now had a fairly good idea what those risks might entail, protested in vain. To underline his determination, Ritchie took 4th Indian Division under his direct command, leaving Godwin-Austen a corps commander controlling a single division. Ritchie's determination, doubtless derived both from memories of the critical moment when Cunningham had faltered and from the presence of Auchinleck at his elbow, was rapidly overwhelmed by the realities of the battlefield. The next day, Messervy reported his division had only forty-one runners, and Tuker weighed in to point out that 4th Indian was in fact not a complete division but had only one brigade group in Benghazi (supply problems held the other two far in the rear). Nonetheless, not until January 28, by which time Rommel had Benghazi nearly encircled, did Ritchie agree to let Tuker withdraw. Only inspired leadership by Brigadier Harold Briggs got the 7th Indian Brigade Group out of the trap. The remnants of Messervy's division were already well to the east of Benghazi, and over the next week, the British pulled back to a line just west of Tobruk. British losses were light (although Messervy lost half his tanks), but the subsequent upheavals, from XIII Corps upward to Downing Street, were considerable.[1]

Godwin-Austen, whose realism in late January was later commended by the official historians, asked to be relieved, since Ritchie had so openly indicated lack of confidence in his judgment. Gott moved from 7th Armoured to XIII Corps, and Messervy took over the 7th, the original desert formation; Alec Gatehouse, also one of the original desert warriors, assumed temporary command of the battered 1st Armoured. In Cairo as well there were changes. Shearer, a talented man with numerous enemies and a reputation for excessive optimism, was replaced by Lieutenant Colonel Francis "Freddie" de Guingand, a very bright—and extremely tactful—staff officer.[2] Auchinleck's chief of staff, Arthur Smith, a holdover from the Wavell era, left about the same time, but the choice of his successor had a less happy outcome. Lieutenant General T. W. Corbett, an Indian cavalryman, was moved from his corps command in Iraq to take over Smith's job. As a Guardsman, Smith had been able to provide knowledge of the British service to his chief; Corbett probably knew less about the British Army than Auchinleck did.

Rommel's comeback deeply shook Churchill's confidence, which was never terribly strong, in the management of the British Army. It came at a moment when the prime minister faced multiple crises at home, in alliance politics, and in the new war against Japan. He took the offensive, his favorite tactic, and demanded a vote of confidence from the House. In the course of defending his stewardship, he paid Rommel a celebrated tribute: "We have a very daring and skillful opponent against us, and, may I say across the havoc of war, a great general."[3] Perhaps he intended his remarks as much to spur his own generals on as to acknowledge Rommel's talents. Four days later, he received from Auchinleck an analysis of what had gone wrong, which included an adverse verdict on British tanks: "I am afraid there are signs that personnel of the Royal Armoured Corps are losing confidence in their equipment."[4] Churchill was not convinced, at that time or later. Remarking that Auchinleck's statements required "careful scrutiny," he subjected the claim to a withering critique in his postwar memoirs, concluding that no one ought to be "misled into thinking that the technical inferiority of our tanks was the only reason for this considerable and far-reaching reverse."[5] Churchill had begun to have fundamental doubts about the skill of British commanders and the resolution of those they led, doubts to which he would give voice repeatedly over the next six months. The rapid collapse in the Far East clearly fed these doubts, but the defeat in Cyrenaica, though far less calamitous (however embarrassing), may have been more chilling. Malaya had been starved of quality troops, Burma more so. Eighth Army, by contrast, had been given the best Britain could provide: "The 1st Armoured Division was one of the finest we had. It consisted largely of men who had more than two years training and represented as high a standard of efficiency as any to be found in our regular forces."[6]

In his explanatory message to Churchill, Auchinleck had actually put his finger on several points beside the quality of German tanks and antitank guns: "I am not satisfied that the tactical leadership of our armoured forces is of sufficiently high standard . . . I am reluctantly compelled to conclusion that to meet German armoured forces with any reasonable hope of decisive success our armoured forces, as at present equipped, organised and led, must have at least a two to one superiority. Even then they must rely for success on working in very closest cooperation with infantry and artillery."[7] Lack of tactical and operational skill, Auchinleck was telling Churchill, was as much to blame as equipment. To be sure, British tanks were still undergunned and mechanically unreliable, but Auchinleck had also begun to realize the need for combined arms training in Eighth Army. Brooke, who had started to feel the results of Churchill's declining faith in the army's leadership, also believed that the handling of British armor left much to be desired, and he too attributed it to faulty leadership and organization. Auchinleck's German opponents saw this complex truth too. In their analysis of the winter battles, they pointed to dispersion of effort and brave but relatively unskilled tactical leadership as the primary British failings. Despite having previously raised the subject of the British approach to battle, Churchill did not specifically discuss this issue with Auchinleck, although it is clear from his coverage of the episode in *The Hinge of Fate* that he regarded issues of organization and leadership as at least as important as technical failings. Yet even though everyone had begun to sense that the problem was at least as much how the Eighth Army fought as what it fought with, there were no further exchanges on the issue between Churchill, Brooke, and Auchinleck. Their argument over the resumption of the offensive revolved instead around the usual issues of numbers—of tanks available, total "ration strength" versus fighting strength, and so forth. This was unfortunate because it meant that the core issue was not addressed at the highest level. But Churchill and Brooke had a host of other troubles pressing on them, as the setback in the desert was followed by catastrophic defeat in the Far East.

Churchill's concern over the possibility of piecemeal defeat in Malaya proved to be all too prescient, but his attention to the campaign unfolding there was transient. As Heath had feared when proposing a deep withdrawal to Percival, the inexperienced 11th Indian Division, trying to conduct that most difficult of military operations, a fighting retreat, was slowly destroyed. A catastrophic defeat at the Slim River in early January finished the division as a fighting force, making a rapid withdrawal from central Malaya imperative. Percival's army, it has often been pointed out, considerably outnumbered the Japanese Twenty-fifth Army. Percival's forces, however, never fought a united battle—with Percival mesmerized by the useless airfields and the need to keep the Japanese away from Singapore, it was consumed bit by bit during the long retreat down Malaya's west coast trunk road. It did not help that command changes made in London and at the Arcadia Conference further handicapped Malaya Command.

Pownall, arriving just before Christmas, barely had time to acquaint himself with his new command before the decisions taken at the Arcadia Conference changed the command structure again, turning Pownall into Wavell's chief of staff. Pownall had enough time, however, to form a reasonably positive view of Heath and a decidedly negative one of Percival (or perhaps simply to confirm a view already formed): "Percival . . . is an uninspired leader, and rather gloomy (as he was in France when B.G.S. to I Corps). I hope it won't mean that I have to relieve Percival, *pro tem*, until someone tougher than he can come from elsewhere."[8] Pownall did not have time to relieve Percival, but he doubtless conveyed this assessment of him to Wavell, who consistently showed scant regard for either the General Officer Commanding (GOC) personally or his military judgments—without, however, making any move to replace him.[9] This raises the whole issue of Wavell's appointment.

Churchill had never been enthusiastic about Wavell, and in June 1941, he had refused his request to return to the United Kingdom on leave.

However comprehensible on political grounds, that refusal was probably a mistake. Wavell was tired when he left Cairo, and New Delhi was not a rest cure. The breakneck expansion of the Indian Army in an equipment-starved environment and the heavy burden of responsibility that fell on the commander-in-chief as a member of the Viceroy's Executive Council made the job only slightly less taxing than the one he had left in Cairo. If Wavell was tired in June, he was by no means refreshed by December. But perhaps more important than fatigue was the attitude with which Wavell approached his new opponent. Put simply, he underrated the Imperial Japanese Army and, even more remarkably, would continue to do so. Playing a round of golf in New Delhi in 1945, he told one of his partners, "I misjudged the Japs. I did not realise for quite a long time what terribly efficient and serious soldiers they were."[10] This, as much as his low opinion of Percival, accounts for the excessive optimism of his orders that the Japanese be held north of Singapore for much longer than the condition of Percival's troops made likely. Wavell's belief that an aggressive attitude would work wonders would be seen again in Burma. His willingness to gamble, which had been evident in the Middle East, when allied with his underestimation of the Japanese, made a significant contribution to the debacles in Malaya and Burma. Defeat in both places may have been virtually certain in the circumstances, but Wavell's interventions did nothing to delay and may even have accelerated those defeats.

As disaster played out in Malaya, Churchill's attention was focused first on the conference in Washington and then on the setback in the desert. His attention to the new war in the Far East was intermittent (as Brooke's seems to have been[11]). What dragged it back was the sudden realization that Singapore was not in fact a fortress and a sharp subsequent clash with Australia over reinforcements for Percival's doomed command.

Anglo-Australian relations had been worsening for some months before Japan attacked. The Australian insistence on the relief of the 9th Division during the preparations for Crusader had left a legacy of prime ministerial annoyance: "I feel this Australian Government is out to make the most trouble and give the least help," Churchill wrote pettishly shortly before Pearl Harbor.[12] The Japanese attack, the loss of *Prince of Wales* and *Repulse,* and the rapid retreat in Malaya, where an Australian division was committed, led the Australian prime minister, John Curtin, to publish a front-page article in the *Melbourne Herald* warning that Australia's traditional links with Britain might have to be rethought in favor of an American orientation to preserve Australian security. Coming while Churchill was in Washington, the article embarrassed and infuriated the British prime minister—but also alerted him to the political weight that now attached to all decisions regarding what increasingly seemed likely to be a rapid endgame in Malaya. Furthermore, as Churchill discovered in Washington, the anxieties of his Australian allies were matched by those of his much more powerful American partners. But American anxieties were centered on China and the port through which China-bound supplies passed—Rangoon. "If I can epitomize in one word the lesson I learned in the United States, it was 'China,'" he told Wavell.[13] This tension between the competing demands of allies was brought to a head by a cable from Wavell on January 16, a missive that finally caused the scales to drop from Churchill's eyes: "Little or nothing [has been] done to construct defences on north side of island to prevent crossing of Johore Strait."[14] There was no Singapore fortress.

Churchill was furious with his staff at the time, and his anger is still apparent in his memoirs. Although the persistence of his illusions about Singapore, uncorrected by his staff, can only be adequately explained by inattention on their part, his painful awakening on January 16 immediately clarified his thinking about further reinforcing Singapore. The British 18th Division, made up largely of Territorials from eastern England, had been rounding the Cape and was bound for the Middle East when Japan attacked. Placed at Wavell's disposal, the unit was now destined for Singapore. However, the Japanese invasion of Burma had begun on the same day that Wavell disabused Churchill about Singapore's prospects. A complete British division might enable Burma's defenders, who were few in number and poorly trained, to hang on to Rangoon. But discussions in London about redirecting the 18th Division to Rangoon quickly reached Australian ears. With Australia's entire field force overseas—the last available, poorly trained reinforcements had just been sent to the 8th Australian Division in Malaya—the reaction from Canberra was volcanic. Curtin sent Churchill perhaps the strongest message he received from any Dominion leader during the war. If the 18th Division was not committed in Malaya, the Australian leader warned, it would be "an inexcusable betrayal."[15] Churchill would deny in his memoirs that Curtin's intervention had been decisive, but obviously it was. Churchill added that there could be "no doubt what a purely military decision should have been."[16] Brooke agreed. Glossing his wartime diaries, he noted, "Looking back on our decision, . . . I think we were wrong to send [the 18th Division] to Singapore."[17] Twice, Churchill had guessed right about the Malayan campaign but to no avail on either occasion. The 18th Division, out of shape after a long voyage and trained for the wrong war, landed in Singapore too late to make a difference to anything except the prisoner-of-war (POW) totals when Singapore fell on February 15.

Churchill's final intervention in the campaign was driven by both his pugnacity and his realization that the final service the doomed Singapore garrison could perform was to conduct a last stand that would both damage the Japanese and impress the United States, Russia, and Australia with British resolve. On February 10, he signaled Wavell that "there must at this stage be no thought of saving the troops or sparing the population . . . the reputation of our country and our race is involved."[18] He had already intervened in a discussion about the destruction of Singapore's ammunition reserves to suggest that firing them at the Japanese would be the best way of disposing of them. It was, of course, unrealistic to expect a heroic last stand in a city with over a million civilians and a failing water supply. But realism had not been a mark of Britain's Far Eastern defense policy for a very long time. Churchill's message to Wavell introduced another note, already heard in reaction to Eighth Army's defeat by Rommel. Was the will to fight lacking in the British Army? Brooke also had his concerns, writing in his diary three days after Singapore surrendered, "Cannot work out why troops are not fighting better. If the army cannot fight better than it is doing at present we shall deserve to lose our Empire!"[19] This haunting fear that British soldiers were not the men their fathers had been in World War I would recur with increasing frequency over the next six months as defeat followed defeat.[20]

Scarcely had the news of Singapore's fall been absorbed when the next major defeat loomed, as the Japanese closed remorselessly on Rangoon. Here, Churchill's intervention centered on two issues: finding reinforcements for the depleted Burma garrison and finding a commander to make the best use of whatever troops were available. With the 18th Division having gone to, and perished at, Singapore and India having been stripped bare (the 17th Indian Division, the least unready to go overseas, had already sent two brigades to Singapore, but the third brigade and divisional headquarters went to Burma), the only troops available were the 6th and 7th Australian Divisions, returning home from the Middle East. Churchill tried to have these diverted to Rangoon, setting off yet another clash with Curtin's government—this one even more intense than the row over the 18th British Division. The Australian official historian would later describe it as the sharpest argument that Canberra had with London during the war. Churchill tried to leverage the commitment of 18th Division to Singapore to get Australian compliance; the Australians refused to rise to the bait. Their temper was not improved when they discovered that, presuming their agreement to his initial request, Churchill had altered the course of the leading convoys carrying units of the 7th Division to speed its arrival at Rangoon. In the end, the Australians prevailed. It is very doubtful whether, even had they agreed, those units that could have been debarked in Rangoon would have made any more difference there than the 18th Division had at Singapore.[21]

As he cast about for troops, Churchill was also involved in selecting a new commander for a theater that seemed set to produce a debacle second only to Singapore. Churchill had always believed in the capacity of human will to bend circumstance. Applying this to Burma, he later wrote, "If we could not send an army, we could at any rate send a man."[22] The man chosen was Lieutenant General Sir Harold "Alex" Alexander, who would end the war as Churchill's favorite among British generals. Alex, the son of an earl, was an Irish Guardsman of great courage, charm, and legendary coolness under fire. A lieutenant in 1914, he was a battalion commander four years later, having won both the DSO and the MC in the interval. In the interwar army, he rose steadily but was not heavily involved in the arguments over the role of the tank. He went to France in 1939 as a divisional commander in Dill's I Corps. After Dunkirk came corps command and then, as a lieutenant general, Southern Command, where he was also commander designate of the British component of Gymnast, the planned Anglo-American attack on French North Africa. Despite his record in World War I and his rapid rise, there were those who questioned whether Alexander was really smart enough for high command. Prominent among them was his fellow Irishman Alan Brooke. In a discussion of who might succeed Wavell as commander-in-chief, India, Brooke considered Alex only to dismiss him—"Has not got the brains."[23] Presumably, Brooke felt that the situation in Burma required more character than brains, and no one ever doubted that Alex had an abundance of that.

The command muddle in Burma, to which Alex was the presumptive answer, was largely Wavell's doing. Told by Churchill after Pearl Harbor to "look east," he looked first at Burma, where the position of general officer commanding had become an end-of-career posting. Wavell descended on Rangoon, took one look at the incumbent, Major General D. K. McLeod, and promptly sacked him. His replacement, however, was Wavell's own chief of staff, Lieutenant General Thomas Hutton, a talented staff officer but not a field commander. Thereafter, Wavell moved to Java, where ABDA Command headquarters was located, trying still to control operations in Burma, although he had only intermittent radio contact with it. He managed only two hasty visits to Burma during ABDA's brief life. The result was a replay of the situation in Malaya. Wavell wanted Hutton to hold the Japanese as far from Rangoon as possible to safeguard the arrival of reinforcements from India. Hutton in turn pressured Major General J. G. Smythe, VC, the commander of the new and inexperienced 17th Indian Division, to hold each of the positions to which the Japanese forced it back far longer than Smythe, all too aware both of the rawness of his troops and of Japanese tactical skills, believed wise or even feasible.[24] As the situation deteriorated in Burma, the viceroy, Lord Linlithgow, and Wavell's temporary successor as commander-in-chief, India, General Sir Alan Hartley, told London that the troops in Burma would fight better if the command was in the hands of a more inspirational figure than Hutton (which raises the question of how much they knew of the actual state of the 17th Division). Churchill immediately responded by offering Alexander. Once Wavell had agreed, Alex was summoned to London, briefed by Brooke (who noted in his diary that "troops don't seem to be fighting well there either which is most depressing"[25]), and given a farewell dinner by Churchill. In his memoirs, Churchill painted a vivid picture of that evening: "Never have I taken the responsibility for sending a general on a more forlorn hope. Alexander was, as usual, calm and good-humored. He said he was delighted to go. . . . Nothing ever disturbed or rattled him . . . all this was combined with so gay and easy a manner that the pleasure and honour of his friendship was prized by all those who enjoyed it, among whom I could count myself."[26] Churchill, of course, had known Alexander prior to that memorable dinner, but it is hard to escape the conclusion that at that table, he found his beau ideal general.[27]

Churchill and Brooke had made a gesture, as much to the Americans as to the situation taking shape on the approaches to Rangoon. But Wavell, now back in India and once again commander-in-chief after ABDA's dissolution, nearly ended Alex's Burma sojourn before it began. Meeting Alexander as he passed through the Calcutta airport, Wavell told him to hold Rangoon. He had finally lost faith in Hutton when his former chief of staff had—correctly—told him that the evacuation of Rangoon might soon be necessary. The possibility became a certainty when, on February 23, the 17th Indian Division was virtually destroyed at the Sittang River east of Rangoon, the last major barrier between the Japanese and the city. Alexander's delay in ordering the withdrawal from Rangoon, the result of Wavell's ill-considered order, nearly resulted in his being trapped there—along with much of the remaining troop strength in Burma. Only a Japanese mistake rescued Alexander from Wavell's error and saved as well a career that ended with a field marshal's baton and a peerage.[28]

Ironically, a much more important appointment than Alexander's passed unremarked by Churchill. To control the forces in Burma, nominally a corps in strength, a corps headquarters, I Burma Corps (or Burcorps), was created, and Major General William J. Slim was summoned from command of the 10th Indian Division in Iraq to head it. Slim was as different from Alex in both background and leadership style as it was possible to be. The son of a not very successful small businessman, he enlisted in 1914, received a wartime commission in the Royal Warwickshire Regiment (Monty's regiment), and served at Gallipoli and in Mesopotamia. His wounds at Gallipoli were so severe that he was lucky to survive. Still technically unfit for active service, he then soldiered for six months in Mesopotamia, winning the Military Cross and collecting another wound. Slim badly wanted to make the army his career, but he lacked the private means necessary for the regular British Army. He therefore transferred, first to the very déclassé West India Regiment—where he could get a regular commission—and then into the 6th Gurkha Rifles of the Indian Army. During the interwar years, he attended the Indian Army Staff College at Quetta (where Hobart was one of the instructors); filled the Indian Army "slot" on the directing staff at the British Army's staff college at Camberley; and then, like Auchinleck, attended the new Imperial Defence College in London. A lieutenant colonel in 1939, he was a successful divisional commander by 1941 and had caught Auchinleck's eye as someone suitable for high command. Slim arrived in Burma shortly after the fall of Rangoon. It was he who would actually conduct the longest fighting retreat in British military history. That long withdrawal, amid a hostile or indifferent population and surrounded by the agonizing exodus of much of Burma's Indian population, placed enormous strains on Slim's leadership skills. Many years later, he wrote a passage about generalship that it is hard to believe was not based on the retreat of Burcorps:

> He [the general] is short of sleep, he is tired, he is probably wet, his nose is running and his sodden map is flapping round in his hands. Before him stand, in a rather forlorn group, some of his staff, a couple of subordinate commanders convinced that whatever eventuates they will have the dirty work to do, and most embarrassing of all, an ally or two, oozing suspicion. If the military situation is bad—and the odds are it will be—they will just stand looking at him, their eyes all asking the same mute question "what do we do now?" . . . They want an

> answer and they want it now. . . . He knows, and they know that unless something pretty brisk and decisive is done quickly neither he nor they will be there in a week's time.[29]

Slim had no difficulty being brisk and decisive. Despite a total lack of air cover, diminishing supplies, attenuating units with no possibility of reinforcement, and the vagaries of his Chinese allies (nominally commanded by an American lieutenant general, Joseph Stilwell, who certainly oozed suspicion), Slim managed the retreat, which teetered several times on the brink of disaster, with skill and determination. In May 1942, just as the monsoon broke, he brought Burcorps into Assam in eastern India, battered and sadly reduced in numbers but still an intact fighting formation. This was the first step in a progress that would see him become the best battlefield commander of all Churchill's generals. The rapid fading of the prime minister's brief attention to Burma is, however, reflected in the relegation of the long retreat to a page in his memoirs.[30] The war against Japan was an exercise in damage control and alliance politics. The real war was in the West; its focus was still the Western Desert.

Before a new offensive against Rommel could be launched, however, there were two issues that the prime minister and his generals had to settle: the American desire to engage Germany directly on the European continent and Auchinleck's determination not to launch another offensive until he was completely ready. It is interesting that Churchill found it easier to move the Americans than Middle East Command. The two arguments overlapped in time but, for clarity's sake, need to be separated. At the Arcadia Conference after Pearl Harbor, Churchill had interested Roosevelt in an Anglo-American descent on French North Africa as a complement to the westward march of Eighth Army after Crusader succeeded. This proposal died when Crusader stalled and then went into reverse. In its place came an American proposal for a 1942 landing in France—Sledgehammer—either to secure a bridgehead for subsequent exploitation or, if the 1942 German campaign in Russia looked as if it was succeeding, as a desperate sacrificial gambit to draw off German forces.

In the end, aided by the flow of events, not least of which was Roosevelt's perceived need to have American troops in combat against the European Axis in 1942, Churchill prevailed, and Gymnast was reborn as Torch. In his memoirs, Churchill would, disarmingly, christen this process Strategic Natural Selection. It was perhaps the obvious feasible operation, but the Allies did not reach agreement easily. Marshall wanted early action in Europe both to vindicate the raising of a vast American army and to keep that force from being siphoned off to the Pacific, where control would be exercised not by the U.S. Army but by either the U.S. Navy or the imperious Douglas MacArthur. As Brooke and Churchill quickly discovered, however, Marshall's thinking stopped short at the French beaches. An exasperated Brooke complained to his diary in a spatter of exclamation points that although the Americans were pushing a September 1942 Sledgehammer, "the total force they could contribute by then only consisted of 2½ divisions!! No very great contribution. . . . His [Marshall's] plan does not go beyond just landing on the far coast!! . . . Do we go east, south or west after the landing? He had not begun to think of it!!"[31]

In the end, because the British (and Canadians) would have to provide the bulk of the forces for any Sledgehammer variant and because Marshall could not satisfactorily answer Brooke's questions, Sledgehammer was dropped in favor of the North African alternative, even though, as a concession to Marshall, the final date was not set until July. Unquestionably, it was the correct decision—there was no realistic possibility of a successful cross-channel attack in 1942. The ill-starred Dieppe raid (code-named Jubilee) in August, which sacrificed a large part of a Canadian division (68 percent killed, wounded, or taken prisoner) without diverting a man, gun, or plane from the Eastern Front, is perhaps the best commentary on the idea of a sacrificial attack to aid the Russians. The Anglo-American argument was nonetheless revealing about what Brooke thought of the state of his army at that moment.

The story of the visit that Churchill and Ismay paid to Camp Jackson, South Carolina, in June 1942 is well known. After observing U.S. training methods, the prime minister asked Ismay for his views. Ismay felt it would be suicidal to put the inexperienced American troops up against Germans. Churchill agreed but felt the raw material was good and, with further training, would be able to face the Wehrmacht, and he told his hosts—Marshall and Secretary of War Henry Stimson—that the training period ought to be two years. That much time had in fact elapsed since Dunkirk, but Brooke, doubtless with the rapid dispersal of the 1st Armoured Division in mind as well as the dismal performances in Malaya and Burma, was by no means sure his army was ready to confront the Germans in large-scale continental warfare. Reflecting on the discussions with Marshall, he later wrote that the Germans were trained and experienced, whereas the British and American formations were "raw and inexperienced."[32] But there was more to Brooke's anxiety than concern over inexperience or the still-deficient equipment with which his army was encumbered. Brooke was seriously concerned about its senior leadership. His problems, he had noted in March, were

> made worse by the lack of good military commanders. Half our Corps and divisional Commanders are totally unfit for their appointments, and yet if I were to sack them I could find no better! They lack character, imagination, drive and power of leadership. The reason for this state of affairs is to be found in the losses we sustained in the last war of all our best officers who should now be our senior commanders.[33]

Later historians would point to selection and training of officers as well as doctrine (or its lack) rather than to a lost generation of leaders, but there is no question that, by the late spring of 1942, both the minister of defense and the professional head of the army were concerned about the British Army's fighting spirit and leadership. Yet Churchill needed that army to produce victory in the desert—to quiet both his critics at home and the clamor for a so-called second front to aid the Russians as well as to maintain Britain's position in the Anglo-American alliance.[34] Instead, by the time Churchill watched those American formations training in South Carolina, the Eighth Army had suffered its greatest defeat at Rommel's hands. Further, the prime minister, having won a costly victory in the struggle over alliance strategy, was now plunged into the worst political crisis of his tenure, and questions were raised about whether, by the time British and American troops were ready to strike at Vichy North Africa, the Germans would be astride the Suez Canal. It was a sorry conclusion to the long discussion over the next British offensive in the desert that had begun as Singapore fell.

Of the pressures on the prime minister, there can be no doubt. On February 15, shortly after Eighth Army settled down west of Tobruk in a position christened the Gazala Line, Singapore fell. Then the German battle cruisers *Scharnhorst* and *Gneisenau*, long pent up in Brest, returned home to Germany, sailing in daylight up the English Channel. The former event was of infinitely greater significance, but the latter probably angered the British public more deeply. Early in March, Rangoon fell, and as the Japanese surged toward the borders of India, a tremor of unrest ran through the Raj. At Easter, the Japanese navy roamed the Indian Ocean, pummeled Ceylon, shelled Indian coastal cities, and drove the Royal Navy back to East African bases, while the Luftwaffe was battering and starving Malta. In January, Churchill had weathered the most intense political criticism he had so far encountered, and in February, he had reconstructed his government in an effort to defuse the situation. Always in the background but never far from the prime minister's thoughts was the one battle he knew that the Allies had to win and that they were currently losing: the Battle of the Atlantic. Churchill's exchanges with Auchinleck from February to May 1942 must be seen against this backdrop. The one cure for many of the problems that beset the prime minister was—still—a victory. And the Eighth Army was still the only force that could give him one.

The fate of British arms in the desert war and that of the prime minister were, as his doctor would note, intertwined more tightly over the next eight months than they had ever been in the past. Churchill would never again be as vulnerable to the political consequences of military defeat. When he wrote his memoirs, he was frank about the degree of pressure he had put on Auchinleck for an early offensive. He had a good case in the steadily worsening plight of Malta. He also hammered at the fact that the inactivity of the 600,000 British troops in Auchinleck's command (the prime minister always cited the ration strength rather than the actual number of fighting troops in these arguments) contrasted sharply with the massive battles on the Russian front. Auchinleck, however, had his case as well. He was determined not to be pushed into a premature offensive, and premature to him was before he had a three-to-two superiority in tanks over his opponent. Moreover, he had already pointed out to Churchill that the training of British armored units left much to be desired. Remedying this deficiency was made more difficult by the arrival of new, unfamiliar equipment. The American Grant tank, with its heavier armor and 75mm gun, was a welcome addition to the Eighth Army, but it brought the problems of familiarizing crews with its operation and maintenance as well as working out tactics for its employment. In addition, Auchinleck could never forget his northern front. Stalingrad lay months in the future. The Germans, stalled in front of Moscow in December, would resume the offensive in the spring. If they erupted into the Middle East from the north, Wilson's Ninth Army in Syria and Lieutenant General E. P. Quinan's Tenth Army in Iraq would have little with which to stop them. Seventeen divisions was the estimate of the forces required. Wilson had two good divisions, and Quinan had two new Indian formations and a raw armored brigade. By the time Churchill wrote his memoirs, the northern front was a minor historical footnote; to Auchinleck, it was an all too real problem.

Some of the argument between London and Cairo involved the disparity between Auchinleck's figures of tanks available in armored units and the number Churchill—and the War Office—thought he should have available for service. It proved impossible to agree on a figure. Part of the problem lay in the continuing need for extensive repairs and alterations to newly arrived tanks (in mid-March, nearly half the tanks in Auchinleck's command were in workshops). Perhaps the larger part of the difficulty, however, came from Churchill's determination to prove to Auchinleck that he could attack (a determination spurred by Ultra information on the steady improvement in Rommel's position as the British, with Malta virtually numb, lost their grip on his supply line). The prime minister invited Auchinleck to return home to resolve the strategic and technical arguments in person. The commander-in-chief—with one experience of the pressures Churchill could generate on his own ground—declined. Churchill then had Sir Stafford Cripps, a member of the War Cabinet who would be passing through Cairo on his way to India, investigate the whole issue. Much to Churchill's annoyance, Cripps pronounced himself satisfied with Auchinleck's arguments.

Lieutenant General Sir Archibald Nye, the vice chief of the Imperial General Staff, who was in Cairo at the same time, was given the job of further probing the commander-in-chief's arguments. He was armed with a list of questions to which he was to get detailed answers—a remarkable inquisition of a theater commander. One asked about Auchinleck's claim that German training and leadership were superior. The answer is interesting, in view of what Auchinleck had already told Churchill. His statement applied to German armor, he replied; the reason for British inferiority was a "failure to recognise until quite recently the vital importance of the closest cooperation between tanks, artillery and infantry in the employment of armoured formations." The remedy was retraining: "Particular emphasis will be laid on training the co-operation of all arms in battle."[35] By the spring of 1942, better equipment had begun to reach Eighth Army. The new 6-pounder antitank gun, which would be used in the desert for the first time in May, represented a quantum leap in firepower. British tanks were still inferior to German tanks in both reliability and weaponry, but growing numbers of American tanks had neither defect. Most important of all, perhaps, Auchinleck had come to realize that the problems that had beset Eighth Army had as much to do with doctrine and training as with equipment. But there was not much time available in which to retrain an army.

There were other clouds gathering around Auchinleck as well. Brooke had begun to have doubts about the choices Auchinleck had made for key positions and therefore about the quality of the advice he was getting. After the war, Brooke noted that he had begun to suspect in late January that

Chink Dorman-Smith had too much influence on Auchinleck, a reflection prompted by a letter in which Auchinleck discussed the need for all-arms cooperation, which would require the reorganization—and retraining—of his armored divisions (the point he made to Nye). In March, the CIGS sent Major General Richard McCreery to Cairo to act as Auchinleck's adviser on armored forces (and presumably to counteract Dorman-Smith's influence). But Auchinleck largely ignored McCreery. By May, Brooke was complaining in his diary both about the unsuitability of Corbett as chief of staff and about the Eighth Army's commander: "I do not feel that Neil Ritchie is a big enough man to command the 8th Army."[36] By that point, it is clear that Auchinleck was on shaky ground with both the prime minister and the CIGS, and the latter distrusted both of Auchinleck's key subordinates and his most influential adviser.

Churchill played with the idea of replacing Auchinleck (rather incredibly, Gort and, again, Nye were two possibilities he considered). Instead, on May 10, he sent Auchinleck a direct order to attack during that month, the latest possible date for a westward advance to acquire landing grounds from which the RAF could cover the passage of a convoy to Malta during the moonless period in June. After nearly a week's silence and another prod from the prime minister, Auchinleck agreed. But Rommel's preparations had moved faster than his. By the time Auchinleck sent his cabled reply to London on May 19, it was clear that before Ritchie could attack, he would have to fight a defensive battle.

Unfortunately, Eighth Army was not well positioned to meet that challenge. Preparing for an offensive, Ritchie had built up huge supply dumps just outside Tobruk, close to the front—close enough to be a liability and embarrassment in a defensive struggle. Gott's XIII Corps held a line from the sea near Gazala south into the desert with two divisions, the 1st South African and 50th British, backed by two army tank brigades. However, the jumping-off point for British armor in the now canceled Operation Buckshot was 50 miles inland, and this had caused the southern end of Gott's corps to be stretched in that direction by putting one brigade of 50th Division in an isolated position, 6 miles south of the rest of the division and 15 miles from the southern anchor of the British line at Bir Hacheim. The intervening spaces were covered by "mine marshes." Gott also had the newly formed and incomplete 2nd South African Division in Tobruk, whose defenses had not been maintained since Auchinleck had decided in February that he would not embark on another prolonged defense of it—either the fighting would move westward, leaving Tobruk a backwater, or, in the worst case, it would be evacuated. Norrie had XXX Corps's two armored divisions positioned behind the Gazala Line.

Auchinleck had decided after the winter fighting that a better balance between tanks, guns, and infantry was needed in his armored divisions, a point he made by letter to Brooke and directly to Nye. To achieve this, each of his armored divisions would be made up of one armored and one motorized infantry/artillery brigade. This transition, however, was not yet complete by May. Lumsden's 1st Armoured, still with the two armored brigades, was roughly behind the center of the line, whereas Messervy's 7th (with one armored brigade conforming, in organization at least, to the new pattern) was south of it, behind Bir Hacheim, which was garrisoned by a Free French infantry brigade under Norrie's command. The new Grant tanks were spread throughout the three armored brigades because, as the British official history puts it, "there were strong psychological reasons for giving every regiment some of the new and powerful Grants."[37] There were significant tensions between the two armored commanders. Lumsden, a British cavalryman, felt Messervy, an Indian cavalryman, had mishandled 1st Armoured when temporarily in command of it during Rommel's January advance. He therefore did not want any part of his division coming under Messervy's command if he could avoid it. If Gott had to worry about his Commonwealth commanders (Major General Dan Pienaar of 1st South African tended to ignore orders he disliked), Norrie had two British divisional commanders between whom cooperation would not be easy. Seldom has the "tribal, parochial nature" of the British Army been more sharply illustrated.[38] At least Gott and Norrie got along well, but together, they were a formidable combination for Ritchie to handle, given his relatively junior rank and the fact that he in turn was under Auchinleck's shadow. Command by committee, a practice that had developed early in the desert war, was now ingrained. All of this would affect the speed with which the British command would react to Rommel in the forthcoming battle.

The timing of that battle had been settled at an Axis summit on May 1 at Berchtesgaden, where Hitler and Mussolini had agreed on a two-stage plan. First, Rommel would launch Operation Venezia in late May, aiming at the defeat of the Eighth Army and the capture of Tobruk. Thereafter, he would go over to the defensive, while an operation was mounted against Malta. With the island conquered, Rommel could resume his drive into Egypt and ultimately to the Suez Canal. His two German panzer divisions, the backbone of his army, had 332 tanks (of which 50 were obsolescent Mark II's). The Italian XX Corps's two divisions had a further 228 medium tanks, of much inferior quality. Ritchie had 573 tanks in his two armored divisions, and the two independent tank brigades had 276 more. (Once again, the British had a clear superiority in tank numbers: Messervy's 4th Armoured Brigade alone was a match, in numbers at least, for either panzer division.) Rommel had a reasonably good idea of the Eighth Army's strength and dispositions, although he somewhat underestimated its size. Even so, his plan reflected a rather low opinion of the proficiency with which the British would fight—the Germans having drawn the same conclusions from past experience as Auchinleck had. Rommel allowed four days for the German armor to swing around the inland flank of Eighth Army, defeat the British armor, and crush XIII Corps between his tanks and the Italian infantry facing it. After that, he would take Tobruk. It was a very ambitious plan and, as usual with Rommel, a logistic gamble. What if, at the end of its four days' supply of fuel, water, ammunition, and food, the Afrika Korps had not routed its opponents?

There has been considerable discussion about the positioning of the British armored brigades at the opening of Rommel's attack.[39] Ritchie's dispositions seem to have been reasonable enough in the circumstances. Even if they were flawed, however, the Desert Fox gave the British an opportunity to retrieve any initial errors because his own overly optimistic plan broke down almost immediately, leaving him in a very vulnerable position. That the British failed to take advantage of this vulnerability and allowed Rommel to recover and then to win his greatest victory led Major General Francis Tuker of the 4th Indian Division, reflecting on it long afterward, to label Gazala-Tobruk "one of the worst fought battles in the history of the British Army."[40]

The 3rd Indian Motor Brigade had been smashed at Mechili in Rommel's first offensive. Rebuilt after that debacle, it had done garrison work in Syria and then three months of desert warfare training in Egypt, only joining 7th Armoured Division on May 22. Stationed on the southern flank of the British position, its commander, Brigadier A. E. E. Filose, had the dubious honor of announcing the opening of the battle of Gazala, telling Messervy at 6:30 A.M. on May 27 that he was looking at a "whole bloody German armoured division." Ninety minutes later, the brigade had been smashed a second time. The Afrika Korps, wheeling north, brushed aside Messervy's motor brigade, crushed his armored brigade, and overran divisional headquarters, taking Messervy himself prisoner temporarily (ripping off his rank badges, he passed himself off as a private and escaped the same day).[41]

Although Ultra had been warning of an imminent German attack for five days, Eighth Army reacted slowly to Rommel's initial move, in part because of Auchinleck's view, expressed repeatedly to Ritchie, that the German commander was likely to make a frontal attack on XIII Corps; this was the shortest route to Tobruk, but Auchinleck's prediction reflected a curious reading of Rommel's approach to battle. When the British at last began to react, 7th Armoured was, of course, without effective command. Nonetheless, Lumsden's two brigades (which considerably outnumbered both panzer divisions together) stopped the Afrika Korps by day's end. Rommel was deep in his opponent's rear, but his forces were scattered, a third of his tanks were casualties, and one of his divisions was already short of fuel and ammunition. Once again, the Desert Fox had gotten himself into difficulties; once again, his opponents were to help him escape. Facing the frustration of his original plan, Rommel pulled his forces together, backed up against the British minefields, and began to clear gaps through them to allow supplies to reach him directly, rather than by the long, precarious route around Bir Hacheim. Only at this point did Rommel discover that the isolated 150th Brigade of 50th Division was in his way. Surrounded by Axis forces, bombed repeatedly, and assaulted by the Afrika Korps, Brigadier C. W. Haydon's three battalions held out until about noon on June 1, while the rest of Eighth Army did little to help it.[42]

Grasping finally, aided by Ultra, that Rommel was not withdrawing but preparing a springboard for further advance, Ritchie and his corps commanders put together what may well be one of the worst-conceived and worst-executed British operations of the war—Aberdeen, intended to pinch out Rommel's beachhead (christened the Cauldron) on the British side of the minefields. Gott's corps would attack from the north, with a brigade of infantry supported by an army tank brigade. From the east, Norrie would launch the main attack under cover of darkness on the night of June 4, using Major General Harold Briggs's 5th Indian Division (hitherto in Ritchie's reserve) to open the way for Messervy's armor—a scheme not unlike Montgomery's for the opening stages of the second battle of El Alamein. The crucial difference was the nature of the command structure. Monty ran his show; no one was really in charge of Aberdeen.

Indeed, elements of three divisions and a tank brigade from two different corps were used without any overall coordination. Norrie handed over his share of the operation to Messervy and Briggs, who were to coordinate their operations (much as Beresford-Peirse had left Messervy and Creagh to work things out during Battleaxe). Gott seems to have taken little real interest: when Major General W. H. C. Ramsden of 50th Division decided that he had already lost one brigade and reduced his contribution to a battalion, the corps commander did not overrule him. The usual Eighth Army conferring and consulting while the attack was being planned took several days. Auchinleck, when informed, was obviously uneasy, urging Ritchie to take even more time if necessary to get the details right. He also warned Ritchie that the infantry would need armored support against the inevitable German counterattack. Incredibly, the operation orders of Lumsden's 22nd Armoured Brigade, under Messervy's command for Aberdeen, would reflect exactly the opposite view—that the tanks need not worry about the infantry, which could look after itself. (This, of course, left the tanks free to pursue the tank-versus-tank, "independent" combat that had long dominated British thinking on the subject.[43])

Faulty planning and poor control led directly to disaster. The location of the enemy's front line had not been correctly identified, so the initial artillery barrage hit empty desert, which was then occupied by Briggs's infantry. The armor, however, advancing through the infantry, ran into German antitank fire, suffered heavily, and sheered away, leaving the infantry isolated. Rommel's daytime counterattack on June 5 dispersed the headquarters of both divisions, which, though located side by side, had been conducting separate battles. The Germans, having driven off the British armor and paralyzed what little command and control there was, went on to mop up three infantry battalions and four field artillery regiments. All the while, the remaining two armored brigades, 2nd and 4th, both put under Messervy's command by Norrie, received no clear orders and remained outside the battle area. For slight losses to himself, Rommel had knocked out 60 of 22nd Armoured Brigade's tanks and cut up two Indian brigades (taking 3,000 prisoners) and four regiments of field artillery.[44] The northern prong of Aberdeen fared even worse. Reduced by Ramsden's nonparticipation to an attack by 32nd Army Tank Brigade, it came to grief on an unsuspected minefield covered by antitank guns, losing 50 of the brigade's 70 tanks. A German staff officer who watched it called this British attack "ridiculous." When Aberdeen came to an inglorious conclusion, Rommel's force for the first time outnumbered XXX Corps in tanks, having about 160 to Norrie's 132. More important, the German had both the initiative and the psychological edge. He never relinquished either until July at El Alamein.

Apart from the courage of the infantrymen and gunners abandoned by the armor, it is impossible to find a redeeming feature in the handling of Aberdeen, which displayed the British command system at its worst. The most measured condemnation is that of the British official history: "The

British system of command was too complicated to deal with the unexpected, and was no match for the strong personal control of the enemy commander. This caused an unfair burden to be laid on the divisional commanders and resulted in many fine troops being thrown away."[45] Watching from afar, through the eyes of Cairo, Churchill did not become uneasy until June 10, when he noted in the casualty figures an "extra-ordinary disparity between killed and wounded on one hand and prisoners on the other," which to him "revealed that something must have happened of an unpleasant character."[46] Nevertheless, he signaled Auchinleck the next day, "We have no reason to fear a prolonged *bataille d'usure* [attrition]. This must wear down Rommel worse than Ritchie."[47] By the time this message reached Cairo, Ritchie had been decisively beaten.

After defeating the Eighth Army's attack on the Cauldron, Rommel turned his attention to the Free French brigade group at Bir Hacheim. While Ritchie's armor licked its wounds, the fiercely defended strong point was taken, although most of the French defenders made a successful breakout. Now Rommel was ready to deal with XXX Corps. Norrie's tank strength was back up to 200, whereas Rommel had 226. Numerically and qualitatively, there was a rough parity for the climactic armored clash of the battle of Gazala. The armor on many German tanks had been upgraded since Crusader, and a few of Rommel's Mark III and IV panzers were "specials," with powerful, long-barreled 50mm and 75mm guns, respectively. By contrast, Norrie's Grants, of which he now had 83, were equipped with good engines and excellent armor (it would stop the standard German 50mm antitank shell), and their 75mm guns were the equivalent of the standard German Mark IV's main armament. It was not, however, on technical issues that the battles of June 12 and 13 turned. To reconstitute armored brigades quickly, depleted units had often been combined, with adverse affects on morale and cohesion. The new 10th Armoured Division forming in Egypt lost both tanks taken to replace losses and two whole regiments from its 1st Armoured Brigade, which were rushed to the front to fill the gaps in 4th Armoured Brigade. But even impaired cohesion does not fully explain the defeat of Norrie's armor. One member of XXX Corps's staff later put his finger on the key: "The blame must fall on Messervy and Lumsden for the dilatory fashion in which they exercised command, and on Norrie for not being firmer in imposing his will on them."[48] By dusk on June 13, Eighth Army had some 50 tanks left. Norrie's defeat left Gott's infantry divisions holding the Gazala Line exposed, and beyond that loomed the question of what to do about Tobruk. At this moment, the prime minister reentered the picture.

Auchinleck had been at Ritchie's headquarters on June 12, and the two men had agreed that Eighth Army should fight it out with Rommel where it stood. The following day, Auchinleck told Churchill of this decision, to which the prime minister replied, characteristically: "Your decision to fight it out to the end is most cordially endorsed. We shall sustain you whatever the result. Retreat would be fatal. This is a business not only of armor but of will-power. God Bless You All."[49]

By the time this response reached Cairo, the crushing of Norrie's armor made new decisions imperative. At 7 A.M. on June 14, Ritchie made one, ordering Gott's divisions withdrawn to the line of the Libyan-Egyptian frontier. It seems clear that Auchinleck intended neither to give up Tobruk nor allow it to be besieged. His plan was for Ritchie to hold the area south and southeast of Tobruk with mobile forces, thus keeping open Tobruk's land communications. Meanwhile, Ritchie would regroup on the frontier and prepare for a counteroffensive. But Ritchie, being closer to the reality of a beaten armored force and the mood of his commanders, was prepared to accept Tobruk's "temporary isolation" if necessary, trusting its garrison to hold it. Alerted by a message from the minister of state in Cairo, Richard Casey (an Australian who had succeeded Oliver Lyttleton), that Gott's divisions would be withdrawing after nightfall, Churchill sent a second signal to Auchinleck late that night asking for reassurance: "Presume there is no question in any case of giving up Tobruk."[50] Auchinleck replied the next day, reiterating his policy of neither abandoning nor allowing the investment of Tobruk. Still dissatisfied, Churchill replied the same day, "War Cabinet interpret your telegram to mean that, if the need arises, General Ritchie would leave as many troops in Tobruk as are necessary to hold the place for certain."[51] This exchange came to an end on June 16. Early that morning, Auchinleck told Ritchie he accepted that the Tobruk garrison might be "isolated" for short periods prior to the British counteroffensive. Then he signaled Churchill: "War Cabinet interpretation is correct."[52] Although uneasy, the prime minister was reassured enough to leave on the night of June 17 for a hazardous transatlantic flight to Washington, where crucial decisions would be made on the future shape of the war. By the time Churchill's flying boat glided down onto the Potomac, Auchinleck's policy of "keeping the door open" to Tobruk was in ruins and Tobruk itself about to be assaulted by the full strength of the Afrika Korps.

As Eighth Army fell back to the frontier, the link with Tobruk became Messervy's division, whose 4th Armoured Brigade had been rebuilt to about 90 tanks, plus 7th Motor and the phoenixlike 3rd Indian Motor Brigades. He was also responsible for a series of "boxes" (defended localities, held by infantry and artillery) scattered between Tobruk and the frontier. One, at El Adem southeast of Tobruk, was held by a brigade of Brigg's 5th Indian Division; two others were east of Tobruk, spaced out between it and the frontier, and were held by brigades of the new 10th Indian Division.[53] Two of the brigades had each detached one of their battalions to create two smaller boxes, giving a total of five to be somehow supported by Messervy, whose armored brigade had not displayed notable aggressiveness since it was roughly handled by Rommel on the opening day of the battle. Such boxes had long been a feature of British operations in the desert. The fate of 150th Brigade was only the latest warning of their weakness: "In their static, all round defensive positions, . . . they could only influence the battle within range of guns sited within the position. They could therefore be ignored [by the Germans]." Moreover, "unless the maneuverings of the armoured formation were successful, all these positions became hostages to fortune."[54] Rommel was about to demonstrate this vividly, at the expense of those five boxes. Something else was going to be demonstrated as well—the inability of either Auchinleck or Ritchie to translate their concept of how the battle ought to be handled into useful action by the corps, divisional, and brigade commanders. On June 15, one of the isolated battalion boxes was overrun; the other single battalion position succumbed the following day. At about midnight on June 16, the brigade holding the box southeast of Tobruk pulled out, its brigadier having gotten Messervy's permission (which Messervy had extracted at the last minute from Norrie). After dark on June 17, Norrie tried to pull another of the Indian brigades back, but two-thirds of it was cut off and gobbled up by the Afrika Korps. (The third Indian brigade, farthest from Tobruk, got back to the frontier intact.) The Germans scarcely noticed the attempts by 7th Armoured Division to interfere. By June 18, Eighth Army was back behind the frontier, and the door to Tobruk had been slammed shut.

Winston Churchill spent June 19 at Hyde Park, Franklin Roosevelt's Hudson Valley estate. "Tube Alloys," the future atom bombs, were discussed, as was the pressing question of when the Anglo-American alliance would launch its first offensive, with Churchill pressing hard for a final commitment to the attack on northwest Africa that had been in his mind for months. In the desert, Rommel's success claimed another victim. Norrie replaced Messervy with Brigadier J. M. L. Renton of 7th Motor Brigade on the grounds that Messervy had failed to provide adequate support for the isolated Indian brigades in their boxes.[55] Rommel himself, meanwhile, prepared to assault Tobruk. The defense was in the hands of Major General H. B. Klopper and his 2nd South African Division. In addition to his two South African brigades, he had one of Tuker's, the 201st Guards Brigade (the motorized infantry brigade of Lumsden's division), and what remained of 32nd Army Tank Brigade. Klopper was newly promoted and had little combat experience. His two South African brigades were new and untried. The defenses of Tobruk had certainly deteriorated since the February decision not to allow it to be besieged again, but what was really wanting when Rommel attacked at dawn on June 20 was the drive and determination that Harding and Morshead had brought to the defense improvised on the heels of defeat in March 1941. As Rommel's armor (with the Desert Fox among the lead troops) broke in and fanned out, the garrison's countermoves were slow and feeble, and by late afternoon, Klopper's control, never very firm, had broken down. Early on June 21, he surrendered 33,000 troops, nearly 20,000 of them British.[56] The booty was enormous—2,000 usable vehicles, 1,400 tons of fuel, and 5,000 tons of food. German losses were light (although German officer losses since the start of the offensive had been high, nearly 70 percent in the Afrika Korps—a good indication of how German tactical performance was attained). The capture of Tobruk was the climax of Rommel's career. An elated Hitler made him a field marshal. For Churchill, Tobruk was the sharpest blow yet and triggered the most serious political challenge he faced during the war.

The prime minister had returned to Washington by train on the night of June 20, gone to the White House, and was standing by the president's desk with Brooke and talking to Roosevelt when General Marshall walked in with a telegram and handed it to Roosevelt. The president passed it wordlessly to Churchill: "Tobruk has surrendered, with twenty-five thousand men taken prisoner." A few minutes later, he had a message from London stating that the commander of the Mediterranean Fleet, Admiral Sir Henry Harwood, was pulling his ships out of Alexandria and sending them through the canal into the Red Sea "to await events." There may have been more painful moments for Churchill during the war, but none was more embarrassing. As he put it, "It was a bitter moment. Defeat is one thing; disgrace is another."[57] It raised again in his mind the fear that the British Army lacked the will to fight that it had shown in World War I. Later that day, he told his doctor, "I am so ashamed. I cannot understand why Tobruk gave in.

More than 30,000 of our men put up their hands. If they won't fight . . . ," and here he broke off.[58]

In January, Rommel had reclaimed in a week most of what had taken the Eighth Army a month to wrest from him. Singapore fell, to outnumbered attackers, in February. March brought the loss of Rangoon (and with it the U.S. link to China). The Japanese chased the Royal Navy from Ceylon to East Africa in April. Now Tobruk, symbol of Britain's lone success against the Wehrmacht, was gone. Roosevelt and Marshall immediately offered Churchill 300 of the new Sherman tanks and 100 self-propelled guns. Although this would, in the long run, help restore British armored strength, the question in the short run was whether the British would still hold Suez when the equipment arrived. There was also the question of whether Churchill would continue to wield the powers he had hitherto enjoyed. By the time he boarded his flying boat at Baltimore on the evening of June 25, he knew that a motion had been placed on the order paper of the House of Commons that day: "That this House, while paying tribute to the heroism and endurance of the Armed Forces of the Crown in circumstances of exceptional difficulty, has no confidence in the central direction of the war."[59]

Rommel wasted no time after the fall of Tobruk. Riding in British vehicles, propelled by British fuel, and often subsisting on British rations, his forces moved east, impelled by the new field marshal's sense of a fleeting opportunity to be grasped. As he drove his tired men forward, Rommel also dragged behind him Axis theater strategy. Hitler had, in any case, been weakening on the planned assault on Malta, which was too dependent for comfort on Italian naval performance. He now endorsed Rommel's request that the Egyptian frontier no longer be considered the limit of his operations. Operation Hercules disappeared, and Rommel headed for Cairo, Alexandria, and the canal.

When the Afrika Korps crossed the Egyptian frontier, it had 44 tanks left. The 7th Armoured had at that point about 100. But Ritchie had already decided that he could not stand on the frontier but had to fall much farther back, to Mersa Matruh (where Wavell had planned to fight Graziani in September 1940). At the same time, his subordinates were making that decision for themselves. Pienaar of 1st South African flatly refused to try to hold his allotted section of the frontier and continued to withdraw (he eventually wound up back in the Alamein position, where a last line of defense was being organized by Norrie's XXX Corps headquarters). Major General T. W. "Pete" Rees, whose 10th Indian Division had already been depleted in the fiasco of the boxes, told Gott, whose XIII Corps had responsibility for the frontier defenses, that he could not hold Rommel for long alone. He was immediately sacked.[60] The impression that Eighth Army's senior commanders were badly rattled is inescapable. The withdrawal continued toward Matruh, where Ritchie was concentrating the New Zealand division and a new headquarters, X Corps, brought forward from Syria. Having sacked Rees for stating the obvious, Gott then had to withdraw 10th Indian to prevent its being cut off. For the third time in its history, 3rd Indian Motor Brigade was badly cut up, as Rommel's columns pushed relentlessly eastward. Clearly, some grip needed to be restored to the British command structure if Rommel was to be stopped. It was at this point that Auchinleck flew up from Cairo, and at about 7 P.M. on June 25, he took over Eighth Army.

Auchinleck would later be criticized for his initial choice of Ritchie and for subsequently supervising him too closely. The former, in the circumstances prevailing at a critical moment in Crusader's fortunes, is more understandable than the latter. Frequent personal visits, exchanges of long letters on operational and tactical matters, and the appearance at Eighth Army headquarters of the commander-in-chief's close personal adviser, Dorman-Smith, all tended to keep Ritchie in the position of a senior staff officer rather than an army commander in his own right. Whether he could have established himself as such in the face of Gott and Norrie (both senior to him), not to mention stubborn divisional commanders such as Lumsden, Pienaar, Ramsden, and Freyberg, is an open question, but Auchinleck's close supervision denied him the opportunity. Churchill certainly felt that Auchinleck ought to have taken command of Eighth Army earlier. At the end of their exchange over a British offensive in May, Churchill told him, "I should personally feel even greater confidence if you took direct command personally, as in fact you had to do [in Crusader]."[61] Auchinleck pointed out that only in Cairo could he keep the sense of proportion necessary for a theater commander, balancing the desert war against the demands of the northern front.[62] In his postwar memoirs, Churchill criticized both Auchinleck's relationship with Ritchie and his refusal to take command of Eighth Army "from the beginning," but he also admitted that Auchinleck was "embarrassed and hampered by his too extensive responsibilities," something that would not be allowed to trouble his successor. "One lives and learns" was as close as Churchill came to admitting that the fault lay in London as much as in Cairo.[63] Perhaps the most telling aspect of the Auchinleck-Ritchie relationship is how it reflected the tribal nature of Britain's armies: Auchinleck, the dominating figure in the Indian Army, simply did not know the British Army well enough to make a better choice. (Perhaps, if Brooke was correct, there were few better choices to make.) Now, however, with his western front shredding and the Germans eating up the miles to Suez, Auchinleck, with Dorman-Smith at his side in the unorthodox position of "chief of staff in the field," had to repair his own mistakes, Ritchie's, and those of many others as well—and salvage a situation far worse than that in November 1941.

His immediate preoccupations were twofold: where to stop Rommel and how best to organize Eighth Army to do it. Ritchie had been planning to delay the enemy on the Egyptian frontier while preparing for a major engagement at Matruh. Auchinleck quickly recognized that Eighth Army was in no shape for a stand at Matruh, and he decided, before midnight on June 25, to conduct a fluid delaying action back to the Alamein Line. Ritchie had also decided, after the fall of Tobruk, that standard-pattern infantry divisions were unsuitable to desert warfare. On June 22, he ordered his infantry divisions split into two components, mobile units that would combine motorized infantry and guns and static troops who would be sent back to the rear (many of these in fact wound up back in the embryonic Alamein position). There had been no opportunity to put this decision into effect. But Auchinleck affirmed it, for which he and Dorman-Smith were later sharply criticized. Actually, as all the desert fighting had shown (most recently in the fiasco of the Indian Army–held boxes), the fate of the armor would decide that of the infantry waiting in a new version of the old British square. The state of British armored formations in late June did not bode well for any infantry formation left to face the Afrika Korps. The real problem lay in the fact that what was required was a change not merely in organization but also in outlook. To turn the infantry into mobile battle groups was one thing; to inculcate the tactical and operational skills that made often ad hoc German battle groups so formidable was another. The British official history accurately pointed this out: "Whether the fluid tactics were appropriate to the occasion or not, they were certainly new and entirely unpracticed."[64] The British were, moreover, trying to both reorganize and conduct a withdrawal under heavy pressure. British doctrine emphasized that withdrawals should be tightly controlled. Such a retreat was precisely what Rommel intended to deny the Eighth Army.

Three days after Auchinleck's assumption of command, Rommel achieved at Matruh what was, if not his most sweeping victory, certainly his most remarkable one. His plan has been described as "rash," but it reflected what he had learned about his opponents over fifteen months of desert war: however bravely they fought, they reacted slowly and often in a poorly coordinated fashion. As he closed up on Matruh on June 25, Afrika Korps had about 60 tanks (few of which were "Specials" and some of which were obsolete light models) and 2,500 tired infantry troops, followed by some 44 more tanks and 7,000 infantrymen in his Italian formations. Rommel was facing Lieutenant General W. G. Holmes's X Corps in Matruh itself, with 50th Division's remaining brigades and 10th Indian Division, whose two surviving brigades had been joined by one taken from Tuker's 4th Indian. South of Matruh, the ground rose in two steps, or escarpments. Above the southern escarpment, Gott had Brigg's 5th Indian (but with only one depleted brigade) and two brigades of Freyberg's New Zealanders; the third remained back at Alamein for lack of transport to make it mobile. (Freyberg had initially been slated to occupy the Matruh defenses but objected to being penned up in a box and was allowed to change roles—he had also invoked his charter to prevent his division being streamlined into mobile battle groups.) Out in the open desert, Lumsden's 1st Armoured covered the southern flank. Its two brigades (4th and 22nd) now had between them about 160 tanks, 60 of which were the formidable Grants. The 7th Motor and 3rd Indian Motor Brigades were also present, having been transferred from 7th Armoured to Lumsden's division.[65] Rommel proposed to tackle this formidable force by driving his 90th Light Division through the gap—which was covered by a minefield and mobile columns from 29th Indian Brigade—between Matruh and XIII Corps and then swinging it toward the sea to cut the coast road. Meanwhile, 15th Panzer and 21st Panzer would drive off Lumsden's armor.

The plan ought not to have worked. Lumsden later said that the Afrika Korps should have been destroyed. But work it did. On the evening of June 26, the Indian mobile columns were brushed aside. The next morning, 90th Light, flogged on by Rommel himself, began to push toward the coast road, while 21st Panzer (with 5 light and 16 medium tanks) took on the New Zealanders. Lumsden held up the skeletal 15th Panzer. Late that afternoon, however, Gott authorized a withdrawal, and Auchinleck approved it (the New Zealanders got away by driving straight through 21st Panzer in a wild moonlight charge that Freyberg likened to Balaclava). Due to a communications breakdown, Holmes learned only the next morning that XIII Corps had gone. He in turn broke out that evening, putting everyone in trucks and in a spectacular motorized exodus, driving 30 miles south into the desert before turning east for the Alamein Line. The next morning, 90th Light entered Matruh. The British official history printed no casualty or loss figures for the battle of Matruh, perhaps because records were lost or not kept, perhaps because the battle and the retreat to the Alamein Line became the subject of an official Eighth Army court of enquiry. German documents claimed 40 tanks captured (although how many had been knocked out and how many had broken down mechanically is uncertain), 6,000 prisoners, and "mountains" of supplies and equipment—enough, it was reckoned, to outfit a division. Rommel had lost a few tanks and perhaps 300 men.

The British withdrawal was now chaotic. German columns were intermingled with British, and in some cases, they were ahead of those they were pursuing. At Fuka, about 50 miles west of El Alamein, 29th Indian Brigade was overrun. Both 50th and 10th Indian Divisions were now mere shells. The New Zealanders had taken nearly a thousand casualties, but due to their unusual cohesiveness, they were still battleworthy. Lumsden's armor got back in reasonably good shape. Ahead of them lay the partially organized Alamein position, the last stop before the Nile Delta. Unusually in the desert war, however, the Alamein Line offered no flanks to be turned, anchored as it was on the sea and the Qattara Depression, impassable to all but the hardiest individual. As his army straggled back, Auchinleck told Dorman-Smith, "The British pride themselves on being good losers. I'm a damn bad loser. I'm going to win."[66]

Behind him in Cairo, a crisis atmosphere, even panic, had set in. The Australian war correspondent Alan Moorehead noted that "the British consulate was besieged with people seeking visas to Palestine. The eastbound Palestine trains were jammed." He also saw all the signs that the British civil and military bureaucrats who ran the war in the Middle East did not expect the panzers to halt at Alamein.

> A thin mist of smoke hung over the British Embassy by the Nile and over the sprawling blocks of G.H.Q.—huge quantities of secret documents were being burnt. All day a group of privates shovelled piles of maps, lists of figures, reports, estimates, codes and messages into four blazing bonfires in a vacant square of land between the G.H.Q. buildings. Some of the R.A.F. papers being bundled down a chute onto another fire blew over the fence and fluttered down into the crowded street outside. I went into one office and the floor was covered in ashes and the smell of burning rag hung over the whole building.[67]

The Cairenes, civil and military, Egyptian and foreign, could be excused their fears perhaps, but clearly, no doubts about the outcome were present in the mind of the decisive actor. Over the next month, Auchinleck carried out his promise: he won, untidily and expensively but decisively.

Two battles opened on July 1. In the desert, the decisive first battle of El Alamein began; in London, Churchill faced his critics on the floor of the House of Commons. Trouble had been brewing for some time. Churchill's reconstruction of his government in February had not stilled the discontent produced by two and a half years of grinding war, punctuated by a series of military disasters. Sir Stafford Cripps, a left-wing Labour leader who had become a War Cabinet member in February, seemed to some a modern, technocratic manager and a good candidate for minister of defense in place of Churchill, who was brave and inspirational but perhaps out of date. On the eve of the desert battle, Harold Nicolson, who idolized Churchill but also saw the political and parliamentary scene with a clear eye, noted in his diary, "I fear Winston's position in the House . . . is not a strong one. This fills me with dismay."[68] Then came the fall of Tobruk. Nicolson told his diary, "The 6 o'clock news tells us that the enemy claim that Tobruk has surrendered 'with 25,000 men and many generals.' The news crashes on us in the lovely evening like a thunderstorm."[69] The next day, the London correspondent of the *Chicago Sun* asked Nicolson whether the fall of Tobruk would produce a political crisis. "I think it may, but I do not say so," he loyally recorded.[70] By June 23, Nicolson was noting a "sullen feeling" in the House and talk of a no-confidence motion, which was in fact tabled two days later. On that same day, Churchill's government lost a dramatic by-election at Maldon by a 6,000-vote margin. The deep frustration that surfaced at Maldon is reflected in a diary entry made on June 25 by a housewife in northern England: "Tobruk has gone—what of Egypt, Suez and India? Nearly three years of war: Why don't we get going—what stops us? Surely by now things could be organized better in some way. . . . If only mothers could think that their poor ones had died usefully—with a purpose. They go out and suffer . . . and then Tobruk falls after all. Valuable lives, time, stores, and effort—gone down the drain. It's shocking. There must be some way out to prevent catastrophes like that."[71]

Churchill returned on June 26 to confront these profound anxieties: "This seemed to me to be a bad time," he wrote in his memoirs.[72] In fact, opinion polls showed his personal popularity at its lowest point since he became prime minister (although with an 80 percent favorable rating, he was still twice as popular as his government). Churchill had urged the merits of the offensive on Auchinleck; he now practiced what he preached. Brushing aside offers by his critics to postpone the debate on their motion, he set July 1 as the date for beginning that debate.

Churchill was fortunate that in opening the debate, Sir John Wardlaw-Milne, who had put down (that is, made) the censure motion, committed a remarkable gaffe. "Wardlaw-Milne is an imposing man with a calm manner which gives the impression of solidity," Nicolson noted. "He begins well enough, but then suddenly suggests that the Duke of Gloucester [the king's brother] should be made Commander-in-Chief. A wave of panic-embarrassment passes over the House. For a full minute the buzz goes round 'But the man must be an ass.' Milne pulls himself together . . . but his idiotic suggestion has shaken the validity of his position."[73] From the prime minister's point of view, what followed was even better. Wardlaw-Milne had attacked him for interfering too much in military matters. Admiral of the Fleet Sir Roger Keyes, VC, seconding the motion, assailed him for deferring too much to the service chiefs. Early on July 2, the day on which the House would vote, Churchill received a brief he had requested on the various issues underlying the unease and criticism. Ironically, it was by Cripps, who, rival and muted critic though he was, gave Churchill the benefit of the analytical mind that had made him one of the most highly paid lawyers in England before the war. Under the heading "Generalship," Cripps wrote: "There is a very general view that with better generalship Rommel could have been defeated. . . . This line of criticism has led to doubts as to whether either the commander-in-chief or the Army Commander has a real appreciation of the tactics and strategy of modern mechanised warfare."[74] Although perhaps somewhat unfair to Auchinleck, this statement was remarkably close to the truth. But Churchill did not try to analyze the desert fighting when he rose to speak. Instead, he painted a grim picture of the extent of the defeats, dwelled upon the need for his government to be strongly supported so that it could deal effectively with its allies, and then virtually dared the House to dismiss him. It was a bravura performance and won him an apparently resounding vindication: Wardlaw-Milne's motion lost by a vote of 475 to 25. Twenty-seven members abstained, however, raising the total of those openly expressing doubts to 52.

Nicolson put his finger on the weak point in Churchill's position. For the present, no one could see any alternative to him, "but the impression left is one of dissatisfaction and anxiety, and I do not think it will end there."[75] A few weeks later, another observer, the Welsh Labour member Ivor Thomas, wrote that "if Alexandria had fallen, Winston would have fallen also. As it is, he will hold his position until we get another major reverse."[76] What had bought time for Churchill was Auchinleck's success in halting Rommel in the first battle of El Alamein.

Rommel's forward elements reached the Alamein Line on June 30, in virtually a dead heat with the last of the withdrawing Eighth Army. He was already feeling the logistic effects of the sudden change of plans after the fall of Tobruk. His supply services had anticipated a pause of several weeks while the attack on Malta was mounted, and Rommel's headlong plunge eastward left them scrambling to keep up. Without the booty captured at Tobruk, in the frontier defenses, and at Matruh, there would have been neither food nor vehicles enough to get Rommel's Panzerarmee to Alamein. But losses in men and tanks could not so easily be made good. A mere 55 tanks and a few thousand weary infantrymen remained with the Afrika Korps when it launched its attack on the Alamein Line on July 1. Rommel's plan was a repeat of the one that had worked so well at Matruh. The 90th Light would swing around the Alamein box, held by Pienaar's South Africans, and cut the coast road while the panzer divisions swung south into the rear of Gott's XIII Corps (whose two armored brigades, with over 100 tanks including about 40 Grants, heavily outnumbered the Afrika Korps). The 90th Light was stopped both by its own exhaustion and by the massed artillery of the South Africans—even Rommel in person could not get it moving again. The Afrika Korps ran into the 18th Indian Infantry Brigade, rushed up from Iraq under an acting commander; with two of its battalions new to combat, the brigade was supported by a scratch force of gunners and nine I tanks manned by crews hastily assembled from replacement depots. The brigade was destroyed, another in the long tally of Indian brigades flung hurriedly into battle in nearly hopeless positions and circumstances, but its stubborn fight blunted what little edge Rommel's panzers had left. On July 2, the Germans tried again, without any success. By day's end, the Afrika Korps was down to 26 tanks. After another day of inconclusive fighting on July 3, Rommel, his three German divisions down to between 1,200 and 1,500 men each and deprived since the Matruh battle of rest and maintenance time by round-the-clock hammering from the RAF, decided to go over to the defensive. The critical moment in the struggle for Egypt had passed.

Auchinleck had given preliminary orders for plans to be made in case the Eighth Army had to retire from the Alamein Line. They included a defense of the populous and fertile delta area of Egypt and a further withdrawal by part of his army to the Suez Canal while the remainder retired up the Nile. (The defense of the delta was entrusted by Auchinleck to Rees, perhaps the Auk's commentary on Gott's claim that Rees lacked a "robust outlook.") In the postwar recriminations between Auchinleck, Monty, and their respective partisans, much was made by Auchinleck's critics of these plans. They showed a defensive-mindedness that unsettled the whole army, the argument went. This argument is not very persuasive. Auchinleck was commander-in-chief, Middle East, as well as Eighth Army commander, and contingency planning was part of his job. Wavell had done the same in the dark spring of 1941 (much to Churchill's fury). In any case, there can be little doubt about Auchinleck's offensive-mindedness. He launched his first counterattack on July 2, and as the fighting died down over the next two days, he began planning his first prepared counterstroke. Over the remainder of the month, he would launch four attacks on Rommel's attenuated German-Italian forces.

In going over to the offensive, Auchinleck had a number of assets. His intelligence was excellent. Ultra information from both Bletchley Park and his own Y service kept him abreast of the enemy's order of battle, supply difficulties, intentions, and reactions to his own moves.[77] He could target the weaker Italian formations, compelling Rommel to use his German units as a kind of fire brigade, rushing from point to point to prevent collapse. The initiative was no longer in Rommel's hands. And as Auchinleck's picture of Rommel became clearer, Rommel's intelligence began to dry up. The Americans changed their attaché cipher, which meant Colonel Fellers's invaluable reports from Cairo were no longer accessible. Then, on July 10, the first of Auchinleck's major attacks, delivered by a brigade of the newly arrived 9th Australian Division behind an artillery barrage that reminded some German veterans of World War I, virtually annihilated the Italian Sabratha Division, overrunning in the process Rommel's 621st Signals Battalion, the radio-intercept unit that provided most of his order of battle and tactical intelligence. Loss of critical personnel and records so reduced the efficiency of the unit that not until March 1943 was it again operating successfully. Morshead's Australians, who had stalled Rommel at Tobruk in April 1941, had again dealt him a savage blow.

Auchinleck had other assets as well. The RAF, flying from bases that were now very close to the front, was punishing the Panzerarmee heavily. On July 3, about 10 tons of bombs an hour were showered down. Although Rommel still had plentiful supplies of captured trucks, he was losing an average of thirty a day to air attacks. As Rommel's supply, replacement, and maintenance situation became more complicated, Auchinleck's became easier, for his forces were fighting close to his depots and stores dumps in Egypt. Furthermore, new formations were arriving to swell the ranks of the Eighth Army. The Australians had been in Syria before joining the Eighth Army. The 8th Armoured Division from Britain began unloading in mid-July. Another British infantry division was following it, and the 300 Sherman tanks were also en route. All Rommel could look forward to in the way of German reinforcements was the gradual arrival of another German light division and, after that, a paratroop brigade. No more panzer divisions could be spared for what was, after all, merely a sideshow to Hitler and the rest of the German army.

Nevertheless, Auchinleck's July offensives, although they pushed Rommel's army near its limit, failed to break his front. The first, launched on July 10 by XXX Corps (now commanded by Ramsden), shattered one Italian division and badly damaged another.[78] The second and third were disasters. In the first battle of Ruweisat (on July 14 and 15), the 4th New Zealand Brigade was smashed. In second Ruweisat (on July 21), 6th New Zealand Brigade lost nearly half its strength, and the newly arrived 23rd Armoured Brigade (of 8th Armoured Division) was decimated. Both these actions were managed by Gott's corps. Auchinleck's final try was made by Ramsden. Once again, in the words of the official history, the execution of the operation broke down in "doubt and muddle." The two attacking infantry brigades, one Australian and one British, hit by German counterattacks while their armored support was still in the rear, took heavy casualties, with two British battalions being overrun. By this time, the infantry, especially the New Zealanders, had become quite cynical about the support they were likely to get from the tanks. The British official historian, writing about first Ruweisat, put his finger on the underlying problem—the failure to achieve an effective integration of different arms on the battlefield, referring to the "dislike of the armoured forces . . . to be tied to the protection of infantry at the expense of their wider role . . . it is fair to say that co-operation between armoured division (as opposed to "I" tank units) and one or more infantry divisions had not really been studied and had certainly not been practised."[79] He then concluded with a generous tribute to an army in which such cooperation was deeply ingrained: "It would be unfair and ungenerous not to recognize the remarkable achievement of the German troops. . . . Small groups of units or sub-units were constantly being flung together for some desperate enterprise—usually to plug some gap—and it is astonishing how often they brought it off. The German soldier always seemed capable of one more supreme effort."[80]

Despite the remarkable battlefield performance of his troops, Rommel understood what had really happened: "The British losses in this Alamein fighting had been higher than ours, yet the price to Auchinleck had not been excessive, for the one thing that mattered to him was to halt our advance, and that, unfortunately, he had done."[81]

Auchinleck sent a signal to London on July 31, indicating that there would be a lull of at least six weeks (while reinforcements were absorbed and desperately needed training and reorganization took place) before he could resume the offensive. Churchill had recently finalized his protracted negotiations with the Americans over future strategy, and an Anglo-American invasion of French North Africa was set for the fall. This meant that Stalin could expect no second front—at least as the Russians defined it—in 1942. Facing a second massive German summer offensive, the Red Army was already reeling backward toward the Caucasus. Churchill's government would not survive another defeat in the field; he desperately needed a victory. Considerations of alliance politics demanded a British victory in the field as well, to buttress Britain's "senior partner" role with the Americans and to demonstrate to the Russians that the British were capable of facing the Germans in the only war that counted in Moscow—the land war against the German army. It was not a good moment to tell the prime minister that the empire's only active field army could do nothing more until early autumn. Brooke had already decided that he needed to go to Cairo in person, continuing on to Iraq and India. These plans were overtaken by Churchill's decision to go to the Middle East and examine matters on the spot, then continue on to Moscow to tell Stalin personally that there would be no cross-channel attack in 1942. Brooke left first, stopping en route in battered Malta. By August 3, he was reunited with the prime minister in Cairo.

Churchill's six days in Cairo produced a major upheaval in personnel and command structure in the Middle East. It was easily the prime minister's most dramatic intervention in the selection of senior army commanders, and it has been so repeatedly described that only a few features need be highlighted. It has been called (by a writer notably hostile to both Churchill and Montgomery) a "purge." That word is unfair. Churchill arrived in Cairo by no means decided on Auchinleck's relief but determined that a vigorous offensive should be launched at the earliest moment. With so much at stake in both domestic and alliance politics, this is unsurprising. Moreover, the natural result of a defeat such as that recently endured by Eighth Army was that senior officers were at risk. Auchinleck had sacked Ritchie; Norrie had removed first Messervy and then himself. On the morning of August 4, Brooke agreed with Auchinleck on further removals. Auchinleck's chief of staff, Corbett, one of his worst choices and widely agreed not to be up to his job (he was described by Churchill as a "very small, agreeable man, of no personality and little experience"), would be replaced.[82] Since Auchinleck himself wanted to return to Cairo and resume control of his vast command and since his proposal to install Corbett at Eighth Army (thus following the Ritchie precedent) was clearly not acceptable, he and Brooke had agreed on Montgomery as the new commander of the Eighth Army, thus setting up what would have been an explosive—and in all probability quite brief—combination. Gott, who was widely admired but also burned out, would go to Syria to replace Jumbo Wilson at Ninth Army, Wilson being, Brooke felt, too old for what might soon become an active command. These arrangements left Auchinleck as the theater commander.

Then things began to go rapidly downhill for Auchinleck. On the evening of August 4, there was a meeting at the British Embassy in Cairo. In addition to Churchill, Brooke, and the three Middle East commanders-in-chief, Casey (the minister of state), Wavell (summoned from India), and the ever-plausible Smuts (who had just lost a division) were there. Churchill pushed Auchinleck hard on the date for the resumption of the offensive; Auchinleck stuck to mid-September. Brooke confided to his diary that it was impossible to shake the prime minister's determination to attack Rommel quickly. What Brooke missed or at least never mentioned even in his diary was the stark political reality put to the prime minister's doctor by Brendan Bracken, a longtime Churchill associate and counselor: "The Prime Minister must either win his battle in the desert or get out."[83] The next morning, Churchill went up to Eighth Army headquarters. Auchinleck, who believed field commanders should live in a spartan fashion, unwisely made no concessions to the prime minister's age or tastes: "We were given breakfast in a wire-netted cube, full of flies and important military personages," Churchill wrote acidly in his memoirs.[84] (Later in the day, when it was the RAF's turn to entertain Churchill, the meal at Desert Air Force headquarters was catered by Cairo's famous Shepheard's Hotel. "This turned out to be a gay occasion in the midst of care—a real oasis in a very large desert," he wrote in appreciative retrospect.[85]) After the inauspicious breakfast, Churchill and Auchinleck conferred in one of the "caravans" (trailers) that provided office space. A staff officer standing outside and hearing the tone of the exchanges was convinced Auchinleck would be replaced. Churchill insisted that Gott ride with him to his next stop. "As we rumbled and jolted over the rough tracks I looked into his clear blue eyes and questioned him about himself," he recalled.[86] When he flew back to Cairo that evening, his mind was made up.

The following day (August 6), Churchill began by offering Auchinleck's job to Brooke, who declined because—although he did not say so to the prime minister—he felt he had developed, painfully, some skills in managing Churchill. Churchill then made a series of changes that were sent out in a signal that evening to Clement Attlee, the deputy prime minister. General the Honorable Sir Harold Alexander would replace Auchinleck; Gott would command Eighth Army. Corbett, Dorman-Smith, and Ramsden were to go. To free the new command team of the distractions of the northern front, the theater was reconfigured. Persia and Iraq would become a separate theater, command of which would be offered to Auchinleck as a sort of consolation prize. Had the northern front become active—and the Germans were by then deep in the Caucasus—this arrangement would have put Ninth and Tenth Armies each under a different theater commander. But the prime minister was now ruthlessly concentrated on defeating Rommel. The invaluable diary kept by Colonel Ian Jacob of Ismay's staff captures Churchill striding up and down his bedroom at the British Embassy "declaiming on the point . . . 'Rommel, Rommel, Rommel' he cried. 'What else matters but beating him'?" Somewhat superfluously, Jacob added: "He [Churchill] means to have his way."[87]

The tribalism of the British Army demonstrated itself clearly in the selection of Gott and the retention of Wilson at Ninth Army. Churchill knew neither; Brooke thought the one too tired and the other too old. Both, however, were from one of Britain's most famous regiments, the King's Royal Rifle Corps. Anthony Eden, Churchill's foreign secretary and designated heir, who had been an officer in the regiment during World War I, had put in a good word for his fellow riflemen. Gott, who had admitted his fatigue to Churchill and whose performance as a corps commander had not been particularly sure-handed, was pressed into the most important field command in the empire, and Wilson continued his puzzlingly steady ascent to the rank of field marshal.

The next day, fate took a hand. Gott, summoned back to Cairo, hitched a ride on a transport that was forced down in flames by a German fighter.

He and the other passengers burned to death. Assessing him nearly two decades later, the official historian wrote that "he was greatly liked and respected for his frank, courteous and unruffled manner, his easy natural leadership and his personal courage. He had more experience of the desert than any other commander. . . . Indeed he is known to have felt that he had been there almost too long. . . . It may therefore be doubted if he would have been the man to breathe new life into the 8th Army."[88] A XXX Corps staff officer, writing years later after all the principals were dead, commented, "Almost all who served under Gott worshiped him," but he went on to note both his shortcomings as a corps commander and his exhaustion by August. "Tragic as it was for him," he concluded "it was fortunate for Eighth Army that he did not assume command."[89] Gott's death enabled Brooke to revert to the candidate he and Auchinleck had agreed upon several days previously: Lieutenant General B. L. Montgomery. In fact, if Brooke's postwar notes are correct, he may have had Montgomery in mind before he got to Cairo. Certainly, Monty's name came up in the conversations Ian Jacob had with army friends soon after his arrival in Cairo.[90]

Only on August 8, with everything settled, was Auchinleck told of his dismissal. Churchill sent Colonel Ian Jacob up to Eighth Army headquarters with a letter relieving him of command and urging him to accept the new Persia and Iraq command. Although a British Army officer, Jacob came from a family that had served in the Indian Army since 1816 (his father had been its commander-in-chief). He wrote in his diary that he felt as if he were going to murder an unsuspecting friend. Auchinleck read the letter, took Jacob for a walk, and told him he believed retirement was better than a face-saving job for unsuccessful generals. The next day, he flew back to Cairo, had a "bleak and impeccable" conversation with Churchill, and prepared to hand over his command to Alexander, who had arrived that morning.

Churchill's thoughts were now turning to his next major task, explaining Anglo-American strategy to Stalin. On the evening of August 10, just before his departure from Cairo for Moscow, the prime minister conferred with Alexander. On a single sheet of British Embassy stationery, Churchill wrote out the new theater directive:

> Your prime and main duty will be to take or destroy at the earliest opportunity the German-Italian Army commanded by Field Marshal Rommel, with all its supplies and establishments in Egypt and Libya.
> 2. You will discharge, or cause to be discharged such other duties as pertain to your command, without prejudice to the task described in

> paragraph 1, which must be considered paramount in His Majesty's interests.[91]

Leaving behind this model of clarity and brevity (which also testified to his clamant need for a victory), Churchill flew off. Early on the morning of August 12, Montgomery's plane landed in Cairo.

5

Monty and His Enemies

Montgomery's arrival in Cairo and his restructuring of the Eighth Army was followed by a limited victory at Alam Halfa (August 30 to September 2) and then his much more impressive—although far from total—success at El Alamein (October 23 to November 4). The battle of El Alamein is remembered, especially in the English-speaking world, as one of the war's turning points. In Churchill's words: "It marked in fact the turning of 'the Hinge of Fate.' It may almost be said, 'Before Alamein we never had a victory. After Alamein we never had a defeat.' "[1]

In the architecture of the prime minister's war memoirs, Alamein occupied a keystone position. Indeed, the memory of Alamein as *the* great British victory owes as much to Churchill as to Montgomery, whose own memoirs, appearing eight years later, had a smaller impact on popular views of the war—although, of course, a major role in touching off an ongoing argument. But Alamein was not the turning point of the war against Germany—that came in Russia and the North Atlantic in the 1942–1943 winter. As one of Montgomery's critics has observed, if the Eighth Army had simply stood on the defensive after Alam Halfa, Panzerarmee Afrika would have been forced into retreat by Operation Torch.

There was, however, a good reason why Churchill treated El Alamein as he did: for him, it resolved the barely contained political crisis triggered by the run of disasters that began with the Japanese attack and ended only with Auchinleck's stopping Rommel in July 1942. Unlike Compass and Crusader, whose significance was unfairly written down by that dismissive "almost," El Alamein was also a victory that Rommel would not quickly erase with one of his lightning ripostes. (Rommel's most significant tactical success after Alamein—his only one, in fact—came at the expense of the Americans in Tunisia.) Most important of all, perhaps, it was an exclusively British and imperial victory—the last one against Germany before the British military effort became inextricably enmeshed in a coalition partnership with an increasingly dominant United States. It was also, however, an important milepost for the British Army, the moment when, with some of its equipment and technique deficits finally overcome, it got to fight the sort of battle it could fight well, a battle whose outcome would ultimately allow Montgomery to put his stamp on the British approach to battle for the balance of the war in the West.

Churchill's need for a victory was underscored when he met Stalin in August. With the German summer offensive grinding relentlessly toward both the Caucasus and Stalingrad, the British Army's unimpressive performance against the handful of German divisions it faced was hardly the best background for the message the prime minister had flown to Moscow to deliver: there would be no second front (at least as defined by the Russians) in 1942. Some 3.3 million German troops were on the Eastern Front. Their summer offensive had been mounted by sixty-five divisions. Stalin, with characteristic verbal brutality, told Churchill that the German army could be beaten in the field if the British Army was willing to fight. Although Churchill's volcanic reaction to this jab impressed Stalin, the episode had underscored for the prime minister the absolute necessity of a clear victory over the German army—and demonstrated how feeble the British military effort appeared from the Russian perspective.

Returning to Cairo, Churchill spent several days in the desert, visiting in Alex's company formations and headquarters, lunching near the battlefield with Bernard Freyberg (as he had in France a quarter century before), and being briefed—"masterly exposition"—by Montgomery, both on Rommel's impending attack and on his own plans for taking the offensive at the end of September. Churchill's report to the War Cabinet on August 21 reflected Monty's view of the situation he inherited—indeed, it was the first edition of what was to become the official Montgomery version.

> I am sure we were headed for disaster under the former regime. The Army was reduced to bits and pieces and oppressed by a sense of bafflement and uncertainly. Apparently it was intended in face of heavy attack to retire eastward to the Delta. Many were looking over their shoulders to make sure of their seat in the lorry, and no plain plan of battle or dominating will power had reached the units.[2]

This assessment, patently unfair to Auchinleck and others, would prompt a good deal of anger when Churchill published it eight years later.[3] But at the time, what concerned the prime minister was the impending renewal of the Eighth Army's struggle with Rommel. He could not afford another defeat, something that became plain soon after his return to London in late August.

The name of Sir Stafford Cripps is largely forgotten today even in Britain, but in 1942, he was a considerable presence in British politics. A wealthy lawyer and Labour politician, his opposition to appeasement had led him, after Munich, to propose an alliance of all Chamberlain's opponents, regardless of party. For this, he had been expelled from the Labour Party. Named ambassador to the Soviet Union by Churchill, he had been largely ignored by Stalin, but when he returned to Britain early in 1942, he was associated in the minds of many, especially on the Left, with Russia's resistance to the Wehrmacht. More important, as dissatisfaction with unending defeat mounted, he came to be considered as a possible alternative for the post of minister of defence, with Churchill becoming an inspirational figurehead. Churchill, of course, had no intention of accepting any diminution of his powers, but a tactical adjustment seemed appropriate, and he offered Cripps the Ministry of Supply. Cripps declined. As pressure on him mounted, Churchill improved his offer: Lord Privy Seal, with a seat in the War Cabinet and the leadership of the House. Cripps's acceptance immediately made him a major player in the War Cabinet and, to some, a possible alternative manager of the British war effort if the tally of British defeats lengthened much further. Churchill very shrewdly got him to agree to head a mission to India that was meant to defuse a growing crisis between the Raj and Indian nationalism, but Cripps's absence was only a temporary respite. By late summer 1942, Cripps was convinced that only a radical reorganization of the central machinery of war direction—and a concomitant reduction of Churchill's role—would improve British military performance.

The fact that he was wrong did nothing to diminish the danger he posed at the moment to Churchill if he carried out his announced intention to resign. Churchill, however, had unusual allies in buying time. Cripps's rise threatened not only the prime minister but also the Labour leaders allied with him, first and foremost Clement Attlee, who was currently party leader and deputy prime minister. Thus, Cripps was prevailed upon by both Churchill and his Labour colleagues to delay his resignation until the impending battles—the Eighth Army offensive and Torch—had gotten under way. Everything now hinged on Montgomery's battle. One of the prime minister's closest associates told Churchill's doctor that if there was not a clear-cut victory, Churchill would have to "get out." As he waited for the opening phase of the battle, Operation Lightfoot, to begin, Churchill must have gone through one of the most anxious periods of his war.[4]

El Alamein is the most written-about British battle of the war. Churchill declared it "will ever make a glorious page in British military annals,"[5] and, at least implicitly, he compared it to Stalingrad—twin turning points in the war against Germany. This is, of course, an exaggeration, for Stalingrad dwarfed El Alamein in significance. Yet the claim, taken together with the Churchill-Montgomery version of the battle and its preliminaries, fueled a controversy that has sometimes come close to obscuring the battle's real significance. Alamein was important not only because it made Churchill politically secure until 1945 but also because it represented a significant change both in the way the British Army fought its war and in the prime minister's relationship to his generals. In this sense, El Alamein was indeed a watershed, even if not quite in the way Churchill and Montgomery claimed in their respective memoirs.

In the first place, Churchill's reorganization of the whole command structure had focused Middle East Command's attention exclusively on the desert war. Alexander was spared the distractions that had beset Wavell and Auchinleck from other directions. In effect, Alex and his able chief of staff, Richard McCreery, were there to see that Montgomery could focus on winning the victory the prime minister so desperately needed. And then there was Monty himself, who remains the best-known and most controversial of Britain's World War II generals, largely because of what he said and wrote after El Alamein had made him famous. It is therefore important to get behind all that and look at what Montgomery actually did and did not do in 1942. It is apparent at once that there were numerous continuities between what Churchill, encouraged by Montgomery, described as "the former regime" and the Eighth Army that Montgomery commanded. The key members of his staff—who would remain with him for the balance of the war—were all in Cairo when Montgomery arrived: Freddie de Guingand, who became his chief of staff; Edgar "Bill" Williams, who would be his intelligence officer; and Charles Richardson and David Belchem, who would end the war as brigadiers responsible for plans and operations, respectively, at Twenty-first Army Group headquarters. Many of the principal actors in the desert war also remained. The Dominion commanders were beyond Monty's reach. The commanders of the 50th Division and the 7th Armoured were replaced—the latter by Harding, one of the original desert warriors. The two corps commands were vacant, and those were quickly filled by officers Monty liked. Brian Horrocks, a lieutenant colonel two years before, took over XIII Corps, and Sir Oliver Leese, Bt., a large, outwardly jovial Guardsman, took over XXX Corps. Herbert Lumsden, whose desert record was spotty at best, became commander of X Corps, in which Monty planned to concentrate his armor. This leads on to the question of the sort of battle he proposed to fight.

Montgomery did not arrive from England with a new doctrine that transformed the desert war. He came on the scene at a moment when many long-standing problems were finally being resolved, and he operated in an environment denied to his predecessors—a theater command structure focused almost exclusively on his army's success and an exhausted, logistically desperate opponent. His predecessors had had to cope with British tanks that were undergunned, underarmored, and mechanically unreliable. Now, however, tanks designed and built in the United States—the Grant and the Sherman—had begun to give British armored formations equipment that was both reliable and had reasonable protection and firepower. The 6-pounder antitank gun, delayed in production after Dunkirk, began to reach the desert in May 1942. Better antitank weapons in turn made it easier to use field artillery in its proper role, something that began to happen when Auchinleck's massed artillery played a critical role in stopping Rommel in the July fighting. Radio equipment, scarce during the post-Dunkirk reequipment and expansion of the army, had become more abundant, making command and control more effective. In addition, more British infantry was available (the 44th and the 51st Divisions), freeing Montgomery from the nearly complete dependence on Dominion units, with their complex and semiautonomous status, that had been the lot of his predecessors.[6] None of this, of course, was Monty's doing—but he was intelligent enough to extract maximum advantage from it.

That, perhaps, is the essence of what Montgomery brought to Cairo: a driving, intelligent professionalism, which is not, of course, the same as inerrancy. He understood that an army commander needed to have and maintain a clear chain of command, responsive to his will. The component parts of his army had to work in tandem to carry out the commander's intentions. He tended to describe these requirements using his own nomenclature—"grip," "no bellyaching," and so forth—but it was evident that he meant to end the loose, argument-prone structure that had hitherto run Eighth Army.

Monty understood other things as well. One of them was the value of the army's most impressive arm, the Royal Artillery. Concentrated, centrally controlled fire plans became a signature of his battles. He had also grasped that there was now available flying artillery whose range and versatility needed to be fully exploited. The nature of the desert war had brought improvements in army-RAF cooperation since the days of Battleaxe, when Beresford-Peirse and his supporting air squadrons had operated from headquarters a hundred miles apart—an apt metaphor for the gap that yawned between the services at that point. Under Air Chief Marshal Tedder, who took over that RAF in the Middle East about the time Auchinleck replaced Wavell, matters improved significantly. Montgomery believed in the closest army-air cooperation, symbolized by his decision to locate his headquarters beside that of the Desert Air Force (commanded by a New Zealander, Air Vice Marshal Arthur "Mary" Coningham). The techniques worked out in the desert and subsequently polished in Tunisia, Sicily, and Italy would produce the air support successes of 1944 and 1945. By that time, of course, Montgomery would be at daggers drawn with the airmen, but that was a function of his personality, not his views on the crucial contributions of airpower to the battlefield.

Finally, Montgomery, though he was a lonely, introverted, egocentric, and exceedingly prickly man, nonetheless understood clearly the soldiers he commanded. The ranks of the prewar regulars had been swamped by citizen-soldiers willing to fight and endure but also raised on memories of their fathers' war and thus needing to be convinced that their lives would not be squandered. This Montgomery managed to do. His oft-criticized cautiousness owes much to his sense of how to get the best performance possible from an army that could not grow larger and indeed would soon have increasing difficulty even replacing casualties. Churchill—and the British public—needed a victory, but the cost of the victory had to be sustainable. For that reason, Montgomery was always casualty conscious, which was something quite different from being casualty adverse. His battles, from Alamein on, were not low-casualty affairs, and his infantry often sustained losses at World War I levels. What Montgomery was intent upon, however, was showing results from his battles, not only for the sake of his own reputation but also to sustain the morale both of his troops and of the blitzed, stringently rationed, and increasingly weary nation that provided them. In the sense of crafting carefully prepared battles that moved his army forward, not at a low cost but at a sustainable one, Montgomery was a World War I general—the heir to the techniques that had made the successes of 1918 possible. Like every other survivor of that conflict, he had seen inefficiently conducted battles of attrition and was determined to do it better. Unless this is fully grasped, Montgomery is hard to understand.

Did the prime minister realize how different a soldier Montgomery was from Alex—or Gott? That seems doubtful. Churchill had met and dined with him in July 1940 when Montgomery was still a division commander responsible for a stretch of Britain's nearly naked south coast. The occasion produced one of the most quoted Churchill stories but probably left the prime minister with no lasting sense of Montgomery's approach to battle.[7] What Churchill did know in August 1942 was that Montgomery was Brooke's protégé—and the commander Brooke believed could deliver victory in the desert. He also knew, during his return visit to Cairo, that another attack by Rommel was imminent, and he flirted with the idea of remaining on the scene.

Conducting his first battle as an army commander with the prime minister in attendance might well have strained even Montgomery's nerve. As it turned out, the battle of Alam Halfa provided him with his first victory and gave Eighth Army an encouraging and clear-cut success. It also prefigured Monty's future performance—right down to the controversy that accompanied it.

In the view of Montgomery's critics, Alam Halfa was a plagiarized victory. Auchinleck and Dorman-Smith had correctly foreseen Rommel's likely course of action: a wide enveloping move to outflank the Alamein Line by breaching the lightly defended minefields that made up its southern half, then swinging north to the sea—a replay of the Gazala and Matruh maneuvers. They planned to counter by holding a position on Alam Halfa ridge, which ran east to west at right angles to the Alamein defenses. Here, Rommel would be met and stopped. Montgomery, the argument goes, took this plan and won a victory with it, and then far from acknowledging its authors, he traduced them as defeatists.[8] This, of course, is a gross and distorting oversimplification. Montgomery's plan was bound to look like Auchinleck's—Eighth Army commanders had changed, but the geography of the Alamein position had not. What Montgomery did, however, was employ his force in a very different manner.

Auchinleck had envisioned a mobile battle. Montgomery, barely two weeks in command and without any experience in handling armor, had no intention of allowing one to develop. Where Auchinleck planned to hold the Alamein Line with boxes in which his artillery would be positioned and which would be pivots of maneuver for his armor, Montgomery opted for a much more conventional plan. More infantry was brought up, and the Alamein Line was solidly garrisoned, while dug-in armor and guns held Alam Halfa. Rather like Wellington in the peninsula, Montgomery intended to let his opponent attack him on ground he had chosen and prepared. When Rommel, ill and short of fuel, moved forward, he was met by round-the-clock bombing and the massed firepower of British tanks and artillery positioned on and behind Alam Halfa. After forty-eight hours of enduring this continuous pounding, Rommel called off his attack. At no point had he even come close to a breakthrough. Montgomery made no attempt to impede Rommel's withdrawal—something for which he would subsequently be heavily criticized.[9] But he had accomplished what he had set out to do—conduct a limited but successful battle in which the whole Eighth Army fought according to his design. That design featured airpower and massive firepower. Churchill, who had accepted from Alex and Montgomery a delay in attacking Rommel that he had found unendurable when proposed by Auchinleck, could derive some comfort from the first performance of his new command team. But the real test still lay ahead.

In his memoirs, Churchill referred to the twelve-day battle of El Alamein as "the great military climax upon which all was to be staked"[10]—an exaggeration of the stakes in the upcoming battle but not, perhaps, of what Churchill himself felt was at issue. That makes his patience with the postponement of Operation Lightfoot all the more remarkable. When Montgomery briefed Churchill at Eighth Army headquarters, he had spoken of late September. In the aftermath of Alam Halfa, that timing slipped to late October. Churchill's reaction, in a message to Alex, was surprisingly resigned—"We are in your hands"—but he also shrewdly pointed out that the delay would mean facing thicker belts of German defenses when the attack finally went in.[11] Montgomery's insistence on delay was based on a desire to give his newly arrived British divisions more training time, as well as the entire army a chance to absorb and become comfortable with new American equipment. It also allowed time for an elaborate deception plan to mislead the Germans about exactly where the attack they knew to be coming would actually fall. Montgomery's signature was the carefully prepared attack, and he had good reason for caution about Eighth Army's next battle. Although some of the British Army's matériel deficiencies were being remedied by new British and American equipment, deeply rooted structural problems remained, and training continued to be a central issue. The vast expansion and reorganization after Dunkirk had had the inevitable side effect of continually disrupting training. Despite Brooke's drive and ruthlessness, this situation improved only gradually between 1941 and 1942. Moreover, as the best study of the subject puts it, "the experience of defeat did not persuade the army to change its basic doctrine of command . . . [that is, a] hierarchical command system that allowed subordinate commanders too little initiative."[12] The fundamental problem of an army with no common doctrine remained. Units fresh from training in the United Kingdom, such as the luckless 2nd Armoured Division in March 1941, had consistently fared poorly in their first desert encounters.

One acute observer, Major General Francis Tuker of 4th Indian Division (one of the only Indian Army officers left in a senior Eighth Army command and a man obsessed with training), put his finger on the problem when, reflecting on the preparations for Alamein, he recalled "how shocked I was at the meagre results of the 2 years of training in the U.K. when I met 44 Div., 51 Div. . . . All these were divisions trained and commanded by Monty and his colleagues—the Horrockses and Leeses." Tuker went on to sharply criticize Monty in particular and the British Army's approach to training in general: "If Monty, instead of making his officers run 7 miles a day, had made them turn out and train themselves on the ground, and teach themselves and their men a little battle-skill, they would have got the same physical exercise and learnt to use their brains." Montgomery, he felt, had been "without any personal effect on tactics other than to keep them where they were in 1918 . . . my opinion . . . was, and still is, that Monty was living in 1918 and never left it." Yet as critical of Montgomery as he was, Tuker recognized that what he saw in him was merely a reflection of a larger problem: "In 1943 I saw [Major General J. A. C.] Whitaker, DMT [director of military training at the War Office], and that interview confirmed to me there wasn't anyone in the British Army who knew how to train infantry for war, how good they could be, and what to expect of them. . . . The mere fact that the British Army had to have things called 'Commandos' damned their infantry at once."[13]

Tuker's analysis contained many elements of truth but overlooked two things. First, Montgomery had to work with what he had and clearly felt a tightly controlled battle plan was the best way to get the maximum out of his troops (thus proving that he fully shared the British Army's "doctrine of command"). Second, his plan for Alamein paradoxically included a very ambitious use of his armor, which did not resemble the situation in 1918 in the least. Believing that the Afrika Korps was primarily an exploitation force (rather than the core of Rommel's army, winning by using effective combined arms tactics), he created a mirror image of it in Lumsden's X Corps, with its two armored divisions. After the infantry of Leese's XXX Corps, supported by massed guns, smashed lanes through the German defenses and cleared them of mines, Lumsden's *corps de chasse* (pursuing force) would pass through the infantry and exploit westward. There were two problems with this. One was (as the prime minister had pointed out) the depth and sophistication of the defenses Leese would face; the other was the complexity of deploying one corps through another, already heavily engaged, and on a very tight timetable at that. Here, there is a faint echo of Operation Aberdeen during the Gazala battle (and perhaps a foreshadowing of another very incautious Montgomery operation—Market Garden in 1944). As with Aberdeen, the plan broke down almost immediately. Unlike Ritchie during Aberdeen, however, Montgomery was able to adjust his plan and move forward, showing a flexibility he later denied having.

Realizing, not least because of the representations of his armored commanders, that he could not force X Corps through, he pulled the armor back and turned the battle into something quite different: an infantry-artillery "crumbling" (Montgomery-speak for attrition) assault designed to remorselessly grind away German-Italian strength before the armor was again launched for the coup de grâce. It is this aspect of El Alamein that reminded observers then and writers since of 1917 and 1918—and it is certainly true that the relatively low Eighth Army casualties (13,500) tended to conceal World War I loss rates among many infantry units at the "sharp end." Crucial to Montgomery's success was the remorseless drive into some of the heaviest Axis defenses by Morshead's aggressive and well-led 9th Australian Division, a role clearly not foreshadowed in Montgomery's original plan.[14]

The failure to achieve a rapid breakthrough produced not only readjustment by Montgomery but also what can only be described as a sudden crisis of nerves in London. Churchill, of course, had a great deal riding on Montgomery's success, Brooke scarcely less. As Monty began pulling formations into reserve to prepare for a renewed breakthrough attempt after attrition had done its work, the prime minister's patience snapped. Sending for Brooke on October 29, he demanded (the CIGS recalled) to know what "my Monty" was doing. (Brooke would later note that Montgomery was always "my Monty" when in Churchillian disfavor.) Summoning a Chiefs of Staff meeting to consider the situation, Churchill opened by asking Foreign Secretary Anthony Eden (who had been stoking the prime minister's anxieties) to lay out his concerns. This was remarkable enough, but equally impressive was the choleric Brooke's restraint in the face of Eden's intervention. He explained the course of the battle to date and what he believed Montgomery's plans to be for the next phase, permitting himself passing sarcastic swipes at Eden's credentials for making an assessment of Eighth Army's operations. The South African prime minister, Smuts, whom Churchill had brought along—and whose military credentials were more obsolete than Eden's—weighed in to say that he agreed with Brooke. Since Churchill valued Smuts's views excessively, the tempest subsided, and a sharp draft message to Cairo was amended into an expression of continuing support. Privately, however, Brooke was deeply concerned. He later recalled returning from the meeting to restlessly pace his office, "suffering from a desperate feeling of loneliness. . . . I had . . . tried to maintain an exterior of complete confidence. It had worked . . . but there was just the possibility that I was wrong and Monty was beat."[15]

Montgomery, however, did not let his patron down. After twelve days of slogging attrition, climaxed in a renewed assault by the formations he had pulled into reserve, Eighth Army finally broke through as the Panzerarmee's front collapsed. Monty had won a clear victory—the one thing Churchill (and Brooke) needed. Being a Montgomery battle, the engagement also ended with a controversy over the failure of the pursuit phase, which had allowed Rommel to get the attenuated remnants of his German formations and some remaining shreds of the Italian units away. The blame for this in fact falls on both Montgomery and his subordinate commanders (and certainly, when next presented with a comparable opportunity to seal a battlefield victory with an annihilating pursuit, in August 1944, Montgomery did much better).[16] But in one sense, it did not really matter. On November 6, Alex signaled Churchill, "Ring out the Bells." The prime minister, accustomed to false dawns in the desert, prudently waited until the success of Torch a few days later. Then Britain's long-silent church bells, never rung for Compass or Crusader, pealed out. The British Army had won the victory Churchill wanted and needed. Rommel would not stage another comeback, at least not against the British. Churchill's control of the war effort would never again be challenged, although this was not as immediately apparent. And the general who was described by the unimpressed Tuker as "self-confident, conceited, very persistent and tenacious, unimaginative" (and who even his official biographer conceded was "flawed, profoundly limited") became the British Army's dominant field commander for the balance of the European war.[17]

Because Montgomery and his favorite subordinates would lead the British Army into battle for the rest of the war, his success at Alamein and the unswerving support of Brooke (who came to regard him as the greatest British field commander since Marlborough) enabled Montgomery, to a considerable degree, to make his own approach to battle something close to British Army doctrine. Alamein was the template. It featured the close integration of ground and air operations, a heavy reliance on massive artillery support, and (after the failure of the initial plan for an armored breakthrough) the use of a succession of "bite and hold" attacks—reminiscent of the action in 1917 and 1918—to gradually grind away the Panzerarmee's defenses. Of course, Rommel had contributed to Montgomery's success. His headlong pursuit of the Eighth Army in June (a long-odds gamble) had, when it failed, left his army in an untenable situation. It was unable to advance or retreat, and lacking reserves, it was prey to exactly the sort of battle Montgomery and his army were best at fighting. Alamein was a template in another regard as well—Montgomery would never be comfortable handling armor. Superimposing X Corps on XXX Corps in the opening stages of Lightfoot asked too much of his commanders and troops and was unsuccessful—as Goodwood, which it resembled in many ways, would later be in Normandy. Critics such as Tuker were therefore correct in contending that much of Montgomery's style derived from 1918. However, in fairness to Montgomery, it is important to note that there were distinctly post-1918 components to a Montgomery battle as well: the recognition of the importance of airpower, of the need for manpower conservation, of the crucial significance of the morale of his citizen army—and of the utility of publicity in sustaining that morale (as well as in advancing his own career). Montgomery's eccentric style was as carefully cultivated as George Patton's and his thirst for recognition as great as Mark Clark's, although he was more balanced than the former and a far better soldier than the latter. In many ways, Montgomery was very up to date.

His tactical and operational style as well as his difficult personality were things with which the British Army, the prime minister, and Britain's allies would have to deal for the balance of the war, for after Alamein, Montgomery and the Eighth Army became for the British people symbols of the martial resurgence of their country. Ironically, Rommel's inflation in British minds into the Desert Fox rebounded to Montgomery's benefit: he had beaten a legendary foe and, in so doing, had given the British a legend of their own. With Alamein and Torch, the war moved into a new phase, one in which the issue for Churchill would be not whether the British Army could win but how to shape victory to support British interests. In this new phase, a soldier such as Alex—charming and emollient—might better have served Churchill's interests. Monty, however, was what he henceforth had.

Montgomery followed Rommel's retreating army cautiously, for which he has, of course, been heavily criticized. Tuker (whose 4th Indian Division was left behind as the Eighth Army moved west, only catching up with the war months later in Tunisia) claimed that Montgomery was intimidated by

Rommel's reputation. Although it would have been impossible for either Eighth Army or its commander not to be aware of Rommel's remarkable recovery in January 1942, that seems an overly simple explanation. Logistics dominates most campaigns and none more so than those in the desert, and Montgomery was always careful about his logistics, as was the British Army generally. Rommel had, after all, contributed powerfully to his own defeat by stranding Panzerarmee Afrika in a logistically unsustainable position. In this, he showed merely an exaggerated version of a standard German military weakness, scanting logistics in favor of tactics and operations (as in France in 1914, Russia in 1941, or Normandy in 1944). It is curious that despite this continuing conceptual weakness, which undercut much tactical and operational brilliance, the German army has been deemed to have had a "genius for war" whereas Montgomery's prudence about logistics is taken as proof of timorous generalship. Montgomery wanted no setbacks, to be sure, and the success he had had was precious not only to him but also to Churchill, the British public, and his army. (It was, as well, already producing an efflorescence of the unattractive vanity that would ultimately damage his reputation more than anything he did or failed to do on the battlefield.) He intended to remain always "balanced," logistically as well as tactically. That care and the skills of Brigadier Sir Brian Robertson, Bt., his logistician (and the son of a World War I CIGS), kept Eighth Army moving steadily westward. Robertson, reflecting on the problems of maintaining an army at the end of a steadily lengthening line of communications, noted: "Having said what he is going to do, a Commander must not cheat. . . . A good administrative staff does not over-insure and cannot be cheated without unfortunate consequences. Some Generals have no morals. Fortunately General Montgomery does not cheat—and moreover he doesn't let other people cheat."[18]

Montgomery's honesty—at least from a logistic perspective—and Robertson's skill took Eighth Army to the eastern borders of Tunisia by February 1943. There, it would face its first major battle since Alamein and enter a new phase of the war, as the British, Dominion, and imperial coalition that had waged the desert war became enmeshed in a larger alliance with the United States. That coalition would present challenges to which Churchill was already turning his mind with an adaptability that, unfortunately, Montgomery could never emulate.

The change in the nature of the war that came with the engagement of ever-growing numbers of American forces and the creation of Allied commands is reflected in Churchill's memoirs. The detailed consideration of tactics and operations that fills so many pages of *Their Finest Hour, The Grand Alliance,* and *The Hinge of Fate* is replaced by a discussion of the formation of alliance strategy and coalition politics—not to mention relations with Russia. One of Churchill's assistants in the compilation of the memoirs, Denis Kelly, told Ismay in mid-1950, "I have passed on to Pownall Mr. Churchill's general observation—'Battles will definitely be noises off in this volume.' . . . Strategy will replace operations when the story is told. The big conferences will be the highlights."[19] In fact, the shifting emphasis is already visible in the second half of *The Hinge of Fate*. Alamein gets a full chapter (mostly by Pownall), but the Eighth Army's next great battle, at Mareth in Tunisia four months later, rates only a few pages. Between Alamein and Mareth, the prime minister had realized that the focus of alliance strategy needed to remain in the Mediterranean in 1943, and he had persuaded his American allies at the Casablanca Conference to accept his logic (although George Marshall was more reluctantly acquiescent than persuaded).[20]

What Churchill now wanted from the British Army was a continuing succession of battlefield victories, at a sustainable cost, for the leverage they would provide with the Americans as well as, of course, for domestic reasons. This Montgomery could provide. The prime minister also needed the closest possible meshing of British and U.S. activities to sustain his vision of a "special" Anglo-American relationship that transcended any mere alliance of necessity between essentially competitive nation-states. To this endeavor, Montgomery could not be a major contributor—indeed, he was rather the reverse. In Tunisia, a template for the Anglo-American military relationship quickly took shape, one that would endure for the balance of the war. Montgomery would form—and, far worse, display—a rather condescending view of the U.S. Army. American officers, in their turn, embarrassed and defensive about their army's showing in its initial encounters with the Germans, would react not only with a hostility to Montgomery that deepened over time but also with disdain for his army's approach to battle. Once formed, those attitudes never changed; they simply became more entrenched. American generals never liked or trusted Montgomery and remained generally critical of the British Army's performance (although not of British courage). And for their part, British officers all too often regarded the U.S. Army as a group of promising amateurs. Thus, as British military performance improved in the second half of the war, that qualitative gain tended to be overshadowed (certainly in American eyes) by issues extraneous to the army's actual performance. Unfortunately, this tendency would creep into much postwar writing, which often resembled extensions of wartime quarrels based on personality clashes as well as on national and institutional pride. That the most influential British writing on the war was—and remains—Churchill's own and that his agenda for the 1943–1945 volumes required that battles be "noises off" helped, ironically, to obscure the fact that the British Army enjoyed a significant, if far from complete, renaissance during the thirty long months that separated Alamein from VE day.

The Tunisian campaign, by the time Eighth Army joined it, was going poorly. The British First Army (commanded by a reserved Scots infantryman, Lieutenant General Kenneth Anderson) had narrowly failed to take Tunis in December and was stalled west of the city. Anderson had begun the war as a brigade commander in Brooke's corps in the BEF. Brooke formed a good opinion of him, and he moved steadily upward in the 1940–1942 army expansion, finally taking over Southeastern Command when Montgomery was summoned to Cairo. As an army commander in the field, however, he proved a disappointment. In December 1942, Churchill mentioned to Brooke that perhaps Alexander should leave Cairo and take over First Army, and Brooke came to believe that "it was very doubtful whether he [Anderson] was fit to command his Army."[21] Whatever his faults, Anderson was afflicted by many things beyond his control: the original Torch design, which handicapped him in the race for Tunis; inexperienced troops; logistic problems on a long supply line; and a weak grip on the campaign by Eisenhower's new, inexperienced, and distracted headquarters hundreds of miles away in Algiers. Yet even if First Army's operations may have disappointed Churchill and Brooke, its failings would be overshadowed by the disastrous debut of the U.S. Army against the Germans.

When Churchill and Ismay had watched American troops in training months before Torch, Ismay had delivered the (fairly obvious) verdict that they were not ready to face the German army, whereas Churchill felt the Americans would learn fast. The Tunisian campaign validated both judgments. The U.S. Army actually was suffering from many of the same problems that had plagued the British between 1940 and 1942. A prewar regular army smaller than that of Britain had begun to grow in 1940 into a massive citizen army—at one point, American planners thought of a 300-division force (later reduced to 90). This meant the progressive dilution of regular cadre as well as the rapid promotion and movement of officers whose peacetime careers, however sparkling, did not necessarily mean fitness for combat leadership. Moreover, unlike the British and Indian armies, nearly all of whose officers had seen extensive combat between 1914 and 1918, fighting experience was more thinly spread in American units, since the United States entered World War I only in 1917 and U.S. troops did not see large-scale combat until the war's closing months. The one area where the U.S. Army was clearly in better shape than the British had been was in its equipment. The quality was reasonably good (although in tank design, the Americans, like the British, never caught up with Germans). The quantity was simply overwhelming.

In mid-February 1943, the American II Corps, commanded by Major General Lloyd Fredenall, holding positions at the southern end of Anderson's First Army front, was hit by a German attack and found itself facing units of the Afrika Korps directed by Rommel himself. The luckless U.S. 1st Armored Division was routed, losing half its strength. Some units simply dissolved. The Germans were amazed at the amount (and quality) of the equipment abandoned by the Americans. The defeat had no operational consequences; Rommel's objectives were tactical—securing his rear as he prepared to again confront Eighth Army. The ramifications of the Kasserine Pass debacle within the Anglo-American coalition, however, were enormous and lasting.

The attack occurred at the moment when a major command change, as settled at the Anglo-American Casablanca summit, took place. To control the Allied forces, a new headquarters—Eighteenth Army Group—was created. Alexander and McCreery moved from Cairo (to replace Alex in Cairo, Jumbo Wilson was moved from Persia and Iraq Command to take over Middle East headquarters). Since the British First and Eighth Armies provided the overwhelming majority of the forces engaged in Tunisia, this arrangement made sense, but Alex and Monty arrived on the scene just as the U.S. Army's debut battle turned out to be an embarrassing shambles. Both decided that the Americans were simply not very good—Montgomery blamed poor training, bad commanders, and, predictably, an American failure to draw on British knowledge and experience. Alex, although he did his best to sideline U.S. troops for the balance of the Tunisian campaign, escaped enduring American hostility, aided by his grace, tact, and charm that had so captivated Churchill. Montgomery's abrasively expressed views and almost total lack of personal charm meant that American irritation, chagrin, and defensiveness arising from Kasserine found in him a focus. Montgomery, moreover, formed the view that Eisenhower was essentially a "political" soldier who understood little about managing battles and campaigns—another first impression with lasting consequences. Kasserine was quickly followed by Montgomery's second major success, in the battles of Medenine and Mareth. These engagements illustrated the Montgomery technique that would henceforth be the signature of British Army battles—and reinforced the sense of superior professionalism that would so bedevil alliance relations.[22]

The Mareth battle was preceded by a German spoiling attack against Eighth Army at Medenine on March 6. As happened at Alam Halfa, Ultra gave Montgomery ample advance warning and Rommel was ill and pessimistic; as the British official history put it, he "took no interest in the details." Montgomery was again content to let the Germans attack on ground the British had thoroughly prepared. XXX Corps's "defense was admirably thought out. . . . The anti-tank guns had at last been sited to kill tanks and not to 'protect' infantry, field guns or anything else."[23] Leese's corps had some 460 antitank guns, many 6-pounder, and some of the new 17-pounder models; it was also backed by some 300 field and medium guns, 300 tanks, and (thanks to Montgomery's care with logistics) abundant ammunition. Rommel attacked with about 150 tanks, but he was met with 30,000 shells and called the battle off, with the loss of about a third of his tanks. A few days later, sick and disillusioned, he left Africa forever.

Eighth Army launched Pugilist to breach the Mareth Line two weeks after Medenine. The line, running from the sea inland to the rugged Matmata Hills, had originally been built by the French to defend the eastern frontier of Tunisia from Italian forces based in Libya. Alex thought it presented as formidable a problem as the Alamein Line. Montgomery chose to make his primary attack a frontal assault, accompanied by a wide outflanking movement by Freyberg's New Zealand Corps (made up of the New Zealand division, a British armored brigade, and additional artillery). Freyberg's maneuver would take some time to develop, was unlikely to be missed by the Germans, and was in any case intended to take advantage of the victory won by the frontal assault. But that assault failed. Leese gave the job to Major General J. S. "Crasher" Nichols's 50th Division and thereafter adopted a hands-off attitude. In the opinion of Francis Tuker (whose 4th Indian Division was to exploit the breach that 50th made), that division was a formation "which learnt nothing, ever, even after years in the Desert." Attacking across a wide, deep, wet ravine (a very bad decision, in Tuker's view) on the night of March 20, the division established a bridgehead in the Mareth defenses, but the accompanying tanks bogged down in the ravine (where the water was about 8 feet deep), no antitank guns could get across, and a German counterattack compressed the bridgehead almost to the vanishing point. Early on March 23, Leese agreed with Nichols's recommendation to break off the attack.[24]

As he had done at Alamein, Montgomery adapted his plan, making Freyberg's left hook his focus while XXX Corps kept the Mareth Line's defenders occupied by the threat of a renewed assault. Freyberg had been moving steadily north outside the Matmata Hills that ran north from the inland anchor of the Mareth Line. By the night of March 21, he was poised before the pass (the Tebaga gap) through the hills that would give him access to the coastal plain and the communications of the German-Italian forces holding the Mareth Line. One of his New Zealand brigadiers and the British armored brigade commander urged him to drive forward. But Freyberg hesitated for several reasons. He knew German armor was moving toward the Tebaga gap, and bitter experience in the desert had left him dubious about the ability of British armor to coordinate effectively with his infantry. Moreover, the casualties his division had suffered in Crete, Crusader, and the July and October Alamein battles had led the New Zealand government to urge manpower conservation. Freyberg therefore waited, and he was still waiting when Montgomery's change of plan made him the spearhead of the offensive. Then, Monty complicated matters by deciding to send Horrocks with X Corps headquarters and 1st Armoured Division to reinforce Freyberg. Although he told Freyberg that Horrocks (who was junior to him both in the army and as a lieutenant general) would "take charge," he never in fact put Horrocks unequivocally in command. Horrocks, for his part, finding Freyberg "grim, firm and not at all forthcoming," made no attempt to assert himself. The resulting command by committee not only violated Montgomery's own precepts about clear command arrangements but also looked very much like the setup that Montgomery had so criticized under Eighth Army's "old regime." Perhaps it was an indication of how flexible—or prudent—he could be that he accepted this rather than confront the formidable Freyberg. A final complication was a monumental traffic jam produced by clumsy Eighth Army staff work (de Guingand was on medical leave). It occurred at Medenine as 1st Armoured and 4th Indian (which was being sent north through the Matmata Hills on a short left hook, its expertise in broken and hilly country having at last been noticed) both tried to use the same road. This cost Tuker twelve hours and robbed his movement of tactical effect.

By March 26, despite everything, Freyberg and Horrocks were finally poised to attack the Tebaga gap in an operation that was named Supercharge by Montgomery, evoking the final phase of Alamein. The actual attack by the New Zealand Corps was a combined arms gem. Air Vice Marshal Harry Broadhurst of the Desert Air Force, utilizing techniques developed in the desert war, had worked out a plan for the massive application of airborne fire support before and during the attack. There was the usual heavy artillery support as well. Attacking in the late afternoon with the setting sun behind them, the New Zealanders, their barrage rolling forward in front of them and tightly aligned with the armored brigade's tanks, quickly reached their final objective, about a mile from their start line. The 1st Armoured Division passed through, driving on through a moonlit night. As at El Alamein, however, the battle ended anticlimactically. An improvised German antitank screen held up British armor, Horrocks decided to wait for Freyberg's infantry, and the German and Italian formations from the Mareth Line made good their withdrawal, to turn and fight again on the next defensible line some miles farther north.[25]

The battle at Mareth, although not as well known as that at El Alamein, revealed a great deal about where the most experienced fighting force in the British Army stood after eight months of Montgomery's "grip." There were still lapses in coordination and leadership failures. Leese allowed Crasher Nichols to make a bad plan. Montgomery quickly got rid of Nichols ("really his fault . . . has not brains and is really stupid"), but his faith in his protégé Leese remained strong.[26] Powerful Dominion commanders such as Freyberg remained semiautonomous. Above all, as shown more clearly at Tebaga gap than at Alamein, a different style had developed. Tactical airpower, added to the heaviest artillery concentration possible, had prepared the way for a coordinated tank-infantry assault, delivered on a relatively narrow front, and it had produced a dazzling tactical success. But that was all. As at Alamein, the enemy had made good his escape. The official historians summed it up neatly: "The British could take full credit for what they had achieved but . . . they had not produced the quality of being what pugilists call 'good finishers.'"[27]

This characteristic would dog Montgomery's armies for the balance of the war. Some of the problem had to do with the personalities of certain commanders. Much of it, however, must be ascribed to a military culture that discouraged initiative and that in training and tactical thinking emphasized consolidation rather than exploitation of gains. Montgomery could get rid of Nichols. But there was not enough time to change deeply embedded traits—not least because they reflected an institutional caution that he fully shared.

The final victory in Africa, a defeat that cost the Germans as many men as were lost at Stalingrad, was a source of immense satisfaction to Churchill—and to Brooke. But it revealed as well more of the tiny cracks that were appearing in the facade of the Anglo-American partnership in arms. "Broadly speaking," Alex had told Churchill after Kasserine, "Americans require experience."[28] Alexander was so convinced of this that he required some prodding before he would give the U.S. II Corps (now commanded by Omar Bradley) any significant role in the final offensive. Alex did not, however, incur any lasting American ill will as a consequence, his charm and style providing him a Teflon coating.

By the time the German-Italian forces, some 250,000 strong, surrendered on May 12, the planning for the leap to Sicily (Operation Husky) was well under way. As the Tunisian fighting drew to a close, Montgomery intervened decisively in the process, rejecting the plans drawn up by a planning staff Alex had appointed (known as Force 141). Its head, Major General Charles Gairdner, was summarily dismissed by Montgomery as "not up to it; he does not know the battle repercussions; he is a bundle of nerves; he inspires no confidence."[29] Monty went on to have Gairdner removed and his own plan adopted. Because it was politically necessary for the U.S. Army to have its own sector in the invasion (Montgomery had wanted U.S. II Corps simply added to Eighth Army), Alexander's Fifteenth Army Group would coordinate the operations of the British Eighth and the U.S. Seventh Armies as the campaign unfolded. The ease with which Montgomery usurped Alexander's role in shaping Husky and brushed aside his staff boded ill for Alex's ability actually to perform that coordinating role. And so it proved.

Brooke had begun to have concerns about Montgomery's tendency to anger allies, noting the worrying signs of rampant egotism in his behavior. In a private conversation with Montgomery in June, he proceeded to "haul him over the coals," noting afterward in his diary that Monty "requires a lot of educating. . . . A difficult mixture to handle, brilliant commander . . . but liable to commit untold errors in lack of tact, lack of appreciation of other people's outlook. It is most distressing that the Americans do not like him and it will always be a difficult matter to have him fighting in close proximity to them."[30]

Montgomery meekly accepted the rebuke from the one superior he respected, but it made no practical difference. As Husky unfolded, Montgomery, hoping to secure more room to deploy Eighth Army, prevailed upon Alex to move the boundary between his army and Patton's in such a way as to marginalize Seventh Army's role. Patton, being Patton, partially overcame the handicap, but by the time the Germans withdrew successfully from Sicily (having displayed the skill at rearguard work that would mark their performance in Italy), the American commanders involved, Eisenhower and Patton, had joined Bradley in having had their fill of Brooke's "brilliant commander."[31] Just at the moment when the strategy Brooke and Churchill had sold to the reluctant Americans produced its greatest success yet with the collapse of Mussolini's regime and Italian peace feelers, the key players on the U.S. side had become completely disinclined to continue to accept the British as senior partners in a theater where, in fact, the bulk of the forces were and would remain British.

Could Churchill and Brooke have avoided this? That seems doubtful. Nothing could erase the disparity in resources between the two allies, which would only grow wider—a disparity that made American dominance in the alliance certain. Nothing, moreover, could change the U.S. Army's deeply rooted suspicion of coalition warfare, based on its 1917–1918 experiences, and the determination of American commanders that the U.S. Army alone had the correct formula for victory: a cross-channel attack. Had the senior British field commander not been the vain and abrasive Montgomery, however, matters might not have become so contentious so quickly (although it must be said that the Americans did not like the dour, reserved Anderson either). To a victory-starved British public, Montgomery—or, rather, the image of him projected by the British press—had become iconic. American commanders resented the British press and BBC coverage that seemed to dwell upon British—and especially Eighth Army—victories to the exclusion of their own contribution. This American attitude seems unreasonable. After all, the British people wanted to hear about their own citizen-soldiers, not the Americans. By the time Axis forces surrendered in Tunisia, many British troops in the Mediterranean and Middle East had been overseas for three years (and much longer for some prewar regulars). As Churchill, having bent alliance strategy toward the Mediterranean in 1942 and 1943, moved to not only exploit the Italian collapse but also shape operations as he had in 1941 and 1942, he came up against the fact that his freedom to manage Britain's war had been sharply constrained, in spite of the fact that the British Army was now a much more effective force.

The prime minister's success in persuading the Americans to make Torch the major alliance operation for 1942, followed by his ability at Casablanca to keep a Mediterranean focus for 1943, came at a price. Marshall, denied a cross-channel attack in 1942 or 1943, was determined to nail the British to 1944. A planning group, under a British general, had been set up after Casablanca to begin work on what became Operation Overlord. At the Trident Conference in Washington in May 1943, the British accepted a May 1944 target date. Moreover, seven divisions, four U.S. and three British, were to leave the Mediterranean for Britain in November. With them would go a significant amount of the amphibious trooplift in that theater. After Trident, Churchill, accompanied by Marshall and Brooke, flew to Algiers to finalize an attack on Italy as the follow-up to Husky. (It was during this stay in Algiers that Brooke, after talking with Eisenhower, read Montgomery the riot act.) Just as, to Churchill's mind at least, a window of enticing opportunity was opening not only in Italy but in the eastern Mediterranean as well, Marshall looked forward to sharply curtailing a commitment that he had always resented, seeing it as a deviation from the only sound strategy for beating Germany—one that also would allow him to deploy and vindicate the huge army he was raising. Whether Churchill really grasped at that point that British preponderance in shaping alliance strategy was waning sharply and the invasion of Italy would be its final manifestation is questionable. Only the assumption of a continued, major British influence would account for the fact that during this period, he thrice promised Brooke the command of the cross-channel operation.[32]

This Anglo-American argument—Mediterranean emphasis versus the earliest possible cross-channel assault—echoed strongly for a generation in postwar historical writing. Even now, the issue resonates. But the passage of time has made several things clear. To have launched Sledgehammer, Marshall's 1942 idea, would have been to invite a larger Dieppe catastrophe, and if Operation Roundup had been launched in 1943, it would have fared little better. Neither the British Army nor the American army was ready. Churchill and Brooke, aware of manpower constraints, knew they would have only one shot at a landing in France. The delay they imposed before such an assault was attempted provided the margin for success that was needed when it finally took place. Nonetheless, just as strategic soundness was not the only issue for Marshall, neither was it for Churchill.[33]

At the end of the Tunisian campaign in May 1943, there were four British armored divisions (plus a separate armored brigade) and seven infantry divisions in the Mediterranean and Middle East. There were also two Indian divisions (and three separate Indian brigades, the equivalent of another division). In addition, there was the New Zealand division and a separate New Zealand armored brigade, plus a South African armored division. Finally, there were five separate British infantry brigades, fifteen unbrigaded infantry battalions (the infantry strength of another one and a half divisions), and three unattached armored regiments. (This tally excludes the growing Polish forces, eventually a corps, that would operate under British command.) Such a huge force could only be moved elsewhere very slowly—and some of it, such as the New Zealander and South African elements, could only be employed elsewhere with their government's approval, which was unlikely to be forthcoming for operations outside the Mediterranean theater. There was, of course, a huge logistic infrastructure in Egypt that could not be moved at all. This aggregation of British, Dominion, and imperial fighting power had to be employed, for several compelling reasons. Its use would, of course, impose attrition on German resources. And doing nothing until May 1944 was unacceptable to the British public (not to mention the Russians). Beyond that, the force and the successes it could win were, in the prime minister's eyes, the most important counter he now had in the game of alliance politics, a game in which Britain's chips were dwindling while its stake remained enormous.

As the Sicilian campaign ground to a close and Eisenhower's forces stood poised to launch Operation Avalanche, the Salerno landing that would, it was hoped, quickly give them Naples with its port and then Rome, two episodes revealed the waning of Churchill's dominance in the alliance: the selection of a commander for the cross-channel assault and the brief, costly, and fruitless Aegean campaign. The latter also demonstrated that, despite the changes wrought by Montgomery (and better equipment), older and deeper problems still persisted in regard to military performance. The Quadrant Conference at Quebec in August gave considerable attention to the stagnant Burma campaign. But the balance between the ongoing Mediterranean campaign and the 1944 cross-channel attack continued to be a major issue. Churchill, facing the reality that the U.S. Army would be preponderant in the cross-channel operation, accepted that an American general would have to be in command. Strolling with Brooke during an interval between conference sessions, he broke the news that the job the CIGS had wanted so badly—and that Churchill had repeatedly promised him—would probably go to Marshall (for whose skills as a strategist Brooke had little regard and who had never commanded large formations in battle). The disappointment and bitterness Brooke felt seems to have escaped Churchill, but it may well be that it never left the CIGS, coloring his views of the prime minister for the balance of the war and beyond.[34] Brooke felt that Churchill had agreed to American command of Overlord as a quid pro quo for Roosevelt's agreement to install Lord Louis Mountbatten, the chief of Combined Operations (of whom he also had a low opinion), as Allied commander-in-chief of the new South-East Asia Command (SEAC).[35] However, it seems more likely that what Churchill was angling for was control of a theater much more important to him than SEAC ever was. "We therefore agreed," he wrote of his talk with Roosevelt, "that an American officer should command 'Overlord' and that the Mediterranean should be entrusted to a British commander."[36] But until these arrangements became operational, Eisenhower would remain in charge of what was now as important a theater of operations as the desert had once been. As Churchill endeavored to involve himself over the next few months as he had once done with Wavell and Auchinleck, however, he was repeatedly stymied and frustrated.

The invasion of Italy—the Eighth Army's attack across the Straits of Messina (Operation Baytown) and the landing at Salerno of the new U.S. Fifth Army under Lieutenant General Mark Clark (Operation Avalanche)—was thought of as the first step in a rapid advance northward, to Rome and onward to the area of Florence by year's end. This notion was based on the assumption that the Germans would withdraw northward behind rearguards, taking a stand on the Pisa-Rimini line—the last mountain barrier before the plains of northern Italy. This assessment was supported by such Ultra intelligence about German intentions as came to hand. In fact, German plans were in flux. Field Marshal Albert Kesselring, the German commander-in-chief, South, favored a prolonged defense of the Italian peninsula, with an initial position well south of Rome. Rommel, now commanding an army group in northern Italy and permanently marked by his encounter in Africa with Anglo-American airpower and overwhelming matériel abundance, cautioned against trying to hold southern and central Italy. Hitler finally opted for Kesselring's theater strategy, encouraged to do so by the slow pace of Allied operations; he was prompted as well as by the realization that Allied assault shipping was leaving the Mediterranean for Britain and that yielding central Italy would give the Allies a springboard for an assault on the economically vital Balkans. By early October, Ultra had told the Allies what the stiffening German resistance north of Naples had already signaled to Fifth and Eighth Armies—there would be no exhilarating drive on Rome followed by a pursuit northward.[37] Instead, terrain, foul autumnal weather, and German tactical skill promised, at best, a slow-motion forward crawl. As autumn deepened, the prime minister faced stagnation in a theater where British and British-controlled formations preponderated—Clark's U.S. Fifth Army was in fact partially British, with Lieutenant General Richard McCreery's X Corps serving alongside the U.S. VI Corps. As Churchill turned his mind to ways to make the heavy British investment in the theater more productive and as Brooke began to worry about keeping enough pressure on the Germans to create the conditions for Overlord, both came up against the limits on their freedom of action set by agreements with the Americans and the alliance command structure in the theater.

At Casablanca, the Americans had accepted an invasion of Sicily; at Trident, they agreed to an assault on the Italian mainland but with a firm date for Overlord and an agreement on a drawdown of British and American troops and shipping from the Mediterranean to make it possible. Thereafter, although the British regarded the agreement as a statement of intent, to be modified as necessary by circumstances, the Americans, led by Marshall, treated it as a lawyer treats a signed contract—binding, unless changed by mutual agreement. And Marshall had no intention of agreeing to the "flexibility" Churchill wanted. Eisenhower, as the theater commander, took his orders from the Combined Chiefs of Staff, but he was no more likely to defy Marshall, his patron, than Montgomery was to cross Brooke. What made this painfully apparent to Churchill was not the course of events in Italy but a minor, if distressing, episode in the Aegean Sea, where the attempt to seize the Italian-occupied Dodecanese Islands failed dismally and the Germans won their last victory over the British.

Churchill believed, and continued to believe long after the war, that the Italian collapse opened the door to great opportunities in the eastern Mediterranean. What those opportunities were can be summed up in a word—Turkey. Turkish entry into the war had long mesmerized him. In the dark spring of 1941, he had hoped for a Balkan front that would include Turkey; Wavell and Auchinleck had both been instructed to earmark RAF squadrons and antiaircraft units to deploy to Turkey should British diplomacy succeed in persuading the Ankara government to join the war. After the Casablanca Conference, he had flown to Turkey, taking Brooke along, to personally lobby for Turkish participation, and Middle East Command was committed to a program of military aid to help the Turks modernize their obsolete army. The Turks, however, were accustomed from the long years of Ottoman decline to avoiding compliance with (while never formally refusing) the demands of the Great Powers, and they were acutely aware that Germany remained powerful while their own army was not; as a result, they evaded the prime minister's embraces. Churchill's concern with securing Turkish belligerency, though based on the correct assumption that it would unsettle Hitler's already nervous Balkan satellites and therefore threaten an area whose retention was crucial to the German war effort, rested on two misconceptions: that the Turks could be persuaded to act before they could do so risk-free (they declared war in February 1945) and that aggressive British action in the Aegean in the wake of Italy's collapse would tip the scales. Even if both assumptions had been correct, the prime minister was about to discover that he no longer controlled the military assets—army, navy, or air—to give effect to his strategic vision.[38]

With the exception of Crete, the islands that sprinkle the Aegean were garrisoned by Italian troops who were in the same state of demoralization as the rest of the Italian military. The Aegean had become a happy hunting ground for a number of the special-purpose units that had flowered in the Middle East between 1940 and 1942. The Long Range Desert Group, having run out of desert to range over, had turned itself into a seaborne raiding force. There was also the Special Boat Service, another tiny group that relied on stealth to carry out its operations. Although these units could accept the gladly proffered surrenders of sometimes quite numerous Italian forces on various islands, they were never intended for prolonged combat. And that was the sort of fighting to which they were about to be committed. Even though the Joint Planning Staff in London (supported by the Joint Intelligence Committee) had urged the merits of operations in the eastern Mediterranean and into the Balkans in the spring of 1943 (seeing the same vulnerabilities that made Hitler nervous), the British Chiefs of Staff were skeptical that the resources could be made available, given the contemplated assaults on Sicily and the Italian mainland. The Americans, of course, were totally hostile to eastern Mediterranean operations. As a result, one of the Trident decisions was that there would be no major operations east of Italy. Middle East Command was told to stand down its preparations for an assault (Accolade) on Rhodes, whose airfields would be crucial in any struggle for the control of the Aegean. There matters might have rested, but Churchill willed otherwise.[39]

General Sir Henry Maitland Wilson had taken over from Alex in Cairo. His command, stripped of troops, planes, and shipping to support the central Mediterranean campaign, actually had little on hand when the Italian surrender opened such tempting vistas before Churchill's eyes. Much of Wilson's trooplift was destined for India, to provide an amphibious capability for projected operations in the Bay of Bengal. The high-quality 8th Indian Division was under orders to join Alexander's forces in Italy. Wilson had little left but oddments when, on September 9, Churchill cabled him from Washington with instructions to "improvise and dare," following this up a few days later by urging him "to think of Clive and Peterborough and of Rooke's men taking Gibraltar."[40] Wilson, however, had little with which to work. The Germans, alive to its importance, took immediate steps to secure Rhodes. From established bases on Crete and the Greek mainland, the Luftwaffe could still dominate the Aegean. The tiny British detachments to whom Italian forces surrendered so readily throughout the Aegean had no hope of holding the islands against the counterattacks that the Germans, showing their usual capacity to improvise, were scraping up troops and shipping to mount. Wilson did have an infantry brigade available, but the 234th Brigade had two battalions that had served in Malta throughout its siege, enduring near-famine conditions for over two years. It had no experience of infantry combat (and probably a considerable number of officers and men who were still mentally and physically tired). Wilson committed the brigade to the island of Leros. The result was a small-scale reprise of the Cretan disaster of 1941. The Royal Navy could not operate without air cover, which the RAF could not consistently provide from its distant airfields, and although both navy and RAF losses were considerable, there could be only one end. A German combined airborne-seaborne assault on Leros began on November 12. On the evening of November 16, the defenders surrendered. Unlike the situation on Crete, there was no successful evacuation, although there were a number of dramatic escapes. The Germans had mopped up the improvised British garrisons with a relatively small commitment of troops. The Aegean remained theirs until the war's end.[41]

Churchill was furious, and his fury shows in the chapter he devoted to the episode in *Closing the Ring*, entitled "Island Prizes Lost." (Originally, there were to have been two chapters, an amount of space quite disproportionate to the importance of the episode from any point of view but Churchill's.) Whereas in the past the anger he felt at what he regarded as opportunities lost fell upon the heads of British commanders, it now it fell upon his American allies. Referring to the refusal of the U.S. Chiefs of Staff to agree to any alteration in the "contract" that pulled some forces back to the United Kingdom and sent others to the new SEAC commander, Churchill bitterly remarked in his memoirs, "The American Staff had enforced their view; the price had now to be paid by the British."[42] What he did not allow to get into print was even more revealing. After Leros fell, he dictated a note full of anger about the rigidity Marshall displayed about Overlord. He was equally angry at Eisenhower, whom he felt had been strongly supported by British resources stripped from Wilson: "Rightly or wrongly, I thought he owed me something."[43]

It was a brutal awakening to what the close alliance with the Americans—for which he had worked so hard—would really mean. An infantry brigade,

6 destroyers, 2 submarines, and 10 lesser vessels plus 113 aircraft had been lost (and 4 cruisers and 4 more destroyers were damaged).[44] The heavy casualties to the New Zealanders serving in the Long Range Desert Group caused the government in Wellington to protest and pull its surviving troops out of the unit. It was an expensive lesson but one from which Churchill drew an important conclusion. In a message to Eden after Leros fell, he complained of "having to fight with both hands tied behind our backs."[45] In a reflective postscript to the whole episode, he wrote: "These experiences made me determine that the command in the Mediterranean in 1944 should be unified, and should pass into the hands of a British Commander-in-Chief free from the detailed control of Washington. This resolve was justified as we had more than two-thirds of all the forces employed in the theatre."[46]

Churchill may also have decided who that commander-in-chief should be. He had been impressed with Wilson's response to his exhortation to "improvise and dare," telling him in mid-October, "I am very pleased with the way in which you used such poor bits and pieces as were left you. *Nil desperandum* [Never despair]."[47] (Brooke was less impressed: "Middle East [Command] have not been either wise or cunning and have now got themselves into the difficult situation that they can neither hold nor evacuate Leros."[48]) It was a long step for Jumbo toward his ultimate field marshal's baton. If there was a moment when the commitment to Mediterranean operations—a necessary strategic preliminary to Overlord for Brooke—became a highly charged issue for Churchill, bound up with Britain's continuing Great-Power status, that moment may well have come as he faced the wreckage of his policy in the Aegean, for no campaign during the war was more his than the Aegean venture.[49]

Contemplating the situation from his static, mud-clogged, and rain-swept front in Italy, Montgomery—about to be moved by Brooke to the position of Allied ground force commander for Overlord—was, as usual, sharply critical of what he saw about him. The Aegean venture he dismissed as "frigging about in the Dodecanese," but he was at one with Churchill about the need to grip and reinvigorate the Italian campaign: "We started brilliantly . . . and in three months we had . . . spectacular results. [But] it was vital to get the Rome line before the weather broke . . . it could easily have been done. . . . But to do so required a very firm grip of the campaign by 15 Army Group. . . . There was no 'grip'. . . . So there we are."[50] For "15th Army Group," of course, read Alexander, about whom Montgomery had become completely disenchanted: "The whole truth of the matter is that Alexander has got a definitely limited brain and does not understand the business."[51] Yet it would fall to Alex (and Wilson as theater commander, though he had been dismissed by Montgomery as "no good") to realize Churchill's dream of British military success in Italy. Much would therefore depend on whether Alex was what Churchill thought him to be—or what Montgomery had decided he was.

6

Alex and the Soft Underbelly

The autumn of 1943 was a turning point in Winston Churchill's war. The tide in the European war was flowing strongly against Germany, and the Mediterranean orientation of Allied strategy had been successfully maintained—at least for the present—in the face of American doubts. But then, failure in the Aegean, quickly followed by the revelation at the Tehran Conference that Roosevelt had his own vision both of relations with Russia and of the future, made the prime minister painfully aware that the United States intended henceforth to steer the Anglo-American alliance in war and to shape the peace. Thereafter, the Mediterranean campaign became, in Churchill's eyes, important not only for the strategic benefits that Brooke had argued would flow from it but also for the political leverage he hoped would come from successful campaigning by the theater's largely British, Dominion, and imperial forces.

In an unused draft on the Aegean campaign, Churchill would say that he felt Eisenhower "owed me something." When it became apparent that whether or not Eisenhower felt any obligation, Marshall certainly did not, the prime minister resolved that the theater "should pass into the hands of a British Commander-in-Chief."[1] The reorganization that followed the naming of Eisenhower to command the cross-channel invasion reflected this determination. Wilson, now high in Churchill's favor because of his willingness to "improvise and dare," succeeded Eisenhower (and was himself succeeded in the Middle East by General Sir Bernard Paget, displaced from his command in Britain by Monty's return to England). Alex remained army group commander in Italy. Even though veteran Eighth Army divisions (the 50th, 51st, and 7th Armoured) were following Monty back to Britain, a British theater command team was now in place and with it, the prime minister hoped and expected, an opportunity for British military successes in what was now the sole "British" theater in the European war.

Between 1940 and 1942, Churchill had also needed victories, from an army ill equipped to supply them. From Alamein to the Italian surrender in September 1943, battlefield success, the prestige of Eighth Army, and the fact that Britain was providing most of the troops in contact with the enemy had given him leverage with the Americans. This situation made his dialogue with the army commanders less intense and less adversarial. From late 1943, however, the prime minister needed British victories in the only British-dominated European theater. The man to whom it fell to deliver those victories was Alex.

Harold Rupert Leofric George Alexander was and remains an enigma. Churchill always admired him, and much of Alexander's wartime career was built on that admiration. Yet by 1943, the dominant figures in the British Army—Brooke and Montgomery—had formed a rather less enthusiastic opinion. Brooke (under whom Alex had served as a divisional commander in France) recognized that Alexander was "charming" but was convinced he was "a very, very, small man" who was "oblivious to his shortcoming!" Moreover, he remarked, "it is hard to advise him as he fails really to grasp the significance of things." Reviewing this judgment after the war, Brooke decided there was nothing he would change, although he phrased his summation more generously: "Unbounded courage, never ruffled or upset, great charm and a composure that inspired confidence in those around him. But when it came to working on a higher plain [*sic*], he was at once out of his depth, had no ideas of his own, and always sought someone to lean on."[2]

Montgomery, as was his wont, was much more blunt. Alex's great—in fact, as far as Monty was concerned, his only—asset was "his charm, and if he lost it he would go right under." Like Brooke, Monty did not think much of Alex's brainpower, describing him as "Not clever." Monty had also spotted something else: "He likes to reach agreement whatever may happen, quite regardless of whether that agreement will win the battle."[3] The argument about Alex would continue, with his ghosted, anodyne memoirs doing nothing to settle it.[4] An admiring official biography by Nigel Nicolson would paint an attractive portrait, but Nicolson would later confess in a private letter, "I began by thinking Alex great and ended by thinking him nice."[5] Alexander's entry in the *Oxford Dictionary of National Biography*, written by Sir David Hunt, a former staff officer, would offer unstinting praise of his generalship, whereas Sir Max Hastings would dismissively refer to his "notorious laziness and lack of intellect."[6] Consensus on Alex may be long in arriving.

As the European war swung in favor of the Allies, no theater would

Alexander (in front with driver), Montgomery, and Brooke in Italy, December 1943. This picture captures something of the relationship of three future field marshals: the CIGS and his protégé in easy conversation; Alex a bit on the outside. (Courtesy Imperial War Museum, image no. NA 9857)

command more of Churchill's interest than the Italian one, where Britain was in command and, moreover, his favorite general led the Allied armies. Churchill's relationship with the handsome, brave, and charming Alex, whose abilities drew such mixed reviews from contemporaries and historians, has not been scrutinized as minutely as his interactions with Wavell and Auchinleck, but it is no less interesting and significant.

Alexander certainly had a number of problems that neither Brooke nor Montgomery made much allowance for. These problems can be grouped under two headings: the nature of his forces and the Americans. Wavell and

Auchinleck had worked with a military instrument that was, at the time, unable to deliver what the prime minister wanted. Alex and Monty had operated in an altered environment, with better equipment making possible better tactics, priority accorded to the empire's premier field army, and an army commander who carefully—and stubbornly—shaped his approach to battle to play to his army's strengths while masking as far as possible its weaknesses. The northern front that had bedeviled Wavell and Auchinleck faded into insignificance after Stalingrad. Alex and Monty also enjoyed the operational initiative, as the alliance as a whole did during the entire post-Torch period, as well as mastery of the air over the battlefield. All this, rather than simply the presence at Alex's side of a first-rate chief of staff in Lieutenant General Richard McCreery (the Brooke-Monty explanation), helps to account for the success the Alex-Monty team enjoyed in North Africa. However, the situation was changing dramatically by the time Alex took over as, in effect, theater commander for the Italian campaign—for Wilson operated, by design, in the stratosphere of strategic and political issues as supreme commander over a vast area stretching from the Middle East to Gibraltar, including support for Balkan resistance.

The cross-channel invasion would be the dominant operation in 1944. The alliance's most experienced senior commanders had moved from the Mediterranean to Britain to organize and lead it—Eisenhower, Major General Walter Bedell Smith (Ike's able chief of staff), Monty, de Guingand, Tedder, Bradley—plus seven combat-experienced divisions. Eisenhower would have been content to have Alex as his land commander, but Brooke, realizing that no British general would hold a more important appointment during the European war's climactic phase, insisted on Monty. Consequently, from the moment Montgomery returned to England, opening his Twenty-first Army Group headquarters and taking up as well his position as overall Allied ground commander for Overlord, his requirements became the first priority for Brooke and the War Office. This was particularly true of calls on what had become the scarcest of all Britain's resources—manpower, especially infantrymen. By late 1943, the British Army was facing a manpower shortage that would grow steadily worse over the war's last eighteen months. The Eighth Army remained Britain's most storied fighting force, but its British infantry would henceforth be a slowly wasting asset, in a theater where the terrain guaranteed that infantry casualties would be high. (During a tour of the theater in October 1943, the adjutant general, General Sir Ronald Adam, warned British commanders that infantry replacements would be a major problem in 1944.) To maintain pressure on the Germans while keeping casualties to a tolerable level would be one of Alex's challenges, just as it would be a major concern for Monty after D day.[7]

The Italian campaign did not, of course, depend simply on British troops, and the heterogeneity of Alexander's forces added yet another complication. The British, Dominion, and empire coalition that had fought in North Africa became steadily more diverse in Italy. A Canadian corps joined the New Zealanders, who had manpower problems of their own, and the South Africans, whose forces committed to Italy were exclusively armored, a way of economizing on South Africa's small pool of white military manpower. (In terms of the nature of combat in Italy, Alex actually had much more armor than he needed.) The Indian Army contributed strongly, as it had done in the Middle East: there were almost as many Indian divisions (three) as Dominion divisions (four) in Italy. Then there was the French Expeditionary Corps, most of whose rank and file were Moroccans, Algerians, Tunisians, and Senegalese. The reborn Polish army was represented by a corps, and there were minor Allies by the score. The British official historians later counted twenty-nine "nationalities" represented in Alexander's command.[8] Monty may have considered Alex's agreeableness a weakness, but it is hard to imagine another British or American officer in the European theater, Eisenhower apart, who could have effectively commanded this Babel of formations (and Ike was also accused of being too agreeable). The twenty-nine nationalities were not, however, the sum total of Alexander's concerns—for the thirtieth was the Americans.

The Italian campaign had never been anything but a sideshow to the Americans, who embarked upon it reluctantly and with a determination to withdraw from it whatever assets might assist Overlord. Four American divisions left the theater in the late autumn and early winter. But Alex's biggest problem with the Americans would not be their lack of enthusiasm for the campaign, nor their desire to withdraw formations for Overlord (and later, more disastrously, for Anvil/Dragoon). It would be a general who remained, Lieutenant General Mark Wayne Clark of the U.S. Fifth Army.

As a young brigadier general, Clark had played an important role in the preliminaries to Torch, landing clandestinely from a British submarine to confer with Vichy officers and officials in an attempt to prevent French resistance to the operation. But he had no combat role in either Tunisia or Sicily. Taking his newly formed Fifth Army ashore at Salerno, Clark faced the German army for the first time, and like the commander of the U.S. II Corps in Tunisia, he found the experience traumatic. Avalanche came as close to failure as any Allied amphibious assault in the European theater.

One of Clark's American corps commanders had to be sacked, and only the massive naval firepower available enabled the beachhead to be stabilized. After the crisis had passed, the arrival of Eighth Army, which had moved slowly north from the toe of the Italian peninsula, produced a picture of Monty leaning down from his command tank to shake Clark's hand. It was vintage Monty but not very helpful to his relations with Clark. Mark Clark was a vain, touchy, ambitious man, uncomfortably aware that Fifth Army's performance at Salerno had been quite shaky. He was also, like many American senior officers (and not a few of their compatriots), profoundly ambivalent about the British. He would become obsessive about "Mark Clark's Fifth Army"—as he insisted war correspondents describe it—and receiving full and abundant credit for its successes; he was equally obsessive about the possibility of being denied that credit by the British. Eventually, this attitude would have seriously adverse tactical and operational consequences.

Therefore, when Alex (under Wilson's benign supervision) became responsible for producing the victories the prime minister wanted as badly as he had wanted Rommel beaten, he faced a daunting task. His army group was a much more complex creature than Eighth Army had been when he and Monty took over in August 1942. He still had formidable Dominion commanders such as Freyberg to deal with, but even more difficult was the task of handling the Americans, especially the prickly Clark. Alex and Monty had had whatever Churchill could give them in that earlier phase of the war, for their campaign was their country's top priority in the land war. Italy would never have that absolute priority—certainly not from the Americans and, with Overlord looming, not even from Churchill and Brooke. In August 1942, Panzerarmee Afrika was in an untenable position, one that Montgomery skillfully exploited. In Italy, however, "Smiling Albert" Kesselring was proving himself a master of defensive warfare, much as the German army had done on the Western Front from 1915 to 1917. There would be no quick breakthroughs followed by dramatic armored pursuits—only slogging infantry combat in terrain and weather conditions even worse than those of the Western Front. Alexander would never have the massive superiority that Montgomery enjoyed—in the 1943–1944 autumn and winter, he would have at his disposal some 18 divisions, whereas Kesselring would control 23, with 15 of these in the battle zone. Stalemated in front of Kesselring's Gustav Line defenses south of Rome, with some of his best divisions leaving the theater, and lacking the three-to-one margin normally considered necessary for attack, Alex was expected (not least by Churchill) to nonetheless produce victory.

Even before Eisenhower left for Overlord, the stagnation of the front had led to consideration of using Allied command of the sea to outflank the Gustav Line, thus opening the door to Rome. It was an obvious answer to the problem, so obvious that Kesselring fretted about it throughout the entire course of the Italian campaign, his concern kept continuously alive by a brilliant Allied deception effort.[9] But sea power conferred less flexibility on the Allies than Kesselring realized. The crucial element was not conventional warships or merchantmen but the highly specialized landing craft, especially the "landing ship, tank," or LST. Much thinking about amphibious warfare and development work on the specialized ships and craft that would be needed had taken place in Britain before 1939 and during the war's early years. The mass production of the huge assortment of amphibious craft, however, fell to the United States, and the distribution of these assets was heavily influenced by the needs of the U.S. Navy's Pacific campaigns. LST availability was therefore always tight in the European war, and most of what was available in the Mediterranean in December 1943 was American—much of it under orders to return to Britain for Overlord. This in turn meant that Alexander could contemplate only a one-division amphibious assault, a force too weak to land near Rome unless the Allied front moved quickly north toward it. But Fifth and Eighth Armies were incapable of doing any such thing. There matters stood, with everyone in agreement on the desirability of the operation but no one quite able to see how it might be done. At that point, Churchill's health intervened decisively.

The prime minister had had a minor heart attack in Washington at the time of the Arcadia Conference and pneumonia after the Casablanca summit. Now, after the stresses of the Tehran meeting and the disappointments in the Aegean, his iron constitution buckled—momentarily. A serious case of pneumonia had his physician, Lord Moran, fearing for his life. Brooke overrode Moran's caution about summoning additional medical help, and that, plus the availability of one of the new antibiotics and his own indomitable will, soon had Churchill convalescent and listening to his daughter Sarah read Jane Austen to him. The prime minister's enforced stay near Carthage and then a further convalescence at Marrakech put him "on the spot" at a crucial moment. Moreover, his illness gave Brooke an opportunity to tour the front in Italy unencumbered by the task of shepherding Churchill. The CIGS quickly summed up the bleak situation: "We are stuck in our offensive here and shall make no real progress till the ground dries, unless we make greater use of our amphibious power. . . . The offensive is stagnating badly and something must be done about it as soon as I get back." Reflecting after the war on his muddy tour of the Italian front (some of it on horseback), Brooke noted, "My visit to Italy had brought home to me the importance of making use of our amphibious power in this theatre by opening up a bridgehead near Rome."[10]

With Brooke back in London determined to restore some mobility to the Italian campaign (and briefing John Harding, who was about to become Alex's chief of staff) and a rejuvenated Churchill hectoring all and sundry on the spot, enough LSTs were found by adjusting the timetable for withdrawals from the Mediterranean to allow for a two-division assault at Anzio, christened Shingle, to be mounted in January. This concession, however, came only after a personal appeal to Roosevelt by the prime minister, and it was couched in language (almost certainly Marshall's) that so hedged it about as to make absolutely clear that the retention of fifty-six LSTs in the Mediterranean for three weeks to make a two-division Shingle possible was the absolute limit of American flexibility. As Churchill summed it up in retrospect: "The American clear-cut, logical, large-scale, mass-production style of thought was formidable."[11] It was this mind-set, reinforced by Marshall's growing power as the balance in the alliance tipped toward the United States, that the prime minister would, with less and less success, confront henceforth. But for the moment, he had won. Now it was up to Alex.

Shingle has become identified with Churchill in the popular memory of the war.[12] But even though he played the key role in breaking the deadlock on LST availability, thus making a two-division operation possible, Shingle actually had a complex paternity. Discussion about an amphibious flanking movement had begun under Eisenhower and Bedell Smith; Alex naturally supported it, as did Mark Clark, whereas Brooke was clear it was the only way to break the deadlock imposed by the Gustav Line. Its failure was similarly the work of many hands.

The most important of those hands were Alex's. Brooke (and Monty) felt that it was crucial to backstop Alex, who had only had two short staff postings in his entire career, with a powerful chief of staff. (Of course, an effective chief of staff was critical to the successes of Eisenhower and Montgomery as well. The Brooke-Monty argument was really that Alex had a pedestrian mind.) McCreery had filled that role from August 1942 until the end of the Tunisian campaign, when he left to command X Corps, which would serve in Clark's Fifth Army. The incumbent when Shingle was planned, Lieutenant General A. A. Richardson, was not, Montgomery felt, of the same caliber: John Harding, chosen and briefed by Brooke to replace Richardson, did not take over in time to make any difference to Shingle's planning, which seems to have been informed by a spirit of excessive optimism. Alex's intention was that the Shingle force (one American and one British division) should move swiftly inland, seizing the Alban Hills and threatening the communications of the Germans holding Clark's Fifth Army in front of the Gustav Line at Cassino. Whether two infantry divisions were force enough—or a force of the right kind—for this role is questionable, but it was clearly the largest contingent that the theater's amphibious resources could put ashore and support, and therefore it would have to do. Much later, Alex would admit to inquiring American official historians that pushing a two-division force inland to the Alban Hills was a gamble but one that he felt sure would lead to a German withdrawal from the Gustav Line. But it is not certain whether Alex had thought through how the force could maintain itself on the Alban Hills if the Germans, instead of withdrawing, counterattacked. It is reasonably certain that neither he nor Brooke made clear to Churchill just how big a roll of the dice Shingle really was.

If the size, composition, and mission of the force were explicable in the circumstances, the command structure and commanders might well have been chosen to negate the effort. Under Alex, Clark's Fifth Army, already waging a major battle around Cassino, was responsible for Shingle. Clark in turn chose Lieutenant General John Lucas to conduct the operation. Lucas had taken over VI Corps after its first commander had been sacked at Salerno. That close-run battle had left both Clark and Lucas cautious; Clark in fact warned Lucas after the virtually unopposed landing at Anzio on January 22, 1944, not to "stick his neck out," and Lucas himself was obviously pessimistic about Shingle. A widely quoted entry from his diary blames everything on the "amateur" prime minister, which is patent nonsense. Although Churchill was an ardent supporter of the operation—and, indeed, made it possible by cashing in one of his dwindling supply of chips with Roosevelt—it was a consensus decision by the prime minister, Brooke, Alex, and Clark that launched Shingle. The command failures that doomed it primarily came down to Alexander and Clark. An unresolved disagreement about the mission of Lucas's corps—the sort of muddle that Alex's "agreeableness" left him vulnerable to and that Monty's ruthless insistence on clarity about objectives was meant to avoid—lay at the heart of the failure at Anzio. Alex (and Churchill) saw Shingle as loosening the Germans' grip on the Cassino position by threatening their lines of communication. Clark considered the attack on the Gustav Line the key—after a breakthrough there, the Shingle force would help complete the victory by threatening the German flank and rear. Hence Clark's advice to Lucas, who was already disposed to caution in any case.

The result was that any window of opportunity Shingle might have presented closed rapidly and, in Churchill's trenchant phrase, the "wildcat" he had hoped to hurl ashore became a "stranded whale." Under pressure from Alexander, who was all too aware of the prime minister's dissatisfaction, Clark sacked Lucas, replacing him with the very able Lieutenant General Lucian Truscott, but the Anzio beachhead remained a besieged enclave until May. Comparisons were made, at the time and later, with the August 1915 landing at Suvla Bay (an attempt to break the deadlock on the Gallipoli peninsula), usually as a way of criticizing Churchill's role. But as the prime minister put it in a letter to Smuts, "My personal efforts did not extend to the conduct of the battle."[13] Brooke, who wrote in his diary on the day of the landing, "Oh! How I hope [Shingle] will be a success! I feel a special responsibility for it . . . I know it was the right thing to do," came sadly to the same conclusion: "Little progress, mainly due to the lack of initiative in the early stages."[14] Shortly thereafter, Brooke decided that "Winston is beginning to see some of Alex's shortcomings," and certainly Churchill's signal to Alex on February 10 (by which time the beachhead was bracing for an imminent German counterattack) was critical—albeit gently so as compared to the messages Wavell and Auchinleck had received: "I have a feeling that you may have hesitated to assert your authority because you were dealing so largely with Americans and therefore *urged* an advance instead of *ordering* it."[15] In the end, the prime minister's affection for Alex was undamaged. "My confidence in Alexander remains undiminished," he told Smuts.[16] Although Churchill's hopes (and Brooke's) had been disappointed, the Italian theater had been kept alive, an important objective for the prime minister, and the Germans had had to commit additional resources to it, a key pre-Overlord consideration for Brooke. Finally, there was the overarching political fact that Churchill noted in a message to Dill: "Even a battle of attrition is better than standing by and watching the Russians fight."[17] But with the effective sealing off of the Anzio beachhead, the restoration of movement toward Rome—the symbolic goal that Churchill was determined to reach before Overlord began—depended on Alexander's ability to crack the Gustav Line at Monte Cassino.

The five-month struggle to take the German Cassino position, from Clark's initial attack across the Rapido and Garigliano rivers in January until Alexander's Diadem offensive in May, was an epic of infantry combat, fought out in ghastly weather and nightmarish terrain.[18] Clark's Fifth Army attack in January—the first battle of Cassino—was mounted with American and British troops already tired by four months of combat since Salerno. In spite of vile weather, there was some limited and expensive success on the front of McCreery's X Corps, but the assault crossing of the Rapido by the U.S. II Corps failed, with casualties to the 36th Division (a Texas National Guard unit) that left lingering bitterness against Clark among its veterans. The French corps, ably led by General Alphonse Juin, had considerable success in the forbidding mountainous terrain on the right flank of Clark's attack, but it, too, was finally stopped by ferocious German resistance allied to the weather. By this time, Shingle had been mounted, stalled, and turned into a besieged enclave facing an imminent and massive German counterattack. Another try at Cassino was necessary to take the pressure off the Anzio beachhead. With Fifth Army's American, British, and French troops exhausted, Alexander sent three fresh divisions over from the Eighth Army, whose front on the Adriatic was quiet. The New Zealand, 4th Indian, and 78th British Divisions would join the Fifth Army, operating as the New Zealand Corps under Freyberg's command. Clark's Fifth Army now included two British corps and, in Freyberg, one of the most formidable soldiers in the theater, a man who had a quasi-autonomous position and the personal admiration of Winston Churchill. The second and third battles of Cassino were not Alex's battles or Clark's but Bernard Freyberg's.

Freyberg, however, had several problems in addition to the Germans. His splendid division had fought on Crete and in the desert from Crusader to Tunisia. Its losses had been heavy, and New Zealand's manpower reserves were slender. Freyberg dealt directly with his government and was left in no doubt about its concern over further heavy casualties. The result, as Brooke put it, was that he conducted operations "with a casualty conscious mind," relying on massive air and artillery support "without risking too much infantry."[19] Yet it was Freyberg's decision to launch Tuker's 4th Indian Division (whose combat record was even longer than the New Zealanders') directly at the monastery that has become the symbol of the battle. Tuker himself, too ill with a recurrence of malaria to remain in command and about to hand over the division to his senior brigadier, was deeply unhappy with the mission. He would have preferred a major turning movement through the mountains by his division and the French corps working together. But faced with the decision for a direct assault Tuker (almost as formidable a personality as Freyberg) insisted adamantly on the heaviest possible air support for his men. Freyberg concurred, as did Clark and Alex.

The resulting obliteration of the monastery, although criticized then and later, must be seen in the context of the command structure that set it in motion: a divisional commander who had seen too many ill-prepared operations in the desert and perhaps the most casualty-conscious corps commander serving under British command. Tactically, the result was a disappointment. Tuker's Gurkhas clawed their way to within a few hundred yards of the monastery but could get no farther. An accompanying assault on Cassino by the New Zealanders was also a failure. Freyberg's next attempt was a renewed assault on the town of Cassino—preceded by another massive bombing and artillery barrage that reduced the town to rubble.[20] The New Zealanders then slowly fought their way into the wreckage (which, like the monastery ruins, provided excellent cover for the defenders—a phenomenon Montgomery would encounter at Caen in a few months). Tank-infantry cooperation had come a long way since the dark days when Freyberg had been repeatedly let down by British armor in the summer of 1942, but hampered by the debris, the New Zealand tanks could not overcome the stubborn German defenders. Loathe as he was to risk a bloodbath among his infantry, Freyberg nonetheless had 36 percent casualties in the four battalions he committed. The 4th Indian Division once again tackled the monastery, and again at great cost, the Gurkhas got tantalizing close, but the German position held. The New Zealanders and the 4th Indian would need months to recover.

Watching the Germans blunt two more attacks, this time by two of the best divisions Alex had, Churchill became increasingly uneasy about what seemed a costly commitment to frontal assault. On March 20, he sent Alex a worried message, notable for its very diplomatic phrasing. The prime minister reiterated that he had "the greatest confidence" in Alex and would back him up "through thick and thin" but commented, almost plaintively, that "it seems hard to understand why this most strongly defended point is the only passage forward."[21] Alexander, by now with Harding at his side, answered the same day with a long, reasoned defense of the Cassino operations, concluding by indicating that they would soon be shut down and preparations put in hand for a very differently conceived and much more powerful attack in the spring. Churchill's response was simply to thank Alex for his "full explanations" and to note, "The war weighs very heavy on us all just now."[22] As Alexander and Harding began to shape Diadem, the El Alamein of the Italian campaign, the prime minister was girding to do battle once again with his American allies to defend the British Mediterranean theater from being completely overshadowed by the great Overlord operation.

The successive attacks on the Cassino position had been conducted by one or two divisions and, because of the constraints imposed by terrain and weather, had often been very weak at the point of attack—a company of infantry inching its way along a narrow ridge toward the monastery. As the failure of the New Zealand and 4th Indian Divisions to breach the Gustav Line became clear, Alexander and Harding rethought their whole approach to the problem. The result was a complex plan that involved an extensive reorganization and the use of both armies together in an army group battle. The aim was the destruction of a large part of the German Tenth Army, which held the Gustav Line, followed by the seizure of Rome before the beginning of Overlord and the pursuit of Kesselring's forces north to the Pisa-Rimini line, the last mountain barrier the Germans could defend before the broad plains of northern Italy and, possibly, a break into the Po Valley. Alexander's plan was developed very differently from the way in which Monty had put his El Alamein design together, something noted by the British official historians: "Alexander issued very little paper in connection with his Spring offensive. Instead he held conferences at Caserta on 28th February, 2nd April, and 1st May, sending out careful agenda for each which outlined his intentions and he informed the commanders and staff officers who would attend of the points upon which decisions would be taken, and of the questions they should be ready to answer."[23] How much of this approach to planning the battle was Harding's and how much was Alex's is hard to say, but the more informal discussion format, so different from Montgomery's technique, certainly reflected Alexander's personality and style, even if it left historians with less grist for their mills.

The core of the plan was the secret transfer of nearly the entire Eighth Army from the Adriatic side of the peninsula westward across the Apennines to form the battering ram that would shatter the German front in the Liri Valley below Cassino and drive toward Rome. Fifth Army would sidestep westward to make room for the Eighth. Some formations were swapped between armies as well. McCreery's X Corps returned to Eighth Army, and the French corps moved to Clark's army. When the shuffling was complete, all the formations in Eighth Army were British, Dominion, Indian, or British-equipped, such as the Polish Corps, whereas Fifth Army was composed of American and American-equipped French units. Though there was administrative logic in the reorganization, it also put the crucial breakthrough in the Liri Valley in British hands, which was as close as the ever-tactful Alex would come to making an open judgment on Clark's generalship.

While all this was happening, tired formations were being pulled out of the line and fresh formations were arriving in Italy (including two more armored divisions and three independent armored brigades for a theater already overstocked with armor). All of this—the movement, the reorganization, the withdrawal of tired units, and the integration of new formations—took time, and the date for the launch of Diadem inevitably slipped back, as happened when Montgomery prepared for El Alamein. And as on that occasion, the prime minister became restless.

Jumbo Wilson had told London that Alexander's reorganization would not be complete until April 15, but clumsy phrasing had led the prime minister to assume that was also the date for the opening of the attack. When Wilson subsequently reported May 15 as the start date for Diadem, the prime minister—deeply involved in an increasingly nasty argument with the Americans over the future of the Italian campaign—reacted sharply, telling Alexander that he was "staggered . . . when your renewed attack was put off for a whole month."[24] A few days later, in a note to the Chiefs of Staff, he spoke of "Alexander's desolating delay."[25] Alex, however, was shrewder in handling Churchill than his critics realized. He had already been given permission to return to England to discuss Diadem, and once exposed to Alex's charm, the prime minister's reservations melted and he pronounced himself satisfied with the proposed timing. (Brooke somehow missed all this, grumbling in his diary about Alexander, "What a small calibre man he is . . . with very little realisation of what he is doing."[26]) On May 1, at the last of Alexander's planning conferences, the attack was fixed for 11:00 P.M. on May 11, 1944.

Because the Italian campaign was overshadowed in less than a month by Overlord—and because Alexander did such a poor job of publicizing his wartime career—the dimensions of Diadem are often overlooked. The largest British battle of the war to that point had been Monty's Alamein attack: one army, three corps, and the equivalent of eleven divisions fighting a twelve-day battle. Diadem was an army group battle: two armies, seven corps, and the equivalent of twenty-three divisions. During the planning for Diadem, Alexander thought it might develop as two El Alamein–style battles—two set-piece battles with a pause between—before he reached Rome. In fact, it was to be a continuous twenty-four-day struggle, with his army group grinding forward at about 3 miles a day, the biggest operation any British or American general had yet attempted. The Diadem plan was complex. Eighth Army would drive up the Liri Valley, with the infantry of XIII Corps under Lieutenant General Sidney Kirkman (Monty's chief gunner at Alamein) seizing crossings over the Garigliano River and opening the way for Lieutenant General E. L. M. Burns's tank-heavy I Canadian Corps to drive forward toward Valmontane. There, a linkup would be effected with elements of the Fifth Army, specifically Truscott's U.S. VI Corps breaking out from the Anzio beachhead. The object was the destruction of most of the German Tenth Army south of Rome, which would then fall to the Allies in due course. As had become usual, a massive deception operation cloaked Alexander's design until Diadem opened with a thunderous barrage by 1,700 field and medium guns, nearly double the number employed at El Alamein. Over the next twelve hours, those artillery pieces fired an average of 420 shells each. Once begun, Diadem required none of the pauses for readjustment that Monty had needed at El Alamein. The attack was relentless, and although the German Tenth Army fought, as usual, stubbornly and well, it had no choice but to give ground. If Diadem so far bore a strong resemblance to El Alamein—and, indeed, to all the Eighth Army's subsequent battles—it was also destined to end ambiguously and in a still-reverberating controversy.

Montgomery's "failure" to cut off and destroy Rommel's tattered army was adversely commented on at the time and has been ever since. In Alexander's design, the bulk of the German Tenth Army was to be trapped between the advancing Eighth Army and the U.S. VI Corps, erupting from the Anzio beachhead and seizing Valmontane, a key point on the main road from Cassino to Rome. This was in fact the plan on which Shingle had been based—the breaching of the Gustav Line followed by a threat to the communications of the retiring Germans. Now, in place of the single corps Clark had used in December, Alexander had smashed through the Gustav Line with two armies. Lucas's VI Corps, almost certainly too small for its task in January, had burgeoned in the intervening months into a force of five American divisions (one of them armored), plus an independent brigade and two weak British infantry divisions (plagued by the lack of infantry replacements, they were short 3,600 men, the equivalent of a brigade). Truscott actually was commanding not a corps but an army, and Alexander had distinctly established Valmontane as its objective. He had also reserved the decision on the timing of the breakout to himself (something that annoyed the ever-touchy Clark). Alexander set May 23 for Truscott's attack. Its object was the German Tenth Army. Churchill, who had kept his suggestions to a minimum in his messages to Alexander, obviously understood Alex's intentions: "A cop [that is, the destruction of the Tenth Army] is clearly more important than Rome, which would anyhow come as its consequence. The cop is the one thing that matters."[27] Unfortunately, it did not matter enough to Clark. Only one division was directed toward Valmontane, while the rest of Truscott's powerful force was swung in the direction of Rome, the prize Clark was determined he would have at whatever cost. The German Tenth Army lived to fight another day.[28]

Churchill had fought hard for Alexander's campaign and had told him at the crucial moment, "The glory of this battle, . . . will be measured, not by the capture of Rome . . . but by the number of German divisions cut off."[29] When he came to discuss Diadem in his memoirs, however, he was surprisingly bland, simply observing of Clark's decision to subordinate Valmontane to Rome: "This was not in accord with Alexander's instructions."[30]

But there was nothing bland about his response, as Diadem ground toward Rome, to an American decision that threatened the future of Alexander's campaign. At one point, Churchill became so irate, due to American actions that would cripple Alexander's exploitation of his victory even more effectively than Mark Clark's free-lancing, that he declared himself willing to end the integrated command structure in the Mediterranean. Anvil, the proposed landing in the south of France to complement Overlord, was the cause of the confrontation. When first discussed at the Tehran Conference, Anvil was either to precede or occur simultaneously with Overlord, in an effort to draw German forces from the Overlord area or at least to hold in place those in the south of France. This design vanished as soon as Montgomery got a look at the existing plan for Overlord and insisted on strengthening the initial assault. This in turn would require more landing craft—which meant that Anvil would have to be postponed (first to July and ultimately to mid-August). The delays, of course, removed its operational relevance to Overlord. Meanwhile, the Italian campaign, stalled in front of the Gustav Line, finally broke into (admittedly slow) movement with Diadem, opening the prospect not only of taking Rome, a largely symbolic victory, but also of driving Kesselring to the Pisa-Rimini line in northern Italy and, perhaps, of breaking into the Po Valley—a development with considerable strategic significance.

Even before Diadem was launched, Churchill and Brooke were arguing for flexibility over Anvil, with Churchill pointing out to Marshall in mid-April that he would "regret having to forgo such an hour of choice" as Diadem's success would present.[31] Once Diadem produced a victory, even one incomplete largely because of Clark's actions, the prime minister became more and more determined to keep the forward momentum of Alexander's campaign going. The Americans, however, were equally determined that Anvil, finally set for August 15, should take place as scheduled, even though it now had deviated from its original aim—indeed, a whole new rationale (the acquisition of the great port of Marseilles) had to be constructed for it. That seven divisions, French and American, would have to be taken from Alexander's order of battle to mount Anvil meant that it inevitably would break the momentum of Alexander's northward exploitation of Diadem.

The Anglo-American argument rumbled on between London and Washington throughout the planning, launching, and culmination of Alexander's offensive. It was finally decided by the refusal of the American Chiefs of Staff, supported by the president, to budge. On July 2, the Combined Chiefs of Staff sent Wilson a directive to mount Anvil on August 15. The prime minister, however, was not prepared to let the matter rest. On July 4, he gave the Chiefs of Staff a draft message he proposed to send to FDR. Brooke, who saw him that evening, noted that Churchill's "vindictive spirits" had been aroused and that his draft was an "awful telegram." The CIGS was sure that the prime minister was "longing to have a good row" with Roosevelt.[32] The anger that had been building in Churchill since the argument over the Aegean the previous autumn boiled over in the draft: "Very grave dissatisfaction . . . exists here at the way in which control of events is now being assumed, one-sidedly, by the United States Chiefs of Staff . . . I consider that we are entitled to press for better and more equal treatment. . . . Otherwise it would be necessary, in particular, to devise some other machinery for conducting the war, including the separation of the commands in the Mediterranean."[33]

As Brooke realized, the consequences of sending this message would have been disastrous, and he and his colleagues eventually talked the prime minister out of forwarding it. Although Churchill dropped the message, however, he refused to concede the point. "I am not going to give way on this for anybody. Alexander is to have his campaign," he told the Chiefs of Staff in a note that also instructed them to see that the Americans realized "that we have been ill-treated and are furious." He closed with a sentiment that would never be allowed to appear in his memoirs: "The Arnold, King, Marshall combination is one of the stupidest strategic teams ever seen. They are good fellows and there is no need to tell them this."[34]

It would be tempting to write this off as an expression of Churchill's increasing exhaustion in the war's fifth year, with the apparent stalemate in Normandy and the rain of "doodlebugs" on London exacerbating matters. But there was much more than that at work. Since the autumn of 1943, he had understood that the relentless erosion of British weight in his Grand Alliance made the achievements of the largely British forces under Alexander's command one of his few remaining assets. To face the clear relegation of that theater to a secondary role—which is what the American insistence on Anvil connoted—was to face the unpalatable fact that Britain was now very much a junior partner, unable to prevent the Americans from riding roughshod over British interests. But what Brooke and his fellow chiefs also saw was that there was no alternative—the Italian theater could not be sustained simply on British assets, so there was no choice.[35] (Concurrently with the crisis over Anvil, a long-running and increasingly acrimonious argument between Churchill and his Chiefs of Staff over the shape of future British strategy in the Pacific was coming to a head. The issue was the same: the prime minister's desire for an independent British strategy, befitting its Great-Power status, versus the only slightly greater realism about the possibilities on the part of Brooke, Air Chief Marshal Sir Charles Portal, and Admiral Sir Andrew Browne Cunningham.) On July 10, Churchill, despite the intensity of his anger—only a pale reflection of which appeared in his memoirs—dropped his idea of withdrawing the Mediterranean theater from the Anglo-American Combined Chiefs of Staff organization set up at the Arcadia Conference in 1941. Anvil, renamed Dragoon, went ahead. Seven divisions were withdrawn from Clark's Fifth Army during July. The impetus of Alexander's advance slackened. Kesselring once again demonstrated his skill, and that of his troops, withdrawing in a controlled fashion to the new Gothic Line in the mountains north of Florence, where he would hold Alexander's forces until their final offensive in the spring of 1945.

What went unnoticed by Churchill in his memoirs and, given his multiple distractions, perhaps at the time as well was that Diadem was the culmination of the transformation of the British Army. It had evolved from a force that was poorly equipped, both conceptually and in matériel, to face the Wehrmacht between 1940 and 1942 into a highly effective fighting force—for the sort of battles it would fight. (A parallel transformation between 1915 and 1917 had prepared the way for the British Army of the "Last Hundred Days," whose achievements have only recently been fully recognized.) El Alamein was the first of the British Army's "new-style" battles, and in many ways, it remained the paradigm. But by 1944, although it was still a reference point (Alex had used it as a yardstick before Diadem), the model had been refined and developed considerably. The equipment deficiencies of earlier years had been largely remedied, even if, in certain aspects, British (and American) equipment remained inferior to that of the Germans. But if quality was occasionally inferior, quantity certainly was not. The oft-criticized British concern with logistics kept the troops involved in Diadem fed and supported without pause during nearly a month of intensive combat.

That combat took place under skies the Allies owned. Army-air cooperation, born in the desert war and developed in Tunisia, was now operating at a peak of efficiency that would again be seen in northwest Europe. Although Allied airpower was never able to cut Kesselring's supply lines completely, it allowed ground operations to proceed unhindered and provided a flying artillery as potent as the Germans had enjoyed in their heyday. But the core of the British battle style remained the infantry-artillery-armor combination. The key element was the gunners. In October 1941, Churchill had called for the restoration of artillery to the dominant role on the battlefield that it had enjoyed in British operations in 1917 and 1918. That process began at Alamein. Monty's chief gunner there, Brigadier Sidney Kirkman, now commanded XIII Corps, whose task was to crack open the German defenses in the Liri Valley below Monte Cassino. Eighth Army's artillery chief, Brigadier Frank Siggers, was coordinating the fire of some 124 regiments (or U.S. battalions) of artillery—by this point, excellent communications and much practice had made it possible to put an entire division's guns at the support of a single infantry company in ten minutes. Siggers's fire plan for Eighth Army required 1,087 guns, and one divisional fire plan ran to forty-six pages. During the first five days of Diadem, nearly half a million shells were fired in support of XIII Corps alone. American officers at the time—and some American writers later—criticized the British Army's World War I–style barrages, but as two British gunners writing about Diadem remarked, the Americans "had not been at Ypres or yet encountered a defence system that could not be infiltrated or outflanked and had to be cracked open by brute force."[36] Kirkman, Siggers, and twelve of the twenty-one artillery brigadiers involved were Western Front veterans. The Germans, who had learned to fear and respect the Royal Artillery between 1914 and 1918, had no doubt that it was back to its 1917–1918 form. Many who had faced the massive artillery concentrations with which the Soviets prefaced their offensives found British gunners far more dangerous.

Despite the massive firepower brought to bear on them, the Germans made the business of cracking the Gustav Line difficult and expensive: Diadem cost 12,000 British, Canadian, New Zealand, and Indian casualties, and those fell primarily on the infantry, the arm in which the British could least afford losses. Three armored and four infantry divisions would be broken up during 1944 to meet the shortfall in infantry, and antiaircraft units were being converted wholesale to infantry in Italy in the aftermath of Diadem. Caution about casualties and concerns over troop morale that reinforced that caution (the Italian theater had a serious problem with desertion), when added to an approach to training that emphasized consolidation over exploitation, meant that the forward movement of Eighth Army after its breakthrough was careful and methodical—about 3 miles a day, or a little over 300 yards an hour, against the very skillful rearguard tactics at which the Germans were, by this time, masters.[37] There were other factors at work as well in the very deliberate advance of Eighth Army in the second stage of Diadem, and these involved the skills of the army commander.

Lieutenant General Sir Oliver Leese, Bt., had been a student at the army staff college when Montgomery was an instructor there. The link forged then made Leese's career. He was a senior member of Gort's staff in 1940, but Montgomery forgave that, pronouncing him the only worthwhile member of that group. Summoned from England, where he was commanding the Guards Armoured Division, by Montgomery in August 1942 to take over XXX Corps, he became Monty's successor at Eighth Army in December 1943, and he did his best thereafter to model himself on his mentor, with mixed results. Despite Montgomery's imprimatur, though, there were questions about Leese. Tuker, a merciless critic of the Montgomery style of command, had questioned the wisdom of the arrangements made by Leese and approved by Monty for the attack on the Mareth line, and the best study of the Italian campaign pronounced him "slow and unimaginative."[38] Certainly, his arrangement for the second phase of Diadem, after Kirkman and the gunners had blown open the German defenses, merited that description. In carefully measured words, the British official historians pointed out that the failure to destroy more of the German Tenth Army, though primarily due to Clark's sabotage of Alexander's design, was also due to "Leese's mistaken choice of the type of division to lead 8th Army's advances, and his failure to judge correctly the nature of the ground."[39] The Liri Valley was only 3 to 4 miles wide and cut by numerous watercourses. Despite this, Leese drove two corps abreast into it; the corps commanders put their armor in front, perhaps to conserve their infantry, a decision Leese approved. The result was colossal traffic jams (in one twenty-four-hour period, 11,542 vehicles passed a checkpoint on Highway 6, Eighth Army's axis of advance, and the average number per day was 8,000[40]) and the army's painfully slow forward movement. The official historians also observed acidly that "ignorance of the nature of the ground was strange. Italy was not unknown. . . . Guide books to Italy had been written for generations."[41]

In fact, the most dramatic action in the breaking of the Gustav Line and the German fallback position in front of Rome (the Hitler Line) was conducted by the North African troops of the French Expeditionary Corps, operating under Fifth Army's command in the wild and hilly country on Leese's left. Accustomed to mountain warfare, supplied by mule trains, and supported wherever possible by armored cars and tanks, they moved with a rapidity that did much to unhinge the German defenders facing Leese's ponderous advance in the Liri Valley. In his memoirs, Churchill noted but did not stress the role of the French Expeditionary Corps. It was left for the British official historians, over thirty years later, to single the corps out in their summation of Diadem and acknowledge its "brilliant performance."[42]

Alex's army, like Monty's in the desert (and soon again in Normandy), had mastered the set-piece attack, followed by a controlled advance—but converting "break in" to "breakthrough" remained a problem. The British Army's most ambitious battle yet, Diadem revealed that in certain types of combat, that army was as good as any in the field, but the repertoire remained limited.[43] After May 1944, deepening manpower problems reinforcing cautious generalship and the increasing dominance of the Americans, both in the alliance generally and on the battlefields of northwest Europe (where the war's focus swung two days after Clark had his Roman triumph), meant that there would be little opportunity or incentive to develop the army's skill set further. In this sense, Diadem, not Monty's Normandy battles, represent the climax of the British Army's journey from the dark days between 1940 and 1942 to consistent battlefield success. Churchill's memoirs, where the focus in *Closing the Ring* and *Triumph and Tragedy*, as he told Pownall, was shifting away from battles, do not reflect this fact. When he told the Chiefs of Staff during the Anvil argument that "Alexander is to have his campaign," it was considerations of alliance parity with the Americans he had in mind. He was no longer giving the detailed attention to the conduct of the British Army's battles that he had in discussing the desert war. That change of emphasis in turn masked what a different army Alexander's was from Wavell's or Auchinleck's.

In the end, one comes back to the enigma of Harold Alexander. Strongly attracted to art as a young man, he was perhaps, like Wavell, a career soldier with some hankerings for a rather different life. Like many young men of his class and time, he seems to have drifted into the army, and even after deciding to make it his career, he failed to impress at least two of his instructors at the staff college. Those two were Brooke and Montgomery—and first impressions proved lasting. Yet Alexander's career moved serenely upward. Churchill was captivated by him, as was a far more cynical and less romantic observer, Harold Macmillan. A World War I Guards officer and, like Alex, possessed of a fine combat record, Macmillan was the British resident minister in the Mediterranean theater from 1942 to 1945. His copious diaries reflect an admiration for Alexander that steadily deepened—above all, an admiration for Alexander's personal style. Staying with Alex in July 1943, during the crucial early stages of the Sicilian campaign, Macmillan noted, "It is rather like a large country house. . . . No fuss, no worry, no anxiety—and a great battle in progress. This is never referred to. . . . The conversation is the usual tone of educated . . . Englishmen—a little history, a little politics, a little banter, a little philosophy—all very lightly touched and very agreeable. . . . I have never enjoyed so much the English capacity for restraint and understatement."[44]

It would be easy to forget that even senior generals need relaxation and to take quotes such as this to produce a caricature of Alexander as simply a charming, elegant, aristocratic lightweight. However much Macmillan admired Alex's style, he also had an opportunity to observe him closely at work, and his admiration remained constant. The weakness of Alex's country-house style was perhaps that it was unlikely to appeal equally to the Americans—or even be fully understood by them, and it was as well prone to create misunderstandings (or give openings for willful misunderstandings) in those who did not share the "capacity for restraint and understatement" that Macmillan so admired. In late January 1944, during Clark's second attempt on Cassino, Macmillan, visiting Alexander, noted, "He has the most effective way of giving not exactly orders but suggestions to his commanders. These are put forward with modesty and simplicity. But they are always so clear and lucid that they carry conviction. It is a most interesting (and extremely effective) method."[45] Alex's approach to command, unlike Montgomery's, opened up areas of exploitable ambiguity that Clark made full use of.

Clark lay at the heart of two major failures—Anzio and the redirection of Truscott's corps in May 1944 (not to mention the failure of his attacks on Cassino). Alexander and Wilson pondered replacing him before Diadem but, cautioned by Macmillan, decided against it. Given the fading American interest in the Italian campaign, the decision was assuredly correct. Difficult and disloyal Clark might have been, but his voice was at least an American voice urging the importance of the campaign. Since Clark and American support were necessary, Alex's methods were almost certainly more useful than the abrasive style of Montgomery. And when dealing with British

Alexander at U.S. VI Corps HQ, Anzio beachhead, 1944. This picture captures the touch of cinematic dash that was part of Alex's persona—and of his appeal to Churchill. (Courtesy Imperial War Museum, image no. NA 11879)

forces, Alexander (and Harding) produced, in the Diadem offensive, an operation that played to the very considerable strengths his army had developed by that point in the war, even if, ironically, Churchill's design for his memoirs did not allow for a full discussion of the feat.

As the balance in the alliance tipped against Britain, Churchill would have supported the "British" theater in the Mediterranean whoever commanded there. That it was Alex made it more pleasant and probably accounted in part for the disproportionate attention the Italian campaign got in *Closing the Ring* and *Triumph and Tragedy*.[46] The prime minister certainly had his moments of irritation with Alex—Brooke, in one of his passages at arms with Churchill over British generalship, reminded the prime minister that he had even "torn Alexander to shreds for his lack of imagination and leadership in continually attacking at Cassino"[47]—but in the end, Churchill always swung back behind the general whose style appealed so strongly.

Perhaps Churchill's instinct was sound for reasons other than Alex's attractiveness as an individual. If the Mediterranean theater had to be sustained, as Brooke understood, because it was an essential preliminary to Overlord and because, in the prime minister's view, British battlefield success was politically essential, it is hard to imagine any British general doing a better job with the complexities, human and geographic, of the Italian campaign than Alexander. The one British senior officer who might have outshone Alex as commander in Italy was, in 1943 and 1944, creating an army of his own—but in a theater as secondary to London as Italy was to Washington. That man was Lieutenant General William "Bill" Slim, and his nascent force was Fourteenth Army. Before long—and on the other side of the globe—he would lead the Fourteenth to the greatest battlefield triumph experienced by any British Army commander in World War II.

7

The Last Sepoy General

As Diadem ground toward Rome, Overlord prepared to launch, and Churchill fought his vain rearguard action against Anvil, a remarkable victory was being won in Britain's other war by the reborn Indian Army, led by the finest British general of the twentieth century, the redoubtable William Slim. Overshadowed at the time by events in Europe and the Mediterranean and almost overlooked by Churchill in his memoirs (until Slim, by then CIGS, protested), the 1944–1945 campaign of Slim and his "Forgotten Army" was the most remarkable feat of arms to take place under the British flag during the war.

Above all, it was the triumph of the old Indian Army on the eve of the demise of the British Raj it had sustained. The transformation of the Eighth Army from its nadir under Ritchie to victories at Alamein and in Diadem is the story of improving leadership, equipment, technique—and circumstances. The transformation of the Indian Army that surrendered at Singapore and then staggered out of Burma into the victorious Fourteenth Army of 1944 and 1945 is even more dramatic, especially since the arrival of the remnants of Burcorps in Assam in May 1942 was far from the low point of its war. That dreary moment came a year later, just as the British armies in the Mediterranean were enjoying the victorious conclusion of their African campaigns.

When Slim's tattered but coherent formations withdrew from Burma into northeastern India, the Raj seemed to be in a desperate situation. Its army had been badly beaten in Malaya and Burma, and Churchill's attempt to defuse rising political tensions in India between the government and the largely Hindu Congress Party had broken down. This set of circumstances would lead to the August 1942 Quit India rebellion—the largest assault on British authority in the subcontinent since 1857.[1] With the enemy on India's eastern frontiers and widespread unrest at home, the Indian Army nevertheless had to begin reorienting its training and doctrine to a new style of war, while simultaneously catching up on the arrears of training and equipment produced by the breakneck expansion between 1940 and 1942.[2]

All of this would have been difficult enough if the Indian Army had been given a respite from active operations in Burma. Even before Burcorps reached India, however, the prime minister instructed Wavell to begin planning a counteroffensive. Because Churchill gave such glancing attention to the war in Burma in his memoirs (as compared to the space devoted to the desert and Italy), it has escaped general attention that in 1942 and 1943, he was heavily, if inevitably intermittently, involved in attempts to redeem the defeats of 1941 and 1942 by a successful counterattack in Burma. The results of these initiatives were unfortunate.

Churchill never repented of the priorities he imposed between 1940 and 1941. He had accepted that war with Japan, if it came, would mean British losses in the Far East but also American belligerency, which in turn would mean an assured victory that would make those losses good—he assumed. He never foresaw the debacle at Singapore and the rapid loss of Burma. Yet he quickly grasped that the restoration of British power in the East required that the prestige lost on the battlefield be regained there—hence his determination to see that a counteroffensive against the Japanese was quickly mounted. Unfortunately, the apparatus of counterattack was nonexistent. An amphibious strategy to retake Rangoon and move on to Singapore required resources that the British could never amass in India until Germany was beaten. But waiting until then was out of the question, both because imperial prestige needed immediate, not delayed, battlefield victory and because Britain's policy and strategy in Asia were hostage to its necessary but demanding American ally. Put simply, China dominated American thinking about the war in South and Southeast Asia and therefore American demands on British policy. Churchill, of course, never shared the views of Roosevelt and the so-called China Lobby in Washington on either Chiang Kai-shek or China's future, but he understood that a failure to support the U.S. desire to restore a land link with China would impose a strain on the Anglo-American relationship that he did not want to risk. He also knew that the Americans were already deeply suspicious of British good faith where China was concerned. Those suspicions were manifest in the way the growing U.S. presence in India was structured.

By mid-1942, an American theater command—China-Burma-India (CBI)—under the acerbic Anglophobe Lieutenant General Joseph "Vinegar Joe" Stilwell, was based in Delhi, reporting directly to Washington and tasked with the twin goals of supporting a trans-Himalayan airlift to supply China and reopening overland communications with that nation. The latter meant the reconquest of north Burma, and it was Stilwell's job not to let the British forget this American goal. Meanwhile, the only force available to mount any offensive—the Indian Army—was in no shape to do anything of the sort. Out of this stew of conflicting aims, inadequate resources, and perceived need to do something came the first Arakan campaign, the absolute nadir for the Indian Army and a very strong contender for the worst-managed British campaign of the war.

An advance down the Arakan coast aimed at Akyab Island, whose seizure would provide airfields to cover a seaborne assault on Rangoon, was originally simply part of a larger plan. When that plan foundered for lack of resources and it became clear that nothing could be done in north Burma during the 1942–1943 winter (the "dry," or campaigning, season), the advance took place anyway—an operation devoid of any strategically relevant objective. That was only the first of its problems. There followed in close succession a theater commander with an unrealistic appreciation of the enemy, a badly flawed command structure, and troops as unready as those who had fought in Malaya and Burma.

Wavell had underestimated the Japanese even as they swept through Malaya and Burma, and quite remarkably, he continued to do so as he planned his first offensive against them. In a memo (entitled "Operation Fantastical") that Wavell sent to his chief of staff, Lieutenant General Sir Edwin Morris, on September 17, 1942, he ruminated, "I have a 'hunch,' which may be quite unjustified, that we may find Japanese opposition very much lower than we expected in Burma if we can only act with boldness and determination," adding that "the Jap has never fought defensively and may not be much good at it. All this is just my private hunch, but I mean to ride it for all it is worth."[3] Wavell's willingness to take risks had produced Compass, the sweeping victory over the Italians, a precedent that he admitted to Morris had influenced him. In the Middle East, however, he had two highly trained regular formations with which to launch his offensive and a weak enemy not given to last-man/last-round defensive tactics. In all of India in the autumn of 1942, there were no units equal in quality to 7th Armoured and 4th Indian Divisions in 1940.

On the day he sent Morris his "Operation Fantastical" paper, Wavell ordered the commander of Eastern Army, Lieutenant General N. M. S. Irwin, to take Akyab. To Wavell's mistakes, Irwin now added his own. A British service officer who had commanded the army units in the ill-fated Operation Menace—the abortive landings at Dakar in French West Africa in September 1940—Irwin had recently been promoted from a corps command. He had a very bad temper and was on poor terms with the corps commander best positioned to handle operations in the Arakan, Lieutenant General William Slim, whose XV Corps headquarters was left on the sidelines.[4] Instead, Irwin proposed to control the operations himself from his headquarters at Ranchi, hundreds of miles away. The actual conduct of the offensive he confided to Major General W. L. Lloyd's 14th Indian Division. This clumsy arrangement—like Wavell's misjudgments—might have mattered less had 14th Indian been the sort of formation the 4th Indian had been when it jumped off for Compass. Unfortunately, it was, instead, a microcosm of everything that ailed the Indian Army in the autumn of 1942.

The 14th Indian Division was part of the 1941 expansion program. Early in 1942, one of its brigades was shipped to Burma and destroyed within a week of disembarkation. A replacement brigade was made up of some troops from the North-West Frontier and others taken from internal security duty. By mid-1942, the division had its three brigades but only half its authorized scale of equipment. Meanwhile, army expansion continued, with all its disruptive personnel moves and constant movement of units between formations. Despite this upheaval, 14th Indian Division, in common with much of the army, began trying to assimilate the lessons of Malaya and Burma, establishing its own divisional jungle-warfare school in midsummer. But when it moved up to the front to begin the push toward Akyab, it was still a work in progress; moreover, the troops were suffering badly from malaria, a problem that was brought under control only in 1943 and 1944.[5]

"My scenario is something like this. We occupy Akyab without much trouble," Wavell wrote in his "Operation Fantastical" paper, an idea he reiterated to Irwin shortly after Lloyd's troops began their slow forward movement in December.[6] That, however, was not how it worked out. The Japanese, though heavily outnumbered, gave ground very slowly, and by early January 1943, they had stalled 14th Division's advance. The prime minister kept close track of the operation, conscious that it was Britain's first offensive venture against Japan, coming six months after the great American victory at Midway and four months after the American landings on Guadalcanal. Wavell, aware of how closely Churchill could monitor military operations and, in any case, still in the grip of his belief that the Japanese were overrated, pushed Irwin; in turn, Irwin fed more semiraw brigades into the offensive. The official historians would later count nine brigades under 14th Division's command, far beyond a divisional commander's span of control.[7]

Meanwhile, Slim's corps headquarters sat on the sidelines, although inserting it was the obvious answer to a major command-and-control problem. Finally, even Irwin recognized that the reinforced 14th Division could do no more against tenacious Japanese defenders whose well-sited bunker complexes were more than a match for the tactics and training the Indian Army could bring to the battle at that point. Wavell promptly overruled Irwin and ordered another attack. Before it could go in, the Japanese struck, and the British house of cards came crashing down.

The rout of the 14th Indian Division (and of the 6th Brigade of the British 2nd Division, which had been added to Lloyd's force) was total—as bad as anything that had happened in Malaya and worse than anything that had taken place in Burma. Watching from afar in mounting fury, Churchill sent the Chiefs of Staff a waspish note: "This campaign goes from bad to worse, and we are being completely outfought and out-manoeuvred by the Japanese. Luckily, the small scale of the operations and the attraction of other events has prevented public opinion being directed upon this lamentable scene."[8] In Churchill's mind, this was the last straw for Wavell. On the day following the prime minister's caustic note, he was summoned home for "consultations."

Irwin finally, in extremis, brought in Slim to manage another debacle. Slim stabilized the front, but in doing so, he once again fell afoul of Irwin, who decided to relieve him—a decision he failed to carry out only because a general shuffle of commanders after the Arakan fiasco removed Irwin himself. Irwin's behavior toward Slim, which helped doom an already shaky operation, was obviously more than simply the result of his loose grip on his temper. Michael Roberts, an Indian Army officer who knew Slim well, served in Burma, and later worked on the official histories, reflected years afterward that there was a "prevalent" belief in the British Army "that the Indian Army was a second class army fit only for what they looked on as guerilla warfare on the N.W.F. [North-West Frontier]."[9] This professional tension had surfaced in Malaya and the desert war, and it would do so again in Burma. In the spring of 1943, however, the failure of 14th Indian Division, coming on the heels of the disasters in Malaya and Burma, might well have seemed to Irwin and other outside observers (including the prime minister) validation of their low opinion of the Indian Army. Even one of Slim's liaison officers, commenting on the state of the units that fought in the Arakan, labeled them as "little better, in a large number of cases, than a rather unwilling band of raw levies."[10] Ironically, as the first Arakan campaign wound down amid defeat and recrimination, a process of renewal had already begun in India that would transform the raw levies of 1942 and 1943 into the great Fourteenth Army of 1944 and 1945. Before that process was well under way, though, Churchill's anger and disappointment over the Arakan failure, buttressing his belief that India and its army were a "welter of lassitude and inefficiency," led to his intervention in the campaign in a way far more dramatic than his descent on Cairo in 1942.[11] In the dreary Indian military scene, the prime minister thought he glimpsed a spark of success, which he meant to kindle into a flame. That gleam came from a raid into Burma led by the strangest figure the British Army produced in World War II, Orde Charles Wingate.[12]

Wavell, although in appearance a stolid, orthodox senior officer, had always harbored some unusual traits. One of them was his openness to unorthodox approaches to military problems. While general officer commanding in Palestine in 1936 and 1937 during the revolt by the Palestine Arabs against the British Mandate authorities, he was favorably impressed by a young gunner officer, Captain Orde Wingate, who had become an ardent supporter of Zionism. Wingate believed that the specially trained counterguerrilla units that he had raised from among Jewish settlers, staffed with British officers and NCOs, christened Special Night Squads, and successfully led into action were a more effective answer to Arab guerrilla tactics than the ponderous "sweeps" by regular infantry battalions. Wingate enjoyed enough success that Wavell remembered him in 1940 and brought him to Cairo from the dead-end posting in Britain to which his genius for making enemies had led him.

Wavell put Wingate to work organizing guerrilla operations against the Italians in Ethiopia. Again, Wingate had considerable success, albeit against a demoralized and disintegrating enemy. And once again, he proved as adept at quarreling with other British officers as at defeating his enemies in the field. At the end of the campaign, worn out by stress and illness, isolated by the hostility he provoked, and without a patron after Wavell's removal by Churchill, he attempted to kill himself in his hotel room in Cairo. Although he recovered, his career would normally have been over. But Wavell again saved him. Faced with the rapid Japanese advance in Burma, Wavell resurrected Wingate, who made the first leg of his trip out to India in the plane carrying Alex to Burma for his brief stint as army commander there. The Japanese moved too fast for Wingate to actually attempt anything in Burma, but during the summer of 1942, he elaborated for Wavell his concept of "long range penetration" (LRP), infantry formations operating deep inside Japanese-held Burma, coordinated by radio and resupplied by air.[13]

Wavell made Wingate a brigadier and gave him three battalions, one British, one Gurkha, and one composed of Burmese hillmen who had remained loyal to the Raj, to try out the concept. As the offensive possibilities for the 1942–1943 campaigning season dwindled, it seemed as if Wingate's proposed operation, reduced from the opening act of an offensive in north Burma to a stand-alone affair, would also be canceled. In a meeting with Wavell, however, Wingate persuaded him to sanction Operation Longcloth (Chindit I) as a trial of LRP methods. In February 1943, with the operations in the Arakan stalemated, 77th Indian Infantry Brigade, the Chindits, crossed the river Chindwin into Burma.[14] In the ensuing two months, the Chindits did some minor and easily remediable damage to Japanese communications, while losing nearly a third of their number plus 1,100 mules and all their equipment. Yet they had gone into Burma, fought the Japanese with what could be represented as success (although in fact, as lightly equipped raiders, they evaded contact whenever possible), and come out again.

The return of the Chindits, coinciding as it did with the depressing conclusion of the Arakan operations, had an impact all out of proportion to its very modest results. There had been only negative news for the British public in the war against Japan since December 1941. Desperate to give the public and the army anything that looked like news of success, General Sir Alan Hartley, acting commander-in-chief, India, in Wavell's absence, lifted the cloak of secrecy that had hitherto shrouded the Chindits. The public relations machine in Delhi leaped upon them, and the unit rapidly became the best-known formation in India. Publicity was, of course, very welcome to Wingate, who was already incubating plans for a much enlarged LRP force that he would lead to the reconquest of Burma. For the second time, however, his patron, Wavell, was removed from the scene at a critical moment. But Wingate had another in reserve (he was quite good at collecting them)—Leo Amery, secretary of state for India and Burma in Churchill's cabinet. Amery, an ardent "gentile Zionist," had known Wingate before the war, and he urged Wavell to make use of him in 1940 and suggested to Brooke that he offer his services to Wavell for use against the Japanese in Burma. Now he became Wingate's "back channel" to Churchill. A copy of Wingate's report on the Chindit expedition went to Amery and from him to Churchill (who had met Wingate at a London dinner party in 1938). It reached the prime minister at a particularly propitious moment—for Wingate, at least.[15]

Almost as soon as Wavell arrived in London, Churchill had taken him off to the May Trident Conference in Washington, venting to him on the way about the failings of the Indian Army going back to the 1857 Sepoy Mutiny. Trident confirmed a May 1944 date for Overlord—and the continuance of Mediterranean operations. It also produced heavy American pressure on Churchill for success in Burma. The prime minister recognized that he needed to respond to this and had come to the conclusion that Wavell, never one of his favorites, was now completely played out. Although not yet formally replaced, Wavell was told after Trident to take some overdue leave in England. In June, he was told that he would be replaced as commander-in-chief, India, and offered its viceroyalty. One of Wavell's last acts as commander-in-chief was also one of his most important. He effectively negated Irwin's sacking of Slim by removing Irwin himself.

Churchill's choice as Wavell's successor was one of his most inspired military appointments. Since his refusal of a consolation prize in the shape of Persia and Iraq Command, Auchinleck had been unemployed. He had been commander-in-chief, India, before succeeding Wavell in Cairo. Now he succeeded him again. In addition to being an Indian Army officer, Auchinleck had, in many ways, come to regard India as his real home. His appointment gave both leadership and further impetus to the military renaissance that had begun slowly and haltingly after the retreat from Burma. But the unglamorous work of reorganizing, retraining, and reequipping the Indian Army was largely invisible from London. All too visible was Auchinleck's reaction to the long menu of offensive operations for India Command sketched out under American pressure at Trident. The reality in India, Auchinleck told Churchill, in terms of both the state of the army as well as of the communications to Assam, meant that it would be necessary to accept much less ambitious operations in 1943 and 1944. Major offensive operations might in fact not be possible until between 1944 and 1945. Churchill must have recollected morosely the arguments between London and Cairo in 1941 and 1942 about the timing of offensives. It was at this moment, having dismissed Wavell and found Auchinleck dampeningly cautious, that Wingate and the first Chindit expedition came to Churchill's attention. The effect was startling. On July 24, Churchill sent a note to Ismay saying that "the commanders on the spot seem to be competing with one another to magnify their demands and the obstacles they have to overcome." A new overall commander for the Burma front was needed, he went on, one "in the prime of life and with the latest experience in the field. General Oliver Leese is, I believe, the right man . . . Wingate should command the army against Burma. He is a man of genius and audacity . . . his force and achievements, stand out . . . and no mere question of seniority must obstruct the advance of real personalities to their proper stations in war." The prime minister concluded by ordering that Wingate be sent home "for discussion."[16]

In the entire war, there may have been no more startling Churchill minute on military affairs than this particular communication. He was furious about the apparent stasis in Indian military affairs (and the problems with the Americans it was producing). That anger was born partly of ignorance about the Indian Army and partly of a failure to grasp the magnitude of the logistic challenges posed by a campaign into Burma from Assam. His solution was to create a new theater command for Burma separate from Auchinleck's GHQ, India, and its depressing habit of confronting him with unwelcome realities. Leese, a Monty protégé and a very orthodox and moderately successful corps commander, was a remarkable choice for this difficult and delicate position—and nothing in his subsequent history indicates that he would have been successful at it. (One general officer who worked after the war on the official history of the campaigns in the Mediterranean gave it as his opinion that Leese's real "ceiling" was divisional command.[17]) But Leese's proposed appointment seems quite reasonable compared to the idea that Wingate, a substantive lieutenant colonel who had never commanded any large formation in action (and whose handling of his Chindit brigade had been none too sure), should become an army commander. This gust of Churchillian enthusiasm was clearly the product of emotion rather than careful consideration, and its only immediate consequence was Wingate's speedy arrival in London. The minute did, however, signal that in his desire to rescue British military prestige in the East as well as meet American demands for action in north Burma, Churchill was willing to take very drastic measures. And certainly, the results that followed Wingate's arrival in London were dramatic enough.

Churchill had always been attracted to maverick personalities (one of the few traits he shared with Wavell). When Wingate, who had undeniable force and charisma, appeared at 10 Downing Street during the prime minister's evening meal, having left India so quickly that he was still in tropical kit, the rapport was instantaneous. Churchill was about to leave for another summit with the Americans, this one at Quebec (the Quadrant Conference). As he himself described it in his memoirs, he decided on the spur of the moment to add Wingate to his party, even arranging for Wingate's wife to be collected from her home in Scotland and put aboard the prime ministerial train on its way to a rendezvous with the *Queen Mary* on the river Clyde.

This remarkable decision caught Brooke (who had already poured cold water on the idea of a Leese-Wingate combination to run the war in Burma) completely by surprise. The CIGS had been briefed on the first Chindit operation by participants even before Wingate reached England, and he saw Wingate himself on the afternoon of August 4 (before Wingate's meeting with Churchill). Listening to Wingate's account of the operation and his plans for the creation of a vastly expanded Chindit force that would gut other army units in India of key personnel and much equipment as well as preempt much of the available airlift, Brooke decided—at least according to his postwar recollections—"that the results of his form of attacks were certainly worth backing within reason." Expecting to confer again with Wingate on his return from Quebec, Brooke was astonished when he boarded the prime minister's train later that evening to discover Wingate was aboard and was also bound for Quebec. He immediately put his finger on Churchill's motivation: "It could only be to bring him over as a museum piece to impress the Americans. There was no other reason to justify this move."[18]

However charismatic and inspiring he was to some, Orde Wingate had never, until Chindit I, commanded in action a force larger than a platoon. And Chindit I had suffered massive losses for little result—indeed, had Hartley not sensed that there was public relations mileage in the operation, it might well have gone unnoticed and certainly would not have produced the earthquake that now ensued. Churchill needed success in north Burma to neutralize the damage that failure to facilitate American goals there might cause in areas he really cared about—such as the Mediterranean. The prime minister's own strategy for the war against Japan had already been articulated and would remain unwavering for another year: amphibious operations across the Bay of Bengal aimed at retaking Singapore, the only objective whose reconquest by British arms would restore the prestige lost in 1941 and 1942. But this would have to await the release of British assets from the European war. Meanwhile, the Americans had to be satisfied that the British were serious about defeating the Japanese in Burma. The latest debacle in the Arakan and bilious reports from Stilwell (who characterized the British, rather puzzlingly, as "pig fuckers") obviously had produced American doubts about whether the British were willing—or able—to be effective where Washington felt it counted. What better way to refute these doubts than by producing the intense, compelling young brigadier whose unorthodox tactics had bested the allegedly invincible Japanese in the jungle that, everyone now said, was their natural environment? Whatever the shortcomings in his knowledge of the actual state of affairs in the Burma theater, Churchill knew passion and commitment when he met it. He had seen a flash of it from Wingate over dinner in 1938; he certainly saw much more at another on August 4, 1943. Brooke had gone straight to the heart of the matter—Wingate was taken to Quebec to impress the Americans. If his ideas involved disrupting units and formations across India, that, in Churchill's mind, was a very secondary consideration, believing as he did that the Indian military establishment was so mired in "lassitude and inefficiency" that it was contributing little to the war in any case.[19]

Nonetheless, the slenderness of the evidence upon which Churchill's conversion to the "Chindit solution" for the north Burma problem was based is startling. In his arguments with Wavell and Auchinleck in 1941 and 1942, he had Ultra intelligence on his side, however optimistically he may have interpreted it. In August 1943, he had only a back-channel copy of Wingate's report, written to buttress the case for more and bigger Chindit operations; his embarrassment at yet another British defeat; his distaste for the Indian Army (he had, after all, once been a British service officer in a good cavalry regiment); his concern with American perceptions—and his personal contact with Wingate, who had an undeniable knack for impressing those he needed as patrons. He certainly had no sense of how Chindit I had looked to some participants. One officer from the Gurkha Rifles (a group with distinct reservations about Wingate) noted, "We did not expect to see any press reports of the expedition. We were wrong, there were banner headlines, about Wingate's expedition had done this and that. We had achieved nothing. We had been kicked out by the Japs."[20] Auchinleck, to whom, as commander-in-chief, India, Wingate's report went officially—long after Amery got it to Churchill—commented in his covering letter to it, "Long Range Penetration Groups must be considered in their proper perspective [which is] an effect on the enemy's conduct of the main battle . . . [they] should be few in number and as small in size as is consistent with the achievement of this object."[21] Brooke, too, thought Wingate's ideas were useful "within reason." It was, however, too late. On the day Auchinleck signed his cover letter, Wingate was already in Quebec and about to be gifted with the largest "private army" of World War II.

The pressures of alliance politics and the need to cultivate an image of British military success obviously were paramount in Churchill's embrace of Wingate (Churchill also took Wing Commander Guy Gibson, VC, of "Dam Busters" fame with him to Quebec for precisely the same reason), but by the time he came to discuss the whole episode in his memoirs, his perspective had changed rather dramatically. The structure of *Closing the Ring* was dominated by the great Allied conferences, the mounting of Overlord, and the Italian campaign. In November 1950, Churchill indicated to his syndicate of advisers for his writings that he could spare only 3,000 words for Burma.[22] He used very few of them on the Chindits. Pownall, who knew Wingate from his time as chief of staff in Southeast Asia Command between 1943 and 1944 (and who had confided to his diary in October 1943 that Wingate was a "nuisance . . . a genius in that he is quite mad . . . can see no good except in his own chosen path"[23]), drafted a chapter for Churchill called "South East Asia Command," which summed up Chindit I pithily: "Wingate had penetrated Burma with a small force. . . . Losses had been severe and, operationally, the operation had brought no results."[24] Another of Churchill's assistants, Denis Kelly, a wartime Indian Army officer decorated for gallantry in Burma, was even harsher about Wingate. Churchill's "attention was so concentrated on crushing Hitler that he could not focus on the other war in the Far East," he later recalled, "but he sensed that the Americans felt we were not pulling our weight and consequently despatched Wingate . . . as a gun toting flamboyant cowboy who could appeal to the Americans of the Middle West. Few of us in the Indian Army will forgive Wingate for deserting and slaughtering his men."[25]

Perhaps because Churchill's syndicate contained powerful critics of Wingate or perhaps because he himself had begun to have second thoughts about the results of his impulsive decision to play Wingate as a card in the complex game of alliance politics, *Closing the Ring* is very vague about Chindit I and the background to Wingate's appearance at Quebec. Pownall's text vanished in favor of a description of the prime minister's meeting with Wingate at 10 Downing Street on the eve of his departure for Quadrant. Thereafter, Wingate is mentioned several times as Churchill discusses the conference but never in a very prominent way. He—and the war in Burma—then disappear for some 500 pages. The reader of Churchill's account gets no real sense of how dramatic and, in many ways, bizarre was the solution Churchill produced at Quebec to the problem of satisfying the Americans that the British would fight in north Burma.

That solution did not comprise merely Wingate and his plan for using a vastly expanded Chindit force to clear the Japanese from north Burma. It also included a restructuring of the theater far more drastic than anything Churchill had done in Cairo in 1942. There, he had altered the boundaries of Middle East Command and changed both the theater commander (and his chief of staff) as well as the army commander. At Quebec, his dissatisfaction with India Command led to the creation of an entirely new theater—South-East Asia Command—based in India and responsible for operations in Burma and beyond, including the planning and mounting of the amphibious operations Churchill hoped would carry the Union Jack back to Singapore.[26] To head the new theater, Churchill choose Admiral Lord Louis Mountbatten, then chief of Combined Operations and a member of the British Chiefs of Staff Committee. Mountbatten was a quite junior admiral, regarded with reserve by his more senior brethren and as a lightweight by Brooke, who took care to appoint as his chief of staff the thoroughly experienced and competent Henry Pownall (then languishing as Jumbo Wilson's successor in the backwater of Persia and Iraq Command).

What made SEAC so badly structured as to be barely workable, however, were the deformations necessary to reassure the Americans about the continued British commitment to clearing north Burma. In practice, this came down to building Stilwell into its structure at several different levels. He was named deputy supreme commander (and, predictably, soon found he disliked Mountbatten). He remained commanding general of the U.S. Army's China-Burma-India theater, in which capacity he reported directly to Marshall in Washington. He also remained chief of staff to Generalissimo Chiang Kai-shek (whom he naturally disliked intensely), another position in which he stood outside the SEAC structure. Finally, he commanded the Northern Combat Area Command (NCAC), the American-Chinese force inching into north Burma, trailing behind it a new road intended to tie into the old Burma Road as soon as the inconvenience of the Imperial Japanese Army was removed. The multiplicity of responsibilities assigned Stilwell were beyond any single individual, and so Stilwell focused on NCAC, relying on deputies to handle matters in Delhi and Chungking. The real point of the whole illogical structure was to position Stilwell to act as a watchdog and check on SEAC, which, in the American view, had as its primary mission the restoration of the overland connection with China lost because of British military failure in 1942.

The Quebec conference resulted in the most radical changes imposed by the prime minister on the conduct of military operations in any theater during the course of the war. India Command was cut out of future military operations. At the same time, it was left with the herculean task of retraining the army that SEAC would use as well as the job of constructing and maintaining not only the logistic infrastructure for the Burma campaign and the airlift to China but also the base structure for the amphibious strategy that was really what Churchill wanted from SEAC. The new theater supreme commander was junior in rank not only to Auchinleck but also to many of the generals, admirals, and air marshals who would be his subordinates—as well as being burdened with a deputy whose job it was to manipulate SEAC to American purposes. (One has only to compare the roles of Air Chief Marshal Sir Arthur Tedder, Eisenhower's British deputy at Supreme Headquarters, Allied Expeditionary Force [SHAEF], to Stilwell's role in SEAC to see how different were the alliance politics of the war against Japan from those of the war in Europe.) Finally, the prime minister's enthusiasm for unorthodox approaches was given free rein in the use made of Wingate. The American Chiefs of Staff were as impressed by the Chindit leader as the prime minister was (another example of Wingate's talent for impressing those whose backing he needed). He arrived in Quebec a brigadier who had conducted—at great cost—a single raid into Japanese-held territory. He left a major general with a commitment that his Chindit force would became a small corps with its own dedicated air component supplied by the Americans. Churchill, playing a very weak hand whose cards were defeats and retreats, had scored a remarkable success: he had convinced the Americans that the British were serious about the Burma campaign. (Brooke, although more skeptical about it all, was definitely not adverse to seeing the Americans satisfied, at least for the moment, about north Burma—like the prime minister, he was focused on the possibilities in the Mediterranean.)

The costs of the Quebec arrangements were heavy, however, and they were paid in India. There, a series of fundamental changes were in progress, changes that would produce a renaissance in the Indian Army and victory in Burma. Two men were crucial to this transformation: Auchinleck and Slim. One of Wavell's last acts, as noted, was to sack Irwin from command of Eastern Army. Wavell's plan was to replace him with General Sir George Giffard, a British service officer who had spent the first part of the war commanding in West Africa. Giffard was a stolid, reserved officer, without an ounce of charisma but with considerable ability. He and Slim, very different types, achieved immediate rapport. But Giffard's stay at Eastern Army was brief. The creation of SEAC brought in its train the setting up of an army group to command all of SEAC's land forces. Giffard moved up to Eleventh Army Group, and Slim took over Eastern Army, soon to be renamed Fourteenth Army. Writing after the war, Slim recalled his own rendezvous with destiny: "As we drove out to Barrackpore [Eastern Army HQ], I watched an army commander's black-and-red flag fluttering over the bonnet of the car, and wondered where I was really going."[27]

Wherever Slim was going, it was the Indian Army that would have to take him there. Despite the creation of SEAC, the war in Burma was still the Indian Army's war. In the months between Wavell's departure and Mountbatten's arrival, the transformation of that army had begun to gather a momentum quite unrecognized in London. In his waning days as commander-in-chief, India, Wavell had appointed a committee to report on how to improve the fighting quality of the infantry and boost army morale. The Infantry Committee, chaired by the deputy chief of the General Staff in Delhi, sat during the first two weeks of June 1943. Its report stressed the need for sounder and lengthier training adapted to jungle warfare in Burma. It also suggested that the numerous doctrinal solutions to the problem of fighting the Japanese produced by various units, from battalion through division, should be replaced by a single doctrine, promulgated by army headquarters and taught by the training divisions, whose establishment it recommended.[28] All of this, in retrospect, seems obvious enough. In mid-1943, it was, in practice, a call for revolutionary change. Serendipitously, the moment for change was ripe.

In his eruption of anger at the Indian Army in May, the prime minister had finally paid close enough attention to realize that the breakneck expansion for which he had hitherto called had ballooned that army while diluting its quality drastically. "It bears no relation to the splendid old time Indian units," he told Amery, without any indication that he understood his own responsibility for this development.[29] A cap was finally put on Indian Army expansion. The total strength was now set at fifteen infantry and two armored divisions. When Auchinleck took over from Wavell, therefore, not only did he have a blueprint from the Infantry Committee (in whose deliberations he had been involved) but he also had the advantage of dealing with a stable army structure. Auchinleck understood the need to move rapidly. To reinforce army headquarters, he thought about bringing Slim to Delhi as chief of staff. Fortunately, Slim became the Fourteenth Army commander instead, but Auchinleck brought another experienced and able Indian Army officer to Delhi, a man whose role was to be absolutely crucial. Major General Reginald Savory's command of the 23rd Indian Division in Assam had been marked by an attention to training and by Savory's production of two long memoranda on jungle warfare and patrolling. As Auchinleck's inspector and then director of infantry, Savory played an overlooked but vital role in shaping the new Indian Army that Slim would lead.[30] In Wavell's final "Despatch" (written after he had moved on to the viceroy's palace), he lamented, "My experience is that our staff system and system of command is too cumbrous."[31] However true of much British Army structure that may have been, there was nothing lethargic about the pace of change in Indian military affairs in the second half of 1943. Two training divisions were quickly set up, and under Auchinleck and Savory at GHQ and Slim at Fourteenth Army (supported by Giffard), myriad changes were set in train: matters of doctrine, training, troop welfare, pay, leave, and medical care were all taken vigorously in hand.

This renaissance owed little to Churchill and Brooke (indeed, there is little evidence they paid much attention to it), something to Wavell, and most to the leadership of a trio of remarkable Indian Army officers—Auchinleck, Slim, and Savory—who were determined to rescue their service from the low point represented by the Arakan campaign. Onto this changing military scene that autumn came first the new SEAC structure and then the impact of Churchill's success in using Wingate to dazzle the Americans.

Wingate had conceived—or perhaps had always had—a very low opinion of the Indian Army (he made an exception for its Gurkha battalions). Churchill had never been an admirer of the Indian Army, and after Malaya, Singapore, Burma, and the Arakan, he was little short of contemptuous of it, a view that can only have been buttressed by the opinions of Wingate. To put together his much enlarged Special Force, Wingate wanted only British or Gurkha infantrymen. At the time, there were only two British infantry divisions in India, and Wingate got one of them, the 70th, for his Special Force. The 70th had trained with Slim's XV Corps, and Slim considered it the best British division available. He later told the official historians quite bluntly,

> If the experienced 70th British Division which I had trained in jungle fighting at Ranchi had been used as a division in the main theatre, it would have been worth three times its number in Special Force. We are always inclined in the British Army to devise private armies and scratch forces for jobs which our ordinary formations with proper training could do and do better.[32]

To lose the best British division available as well as four Gurkha battalions would have been bad enough for Slim and Giffard. But Wingate, buoyed by his success at Quebec and armed with Churchill's incautious authorization to communicate directly with Downing Street if he encountered any obstruction, was disruptive over a very wide field, playing the role of embattled prophet to the hilt. The orthodox—and shrewd—Henry Pownall noted that Wingate

> [is] resentful of anything that is normal, deliberately runs counter to authority, demands first priority for his affairs and if he thinks he isn't getting it (and he is very touchy) threatens to wire direct to the prime minister. I don't doubt the P.M. has invited him to do so, he does it to many people including myself in the past. But Wingate, being abnormal, doesn't see that he simply cannot go about cracking that whip.[33]

It is most doubtful that Churchill ever realized that, in empowering Wingate as he had, he retarded rather than advanced the military changes necessary for victory in Burma and added another intractable complexity to a theater that already had more than enough of them.

Through all this, meanwhile, the rejuvenation of the Indian Army continued. When Slim later wrote about Giffard that he "understood the fundamentals of war—that soldiers must be trained before they can fight, fed before they can march, and relieved before they are worn out," he was criticizing not only Giffard's predecessor, Irwin, but also the whole state of affairs produced by overexpansion and politically driven operations such as Wavell's Arakan offensive.[34]

Slim's own approach to battle was built on three things: a retrained army, the potential of air supply, and a shrewd assessment of the Imperial Japanese Army. The mechanism put into place by Auchinleck and Savory was providing the first; the American-built Dakota, the military version of the redoubtable DC-3 and the most important piece of equipment in Fourteenth Army (even if much of it was American owned), was providing the second.[35] And Slim's own experience and reflection provided the third. The Imperial Japanese Army was committed to a relentless and inflexible tactical aggressiveness, and it was logistically careless. This had not been a handicap for the Japanese in Malaya, Burma, or the first Arakan campaign, where they faced shaky, inexperienced opponents and could subsist off captured British supplies, dubbed by them "Churchill supplies." The Japanese advanced to contact and then worked around their opponents' flanks; they were always attacking and searching for their opponents' communications, which, if cut or even threatened, produced a retreat—usually disorderly—by the largely road-bound British and Indian formations. With each defeat and retreat, losses of men and equipment mounted and morale and unit cohesion sank. Slim, with troops better trained and (as a result of reorganization) much lighter and less road-bound, promulgated a new doctrine for Fourteenth Army: if cut off, units would go into an all-around defense (known as "boxes") and stand fast. The Dakotas would handle resupply, and the Japanese could, like the dervishes at Omdurman, batter themselves to pieces on a new version of the old British square, while reserve formations moved up to hammer them on the anvil of the boxes.[36]

By the 1943–1944 winter, as Wingate put together his Special Force and Mountbatten's SEAC staff wrestled with the first of a long series of amphibious schemes destined never to be implemented, Slim had his new army poised for its first test. Far better trained on much sounder lines, shorn of the excessive mechanization that had so hobbled it in 1941 and 1942, leavened by the return from the Middle East of veteran units such as the 5th Indian Division, and with a very high proportion of its officers down to brigade level known personally to Slim, Fourteenth Army was a far different force than the Japanese—or Winston Churchill—realized. In addition to the revolution in training, organization, doctrine, and logistic support, Slim's army bore witness to another revolution: in the twilight of its long history, the Indian Army was increasingly officered by Indians.

The process of "Indianizing" the officer corps of the Indian Army began after World War I in tandem with the concessions to Indian nationalism embodied in Britain's 1919 Government of India Act. Progress was very slow—many of the Indian Army's British officers were convinced that Indian officers could never develop the command skills needed to effectively lead their men. By the time India went to war, of the army's 4,424 officers, only 396 were Indian, and those were largely in subaltern ranks or were medical officers.[37] What really changed the rate at which Indians were commissioned was, of course, the open-ended expansion program adopted in the summer of 1940, at the same time the British Army was growing rapidly and unable to provide large numbers of junior officers for India. The only way to find the officers needed was, therefore, to commission more Indians. Auchinleck, in his first tour as commander-in-chief, India, strongly supported this and laid down what he saw as the necessary corollary: "Equal treatment, regardless of colour."[38] From that point on, the number of Indian officers steadily grew, and though equal treatment was not easily attained, considerable progress had been made by the time Auchinleck returned to GHQ in mid-1943 to again add his powerful support to the process. Savory, too, who played a crucial role under Auchinleck, had been a strong supporter in prewar days of commissioning Indians. And after one episode in which an Indian officer posted to Fourteenth Army headquarters was gotten rid of by midlevel staff officers, Slim made it especially clear to every unit and formation that such an episode would not occur in his army again. By the war's end, the Indian Army carried some 43,000 officers on its rolls, of whom 14,000 were Indians, and by that time, they were commanding up to brigade level.[39]

Churchill's attitude toward Indian politics is too well known to require comment here. His view of the Indian Army was, as noted, similarly jaundiced. He remembered the 1857 mutiny too well and distrusted Indian units, unless commanded by British officers and brigaded with British units to guarantee loyalty. It is one of the greatest ironies of his career that policies adopted in order to fight on in 1940 made the demise of the Indian empire virtually certain. GHQ, India, recognized by 1942 that postwar independence was a goal cherished by most of its soldiers. Six months after Slim's great victory in Burma, Auchinleck observed, "Every Indian officer worth his salt is today a nationalist."[40] In the rapidly changing wartime structure of the Indian Army lay the key to the speedy termination of the Raj after its last great military triumph.

In 1943, however, all this was in the future. There is little indication that Churchill fully grasped the significance of the changes in the Indian Army set in motion by the decisions taken in 1940. He wanted success in Burma and expected it from Wingate, not from the work of Auchinleck, Savory, and Slim. Nonetheless, it was the Indian Army he so mistrusted and its officers who were a closed book to him that produced the first glimmering of light in the East and in the Arakan, where failure had prompted him to embrace Wingate.

The Japanese plan for the 1943–1944 dry-weather season called for a preemptive attack on the British base area in the Imphal plain of eastern Assam, the jumping-off point for any British counteroffensive into Burma. (Increased Japanese sensitivity to the vulnerability of their frontier with British India was perhaps the most important result of Chindit I.) This operation had two parts: a preliminary strike in the Arakan to draw in British reserves and then an attack on the Imphal plain and its road link to the railhead at Dimapur. The Arakan operation would be mounted by the Japanese Twenty-eighth Army (a reinforced division, with another moving up behind it—some 30,000 men). The attack would fall on the 7th Indian Division, commanded by Major General Frank Messervy, whose Middle East experience had accustomed him to difficult situations. The Japanese assumed that, attacked from the flank and rear, the Indian formation would collapse into retreat as it had in the past, leaving behind the expected Churchill supplies. When the Japanese launched their attack in February 1944, however, only the first part of the operation went according to plan. "The Japanese main column walked through my brigade in a dense column 8 abreast in the darkness and early morning mist. We caught the supply column and rearguard and destroyed it. The main column made no attempt to help it and carried straight on," wrote one Indian Army brigadier.[41] The Japanese had lost none of their skills at infiltration—nor the logistic carelessness that now turned obsession with attack into ruin. Although its headquarters was overrun, Messervy's division neither collapsed nor withdrew.

The crux of the battle was the defense of the division's support base, called the Admin Box, by a medley of combat and support units. The Japanese hammered at it, but the improved fighting skills of the British and Indian units defending it and the supplies sustaining them showered down by the Dakotas turned the Japanese assault into a killing ground on which the legend of Japanese invincibility was destroyed. Some 5,000 of the 7,000-strong Japanese strike force died as Slim moved up reserve formations to relieve the siege of the Admin Box and pulverize the attackers. Years before while a student at the Indian Staff College at Quetta, Slim had been criticized by an instructor for a tactical solution that involved "using a sledge hammer to crack a nut." His reply foreshadowed what he did in the Arakan: "Sir, have you ever seen a nut that has been cracked by a sledge hammer?"[42] He had created in the Arakan the paradigm for the much greater struggle opening in Assam.

The battle of Imphal, which opened in March and lasted until the shattered Japanese Fifteenth Army withdrew in June, was the most complex battle handled by a British Army commander during the war. Sprawling across a front that stretched for over 500 miles from the Arakan to Dimapur, it was tied together by the Dakotas that made it possible for Slim to switch formations from one battlefield to another and by his own grasp of all the pieces on the intricate chessboard of the theater. But the fundamentals were simple—Slim met the Japanese attack by slowly pulling back the three Indian divisions of his IV Corps to the edge of the Imphal plain, where they stood, supplied again by the tireless Dakotas. Slim allowed the tenacity exhibited by Japanese commanders in pursuit of an objective, regardless of the

"Bill" Slim speaking with a Gurkha rifleman near the front in Burma, 1944. The road is one of the better parts of his line of communications. (Courtesy Imperial War Museum, image no. SE 2952)

logistic or tactical situation, to destroy Fifteenth Army as it tried desperately to prevail against well-trained troops, effectively commanded, adequately supplied, and backed by superior artillery and airpower. In the end, the Japanese lost 53,000 of the 84,000 men they committed. It was the most shattering victory yet won by a British general—and, unlike Compass, no Rommel lurked in the wings to redeem failure.[43]

Amid all this, the force Churchill had given Wingate was launched on Operation Thursday (Chindit II). It had been originally envisioned as opening the way for Fourteenth Army to advance (although in Wingate's view, Special Force troops would retake north Burma, with the inferior Indian Army units simply mopping up behind them). Once Slim decided that he would meet the impending Japanese offensive on ground of his own choosing, however, Special Force was launching itself into an operation without a clear objective. Canceling Thursday was not an option: nearly a sixth of the best infantry units in the theater were already committed to it, and the

American reaction if the British reneged on an operation Washington had underwritten heavily—and saw as a pledge of British commitment to retaking north Burma—did not bear thinking about. Nor was Wingate, brandishing his "special relationship" with Churchill, about to move quietly to the margins. A few days after Special Force began its "fly-in" to airheads deep inside Burma, Wingate gave a demonstration of just how perceptive Pownall had been about him. In a "personal" signal to Churchill on March 22, 1944, Mountbatten stated that, "in view of your instructions that Wingate be allowed to communicate direct with you in certain circumstances," he was passing on a message from Wingate asking for four additional Dakota squadrons for Special Force (which already had its own dedicated American air component). Wingate then went on to complain of "distorted accounts" and to demand, "Let the truth be told about what has happened and is happening." Mountbatten's appended comments were that he, Air Chief Marshal Sir Richard Peirse (the theater air commander), and Giffard had no idea why Wingate thought he needed four more squadrons but that Giffard and Slim warmly endorsed more transport aircraft for the theater as a whole. Mountbatten concluded the message rather mildly: "I do not understand what Wingate means by 'distorted accounts' and 'let the truth be told' because full and accurate accounts of the fly-in of his force have already been given by competent British and American observers."[44] It was probably this signal that led Brooke to note in his diary, on March 23, "Wingate is now wiring direct to the PM. . . . It looks as if the strain of operations had sent Wingate off his head."[45] Two days later, Wingate was dead, killed when the American aircraft on which he was traveling crashed.

In August 1944, Churchill, speaking in the House of Commons, referred to Wingate as "a man of genius who might well also have become a man of destiny."[46] Perhaps a better summary of this strange man was penned a few weeks later by Brigadier Bernard Fergusson, who had commanded a column in Chindit I and a brigade in Chindit II: "I think he really was a genius. . . . He was thoroughly hated by almost everybody. He loved making enemies and lived on intrigue. . . . He had no instincts of charity or kindness at all. . . . In a word he was mad."[47]

Without Wingate's fiery, demanding presence to keep it in the center of the picture, Special Force, perhaps inevitably, drifted to the margins of the theater. Its application against the communications of the Japanese Fifteenth Army, as Pownall noted in a draft that he prepared for *Closing the Ring* (which Churchill did not use), ran up against the peculiarities of Japanese logistics: "Their diversionary effect was not so great as had been hoped. The enemy withdrew nothing from the Imphal front and only one battalion from Stilwell's."[48] In the end, as befitted the circumstances of its birth, Special Force was assigned to Stilwell's NCAC, where his Chinese-American force followed by American road builders was still inching south against tenacious Japanese resistance. By the time the last of Special Force was withdrawn, exhausted, in July, it had written an epic of courage and endurance, but its contribution to the decisive victory Slim won at Imphal was marginal and certainly fell well short of Churchill's hopes in August 1943. The measured verdict of the official historians, however much resented by Wingate's partisans, seems just: "Special Force was a military misfit; as a guerrilla force it was unnecessarily large and, as an air transported force, it was too lightly armed and equipped either to capture strongly defended vital points or to hold them against attacks by forces of all arms until the arrival of the main forces . . . in spite of the fortitude and gallantry of the . . . troops, the results achieved were not commensurate with the resources diverted to it at the expense of the 14th Army."[49]

Churchill was central to launching Wingate and the Chindits into the center of the Burma campaign. It is interesting to note how soft are the echoes of this in *Closing the Ring*. Churchill had allotted a mere 3,000 words to the crucial year of the Burma campaign. He wrote a vivid description of his meeting with Wingate at Downing Street, but thereafter, Special Force and its leader fade from the narrative. Pownall produced a draft chapter with some trenchant assessments of both Chindit expeditions, but Churchill chose not to use them. The Japanese attack in the Arakan in February 1944 gets a paragraph, Imphal little over a page. Although two corps commanders are mentioned by name, Slim is not. The Fourteenth Army is never mentioned by name (a fact the veterans of the Forgotten Army noticed and Slim brought forcibly to Churchill's attention). The launch of Chindit II gets as much space as all the Fourteenth Army's battles, much of it devoted to Churchill's telegram to Roosevelt describing the fly-in of the Chindit brigades. His brief account of Wingate's death—"With him a bright flame was extinguished"—is considerably less fulsome than his House of Commons tribute.[50] No further space is given the Chindits, nor is there any assessment of their impact.

The one intervention Churchill made in Slim's sprawling battle was over the use of transport aircraft. Mountbatten and Slim had to constantly juggle Dakotas to move two divisions from the Arakan to Assam, sustain Special Force, and support Stilwell. The only way to do this was to borrow from the large pool of American transports dedicated to the China airlift. This situation led to problems with Washington. Feeling that there would not have been a north Burma campaign if he had not had to satisfy the Americans, Churchill told Mountbatten, "Let nothing go from the battle that you need for victory. I will not accept denial of this from any quarter, and will back you to the full."[51] Unlike in his equally adamant stand against crippling Alex's campaign for Anvil, Churchill prevailed on this issue. But, of course, the Americans wanted success in north Burma.

Churchill's perfunctory and detached account of the war in Burma in 1943 and 1944 faithfully reflects his priorities. He did not want to fight there but rather to craft an amphibious strategy that would reclaim Singapore. North Burma was a problem in alliance politics that Wingate was supposed to alleviate. Churchill was very candid about this both to his inner circle in London at the time and later in his memoirs: "We of course wanted to recapture Burma, but we did not want to have to do it . . . across the most forbidding fighting country imaginable. . . . I wished, on the contrary, . . . our whole British-Indian Imperial Front would . . . advance across the Bay of Bengal."[52] In fact, during the months that Slim won in the Arakan and Imphal, Churchill was pursuing this objective in a bitter confrontation with his Chiefs of Staff, who wanted a "Pacific" strategy based on Australia. To this unreal argument over strategic options for which the British lacked the resources, Churchill devoted an entire chapter in *Closing the Ring*, more than he devoted to a year of fighting in Burma.

The rebuilding of the Indian Army and Slim's Arakan and Imphal victories were demonstrations of the aggressive determination and imaginative leadership Churchill had always called for and whose lack he so frequently lamented. But those qualities were being displayed by an army he had always undervalued and in a campaign he had never wanted to fight. His embrace of Wingate (unlike his resuscitation of Hobart in 1940) represented not so much an understanding of Wingate's highly unorthodox (and only partially workable) ideas as a recognition, which Brooke saw clearly, that here was a trick pony to dazzle the Americans. Brooke, although not as detached as the prime minister, was not really focused on Fourteenth Army's campaign either. It is doubtful if either man ever fully realized that the greatest British feat of operational maneuver, not only of the war but of the twentieth century, had been the work not of Monty or Alex but of Slim. But such, in 1944 and 1945, would be the case.

8

Three Victories

In midsummer 1944, Britain was approaching the end of its fifth year at war. Mobilization of people and resources had already peaked and henceforth could only inexorably decline. The British public—rationed, bombed, and overworked—was bone weary. During the 1944–1945 V-1 and V-2 attacks, observers would note that the resilience shown in 1940 and 1941 during the Blitz was no longer there. The key decision makers were tired as well. Churchill was in his seventieth year, and the diaries of his doctor and of the CIGS are full of references to his mounting fatigue and irritability. (At that point, no one, almost certainly including the prime minister himself, would have imagined that his final retirement lay a decade in the future.) Britain had three armies in the field: the Second, the British component of Montgomery's Twenty-first Army Group in Normandy; the Eighth, with Alexander's forces in Italy; and Slim's Fourteenth in Burma.

In the remaining months of the war, the Second and Eighth would exhibit both the continuities with the army of 1940 and the very considerable changes brought about by the pressures of war, and Brooke, Monty, and Alex would become field marshals. The Second Army, however, would play a steadily smaller role in the campaign in northwest Europe as the American forces grew massively in numbers and assurance—and as Britain finally ran out of men. The Eighth Army played a major role in Italy to the end, spearheading the final offensive there, but the theater had been marginalized, first by Overlord and then by the American insistence on Anvil. Alexander would become theater commander when Jumbo Wilson succeeded Dill in Washington, but by then, the high hopes Churchill had had for the campaign had evaporated. Indeed, there was little Churchill could do to influence the British Army's final European campaigns, much as he may have wanted to do so.

In Burma, the picture was very different. Slim and Fourteenth Army, whose British component had dropped by the campaign's end to only about 13 percent of the total force, would carry out the finest operational maneuver of the war by a British general. And in a campaign he had never wanted to fight, Churchill would deliver his last effective intervention in military affairs during World War II.

The Second Army, commanded by one of Montgomery's most self-effacing protégés, Lieutenant General Sir Miles Dempsey (another of Monty's staff college students), was made up of units that for the most part had spent years training in Britain.[1] To leaven these troops with battle experience, three Eighth Army formations had been brought back from the Mediterranean in the 1943–1944 winter: the 50th and 51st (Highland) Infantry Divisions and the 7th Armoured Division. Despite this—and Montgomery's replacement of many officers in the home-based formations with his own choices—the British Second Army's performance in Normandy has been regarded by many subsequent commentators as disappointing. Some of this criticism, of course, is bound up with Montgomery's controversial personality and the increasing anger of the Americans at his conduct of the battle, all of which spilled over into a postwar historiographical controversy only now beginning to give way to more balanced analysis. There is, however, much more to the story than Monty.

The veteran Eighth Army divisions had unquestionably lost something of their edge. One treatment of the Normandy campaign argues that Second Army was a tired army, especially among the ranks of its desert veterans.[2] Certainly, none of those divisions distinguished itself in Normandy. Francis Tuker was later to say of the 50th Division that it "learnt nothing, ever, even after years in the Desert," and 7th Armoured's performance in Normandy was so weak that Dempsey eventually sacked its commander, his chief staff officer, the divisional artillery commander, and the armored brigade commander. (The commander of XXX Corps, in which 7th Armoured served, went as well.[3]) A New Zealand observer, Brigadier James Hargest, another desert veteran with bitter memories of the shortcomings of British armor, attributed its failings in Normandy to the "cavalry mentality" of some armored units. But the problem, as is now clear, went deeper than a stubborn infantry division, a badly handled armored unit, a weak corps commander, or the horsey background of some armored regiments.

The British Army at the beginning of the war has been described as slow and reactive. Similar charges were still being made in 1944. It might seem as if nothing much had changed, but actually a good deal had. British equipment had improved, although it continued to be inferior to that of the German forces in some respects. For example, the workhorse Shermans that made up the bulk of the armor were no match for German Panthers and Tigers, and other, humbler items of equipment were also inferior, especially the weapons carried by the average infantry company. Rifles, machine guns, and antitank weapons that were not as effective as those of the Germans tended to slow down the pace of British operations, reinforcing a tendency created by the training system. Most of British Second Army in Normandy was composed of units that had been trained in Britain for years. As a young platoon commander observed in retrospect, "We lacked two things: comprehensive and imaginative training and personal experiences of battle. . . . Too many junior officers did not think for themselves and persistently relied on the narrow teaching of the Battle Schools, whose dogma had assumed the proportions of holy writ."[4]

In fact, the training system and the doctrinal confusion that it reflected may have been as responsible as defects of weaponry or cumulative fatigue for the performance of Monty's army in Normandy and, indeed, on to the end of the war. The most careful study of how the British Army at home actually trained between 1940 and 1944 concludes that it was "disgraceful" that "infantry tactics ultimately advanced little from the standards of 1916"—that is, before the tactical revolution that produced the very effective army of 1918.[5] If infantry tactics were weak, tank-infantry cooperation was initially no better, and much of this is attributable to Montgomery himself.

Brigadier Harold Pyman (the brigadier General Staff for training in Twenty-first Army Group), who had served in the desert, produced a good pamphlet that provided training guidelines for tank-infantry cooperation. But its dissemination was canceled when Monty arrived home to take over the army group from General Sir Bernard Paget. In its place, another pamphlet appeared in February 1944, based on one produced by Eighth Army. Montgomery had already informed the vice chief of the Imperial General Staff (VCIGS), Lieutenant General Sir Archibald Nye, that he regarded Eighth Army practice as the new doctrinal norm for the British Army. The VCIGS rejected this claim, but the only person who could have overruled Monty with actual effect on his behavior was Brooke. The CIGS, feeling that Montgomery was the greatest British soldier in several centuries, never did so. All this might have mattered less if Montgomery had been correct. Unfortunately, he was not. As the historian of British Army training has observed, "It became the doctrine of 21 Army Group that in combined tank and infantry attacks, the tanks should lead and infantry should follow. Three years of experience had taught everyone, except apparently Montgomery and his lieutenants, that such tactics were ruinous. Montgomery's intervention ensured that the lessons of BATTLEAXE would have to be learned all over again in Normandy."[6] Pyman might well have suffered the fate of many officers whose work Montgomery disliked, but his previous connection with Eighth Army gave him a soft landing. His job was abolished, but Monty moved him to XXX Corps as brigadier General Staff, and eventually, he became Second Army chief of staff. Although largely overlooked in most discussions of Montgomery's career, this episode seems to merit the castigation delivered by one historian when he denounced "Montgomery's conceit, arrogance and vanity, his supreme faith in his own qualities and tendency to deny merit in those who were not of his circle."[7] Francis Tuker, a man obsessive about good training, offered a similarly dismissive judgment: "If Monty is the best commander we had in the last war, then our standard could not have been very high."[8]

Many armies have compensated—or tried to—for inadequacies in matériel, training, and doctrine by a ruthless use of manpower. But this option, used by the Red Army in 1941 and 1942, was simply not available to the British Army. And even had the will to expend men prodigally been present, the men were not. By the end of 1942, the flow of recruits to the army was insufficient to keep formations on active service up to strength. Before the end of the post-Alamein pursuit, two divisions had to be "cannibalized" in Eighth Army. In 1943, that army was chronically short of replacements, and four divisions' worth of formations were broken up in Britain. The assumption that the war would end by December 31, 1944, accepted for planning purposes in late 1943, gave the army only 150,000 new recruits for that year. By the eve of D day, yet more units had been broken up in the United Kingdom, and six "Lower Establishment" divisions (formations already trimmed drastically in men and equipment) were reduced to mere cadres. Even so, the War Office could only promise to cover expected casualties in Montgomery's army group for the opening phases of the campaign. By the end of 1944, Monty had cannibalized two more divisions (one of them the veteran but disappointing 50th). Ultimately, the manpower problems, the equipment issues, and the difficulties created by faulty doctrine leading to the wrong sort of training all pointed to the necessity of fighting manpower-efficient set-piece battles—"crumbling" battles (or "colossal cracks," in Monty argot) that took advantage of the firepower available to the Royal Artillery and the Allied tactical air forces. Fortunately for Montgomery, this was the sort of battle with which he was most comfortable.

It seems doubtful that Churchill was aware of the doctrinal and training issues that affected the Twenty-first Army Group's readiness for Overlord. The months between Monty's return to Britain and D day were also the months that saw the Anzio operation, the intensification of the Anglo-American argument over Anvil, the quarrel over Pacific strategy with the Chiefs of Staff, and Diadem. Churchill was no doubt aware of Montgomery's changes to the plan he had inherited and aware also of Monty's program of public appearances (intended as morale boosters), which, at one point, he suggested were being overdone.[9] But the only recorded clash between the prime minister and Montgomery was on the very eve of D day, when Churchill, startled by the enormous number of vehicles that would be landed in the first three weeks, had Ismay raise the matter with Montgomery. The subject was certainly discussed by Monty and Churchill when the prime minister dined at Twenty-first Army Group headquarters on May 19. Montgomery's version of events—that he refused to allow Churchill to speak with his staff about the issue and threatened resignation, whereupon the prime minister backed down, tearfully—must, like many of Monty's recollections, be taken with a cellarful of salt.[10] Churchill had "teeth versus tail" arguments throughout the war with senior generals. He was at his weakest in dealing with logistics, although accurate about the general tendency of the British Army to overinsure itself in this area. If Churchill had little direct input during the tense countdown to D day, his role became much more important once the battle was joined in Normandy, stalemate settled over the bridgehead, and Montgomery came under heavy criticism from his numerous American and British enemies.

The argument over Montgomery's conduct of the Normandy battle has generated a considerable literature that has focused more on personalities than on the nature of the army he commanded and the problems it faced.[11] Forced to fight on the offensive against a skillful and determined opponent in terrain that aided the defense, the British Army confronted a situation in which infantry casualties were bound to be high—an extremely serious matter for an army running out of infantry replacements. Tank-infantry cooperation, which might have limited casualties, was poor, a result of defects in doctrine and training; not until well into the campaign did experience begin to compensate for the shortfalls in pre–D day training, some of which, as has been shown, were directly attributable to Montgomery him-

Churchill and Montgomery in Normandy, July 1944. While there was never the warmth between these two that marked Churchill's relations with Alex, Monty and the prime minister needed one another. (Courtesy Imperial War Museum, image no. B 7767)

self. The set pieces that characterized the Montgomery approach to battle, although not capable of producing a spectacular breakthrough, imposed an unbearable cumulative attrition on the Germans. Monty was, as Tuker acidly noted, a 1918 general in many ways, but his version of attrition was for the most part carefully and intelligently managed to produce victory at an acceptable cost. No one was more conscious of the need for this than the prime minister, who understood that Britain's diminishing influence in the Grand Alliance would erode even more rapidly if the drain of casualties made the British Army unable to bear a significant share of the fighting in northwest Europe.

For that reason, the whole discussion about whether Montgomery's position was in jeopardy in July 1944 is rather artificial. Certainly, stalemate seemed to settle over the beachhead, and successive British and Canadian attacks moved the front forward only slowly and at considerable cost. The RAF, led by the deputy supreme commander, Tedder (who had come to dislike Monty intensely), was deeply critical. The Americans had never liked Montgomery to begin with, and now they found a new cause for resentment in British press coverage of the beachhead fighting (although why the American generals should have been surprised that British newspapers focused on British efforts has never been explained). Churchill himself, tired and increasingly apprehensive about the future, roundly abused "your Monty" to Brooke on several occasions (and he even berated Alex to his cabinet at one point).[12]

Yet the reality was that Montgomery was the only British general who had become a household name in Britain, that his soldiers had confidence in him, that Brooke stood firmly behind him, and that Churchill understood all this.[13] The prime minister also understood the manpower problem. When Monty's major assault east of Caen (Goodwood), launched on July 18 behind 7,700 tons of bombs and using all three available British armored divisions, did not produce the decisive result he had incautiously seemed to hint at, his critics redoubled their assault. Goodwood, however, provided a perfect example of why Montgomery's style of battle was now inevitable. In a subsidiary operation by II Canadian Corps, named Atlantic, the infantry suffered 76 percent casualties; the accompanying armor, operating much as British armor did, lost only 7 percent. The three British armored divisions lost some 400 tanks—all replaced within forty-eight hours—but only suffered 521 casualties. Although British infantry took World War I–level casualties on occasion, they simply could not afford to do so often (nor could the manpower-poor Canadians). A cautious, firepower-intensive approach to battle was absolutely inevitable at this point, and that being the case, there was in fact no British general better suited to conducting it than Monty. Even if Goodwood and other operations in Normandy revealed how faulty British doctrine still was, the army with which Montgomery would fight the rest of the war was now past major structural and doctrinal change.[14] All that could be done was to use it cautiously, husbanding its strength to maintain a credible British military contribution. Wellington had once quipped that his army was Britain's last. In Montgomery's case, that was literally true. Churchill, gusts of anger apart, knew this perfectly well. He had noted in his biography of Marlborough that the maddeningly cautious Dutch "Field Deputies," who controlled a sizable contingent of the duke's Anglo-Dutch army, were very conscious of the need to conserve the dwindling resources of their nation. Monty played a similar role in 1944 and 1945, and this made him much safer than perhaps anyone, including himself, fully recognized at the time.

A great deal of energy has been expended in praising the German defenders of Normandy and contrasting their undoubted tactical skills with the shortcomings of the British (and Canadian and American) troops who ultimately defeated them. Here, two observations seem pertinent. Few of the British formations were combat experienced; most of the Germans were—and the British were attacking. The three-to-one ratio usually sought by attackers over defenders represents a reasonably good measure of which role presents greater challenges. Moreover, behind many of the criticisms of British military performance in Normandy and elsewhere, there seems to lurk the curious assumption that a victory through firepower is somehow less of a victory than success in a straightforward *mano a mano* infantry contest. A young British platoon leader in Normandy who later reflected on this argument sensibly observed,

> It is, of course, very much in [the Germans'] interest to encourage the theory and myth that, although superior as fighting men, they were beaten only by numerically superior forces and firepower. In my experience this was not so. In many attacks the prisoners we took outnumbered our attacking force. . . . Unlike us, they rarely fought at night. . . . Where we patrolled extensively, they avoided it. . . . If our positions had been reversed, I doubt if they would have performed better than we did . . . some Wehrmacht formations were extremely . . . competent but many were not. . . . Some . . . fought with fanaticism but most did not.[15]

American, British, and Canadian hammer blows as well as Hitler's refusal to countenance any withdrawal and the logistic failings that the German army's admirers prefer to ignore led to the progressive collapse of the German front in August. Mobile warfare suddenly became possible—largely because there was a vacuum behind the German front, into which British and American armor surged. Patton's dash eastward to Lorraine is much celebrated by American military historians, but the drive from Normandy to Brussels by Dempsey's armor was equally dramatic. Like Heinz Guderian's rapid passage in the opposite direction four years earlier, the challenges were more logistic than tactical. And it was logistics that caused both Patton and

Dempsey to pause for breath (and fuel, ammunition, repairs, and replacements) at the beginning of September.

During that pause, Montgomery made his greatest mistake as a commander, fumbling away the last chance for his army to make a decisive contribution to the shape of the subsequent campaign. The great port of Antwerp, logistically vital, fell to Major General Pip Roberts's 11th Armoured Division without resistance. Its port facilities were unscathed, but Antwerp lies 80 miles from the sea. To make use of the port, the Allies needed to control the banks of the river Scheldt from Antwerp to the North Sea. The chance to do that cheaply—and to cut off the 100,000-strong German Fifteenth Army—was there, albeit briefly. Roberts, however, like Second Army as a whole, was looking east, toward a pursuit to the Rhine. Moreover, his men were tired, his tanks were in need of maintenance, and his fuel supply was low. He would later blame himself for not having grasped the situation, but the real responsibility lay with Montgomery and Dempsey.[16] At Montgomery's level, however, other considerations predominated.

On September 1, 1944, Eisenhower assumed direct command of his army groups, ending Monty's tenure as Allied land forces commander, a role that had become increasingly nominal since the Normandy breakout. Simultaneously with Ike's taking direct command, Montgomery was made a field marshal. The baton, however, was no compensation for his diminished role. Neither Monty nor Brooke could ever accept that Eisenhower's decision to assume direct command was the inevitable consequence of the shifting balance of forces in the alliance. To them, it was a dreadful mistake—putting the conduct of the campaign into the hands of a man who, however charming, had never commanded any formation in battle. They would persist for months in their attempts to reinsert a ground forces commander between Eisenhower and the army group commanders, to the vast annoyance of the Americans. But in early September, Monty's piqued vanity, coupled with his sense that Britain's strength and manpower alike were nearing exhaustion—"The British economy and manpower situation demanded victory in 1944. No later."[17]—led him to direct his attention eastward to the Rhine and Ruhr.

Getting across the Rhine might mean victory in 1944—a victory in which Twenty-first Army Group would play a leading role. In the heady atmosphere produced by the Normandy success, this possibility glimmered enticingly, and the problem of opening Antwerp became a secondary matter. The resulting and most un-Montgomeryesque Operation Market Garden (to seize the bridges across the lower Rhine in Holland, opening the way to the Ruhr) failed spectacularly, and Antwerp was not opened for two more months. Monty's later admission of error—itself a rare event—had a distinct air of rationalization: "I must admit a bad mistake on my part. I underestimated the difficulties of opening up the approaches to Antwerp so that we could get free use of the port. I reckoned that the Canadian Army could do it *while* we were going for the Ruhr. I was wrong."[18]

Beyond the manifest unfairness of this remark to the Canadians (with whom, Lieutenant General Guy Simonds apart, Monty's relations were never very warm), his assessment of Market Garden's failure is notable for its lack of any attention to the flaws in British Second Army's performance, flaws that reprised themes from the past four years.[19] Despite approval by the apostle of "grip" and "balance," the Market Garden plan displayed some of the incoherence of Ritchie's Aberdeen operation in the desert in June 1942. The grip of Monty and Dempsey on the battle is not very evident. Lieutenant General Brian Horrocks, whose XXX Corps was to drive over the "airborne carpet" to Arnhem, does not seem to have been much more effective. His leading division, Major General Alan Adair's Guards Armoured Division, demonstrated the same weaknesses in tank-infantry cooperation that had characterized its pre–D day training (and that had, of course, been reinforced by Monty's ill-advised doctrinal fiat on the subject). Montgomery had actually formed a poor opinion of Adair in England before D day but had been unable to remove him in the face of the Guards establishment, the most formidable of the British Army's regimental tribes. The belief underpinning Market Garden—that the Germans were at their last gasp—was false; so, therefore, was the assumption that Second Army could make a lightning thrust to Arnhem on a front that was only one Sherman tank wide. The mistaken focus on getting across the Rhine, moreover, led to the necessity for a bitter two-month struggle to open Antwerp in brutal infantry fighting that cost yet more irreplaceable British and Canadian rifle company casualties. Thereafter, Montgomery's British and Canadian divisions would fight a series of grinding battles (Operation Veritable) to close up to the Rhine, then cross it at Wesel in Monty's last great set piece (Operation Plunder, on March 24, 1945), and drive across north Germany to the Baltic against incoherent but often bitter resistance in the war's dying weeks. But after the autumn of 1944, the Twenty-first Army Group and its commander were no longer able to play the role that Monty and Brooke sought and the prime minister had hoped for.

Churchill, Brooke, and Montgomery argued at the time and in postwar publications that Eisenhower's "broad front" strategy imposed an unnecessary constraint on Allied progress and that a concentration on the left, where Twenty-first Army Group threatened the Ruhr (the heart of German war-making power), was the strategically correct course of action. Behind this lay not only Churchill's desire for a role for the British Army commensurate with the position he was trying to maintain for Britain in the alliance but also Brooke's belief that the Americans simply did not understand strategy. Working against the British leaders, however, were the increasing self-confidence of the Americans, their determination to fight the war their way (not to mention their intense dislike of Monty), and the brute facts of manpower. The fighting in February and March, as Twenty-first Army Group hammered its way to the banks of the Rhine, cost the equivalent of thirty-five to forty battalions of infantry. There were no replacements for these men—only expedients such as shuffling naval personnel into static infantry roles. By the time Monty crossed the Rhine, there were about 870,000 "British" troops in Eisenhower's command (many of them, of course, Canadian and some Polish)—and roughly 2.5 million Americans.[20] Even under Montgomery's (usually) cautious management, the British Army was slowly melting away. Its equipment and tactical skills had certainly improved, even if they were still inferior to those of their opponent in some respects. (There is no evidence to indicate that the British were in any appreciable way inferior to their American allies except, perhaps, in mobility.) Yet what Monty's army could not deliver in the war's closing months was the political leverage that came with dramatic battlefield success, such as Eighth Army had given the prime minister in 1942 and 1943. In the circumstances, that was beyond reach.

Addressing the officers of Eighth Army HQ at Tripoli in February 1943, in the wake of the success at Alamein, Churchill told them, "You have nightly pitched your moving tents a day's march nearer home."[21] The Eighth Army's tortuous road led it to Italy, where its war would end triumphantly on the battlefield, but its victory would be shadowed by a sense of what might have been. Unlike Montgomery, however, who for decades argued the superiority of his operational concepts, the ever-tactful Alexander avoided such confrontation not only during the war but to the end of his life.

The crucial decision that governed the last act in Italy had, of course, been taken in July 1944, when the Americans refused to reconsider Anvil—ironically, four days after Kesselring had decided that he would need to withdraw farther and faster. Alexander's forces, stripped of seven divisions (as well as the amphibious trooplift that would have given him operational flexibility), simply lacked the punch to break through the last but very formidable barrier—the Gothic Line in the Apennines, which stood between them and the plains of northern Italy. (Brooke also blamed Alex and Leese for not conducting the pursuit to the Apennines well enough.) Stalled before the Gothic Line, Alex's armies would remain there until spring. By the time that they mounted their final offensive in April 1945 (Operation Grapeshot), the command structure had changed—and the secondary nature of the theater had been repeatedly underlined.

The death of Sir John Dill in November 1944 had set off a major reshuffling in the Mediterranean. Wilson was sent to Washington, and Alexander (a field marshal since September) became theater commander. To replace him, Churchill suggested Mark Clark—even though the bulk of the troops in what was once again designated Fifteenth Army Group were British, Commonwealth, and empire formations. If the prime minister thereby hoped to keep American interest in the theater from dwindling further, he was doomed to disappointment. Clark, avid as ever of renown, certainly agreed with the idea, developed by Alexander's staff, of Fifteenth Army Group's breaking into the Po Valley and then swinging to the right through the "Lubljana gap" into central Europe—especially since he saw himself leading the thrust. The problem was that Clark's advocacy was not important in Washington, where Marshall remained adamant in his concentration on northwest Europe (Brooke was also skeptical about a drive to Vienna). For the last six months of the war in Europe, the British forces in Italy would be commanded by an American who disliked British generals, distrusted the fighting qualities of British troops, and was focused on a triumph for American arms. The U.S. Fifth Army passed into Truscott's capable hands. Eighth Army also changed commanders. Leese—who had come to dislike Clark so much that he did not want a common boundary with Fifth Army—left for South-East Asia Command, to become Mountbatten's ground forces commander.[22] Lieutenant General Richard McCreery succeeded him and would lead Eighth Army into its last battle. Harding, anxious to hold a field command (which was essential for further promotion), moved from Alexander's side to take over XIII Corps when Kirkman, ill and worn out by dealing with Clark, under whose Fifth Army the corps had operated for several months, returned to the United Kingdom. Alex's final chief of staff was Lieutenant General Sir William Morgan, who had been his BGS when he commanded the British rear guard at Dunkirk.

The shuffling at the top was matched by changes in the order of battle.

The Canadian Corps left over the winter to join the First Canadian Army in Twenty-first Army Group. A British division also left for Montgomery's command. Churchill's decision to intervene against the Communist resistance in Athens in December 1944 moved several of Alexander's divisions to Greece. The drought of replacements, particularly for infantry rifle companies, persisted, and the wholesale conversion of antiaircraft and even RAF ground staff to infantry roles brought into units men with minimal training for their roles and often indifferent morale. Not surprisingly, desertion continued to plague Eighth Army. There was also very serious concern about the morale of the Polish Corps as news of the Yalta agreements spread—although these troops in fact would fight effectively to the very end.[23] Allied air- and firepower superiority was unchallengeable, however, which was fortunate because Alexander's armies had nothing like the three-to-one superiority for which attackers aimed: his seventeen divisions (one of them a Brazilian cavalry division of minimal use) faced twenty-three German divisions, most at full strength, with a reasonably good supply situation, albeit little fuel. The sophisticated deception efforts employed to mislead the Germans about Allied intentions were seldom more needed.

In its last battle, Eighth Army, still a microcosm of the empire (three British and two Indian divisions plus the New Zealanders; the South African armored division had been loaned to Truscott), displayed considerable tactical skill, producing first a breakthrough and then a vigorous exploitation. Clark had not intended for Eighth Army to play anything but a subsidiary role, but by the time Truscott's weather-delayed attack got rolling, McCreery had already decisively breached the Gothic Line. Thus, in April 1945 in the campaign's waning moments, the 6th Armoured Division enjoyed the sort of exhilarating cavalry pursuit that Dempsey's armor had experienced the preceding August. McCreery opened with the Eighth Army signature artillery barrage: 1,020 guns, with 2 million rounds of ammunition available to them. But there was also tactical innovation—a crucial flanking attack across a marshy lake with the infantry carried forward on tracked amphibious carriers. It was a fine professional finish for Eighth Army after twenty months of bitter and often frustrating combat. "There have been few campaigns with a finer culmination," Churchill would later write.[24] But the hopes he had invested in the campaign had run into the sand months before. The prime minister had always looked to military performance to help maintain Britain's position in the alliance, and in fact, that performance had quite perceptibly improved since the frustrations of 1941 and 1942. But the improved British military performance had turned out to mean surprisingly little to the Americans.

The first two Victoria Crosses won in the Eighth Army's last battle were awarded to sepoys of the Indian Army, which began its war against the European Axis in the Western Desert with O'Connor's Compass offensive and finished it triumphantly on the river Po. As the Italian campaign wound down in the shadow of the final German collapse, that army was consummating in Burma the sort of spectacular operational success for which Churchill had always yearned—but in a theater to which neither he nor anyone else was, by that point, paying much heed.

The Japanese Fifteenth Army—beaten, diseased, and starving—recoiled from Imphal in July 1944, with monsoon rains completing its misery. The theater's equivalent of winter quarters, the monsoon months had always been closed season for campaigning. Slim, however, intended to maintain his army's momentum by continuing operations throughout the monsoon. When the dry weather began in the autumn, he wanted Fourteenth Army poised to break out into the plains of central Burma, where his superiority in armor, artillery, and tactical airpower would have full play. The monsoon pursuit would also keep his campaign going at a time when, as he knew full well, there were still hopes in London and at SEAC headquarters that a primarily amphibious strategy would replace the slog in Burma.[25]

As the rainy season wore on and Slim's men squelched forward, however, it became more and more apparent that Fourteenth Army's campaign was all that SEAC and London were going to be able to mount during the 1944–1945 dry season. The long, bitter argument between the prime minister and the Chiefs of Staff had finally come up against the reality that the British, in the absence of an end to the European war, simply did not have the resources to undertake the preferred amphibious strategy. Indeed, without American help, they did not have even the assets in certain crucial categories (such as transport aircraft) to sustain the strategy that circumstances had forced on Churchill and Mountbatten: the overland reconquest of Burma from the north, the one option the prime minister had always hoped to avoid. As Fourteenth Army ended its monsoon campaign and prepared for the destruction of the Japanese Burma Area Army in central Burma followed by an advance on Rangoon, it was therefore unfortunate that American interest in the campaign waned sharply even as a SEAC reorganization complicated its operations—or, rather, it would been unfortunate if the army commander had been anyone but Slim.

American interest in Burma had always been limited to its role in supporting China's war effort. By the autumn of 1944, north Burma was in Allied hands, and Stilwell's road—the Ledo Road—had linked up with the old Burma Road. Stilwell himself had departed, to general relief, and his hats were distributed to three American generals. From that point on, however, American interest in Burma plummeted. Slim would conduct his 1944–1945 campaign under the shadow of the possible loss of the American air transport squadrons needed to make it possible. Another shadow was cast by the reorganization that removed Giffard—who had supported Slim and ridden him on a light rein—and replaced Eleventh Army Group with Allied Land Forces South East Asia (ALFSEA), commanded by Leese. This lit a fuse that would explode in May 1945. Although a Monty protégé, Leese was a general of, at best, average attainments. He also, Slim noted later, had a great deal of "desert sand" in his shoes. He brought with him much of his staff from Eighth Army (something Alex shrewdly cautioned him not to do) and the ALFSEA atmosphere became suffused with the assumption that Eighth Army was the metric by which matters should be judged. This also meant that the headquarters to which Slim reported was heavily British Army, though Fourteenth Army was as heavily Indian Army. The almost predictable result was described thirty years later by one member of the team that wrote the official history of the war in Burma (himself a former Indian Army officer): "Mountbatten got a bad bargain when he swapped Giffard for Leese. Bill was quite frankly insubordinate in his dealings with Leese, but he was an expert in knowing when he could be insubordinate—and for 'could' you could substitute 'should.' "[26] The same officer put his finger on the root cause of the antipathy: "In common with many British Service Generals [Leese] disliked the Indian Army."[27] Slim began his final campaign with a precarious supply situation and an unhelpful (to say the least) superior whom he would do his best to keep at arm's length—and then there was the Imperial Japanese Army.

He had one immense asset—his own remarkable army, which had become, in the words of two recent students of the campaign, "a cold, efficient killing machine."[28] The Indian Army's renaissance between 1943 and 1944 was a very complicated process, and a great many individuals contributed, from Auchinleck and Savory through formation commanders to staff officers who toiled on doctrinal pamphlets and training schemes. But Slim put the capstone in place when he led Fourteenth Army to victory, first in the Arakan and then at Imphal. That army now had the collective sense of mastery on the battlefield that all of history's great fighting forces develop. It was, moreover, an increasingly Indian force at every level. The British manpower crisis afflicting both the Second and Eighth Armies in Europe was felt with particular intensity in Burma. In June 1944, Fourteenth Army's British infantry battalions were some 3,500 men short; by October, the figure was 10,000. Some of this was due to a War Office decision to shorten the period of overseas service that qualified for repatriation from five years to three years and eight months.[29] Clearly, Slim's two British divisions (one composed of two brigades instead of the normal three) were now wasting assets. In the 1944–1945 campaign, the 2nd and the 36th Divisions would be gradually phased out and returned to India, and British battalions in Indian divisions would be swapped out as well for Indian units. By the time Rangoon fell to Fourteenth Army, its British strength was down to 13 percent of the total. Moreover, the Indian units and formations were increasingly officered up to field grade by Indians. This transformation augured the end of the Raj even more surely than did the fall of Singapore. None of this, of course, registered on the prime minister's personal radar, though it undoubtedly would have agonized—and enraged—him if it had. It was also past altering. Slim had a superb weapon at hand, and he meant to reconquer Burma with it. Recalling the mood of his army after Imphal, he wrote later, "Some of what we owed we had paid back. Now we were going on to pay back the rest—with interest."[30]

Recognizing that the European war could now not end until the spring of 1945, delaying the release of assets for SEAC's war, Churchill and the Chiefs of Staff, in early October, once again postponed SEAC's amphibious plans until after the 1945 monsoon. By that time, Slim and his staff were already elaborating the plans for Operations Capital (the destruction of Burma Area Army in the plains around Mandalay) and Extended Capital (the drive to Rangoon, also known to Slim's staff as SOB—Sea or Bust). The Japanese had pulled back behind the Irrawaddy, which was up to a mile wide in places and with its only bridge down (blown by Slim during the 1942 retreat and unrepaired by the Japanese). To get across, Slim resorted to large-scale operational deception. His XXXIII Corps would simulate the main advance, closing up to the river, putting bridgeheads across, and threatening Mandalay from the north. Meanwhile, IV Corps—now commanded by Lieutenant General Frank Messervy—observing radio silence and screened by a complex of deception measures known as Operation Cloak, would approach the river well below Mandalay, cross, and strike for the communications center of Meiktila. With that in hand, the entire Japanese position in central Burma would be unhinged. It was an operational design as bold as the German Ardennes thrust of 1940—and equally as risky. As the design began to take shape, Slim was finally given some recognition: he was knighted at Imphal on December 15, 1944, by Wavell, acting for the king. (He was still only a lieutenant general, two and a half months after Monty and Alex had become field marshals.)

A remarkable fact about the battle that was about to begin in central Burma was how little it resonated in London. Churchill, tired and preoccupied, sent no telegrams of the sort that Monty and Alex received before major offensives. Brooke's diaries contain none of the anxiety-wracked entries that preceded Anzio or Overlord. In truth, London's interest was not much greater than Washington's in what had become almost a private war between Fourteenth Army and its Japanese opponents. Much more surprisingly, Leese, his patronizing attitude deeply resented at Fourteenth Army, was nearly out of the loop as well. "I always went on the principle that my plans, as long as they carried out the general directions I had received from above and did not require more resources than I had under my control, were my business and did not require anybody's approval or sanction," Slim later declared.[31] As Capital was planned, Slim's mind was already leaping ahead to the exploitation phase, the drive to Rangoon and the sea known as Extended Capital. Brigadier Michael Roberts, who was both an official historian and Slim's researcher for his memoir, *Defeat into Victory*, later told Ronald Lewin, Slim's official biographer, "In a casual conversation I once asked Bill when he first thought of Meiktila. . . . His answer was he didn't think he did think of it first: the whole Fourteenth Army staff was continually thinking about it and he didn't know who first said Meiktila. The result of their joint thinking and discussing was Extended Capital."[32] The degree to which Slim was ignoring Leese at this point is indicated by Roberts's further remark that "Fourteenth Army HQ's behaviour in not telling ALFSEA about Extended Capital until the last moment was of course most reprehensible but Slim was not taking any interference from any higher formation. He mystified and misled ALFSEA, the British Press and the Japanese."[33]

Slim's design, backed by the flexible and improvisational logistics that had become his army's hallmark, worked brilliantly. Mesmerized by XXXIII Corps's crossings north of Mandalay, the Japanese were totally caught off guard by IV Corps's leap across the Irrawaddy on the night of February 13, 1945. For the subsequent push to Meiktila, Messervy had chosen D. T. "Punch" Cowan's 17th Indian Division. (Slim later said, "If you wanted an 'up guards and at 'em' show you couldn't do better than give it to Punch."[34]) Reorganized after Imphal from its jungle-fighting "light" configuration into a motorized infantry division, the 17th proved its adaptability by swiftly moving across the country and taking the lightly defended linchpin of Burma Area Army's communications system. Reinforcing formations were immediately flown in to consolidate Cowan's position. Surprised, off balance, and with their communications—and with it, their command and control—fatally compromised, the Japanese nonetheless reacted with their usual ferocious determination, throwing in counterattack after counterattack and destroying themselves as they had at the Admin Box and Imphal. By the end of March, Burma Area Army had shot its bolt and begun to retire. SOB jumped off on April 11, with 300 miles to go and a one-month window before the monsoon was expected to begin. Using two very aggressive divisional commanders, Cowan and Pete Rees of 19th Indian Division, Messervy launched a drive that, had anyone noticed, ranked with anything the British or American armies had done in Europe. Tank-infantry spearheads drove over or around the disorganized but still furiously resisting Japanese; every 50 miles or so, engineers hacked out an airstrip. Then the Dakotas appeared, and the drive went on. What the Japanese could no longer do, however, an early monsoon did. Cowan's division was only 50 miles from Rangoon—and not far from the Sittang, where it had almost been wiped out three years before—when torrential rains and flooding halted it. But the Japanese had already left Rangoon, which was officially "liberated" on May 3, 1945—in the shadow of the German surrender in Italy and with VE day looming. This guaranteed that Fourteenth Army's victory was barely noticed in London.[35]

There was one aspect of the 1944–1945 campaign about which Slim had not been candid when he claimed that he felt entitled to plan and carry out operations as long as they did not require "more resources than I had under my control." He did not control anything close to enough air transport. Only the Americans could make up the difference. Churchill's papers for 1945 contain no references to Slim, but on one occasion, the prime minister intervened with decisive effect to sustain SOB.

Waning American interest in Burma had an immediate impact on Slim's campaign when, in December 1944, three squadrons of American transports were suddenly shifted, at the behest of Chiang and his new American chief of staff, Major General Albert Wedemeyer (previously Mountbatten's deputy chief of staff), from supplying Fourteenth Army to transferring to China the American-trained Chinese divisions that had served under Stilwell in NCAC. This move cost Slim two to three week's time, he later estimated, through loss of logistic support. It also reduced pressure on the Japanese in north Burma, allowing them to transfer units to face Fourteenth Army. Brooke, in the only reference to Slim's campaign in his diary between January and May 1945, noted sadly but accurately, "The transport aircraft belong to the Americans, and . . . the reconquest of lower Burma does not interest them at all. All they want is north Burma and the air route and pipeline and Ledo road into China. They have now practically got all these, and the rest of Burma is of small interest to them."[36]

London, preoccupied with other things, was very slow to respond to Mountbatten's appeal for support in getting the squadrons back. Mountbatten sent his chief of staff, Lieutenant General Sir F. A. M. "Boy" Browning (who, after commanding the airborne component of Market Garden, had replaced the ailing Pownall) to reinforce his plea, and finally, on January 18, the Chiefs of Staff asked the Americans to send the planes back. On January 21, Wedemeyer agreed to return two of the three squadrons. The lost weeks were, it turned out, the difference between reaching Rangoon overland and being caught short by the monsoon.

On the eve of Extended Capital, the Americans almost did it again, for they were planning to shift the lone U.S. combat formation in north Burma to China at the expense of Slim's logistics, just as Slim was about to drop overland supply and rely on the by now desperately overworked Dakotas to sustain Messervy's drive to Rangoon. Appeals from SEAC to Washington fell on deaf ears. Then, on March 30, less than two weeks before Extended Capital's start, the prime minister intervened. He had lost the struggle over Anvil the preceding year, but this time, he meant to win his battle for a British victory. He took his argument directly to Marshall, by that point the real manager of the American war effort, and put his case with total candor:

> As General Marshall will remember from our talks . . . we greatly disliked the prospect of a large scale campaign in the jungles of Burma, and I have always had other ideas myself. But the United States Chiefs of Staff attached the greatest importance to this campaign against the Japanese, and especially to the opening of the Burma Road. We therefore threw ourselves into the campaign with the utmost vigour. . . . I therefore feel entitled to appeal to General Marshall's sense of what is fair and right between ourselves, in which I have the highest confidence, that he will do all in his power to let Mountbatten have the

> comparatively small additional support which his air force now requires to enable the decisive battle now raging in Burma to be won.[37]

Jumbo Wilson was told to pass this to Marshall "orally and unofficially," but it was clear that Churchill was calling in a debt. It worked. The prime minister in effect embarrassed Marshall into agreeing to leave the vital air transport squadrons with Fourteenth Army until Rangoon fell or June 1, whichever came first. Churchill, of course, had never met Slim—to him, it was Mountbatten's battle. But it was Slim with his iron determination and unbreakable confidence in himself and his army, in the face of repeated threats from his allies to his rickety supply system, that drove the campaign on, pulling Leese, Mountbatten, London, and ultimately Marshall after him. Years later, commenting on the draft of the official history volume covering 1944 and 1945, Slim mildly observed that the equipment with which he mounted the assault crossing of the Irrawaddy would have been considered "ludicrously inadequate in any other theater." He might have said the same of his resources throughout the campaign. He went on to point out some other features "not always noticeable in British battles of the Second World War": no overwhelming ground superiority; a front of enormous width (200 miles); the creative use of surprise and deception; and the use of operational maneuver (that is, the thrust to Meiktila).[38] Slim's pride in his army was understandable—he and it had first broken the opposing army and then virtually annihilated it in a devastating pursuit. Only O'Connor's Western Desert Force had a comparable victory—and the opposition Slim faced was more formidable by far. He was, of course, also contrasting Fourteenth Army's style with the Montgomery pattern. This swipe at Eighth Army, from a usually generous man, may reflect the fact that, as Rangoon fell, Leese tried to sack him.

This incident was one of the strangest episodes in a campaign that was full of them. It also did not become general knowledge for many years. Slim drafted and then elected not to use an account of it for his *Defeat into Victory*. The official history likewise passed over the episode in silence.[39] Only with the publication of Ronald Lewin's official biography in 1976, after Slim's death, was a fuller (but still not complete) account available.[40] Mountbatten was alive when Lewin wrote, and his role consequently remained unclear, as to some extent it still does.[41] What is clear are the facts that Slim recorded in his draft: Leese arrived at Slim's headquarters, "and, after congratulating me on the success of Fourteenth Army, he abruptly said he had decided to

Slim at Fourteenth Army Headquarters, March 1945. The finest British general since Wellington, Slim built the Fourteenth Army into one of the great fighting forces of the war. The forceful expression faithfully mirrors Slim's determination, as those who clashed with him discovered to their cost. (Courtesy Imperial War Museum, image no. SE 3311)

make a change in its command."[42] Slim was shocked, as well he might have been—army commanders are not usually dismissed in the aftermath of spectacular victories. He noted in his diary, "Sack. 15:30," then announced he would retire.

His calmness may have been shrewdly calculated. His staff and senior commanders were outraged by the action of "an affected silk-handkerchief-waving guardsman," as one of them described Leese. Slim's chief of staff, Brigadier J. S. "Tubby" Lethbridge, was prepared to lead a sit-down strike at Fourteenth Army headquarters to force the issue into the open, even at the cost of a court-martial. A corps commander and two division commanders threatened resignation. Auchinleck, the professional head of the Indian

Army who was then in London for consultations, took up the subject with Brooke. The CIGS had spent years cleaning up the broken crockery left by Monty's gaffes, but he deeply admired his protégé. Leese was a different matter. Brooke had also paid enough attention to the Burma campaign to know who had won it. At this point, Mountbatten, if he was behind Leese's actions, sharply reversed field. Leese was told he had overreached, and ALFSEA's (notoriously tactless) chief of staff was sent to tell Slim it had all been a mistake. Meanwhile, Brooke had gone to Churchill. Leese later told Lieutenant General Sir Philip Christison (a British Army officer who had been named by Leese as Slim's successor): "Brookie went to Churchill and told him the Indian Army wouldn't fight without Slim. 'Who sacked Slim?' said Churchill. 'Leese' said Alanbrooke [*sic*]. 'Well, sack Leese.' "[43] Shortly thereafter, Slim went home on leave. When he returned, he was a full general and Leese's successor at ALFSEA—despite telling Churchill, at his first meeting with the prime minister, that the remaining British troops in Fourteenth Army would be voting Labour in the impending general election.

Obviously, Leese, quite possibly encouraged by Mountbatten, had decided to "put Slim in his place."[44] It was the climax of a long history of tension between Fourteenth Army and ALFSEA, on one hand, and between two armies whose officers had very different professional traditions (and social origins), on the other. In Burma, the Indian Army had finally won the great victory that effaced the bitter memories of 1941 and 1942—and Slim had outmaneuvered not only the Japanese but also the condescension of the regular British Army.

Apart from insisting that the Americans not be allowed to cripple Fourteenth Army's supply system and backing Brooke's decision on Leese, Churchill paid little heed to Burma in 1944 and 1945. This was reflected in the way the triumphant end of that campaign was treated in his memoirs. The great battles of 1944, as noted previously, were covered in *Closing the Ring* (mostly in Pownall's prose), but neither Slim nor Fourteenth Army were mentioned by name. Veterans of the Forgotten Army took note, particularly the veteran who was now a field marshal and CIGS (despite an attempt by his predecessor, Montgomery, to block his appointment because he was a former Indian Army officer). Slim spoke to Churchill, once again prime minister, about the omissions, and Churchill took the point. In *Triumph and Tragedy,* Burma got the best part of two chapters, and the "famous Fourteenth Army, under the masterly command of General Slim,"[45] was duly acknowledged. But the narrative was Pownall's, and Churchill highlighted only his (very significant) interventions to safeguard Fourteenth Army's all-important stock of Dakotas. There was a rather pro forma feel about it all, especially when contrasted to the treatment of Alex's campaign. There was no tribute to the Indian Army—indeed, there was no recognition that the "famous Fourteenth Army" was a largely Indian Army in which British troops were by that point far outnumbered not only by Indians but also by Africans.

Through the war, Churchill had questioned the aggressiveness of British Army commanders and what he saw as their consistent logistic overinsurance. Slim had the former in abundance—"he simply exuded determination," one of his divisional commanders recalled[46]—and never had the luxury of the latter, producing instead a miracle of logistic improvisation that used everything from Dakotas to elephants and porters with headloads. He held a beaten army together on the longest retreat in British military history, helped rebuild it into the victorious force of 1944 and 1945, and demonstrated the ability to switch from jungle combat to mobile warfare without missing a beat. As he later told the official historians with considerable understatement, the design for Capital and Extended Capital showed that his army's "grand tactics of battle . . . were rather bolder than usual."[47] He had a shrewd appreciation of the strengths of subordinate commanders, switching from the cautious infantryman Geoffrey Scoones (who had managed the defense of Imphal) to the cavalryman Messervy to lead IV Corps in the Meiktila "masterstroke." His impact on those who served under him was striking, as witnessed by the reaction of his staff and commanders to Leese's attempted coup. Much further down the chain, a young British soldier recalled, forty years later, "the burly man who came to talk to the assembled battalion . . . it was unforgettable. Slim was like that: the only man I've ever seen who had a force that came out of him."[48]

Recent historical writing has tended to see Slim's 1944–1945 campaign as foreshadowing later doctrines of "maneouvre warfare."[49] He was clearly the outstanding British Army commander of World War II and Britain's best field commander since Wellington. Yet Churchill never seems to have noticed. Writing to the Australian prime minister, John Curtin, shortly after Pearl Harbor, Churchill had noted that "so far the Japanese have only had two white battalions and a few gunners against them, the rest being Indian soldiers." Slim, unfortunately, was fighting in the wrong place and came from the wrong army.[50]

9

Winston and His Generals

The British Army went to war in 1939 handicapped in a variety of ways. Directed to focus on imperial defense for much of the interwar period, it was only at the last minute given a "continental commitment" role. It had unresolved doctrinal issues concerning the role of armor and an institutional culture that encouraged caution. Training reflected doctrine—or, rather, the arguments over it. Some equipment, based on faulty assumptions, was inadequate. The latitude allowed senior officers in training their commands introduced another complication. There had been few large-scale exercises during the "long weekend" between the wars, and the very belated decision by the Chamberlain government to introduce conscription in the spring of 1939 caused personnel turbulence just as the army went to war.

Despite all this, the British Army might well have been able to operate with considerable effect if the war had take the course that the Anglo-French alliance forecast, with Franco-British forces standing on the defensive as blockades sapped Germany's ability to support a war and then opening a careful offensive to defeat the (already weakened) German army. Instead, a brilliantly bold (almost foolhardy) conception, executed with great skill—and not a little luck—won for the Germans one of the most stunningly complete tactical and operational victories in the annals of war. The British Army survived due to the cohesion of its regular core, Gort's moral courage, German mistakes—and a miracle of improvisation by the Royal Navy.

But although it survived, the experience had been traumatic for the army. Now, virtually weaponless, that army had to reorganize, reequip (initially with weapons known to be inferior to the enemy's), and grow, absorbing a flood of conscripts—while at the same time preparing to meet invasion. It had also to cope with the arrival at 10 Downing Street of the first prime minister since Wellington in 1829 to have been a regular soldier (albeit briefly and forty-five years before). Winston Churchill was sure he "knew a great deal about it all"—and so he did. Articulating the nation's will not only to survive but also to win, he was incomparable at presiding over a total mobilization of people, resources, and willpower. His strategic instincts were often as good as the professionals, but the correlation of weapons, equipment, doctrine, training, and leadership that produced battlefield success had moved on since his last close acquaintance with them as a battalion commander in 1915 and 1916. Administration ("logistics" to the U.S. Army) would never be his strong point (and Britain's other army, the highly professional Indian Army, evoked from him neither admiration nor sympathy). Nonetheless, it was Churchill who would determine much about the way the British Army fought World War II and, later, how that war would be perceived.

One of Churchill's major early decisions—that Britain would retain its position in the Middle East—shaped much of the British (and Indian) Army's war. From that point on, there were really three "British" armies. There was the army at home, initially struggling to ready itself to meet an invasion and then to prepare for the day it would reenter Europe. The dominating figure in this army was the able, acerbic, cautious gunner Alan Brooke, on whose mind the power and skill of the 1940 Wehrmacht was indelibly stamped. Then there was the army in the Middle East, a polyglot, multinational coalition of British, Dominion, and Indian formations, with minor allies (Poles, Free French, Greeks) added in. Until 1942, there was no dominating figure like Brooke in this army—but quite a few powerful, semiautonomous Dominion commanders and a large number of Indian Army officers. The Army's apostles of mobility had their greatest impact in this theater, where the approach to battle between 1940 and 1942 was an amalgam of what successive theater commanders felt possible, London (read the prime minister) wanted, the powerful Dominion generals were willing to do, and believers in the supremacy of the tank took to be its correct role (beliefs reinforced by the misleading early success against the Italians). Since the Middle East style did not include combined arms warfare (whereas the Germans practiced it skillfully), the stage was set for a series of disappointing battles in which the British were consistently defeated, despite an often impressive superiority in numbers. Coming at a time when the prime minister needed victories for domestic morale (and to buttress his political position) as well as to impress neutrals and the Allies, preeminently Americans and Russians, it drew the not unwilling Churchill deep into the management of the war in the Middle East, changing theater commanders twice and trying to find the right commander for the much-tried Eighth Army.

Meanwhile, there was the Indian Army, engaged in an expansion process to support the war in the Middle East that was even more complex than the British Army's. Scanted for resources and regarded with suspicion by Churchill (when he bothered to notice it at all), the Indian Army made possible British control of the huge Middle East theater, contributing more divisions until 1942 than the British Army did. But a terrible price was exacted. Overexpanded, its quality impaired by the process, and trained for one war only, it suddenly faced a second, different war in Malaya and Burma against a ferocious opponent whose threat had been underestimated and regarding whom Churchill had taken a coldly calculated risk. The result was a series of disasters. These failures confirmed Churchill's low estimate of the Indian Army (a view shared by a number of senior British Army officers), but they also were the prelude to a remarkable institutional renaissance.

The second half of 1942 was the crucial moment in the British Army's war and in its relationship with the prime minister. Brooke, CIGS since December 1941, was made chairman of the British Chiefs of Staff Committee in March, thus becoming Churchill's principal military collaborator and sparring partner for the rest of the war and giving posterity his often unfair but invaluable record. In August 1942, Brooke was able to place his protégé, Montgomery, in command of the Eighth Army and the desert war. Brooke admired Monty and thought him the greatest British general since Marlborough had commanded Britain's forces during the War of the Spanish Succession (1703–1713). Indeed, Montgomery's career would have been inconceivable without Brooke's patronage and support. In October 1942, Monty delivered the most important victory of the war from the prime minister's point of view, solidifying the Brooke-Monty grip on the British Army for the balance of the conflict. El Alamein was, in many ways, a 1918 battle of controlled attrition. But Monty did understand the integration of airpower into his battle plan (however much senior RAF officers came to loathe him). He was never comfortable with armor, exploitation, or improvisation—and took good care to avoid situations that would require those skills. But the trend of the war after the autumn of 1942 favored him. What Britain needed and what Churchill required was victory at an acceptable price, especially as British manpower dwindled from 1943 to 1945.

When Churchill later told the syndicate of assistants working with him on his memoirs that the focus from 1943 on would be conferences and not battles, he was also indicating his changed perception of the army's role. That role the Brooke-Monty army fulfilled: the lavish use of firepower to keep casualties down while delivering the victories that Churchill felt were so important to sustaining Britain's position in the Grand Alliance, which the prime minister felt was essential to his nation's future as a Great Power. That this policy was a failure (and never very realistic) ought not obscure the fact that the British Army became quite proficient at delivering those sort of victories. As long as it could fight the kind of battles it was good at, its performance was very solid and at least on a par with that of its American allies (and rivals). The structure of Churchill's memoirs, by spending more time on the battlefield in 1941 and 1942 and less thereafter, tended to obscure the transformation in the British Army's effectiveness in the second half of the war. Although the flaws in doctrine, training, and equipment—some of prewar origin, a few added by Montgomery himself—were visible to the end, the forces Montgomery and Alexander led between 1943 and 1945 did as much and performed as well as could be expected of a shrinking and increasingly weary citizen army.[1]

The able and critical Francis Tuker felt that Montgomery had not advanced beyond 1918 tactically; rather more harshly, William Slim later said he was the "legitimate descendant" of the generals of 1914 to 1918.[2] The "British" army that broke with that style of warfare was the army from which Tuker and Slim came. The Indian Army was at the end of the pipeline for equipment and British personnel. It would never fight the equipment-rich war possible in Europe from 1942 to 1945. And even if lavish supply levels had been available, the line of communications to Fourteenth Army would never have supported their movement, first to Assam and then onward into Burma. The result was an epic of improvisation, from creating cargo parachutes out of jute to wrangling elephants trains and building a fleet of river transports. But at the core of Fourteenth Army's success was Slim's belief that well-trained and well-led infantrymen were the key to victory. The institution of appropriate training based on sound common doctrine, the development of good junior leaders, the application of combined arms techniques, and a sophisticated use of air supply far beyond anything attempted in Europe, plus flexible and imaginative leadership—all these were essential to the military renaissance of 1943 and 1944 and the victories of 1944 and 1945 by an army that was, by then, overwhelmingly Indian.

Burma fit awkwardly in Churchill's narrative strategy, however, and the revitalization of the Indian Army even more so. As a result, the truly remarkable campaign there never received the attention it deserved from him, and despite Slim's very successful memoir history, a generation passed before serious historical study of it began.

The story of the British Army in World War II is also the story of the limited impact Churchill could have on how it fought, as opposed to where, under what conditions, and (to some extent) under whose command. Issues of training, doctrine, and, for the most part, equipment were really outside Churchill's purview, and in spite of the impression his minutes sometimes give, they were driven by an internal dynamic. After the early years of defeats, retreats, and evacuations, the ascendancy of Brooke and Montgomery meant a return to tactical and operational caution (reinforced by manpower concerns). Victories through firepower at an acceptable cost in lives were the aim—and the British Army delivered those (aberrations such as Market Garden apart). Churchill had hoped to parlay those victories into continuing British influence in the Grand Alliance, especially with the Americans. That this did not work out is chargeable more to the situation than to the army: even a totally, ruthlessly mobilized Britain simply could not match American resources or avoid American dominance. But its battlefield performance, if weak initially, was impressive enough at the end.

The Indian Army's performance was even more striking. From a low point between 1942 and 1943, it had remade itself by 1944 and 1945, perhaps in some ways aided by the quasi autonomy that allowed Auchinleck, Savory, Slim, and many others to get on with the business of forging a battleworthy weapon, with few interventions from above (although Churchill's fervent embrace of Wingate was a significant distraction with little payoff). No matter what amphibious return to Singapore Churchill might dream about or Mountbatten plan, the war in Burma was the war the Indian Army had, and it got on with preparing to win it, accepting whatever new structures or doctrines were necessary. It seems safe to predict that Slim's campaigns will be deemed examples of the military art far longer than any of Monty's victories.

This book began with a question: how valid were Churchill's criticisms of his generals? The evidence indicates that the problems the British Army faced were no more attributable to the inadequacies of its commanders than to inadequacies of doctrine, training, and equipment (some inherited from the prewar army, some of wartime origin) as well as the impossible situations in which it often found itself. (Of course, the failures of Cunningham, Ritchie, Percival, and Irwin were real enough, if no more real than those of many failed American commanders.) Gradually, improvement in all these areas, even if uneven and never complete, made the British Army a much more effective force, but Churchill's memoirs had no room for the detail that would have shown this. The remarkable transformation of the Indian Army, which took it from a nadir in 1943 that was lower even than the Eighth Army's in mid-1942 and made it into one of the great fighting forces in British history, was, sadly, not something Churchill ever wanted to chronicle. War for him had a political purpose, and the triumphant end of the Indian Army's war was the prelude to Indian independence.

The British Army's military performance in the twilight of Britain's power was as good as could be expected, given the situation and the nature of the instrument, whereas the Indian Army's performance was astonishing. It is ironic that Britain's indispensable war leader did not fully grasp those facts and thus did both armies something less than justice.

Notes

Prelude

1. General Sir Archibald Wavell was commander-in-chief, Middle East, 1939–1941.

2. Admiral John Byng was executed for cowardice after he failed to relieve the besieged garrison of Minorca at the outset of the Seven Years' War. If Brooke's memory was correct, Churchill's view of the Byng affair had changed. In *A History of the English-Speaking Peoples,* vol. 3, *The Age of Revolution* (New York, 1957), the text of which had been written before the war, he referred to the admiral's execution in this way: "The Government shifted the blame on to Admiral Byng, whose ill-equipped fleet had failed to relieve the Minorca garrison. By one of the most scandalous evasions of responsibility that an English government has ever perpetrated Byng was shot for cowardice" (138).

3. During Rommel's March–April offensive in the desert, two generals had been captured when their unescorted staff car blundered into a German patrol at night.

4. Kennedy's account is in *The Business of War,* ed. Bernard Fergusson (New York, 1958), 106–107. Churchill's April 28 directive is in Martin Gilbert, ed., *The Churchill War Papers,* vol. 3, *The Ever Widening War, 1941* (New York, 2001), 556–557. Brooke's contemporary diary note and postwar gloss are in Alex Danchev and Daniel Todman, eds., *War Diaries, 1939–1945: Field Marshal Lord Alanbrooke* (London, 2001), 154. Kennedy did not print his subsequent exchange of letters with Churchill. They appeared only in 1983: see Martin Gilbert, *Winston S. Churchill,* vol. 6, *Finest Hour, 1939–1941* (London, 1983), 1071. Kennedy's account is the basis for an episode in a British television production in which the prime minister is depicted, sitting at a luncheon table plentifully adorned with empty bottles, threatening to shoot generals. The unmistakable implication is that Churchill made the threat while under the influence of alcohol. Wrenched from its context and presented for dramatic impact, it is a case study in the perils of docudrama. Churchill's own memoirs are silent on the episode.

Kennedy, who held the position of director of military operations longer than any previous incumbent, was a very able staff officer who found himself in an anomalous position: throughout his tenure, real control of military operations lay with the theater commanders. The result, as Lieutenant General Sir Ian Jacob pointed out to me in several conversations, was that he had less to do than either his title or his abilities might have warranted. This may account for the waspish tone of his memoir. After retiring because of ill health in 1944, Kennedy became governor of Southern Rhodesia.

5. Sir Arthur Bryant's *The Turn of the Tide* (London, 1957) and *Triumph in the West* (London, 1959) were essentially a narrative history by Bryant (who in 1940 made a remarkably adroit transition from Germanophile appeaser to ardent Churchillian) into which were embedded selections both from Brooke's wartime diaries and from his post-war "Notes on My Life." A. J. P. Taylor perceptively characterized the result as "a mixture of arrogance and pettishness, . . . unfair to Brooke and to others"; see Taylor, *English History 1914–1945* (Oxford, 1965), 637. Churchill was deeply hurt, and his personal circle enraged, by the books. Sir John Colville, a Churchill intimate, later wrote that Brooke was the only man on whom he ever saw Churchill turn his back. Brooke—who became Lord Alanbrooke in 1946—deserves, however, to be judged not on the more spectacular outbursts in his wartime diaries (which were his personal safety valve as well) but also on the basis of his accomplishments. The study by Sir David Fraser, *Alanbrooke* (London, 1982), is a good starting place. Brooke allowed his papers to appear as they did in part because he felt Churchill's memoirs paid little heed to his role—and in part because he needed the money. There is now a reliable edition by Alex Danchev and Daniel Todman, and Brooke's papers are available at the Liddell Hart Centre for Military Archives, King's College, London.

6. Bernard Law, Viscount Montgomery, *The Memoirs of Field Marshal the Viscount Montgomery of El Alamein* (London, 1958), tells the reader much more about Monty than about the events he describes.

7. A good example of this is Eliot Cohen's *Supreme Command* (New York, 2002), 95–132. The chapter concludes with the words quoted here.

Chapter One. Legacies

1. Anthony Storr, a noted British psychoanalyst, has done the only serious personality analysis of Churchill to date, in his essay "The Man," in A. J. P. Taylor, ed., *Churchill Revised: A Critical Assessment* (New York, 1969), 229–274. Among other things, Storr argues that Churchill's almost manic level of energy derived from a lifelong struggle to keep depression at bay. The finest overview of his life is Geoffrey Best, *Churchill: A Study in Greatness* (London, 2001).

2. For example, Peter Gretton, in his *Former Naval Person: Winston Churchill and the Royal Navy* (London, 1968), argues that Churchill's fondness for "offensive sweeps" by destroyers as an anti-U-boat tactic had its roots in his cavalryman's training.

3. Winston S. Churchill, *The World Crisis,* 5 vols. (New York, 1923–1931).

4. Winston S. Churchill, *Marlborough: His Life and Times,* 6 vols. (New York, 1933–1938).

5. Winston S. Churchill, *The Second World War,* vol. 2, *Their Finest Hour* (Boston, 1949), 43.

6. This is a good point at which to note some of the more significant decorations held by British officers during World War II. The Victoria Cross (VC) was, of course, the premier award for valor. The Military Cross (MC) was given for outstanding gallantry on the part of officers of the rank of major or below; the Distinguished Service Order (DSO) was awarded either for courage just below the Victoria Cross level by junior officers or distinguished leadership by senior officers—hence the slightly cynical observation that your men could win the DSO for you, but you had to earn the MC yourself.

Lieutenant General Sir Bernard Freyberg, the formidable commander of the New Zealand Division throughout the war, received a VC and the DSO with two bars (that is, three DSOs) as well as six mentions in dispatches and nine wounds between 1914 and 1918.

7. Of the 35 divisions available to the British in 1944, 25 were infantry, but only 17 of those were field-force quality. By contrast, the U.S. Army raised some 90 divisions, the Germans about 300, the Russians 400, and the Japanese 100. "Division," of course, meant something different in each of these armies. The figures nonetheless indicate the basic poverty of Britain in what was and is still the most fundamental of all resources for war—people.

8. Brian Bond, *British Military Policy between the Two World Wars* (Oxford, 1980) is a very good survey; David French, *Raising Churchill's Army: The British Army and the War against Germany, 1919–1945* (Oxford, 2000) is an incisive analysis, to which I am much indebted.

9. Liddell Hart developed his arguments in dozens of publications, but they are perhaps best sampled in his *The Tanks: The History of the Royal Tank Regiment,* 2 vols. (New York, 1959) and in his *Memoirs,* 2 vols. (New York, 1965–1966). The latter work is a sophisticated exercise in the denigration of everyone who ever disagreed with or disappointed him. Liddell Hart's much-inflated reputation badly needs revision. There are studies by Brian Bond, *Liddell Hart: A Study of His Military Thought* (London, 1977), and Alex Danchev, *Alchemist of War: The Life of Basil Liddell Hart* (London, 1998). The whole question of the development of armored doctrine in the interwar British Army is best covered by French, *Raising Churchill's Army,* and in two works by J. P. Harris, *Men, Ideas and Tanks: British Military Thought and Armoured Forces, 1903–1939* (Manchester, UK, 1995) and "British Armour, 1918–1940: Doctrine and Development," in J. P. Harris and F. N. Toase, eds., *Armoured Warfare* (London, 1990), 27–50.

10. The development of combined arms tactics during the interwar years and their application during World War II have been described very thoroughly by Jonathan House, *Combined Arms Warfare in the Twentieth Century* (Lawrence, KS, 2001). This book is essential reading for understanding military effectiveness—or the lack of it—in World War II.

11. The phrase is the title of Field Marshal Lord Carver's 1979 Lees Knowles Lecture, published as *The Apostles of Mobility: The Theory and Practice of Armoured Warfare* (London, 1979).

12. On the eve of the war, Britain's one experimental "mobile division" morphed into the 1st Armoured Division. It had 321 tanks but only one infantry battalion and thus faithfully reflected the tank-heavy doctrines of the apostles of mobility. This contrasted sharply with the more balanced German panzer divisions, whose tank brigade was accompanied by a four-battalion rifle brigade as well as gunners, signals, and an air liaison detachment. Eventually, after much expensively purchased experience, British armored divisions would be similarly balanced.

13. Harold R. Winton, *To Change an Army: General Sir John Burdett-Stuart and British Armored Doctrine, 1927–1938* (Lawrence, KS, 1988), 229–231, has a good discussion of the imperial factor as it affected British Army structure and thinking during the interwar years. Winton's study of Burdett-Stuart is very important for understanding the interwar army.

14. The case against British manufacturers has been made most strongly in Correlli Barnett's *The Audit of War: The Illusion and Reality of Britain as a Great Nation* (London, 1986). French provides a needed corrective in *Raising Churchill's Army*. It is nonetheless remarkable that British manufacturers never managed to produce a gasoline container as good as the standard German item, christened the jerrican; jerricans were gratefully used by those British units fortunate enough to acquire some.

15. Shelford Bidwell and Dominic Graham, *Tug of War: The Battle for Italy, 1943–45* (London, 1986), 190. The observation about the staff college commandant was made to the author by Lieutenant General Sir Ian Jacob. There is, however, evidence that even though young public school boys in the 1920s and 1930s yearned to be horsed cavalry officers, they knew all too well the future would be different. Patrick Leigh Fermor, who would have a colorful war behind enemy lines, recalled schoolmates "vowed . . . practically from birth, to paternal cavalry regiments and . . . cast down by the thought that, . . . the cavalry was being motorized fast. Wheels, armour plating, nuts, bolts and caterpillar-tracks were closing in and soon, . . . there would not be a whinny within earshot"; see Fermor, *Time of Gifts* (London, 1977), 124.

16. Sydney Jary, *18 Platoon*, 5th ed. (Winchester, UK, 2003), 20. This book fully deserves the overused label "minor classic."

17. Quoted in Bond, *British Military Policy*, 68. It is interesting to note that French, in *Raising Churchill's Army*, 45–47—generally a revisionist account that seeks to explain the wartime performance of the British Army in terms of concrete problems in doctrine, organization, training, and equipment rather than in sociological terms—nonetheless also points to imaginative failures that echo Chetwode's strictures.

18. David Fraser, *And We Shall Shock Them: The British Army in the Second World War* (London, 1983), 53. Fraser retired a full general.

19. However, in judging the impact of the regimental system on how the British Army fought, it is important to note what it could mean to a British soldier. Alex Bowlby, who fought in Italy in 1944 and 1945 (a campaign as viciously demanding of infantry as the Western Front had been in an earlier war), recalled a moment when "I had never felt so conscious of my regiment as I was then. This was the way to risk one's life. There was no King and Country about it—it was the regiment. And I wouldn't have changed places with anyone"; see *The Recollections of Rifleman Bowlby* (London, 1991), 129.

20. Barnett, *Audit of War*, 190.

21. In virtually every British campaign of the war, British units fought alongside Dominion and empire formations. Canadian, Australian, New Zealand, and South African formations, most of whose senior officers were also Western Front veterans, were very heavily influenced by British patterns of organization and training as well as British doctrine. They also used British equipment, at least initially. There were obvious individual national characteristics about these forces—especially marked in the case of the Australians—but nonetheless, all had a strong family resemblance to their British model. In most cases, this made integration with British forces and service under British commanders technically easy; it was the clash in attitudes between British generals and Dominion commanders conscious of commanding distinct national formations that made for great complexity, as will become apparent in the narrative. The Indian Army, bigger than any Dominion force—indeed, larger than all the Dominion forces taken together—

and with its own history, traditions, and separate officer corps (not to mention a strong sense of its own professionalism), was yet another complication. It too drew on British patterns, but it was quite different in many ways from the British Army. This situation led to tensions between its commanders and British Army generals that were never fully resolved, which will be discussed in greater detail. Senior British officers commanded difficult coalitions before they ever had the Americans to deal with.

Chapter Two. Retreats and Evacuations

1. Winston S. Churchill, *The Gathering Storm* (Boston, 1948), 608.

2. Auchinleck, an Indian Army officer who had been called home to command a new corps forming for the BEF, took over the effort against Narvik in northern Norway and finally took the town—only to evacuate it almost immediately as the defeat in France deepened. Paget successfully extricated the largest of the two forces landed in central Norway. Colin Gubbins, who would end the war as a major general and the operational head of Special Operations Executive (SOE), led "independent companies," precursors of the Commandos, in Norway as well.

3. Churchill, *Gathering Storm*, 649.

4. David Fraser, *And We Shall Shock Them: The British Army in the Second World War* (London, 1983), 52–53. The official history is T. K. Derry, *The Campaign in Norway* (London, 1952). Francois Kersaudy's *Norway 1940* (London, 1990) is a very good account by a French scholar that does justice to the coalition dimension of the campaign, which is often overlooked.

5. Churchill, *Gathering Storm*, 667.

6. The defeat of the French army in 1940 is still a very controversial subject. A good recent summary is Julian Jackson, *The Fall of France: The Nazi Invasion of 1940* (New York, 2003).

7. Winston S. Churchill, *The Second World War,* vol. 2, *Their Finest Hour* (Boston, 1949), 65.

8. Ibid.

9. Winston S. Churchill, *The World Crisis,* 4 vols. (New York, 1927), 3:106.

10. L. F. Ellis, *The War in France and Flanders* (London, 1953), 149.

11. The minutes of the 10 P.M. meeting of the War Cabinet Defence Committee are in Martin Gilbert, ed., *The Churchill War Papers,* vol. 2, *Never Surrender, May 1940–December 1940* (New York, 1995), 147–149 (hereafter *CWP2*).

12. Churchill himself said nothing of this in *Finest Hour.* Only as the records began to open in the 1970s could the story be reconstructed. I explored it briefly in *Churchill: Retreat from Empire* (Wilmington, DE, 1984), 1–9. Churchill's official biographer, Sir Martin Gilbert, tells the story a bit diffusely in *Winston S. Churchill,* vol. 6, *Finest Hour, 1939–1941* (London, 1983). It can be tracked almost minute by minute in *CWP2*, 147–187. There is a colorful account in John Lukas, *Five Days in London: May 1940* (New Haven, CT, 1999).

13. In addition to Brooke, Adam, Montgomery, and Alexander, the two successive Eighth Army commanders after Monty, Oliver Leese and Richard McCreery, were brigadiers, as were Kenneth Anderson, who commanded the First Army in Tunisia, and Miles Dempsey, who commanded the Second Army in northwest Europe from D day to

VE day. Brian Horrocks, who became Montgomery's favorite corps commander, was a lieutenant colonel.

14. Both Brooke and Montgomery would later be very critical of Gort—Brooke in his wartime conversations and diaries, Montgomery in his postwar memoirs. Gort never held another field command after Dunkirk, although he served briefly as inspector general of training, then as governor of Gibraltar (1941–1942) and Malta (1942–1944), and finally as high commissioner in Palestine (1944–1945). None of these were sinecures. His health collapsed in Palestine, and he died in March 1946. Churchill seems never to have forgotten him. He pushed to have Gort made a field marshal (1943) and in *Finest Hour* (84) acknowledged Gort's crucial decision. The official history, published in 1953, also recognized how important Gort's actions were, but few seemed to notice. Gort was rescued from oblivion only when Sir John Colville, one of Churchill's wartime staffers and a close postwar associate, published *Man of Valour: The Life of Field Marshal Lord Gort, V.C.* (London, 1972). Even now, he remains little known outside the ranks of specialist historians.

15. When Churchill succeeded Chamberlain as the battle of France opened, he decreed that there would be no change of residence for a month. Until after Dunkirk, he continued to live and work at Admiralty House.

16. Churchill, *Finest Hour*, 72.

17. Ibid., 73. Ironside, who died in 1959, left no memoirs, nor is there a biography. His 1937–1940 diaries have, however, been edited by R. McLeod and Denis Kelly, *The Ironside Diaries, 1937–1940* (London, 1962). Perhaps the most striking thing about them is that they show Ironside, like Brooke, tended to vent in his diaries about the political figures with whom he dealt. He is supposed to have been the inspiration for Richard Hannay, the hero of several of John Buchan's thrillers, including *The Thirty-nine Steps*. Alex Danchev, drawing on the memories of General Sir Leslie Hollis, argues that Ironside actually was pushed by Churchill: see his "Waltzing with Winston: Civil Military Relations in Britain in the Second World War," in Paul Smith, ed., *Government and the Armed Forces in Britain, 1856–1990* (London, 1996), 197. The evidence comes from James Leasor's *War at the Top* (London, 1960), an "as told to" book. There seems to be no surviving contemporary evidence with which to make a definitive verdict.

18. Dill died in 1944, so there is no postwar memoir, nor is there a biography. Alex Danchev has examined his role as CIGS in several essays, especially "Waltzing with Winston," and has produced a full-scale study of his time in Washington as the senior British representative there from 1941 to 1944, *A Very Special Relationship* (London, 1986). But the materials for a full study of his time as CIGS seem to be lacking, which leaves a void in our understanding of how policy and strategy was formulated in London in 1940 and 1941. The closest thing we have to a study of how Dill functioned as CIGS is B. Fergusson, ed., *The Business of War: The War Narrative of Major General Sir John Kennedy* (New York, 1958). Kennedy was director of military operations during Dill's tenure—and a central player in the spectacular clash with Churchill at Chequers in April 1941.

19. Ismay wrote *The Memoirs of General Lord Ismay* (New York, 1960). It breathes barely a whisper of criticism of Churchill but is very interesting on how the machinery he ran actually worked. There is an affectionate biography by Sir Reginald Wingate, *Lord Ismay: A Biography* (London, 1970). One of the great problems with assessing Ismay was summed up by Ian Jacob: "Staff officers have no lives—what they do becomes part of

the story of those they serve." Jacob himself, who retired as a lieutenant general and went on to be director general of the British Broadcasting Corporation (BBC), has been profiled by General Sir Charles Richardson, *From Churchill's Secret Circle to the BBC: Biography of Lieutenant General Sir Ian Jacob, GBE, CB, DL* (London, 1991). Hollis, who ended his career as a full general and commandant of the Royal Marines, published a memoir, *One Marine's Tale* (London, 1951), and, with James Leasor, *War at the Top* (London, 1959). The general blandness of the writing by and about these central figures reflects both the ingrained discretion that made them so successful and the point made by Sir Ian Jacob. It is quite hard to discern the fingerprints these three left on Churchill's success, but as Ismay pointed out in *Memoirs* (164–166), it is instructive to compare the handling of the Dardanelles venture of 1915, when nothing like the Defence Secretariat existed, with the way Churchill's ideas were staffed and vetted from 1940 to 1945.

20. David French, *Raising Churchill's Army: The British Army and the War against Germany, 1919–1945* (Oxford, 2000), 107. Territorial divisions were roughly analogous to contemporary U.S. National Guard divisions. These units of "weekend soldiers" lacked the training and equipment of regulars and were expected to require equipment upgrades and additional training upon mobilization. Their officers were regarded by the regulars much as reserve officers are universally by career professionals. One of the Territorial divisions in the BEF—50th Division, from the depressed mining communities of northern England—distinguished itself in France and then served in the Western Desert to mixed reviews.

21. Of course, the oil fields of Iran and Iraq (the Saudi and gulf fields were not yet major producers) were extremely important to the British war effort, since the British did not have to spend precious hard currency to pay for their output. However, there can be little doubt that the reason for Churchill's reaction in June 1940 to the proposal to pull the fleet out was based primarily on the psychological impact at that moment of a tacit admission by the British that they doubted their ability to maintain a crucial imperial position. Cunningham's signal of June 18, 1940, is quoted in S. W. Roskill, *Churchill and the Admirals* (London, 1977), 150.

22. Slim would come close to duplicating this feat in Burma in 1945—against a far tougher opponent. But Slim was not outnumbered as badly as O'Connor had been.

23. Liddell Hart, however, writing in 1938 of generals who would hold high command if war came in the next few years, expressed some doubts about Wavell: "Formerly . . . a man of marked originality of thought, with a gift for surprise . . . but seemed to have gone off in the last year or two"; see Liddell Hart, *The Liddell Hart Memoirs*, 2 vols. (New York, 1965–1966), 2:238. Was Wavell past his best in 1940? Perhaps he was, but Liddell Hart was very catty.

24. In his fine biography of Wavell, *The Chief: Field Marshal Lord Wavell. Commander-in-Chief and Viceroy, 1939–1947* (New York, 1980), Ronald Lewin, comparing Wavell to Montgomery, speculates on whether Wavell "really possessed the instincts of a killer" (27). One can imagine Wavell as the sort of academic whose ability, ambition, and drive would take him to the top of a university. That is not a career in which it is easy to imagine Monty—indeed, Lewin's question would not occur to a biographer of Montgomery. Even Wavell's admiring official biographer, John Connell, subtitled his work *Soldier and Scholar.* A seldom-noted oddity of Wavell's career is that he reached the rank of field marshal without ever having commanded a unit in combat.

25. Wilson was described by Major General Sir Edward Spears, who intensely disliked him, as "an enormous, bald man . . . like an outsized child's balloon. . . . As for wisdom, military historians may discover in his decisions a sagacity which my own shortcomings no doubt prevented me from seeing"; see his *Fulfillment of a Mission: Syria and Lebanon, 1941–1944* (London, 1977), 89. One of those military historians, Ronald Lewin, in *The Chief*, wrote that Wilson "reached the rank of Field Marshal for reasons which are difficult to identify and have never been explained" (57). (But Wilson did conduct a reasonably successful withdrawal from Greece, as noted in the text.) There is an engaging portrait of "General Jumbo"—which, however, does little to answer Lewin's question—in Hermione Ranfurly, *To War with Whitaker: The Wartime Diaries of the Countess of Ranfurly, 1939–1945* (London, 1994). Ranfurly followed her husband, a Territorial Army cavalryman, to the Middle East in 1940 and, after his capture, contrived to attach herself and her husband's Jeeves-like manservant, Whitaker, to Wilson's staff, on which she remained until 1945. Hobart, spurned by the army establishment (in addition to being "difficult," he had been involved in a divorce), was a lance corporal in the Home Guard when Churchill insisted on his reemployment. He spent most of the war with the 79th Armoured Division, an experimental and development formation that was the parent of many of the specialized tank units (mine-clearing, amphibious, flame-throwing, and so on) that played such an important part in the second half of the war. He was never given the opportunity to command in the field against the Germans. There is a biography by Kenneth Mackesy, *Armoured Crusader* (London, 1967).

26. Yet the division had only two of its three brigades, and only one of those was an Indian Army brigade. Its brigadier was a very formidable soldier, Reginald Savory. After commanding a division, Savory would become inspector and then director of infantry in India in 1943 and play a vital, if unheralded, role in shaping the army Slim led to victory between 1944 and 1945. He was the last adjutant general of the old Indian Army.

27. These British "columns," made up of guns, motorized infantry, and armored cars, succeeded perhaps too well against the Italians. The British became wedded to this sort of formation, which proved of little use against the better-trained, better-equipped, and better-led Germans.

28. Even before the war, Anglo-French planners, contemplating a long period of attrition before an offensive against Germany would be possible, had intended to strike at Germany's weaker Italian partner first.

29. Churchill, *Finest Hour*, 422. Volumes 2 through 4 of Churchill's memoirs track events in the Mediterranean and Middle East very closely, an indication of the author's identification with the campaigns there. The same would be true of the Italian campaigns in volumes 5 and 6.

30. Churchill, *Finest Hour*, 425.

31. Churchill printed the directive in ibid., 428–432. There is no hint in *Finest Hour* that he thought of replacing Wavell almost the moment he met him—although there was in early drafts. See David Reynolds, *In Command of History: Churchill Fighting and Writing the Second World War* (London, 2004), 190–191. Freyberg had received his first commission in 1914 in the Royal Naval Division, with Churchill's help. His VC, won on the Somme, ensured him Churchill's lifelong admiration. British by birth, he had grown up in New Zealand and had been invited by the New Zealand government in November 1939 to take command of the New Zealand Expeditionary Force, more commonly

called the 2nd New Zealand Division. (New Zealand had only one division at that point—the numeral meant that it was the successor of the World War I New Zealand Expeditionary Force.)

32. John Connell, *Wavell: Soldier and Scholar* (London, 1964), 265. A careful reading of the account of the Somililand episode in the official history, I. S. O. Playfair, G. M. S. Stitt, C. J. C. Molony, and S. E. Toomer, *The Mediterranean and Middle East*, vol. 1 (London, 1954), 171–179, indicates that, in fact, Godwin-Austen had handled his badly outnumbered force (the Italians had a five-to-one margin) quite well. The only real question seems to be whether Wavell was right to make the effort to mount a defense, and on this point, the official historians, writing after Churchill's memoirs appeared, go out of their way to argue for Wavell's policy.

33. Harding would later command the 7th Armoured Division, serve as chief of staff to Alexander in Italy, and end his career by succeeding Slim as the professional head of the British Army in 1952. There is a biography by Michael Carver, *Harding of Petherton* (London, 1978). Harding's given names were Allen Francis, but he was always known as John.

34. Wavell's official biographer, John Connell, points out that Wavell had been a junior officer on the staff of Major General Henry Wilson, the director of military operations at the War Office, at the time of the Curragh Mutiny of March 1914. At that point, a bill conferring home rule (limited self-government) on Ireland was passing through Parliament. As always when Irish affairs intrude into British politics, tempers were running high. Under the impression that there was a plot to use the army to compel Ulster to accept home rule (that is, membership in a Catholic-dominated, quasi-autonomous Ireland), officers of a cavalry brigade stationed in Ireland threatened mass resignation. Churchill, then a Liberal cabinet member, was supposed to be one of the principal plotters. Wilson, Wavell's boss, was a rabid opponent of home rule. Connell's comment—that Wavell, as a result of this episode, developed "a suspicion of professional politicians, however talented, however versatile, which deepened and strengthened as the years passed"—may be true but hardly seems sufficient to explain his behavior over Compass; see Connell, *Wavell,* 82–89. David Reynolds, in his indispensable study of Churchill's memoirs, *In Command of History* (193–195), points out that Churchill, to be sure the War Cabinet accepted the policy of limited military aid to Greece, did not reveal that Wavell was planning an offensive until after Eden's return and maintained the pretense that he had not known until then in his memoirs. This is a good example of why Churchill's memoirs need such careful handling. It does not, of course, fully explain why Wavell acted as he did.

35. Brooke later withheld from Churchill the detailed final plan and start date for Montgomery's El Alamein attack when he received them two weeks prior to Lightfoot, but, of course, Churchill had known since Montgomery's appointment in August that an attack was being planned; see Alex Danchev and Daniel Todman, eds., *War Diaries, 1939–1945: Field Marshal Lord Alanbrooke* (London, 2001), 329. This comes not from Brooke's contemporary diary but from his postwar "Notes on My Life" and is a gloss on his October 14, 1942, entry.

36. The Germans had in fact offered help, but Mussolini had rejected it. General Georg Von Thoma's unflattering assessment of Italian armor—"moving coffins"—was made during these discussions between the Axis partners.

37. The paved road built by the Italians, the Via Balbia, hugged the coast, which meant that it followed a roughly semicircular path at this point. A force cutting across the desert thus was able to use the diameter while its opponents crept around the rim of a circle.

38. O'Connor's total striking force at this point was composed of 67 tanks (only 22 of them cruisers), an armored car regiment, a battalion of motorized infantry, and 24 field guns. The Australians were far away, following the Italian retreat along the coastal highway. In addition to the official history—Playfair et al., *The Mediterranean and Middle East*, vol. 1—there is a very readable account of Compass in Barrie Pitt's *The Crucible of War: The Western Desert, 1941* (London, 1980).

39. Since the Balkan armies were also less modern than the Polish, which the Germans had finished off in two weeks, it is clear that a certain amount of wishful thinking was indulged in by British enthusiasts for a Balkan bloc, including the prime minister. If the British were unrealistic, the Turks were not. An interesting book could be written about the British attempts to cajole the Turks into the war and the Turks' skill in inveigling aid out of the British while making no concrete move until it was quite safe. (Turkey declared war on Germany after the Yalta Conference in 1945.)

40. When Dill returned to London, he told his confidant, Major General John Kennedy, the director of military operations at the War Office, that "he feared a bad mistake had been made" over Greece; see Fergusson, *The Business of War,* 90. If he felt that way, why did he not try to prevent it instead of venting to Kennedy? He was, after all, the professional head of the British Army—although junior as a general to Wavell. Alexander's insight that Dill was indecisive and gloomy is amply borne out by Kennedy's narrative. Churchill's progressive disenchantment with him seems understandable. Interestingly, a young staff officer in Cairo at the time spotted Dill's missed opportunity: "Churchill had made clear his uncertainties; on the face of it WSC was almost seeking a convincing reason for calling the whole operation off"; see Major General R. F. K. Belchem to Ronald Lewin, August 6, 1979, Lewin Papers, RLEW 2/13, Churchill Archive Centre, Churchill College, Cambridge (hereafter CAC). Belchem (always known as David) was a captain in 1941; he ended the war a brigadier on Montgomery's staff.

41. The British record of the conference where the agreement was made is clear that the Greeks would pull back to a more defensible line. The Greek record has disappeared. The Greek army had very limited mobility. Quite apart from the political implications of giving up not only the ground won against the Italians in Albania but also Greece's second city, Salonika, the Greek commanders may have feared being caught by the Germans while redeploying. Even had they fallen back as the British wished, it is questionable how long their already overstrained army, incapable of maneuver and with little artillery, could have stood up against what was then the best combined arms force on the planet; see Playfair et al., *The Mediterranean and Middle East*, 1:377–388. It is interesting to speculate on what might have happened had the Greeks shortened their line. The Germans would have won, but a longer, harder fought campaign would have meant much higher losses to a largely Dominion force, not to mention the RAF squadrons and shipping that supported Wilson. Perhaps the Greek commander-in-chief, General Alexander Papagos, did the British a favor.

42. Harold E. Raugh Jr., *Wavell in the Middle East, 1939–1941: A Study in Generalship* (London, 1993), demonstrates at length how crucial Wavell's role was—but then sums up:

"It was Churchill's silent hand on the rudder which steered the course unswervingly to inevitable military defeat in Greece" (167). Raugh does not seem to notice the contradiction. A much better assessment is Lewin's *The Chief.* Lewin concludes that the charge "that Churchill forced Wavell into Greece against his will" is a "myth" (107).

43. F. H. Hinsley, E. E. Thomas, C. F. G. Ransom, and R. C. Knight, *British Intelligence in the Second World War* (London, 1979), 1:407, 409.

44. The British armored car was commanded by Lieutenant Edgar Williams, who would end the war a brigadier and Montgomery's intelligence chief.

45. A young staff officer in military intelligence later observed, "John Shearer was one who had such reverence for his Chief [Wavell] that he would never attempt even respectful argument with him"; see Belchem to Lewin, July 22, 1979, Lewin Papers, RLEW 2/13, CAC.

46. The northern, coastal belt of the Italian colony of Libya was subdivided into two provinces. The eastern, or Cyrenaica, was the scene of most of the desert war. The western province was Tripolitania.

47. This technique was a hallmark of Wavell's command style. Later in Malaya and again in Burma, Wavell would overrule decisions by local commanders, demonstrating a lack of confidence in them—but then leave them in place.

48. This incident doubtless lay behind Churchill's April 28 directive that "Generals and Staff Officers surprised by the enemy are to use their pistols in self-defense." Ironically, as they drove through the darkness, O'Connor was sure that Neame's desert navigation was wrong, but the car was Neame's. Wavell wanted to trade any six Italian generals for O'Connor, but he was overruled by the War Cabinet, whose members feared accusations of discrimination in favor of generals. Although his captors were German, O'Connor was turned over to the Italians—North Africa was, by Axis agreement, an "Italian" theater. He escaped at the time of the Italian surrender in 1943 and subsequently commanded a corps in Monty's Twenty-first Army Group. But the dash and fire of 1940 were gone. O'Connor never wrote memoirs, leaving a significant gap in the literature of the desert war. But there is a biography by John Baynes, *The Forgotten Victor: General Sir Richard O'Connor* (London, 1988).

49. The 2nd Armoured Division was never reconstituted.

50. Churchill described the decision in *The Grand Alliance* (Boston, 1950), 244–252. He, of course, had wanted to send reinforcing armor to the Middle East directly through the Mediterranean in August 1940. His ability to override professional reservations in April 1941 is an indication of the ascendancy he had established by that time.

51. See the Prelude.

52. Churchill to Lord Moyne [secretary of state for the colonies], March 1, 1941, in Churchill, *Grand Alliance*, 742.

53. Churchill to Wavell, December 2, 1940, *CWP2*, 1171. Wavell had also opposed the prime minister's desire to raise a Jewish brigade in Palestine—a project Churchill drove through against intense bureaucratic opposition, although it took him until 1944 to prevail. David Reynolds points out that in an early draft of *Finest Hour*, Churchill had been much blunter: "All our military men disliked Jews and loved Arabs. General Wavell was no exception"; see Reynolds, *In Command of History*, 191.

54. Churchill recounts this in *Grand Alliance,* 202, adding, rather mildly, "This was not in harmony with any statement he made to us."

55. Fergusson, *The Business of War*, 135.

56. Hinsley et al., *British Intelligence,* 1:261–264; Churchill, in *Grand Alliance*, 356–357, has a dramatic description of how a single item of Ultra intelligence, reaching him toward the end of March, clarified his thinking about Hitler's 1941 objectives. He had, of course, always insisted on seeing "authentic documents — in their original form." In this case, a decrypt from Bletchley Park confirmed the suspicion that had long lurked in his mind: the failure to knock Britain out in the summer of 1940 would be followed by an attack on Russia.

57. Dill's May 6 minute to Churchill is (mostly) reproduced in Churchill's *Grand Alliance*, 420–422; Churchill's May 13 answer is in Martin Gilbert, ed., *Churchill War Papers,* vol. 3, *The Ever Widening War, 1941* (New York, 2000), 660–661 (hereafter *CWP3*). The bulk of it appeared in *Grand Alliance*, 422–423. Dill's final shot was printed in full by the official historian of British strategy, J. R. M. Butler, *Grand Strategy,* vol. 2, *September 1939–June 1940* (London, 1957), 580–581. Kennedy's role is described in Fergusson, *The Business of War*, 115–116. A study of Kennedy's role at the War Office would be most useful—he served as director of military operations longer (from 1940 to 1944) than any previous incumbent and clearly played an important role in stiffening Dill to confront Churchill in April and May 1941, a clash that was decisive in preparing the way for the ruin not of the Middle East but of Singapore. On this, see Raymond Callahan, *The Worst Disaster: The Fall of Singapore* (Newark, DE, and London, 1977), 81–93. The presentation of this episode by Churchill in his memoirs is an interesting example of how he structured them. Both Dill's May 6 memo and Churchill's May 13 reply are reproduced almost in their entirety but appear in the chapter in which he discusses the preparations for the Atlantic meeting with Roosevelt, several months later. This placement divorces the whole exchange from its context—the springtime freshet of disasters in the Balkans and the desert—and tends to obscure the fact that those disasters led to a parting of the ways between the prime minister and the CIGS.

58. Quoted in Wingate, *Ismay*, 57.

59. I. McD. G. Stewart, *The Struggle for Crete* (London, 1966) is a model battle study by a New Zealand historian who wrote before the intelligence background of the battle became known. His conclusions about the tactical handling of the New Zealand division, however, remain valid. Curiously, the British official intelligence history (Hinsley et al., *British Intelligence,* 1:421), though it makes clear Churchill's constant monitoring of the German intentions Ultra was laying bare and his expectations for British success, is rather reticent in assigning responsibility for the British failure: "The British, whether from weakness or for other reasons, were not in a position to make better use of an intelligence service that was at last getting into its stride." "Other reasons" was a euphemism for Freyberg's failure to (as Monty would doubtless have put it) "grip" the battle. Freyberg was sharply criticized by some of his brigadiers following the battle, and the argument, reinforced by what is now available on the intelligence dimension, has reverberated in recent writing on the battle. Anthony Beevor, *Crete: The Battle and the Resistance* (London, 1991), is critical of Freyberg—as was Stewart. Freyberg has been defended by his son, Paul Freyberg, in *Bernard Freyberg, V.C.: Soldier of Two Nations* (London, 1991), and by Laurie Barber and John Tonkin-Covell, in *Freyberg: Churchill's Salamander* (London, 1990). Barber and Tonkin-Covell are particularly critical of Freyberg's brigadiers. The reality is that the failure at Maleme was the result of multiple errors, from Freyberg

down to the battalion level; it had far more to do with the structure of command in the division than with any failure to understand and utilize Ultra.

60. In thwarting the German attempt to bring men and matériel to Crete by sea and then in saving what could be saved of Freyberg's men, the Royal Navy paid a price that temporarily put it all but out of action in the eastern Mediterranean. Tradition can be numbing, but it can also be magnificently inspiriting. There are few better examples of the latter than Admiral Sir Andrew Browne Cunningham sending his battered ships and exhausted crews to save the garrison of Crete with the words "It takes the Navy three years to build a ship. It would take three hundred to rebuild a tradition"; see S. W. Roskill, *The War at Sea, 1939–1945,* 3 vols. (London, 1954–1961), 1:419.

61. Paulus sent his signal through Luftwaffe channels. It was thus transmitted in the Enigma cipher most easily read by Bletchley Park.

62. One of the many anomalies of Britain's war against Rommel is that Egypt, the base for that war, was not at war with either Germany or Italy. Moreover, Egyptian nationalists were strongly anti-British and pro-German. This fact and the general sympathy felt throughout the Arab world, at least among militant nationalists, for Britain's German enemy (of which the Iraqi revolt was a manifestation) made the political dimension of Wavell's task particularly delicate. In assessing the relationship between London and Cairo, it is important to keep the peculiar atmosphere of Cairo in mind. Markedly different from the grimly focused London of those years, this colorful, cosmopolitan city, officially the capital of a friendly neutral, was the seat of Britain's sprawling "informal empire" in the Middle East. Olivia Manning's "Levant Trilogy" novels catch the atmosphere. Artemis Cooper's *Cairo in the War* (London, 1989) is a readable social history of this strange moment in British and Cairene history.

63. Lord Louis "Dickie" Mountbatten certainly had an immense load of responsibility in South-East Asia Command (SEAC) from 1943 to 1945, but SEAC was far more marginal to the British war effort than the Middle East between 1940 and 1942.

64. Operation Brevity suffered, as would Battleaxe and subsequent British operations for the next year and more, from poor British signals security. While Bletchley Park was providing strategic and operational intelligence by reading Enigma traffic, Rommel's radio-intercept unit was taking advantage of British on-air carelessness to provide him with a wealth of tactical intelligence.

65. This improvement included the installation of a number of the 88mm guns that would become perhaps the most famous—and most feared—of Rommel's weapons. Developed as an antiaircraft gun, the 88 was first used in Spain in 1936. Its existence therefore was no surprise to the British; its tactical utilization was. German doctrine put the 88 into the battle line with the panzers, where it could devastate British armored formations. On its high trailer mounting, the 88 ought to have been a good target for British artillery, but British guns were used to support the infantry while the tanks fought alone—a legacy of Hobart's disdain for all-arms cooperation. In the frontier defenses that were developed after Brevity, the Germans mitigated the vulnerability of the 88 by digging it in.

66. Once the Luftwaffe had established itself in Crete, the problems of running supply convoys to Malta from Egypt or of interdicting Rommel's supply line to Tripoli became much more complicated. The need for RAF bases in western Cyrenaica to allow air cover for Malta-bound convoys became a major factor in British planning for over a

year. If Rommel could not be beaten, Malta might fall, making the Axis powers the masters of the central Mediterranean. That in turn might mean a buildup of German strength in North Africa to a point that would not only foreclose the possibility of a British victory there but perhaps also threaten the survival of the Middle Eastern empire as well. The fact that we know now the Germans had no such plans in 1941 and 1942 should not obscure how threatening such a sequence seemed then to the British, fighting alone.

67. Creagh's other armored brigade, the 7th, was equipped with the Crusader, a fast, lightly armored, undergunned tank. How the technically very different tanks of the two brigades were to cooperate on the battlefield—something they had never had to do during Compass—is not clear. Certainly, there had not been time for them to train together before Battleaxe.

68. The Germans had captured a number of Matildas in France in 1940. In August of that year, they ran tests that showed that only the 88's 16½-pound shell had any effect on its 78mm frontal armor; 88s therefore accompanied the first German units to arrive in Africa in February 1941. Because there was little serious tank fighting in Rommel's first offensive, it was not until Battleaxe that British tanks faced the 88 on the battlefield.

69. The backbone of Rommel's two panzer regiments was the Panzer Mark 3. Originally, the Panzer 3's specifications had been roughly comparable to those of the Crusader, but by the time Rommel went to Africa, new models with a more powerful gun (50mm instead of 37mm) and upgraded armor (double the original thickness) were available. The British were unaware for some time of either development.

70. Since the final total of British tank losses in Battleaxe was 91 (of 190) tanks, the sharp reduction in Creagh's force by the morning of June 17 was obviously due in part to breakdowns that were repaired in time for the tanks to be withdrawn.

71. Brigadier John Harding, Beresford-Peirse's chief of staff, later told the historian Ronald Lewin that Wavell had tears in his good eye when he took this decision. A more junior staff officer present at the conference recalled that Wavell gave no orders, offered no advice, merely listened, and then told Creagh, "Well you've got a lot of 25-pounders, if you can't stop them I don't know who can." Then he left. See G. P. B. Roberts, *From the Desert to the Baltic* (London, 1987), 50.

72. It may not be without significance that one of Wavell's friends and admirers in London was Henry "Chips" Channon, who was well connected with the Chamberlainite remnant in the Conservative Party—precisely that political circle least enthusiastic about Churchill.

73. Neither Creagh nor Beresford-Peirse ever received active commands again. Harding felt Beresford-Peirse's infantry background made him very uncertain when handling armor. Gatehouse was much more critical. According to him, the XIII Corps commander not only made elementary mistakes but also tended to bluster and insist on obedience to his orders whenever questioned. In Battleaxe, all the armored units came from the Royal Tank Regiment and might well be assumed to have regarded an outsider such as Beresford-Peirse warily. It is interesting to note that Rommel, after he failed to take Tobruk in May, had sacked a divisional commander and two panzer regiment commanders, court-martialing one. British heads were not the only ones to roll after a desert

failure; Rommel, though, seemed to get better results from the examples he made—at least until Monty arrived on the scene.

74. Correlli Barnett, *The Desert Generals* (London, 1960), 67. In 1981, Barnett produced a revised edition, adding lengthy appendixes in which he discussed material that had become available in the intervening twenty years, especially that contained in the first two volumes of Hinsley et al.'s official history of intelligence. Vividly written, Barnett's strong anti-Churchill and anti-Montgomery biases make *The Desert Generals* a book to be used with care, however.

75. David Belchem later described just how raw formations newly arrived from the United Kingdom were. Visiting a unit detached from 2nd Armoured Division and sent to Greece, he met "a territorial battalion of motor infantry from the Armoured Brigade. The C.O. [commanding officer] was a most charming man—I think a stockbroker. His Adjutant (Regular) was a drip. I doubt if any of them could distinguish between a German and an Evzone!"; see Belchem to Lewin, July 22, 1979, Lewin Papers, RLEW 2/13, CAC. (An Evzone is a colorfully costumed Greek soldier, still seen performing ceremonial duties in Athens.)

76. On the Indian Army, see Chapter 3. As noted in the text, the destruction of the 3rd Indian Motor Brigade at Mechili in Rommel's first offensive is an example of the problems the Indian Army faced at this point.

77. It was easier for Britain, a heavily industrialized country, to raise the numerous support formations needed in the Middle East, whereas the Dominions concentrated their manpower in "teeth" formations. But this meant that despite the large number of British troops in the theater, Dominion and Indian formations preponderated among fighting units. As casualties mounted, this situation became another concern both for British commanders and for Churchill.

Chapter Three. Rommel's Victims

1. Some of this was doubtless due to the comparative poverty of many of the Irish Protestant landowners, which made a military career, particularly one in India where it was possible both to live on one's salary and to save money, quite attractive. It is also true that the professions that absorbed some landowners' sons in England were much smaller in Ireland—another incentive for an army career.

2. The Montgomerys, like the Auchinlecks, were Protestant Irish. Monty's father was a missionary bishop, and family resources were comparatively slight. Monty's brother Brian did make it into the Indian Army, however, retiring as a colonel.

3. It is interesting to speculate on whether the qualitative decline of the Indian Army would have been quite as severe by 1942 if Auchinleck had remained uninterruptedly in Delhi. Many of the problems were beyond any single individual's control, but Auchinleck, who had a much more acute sense of the realities of his service than any British service officer could have, might not have made the mistake of assuming, as did his successor Wavell, that the Japanese were not a serious problem.

4. Indeed, the concern of the British authorities in India about the area went back to the East India Company's involvement in the Persian Gulf, which began in the eighteenth century.

5. Lieutenant General W. G. H. Vickers, who became quartermaster general in India during the war, later remarked to Slim's official biographer that Slim was a grammar school boy "and very conscious of this in the Indian Army context," adding rather artlessly, "I was Public School, Sandhurst and Cavalry, and I could see this"; see Ronald Lewin, note of conversation with Vickers, December 9, 1972, Lewin Papers, RLEW 3/6, Churchill Archive Centre, Churchill College, Cambridge (hereafter CAC). This may have been a factor in Slim's difficult relations with two British Army officers, Lieutenant General Noel Irwin and General Sir Oliver Leese, Bt. See Chapter 7. Grammar schools were often old and educationally distinguished but definitely less socially prestigious than Britain's public schools, and they were attended by students of a different background from those populating the public schools.

6. To some extent, this decision was driven by finances. Horses and fodder were plentiful in India, whereas machines were scarce and expensive.

7. The 1940 expansion program (devised after the French collapse) called for five infantry divisions, subsequently increased to six, and an armored division. The 1941 program, launched while the 1940 scheme was not yet complete, added four more infantry divisions and a second armored division. Toward the end of 1941, the next (1942) program began; it called for another four infantry divisions and a third armored division. By the time Auchinleck left for Cairo, India was raising armored divisions for which no tanks were yet available and antitank units without up-to-date antitank guns.

8. The British staff system, created shortly after the Boer War, was not, like most European staff systems, a fairly close copy of the German system evolved under Helmuth von Moltke in the mid-nineteenth century. The functions, of course, were similar, but the titles—brigade major; brigadier General Staff, and so on—can be, like much British practice and nomenclature, a bit puzzling to outsiders. It is important to note that before Ritchie became BGS to Auchinleck at Southern Command, he had held the same position under Brooke in the BEF's II Corps. Brooke became Ritchie's patron, as he was Monty's, with important consequences.

9. Wavell had used Brigadier Eric "Chink" Dorman-Smith, the commandant of the wartime Middle East Staff College at Haifa, as an unofficial adviser, a sort of one-man brain trust. Auchinleck (who had known Dorman-Smith in India when he had been director of military training while Auchinleck was deputy chief of staff) continued this practice. He may have been more influenced by Dorman-Smith than Wavell, since his contacts in the British Army were so sparse. Dorman-Smith had a sharp mind, allied to a sharp tongue. He had also had a meteoric rise—captain to colonel in six years. He was not, as a result, a very popular figure.

It is a measure of the remoteness of the British and Indian armies from one another that more than a quarter century later, Major General David Belchem, a British regular who had been a young staff officer in Cairo in 1941, could refer to Auchinleck as "a splendid leader of Gurkhas." In fact, Auchinleck had joined the 62nd Punjabis in 1903. Belchem would not have confused British Army regiments in the same way. (Belchem is also the source of the observation about Arthur Smith and Auchinleck.) See Belchem to Ronald Lewin, July 22, 1979, Lewin Papers, RLEW 2/13, CAC. (Belchem's given names were Ronald Frederick King, but he was always known as David.) Yet Auchinleck may have been rather impolitic in letting his own prejudices show. He is reported to have remarked at one point that well-trained and well-commanded British soldiers could be as good as Indian units. See Anthony Clayton, *The British Officer: Leading the Army from 1660 to the Present* (London, 2006), 227n5.

10. Dill to Auchinleck, June 26, 1941, in John Connell, *Auchinleck: A Critical Biography* (London, 1959), 246–248; the quoted passages are on 247, and the italics are in the original. Interestingly, the official historian of British strategy, J. R. M. Butler, also quoted the letter in full, in *Grand Strategy,* vol. 2, *September 1939–June 1941* (London, 1957), 530–532. Lengthy quotations from private papers are rare in the official histories, and in this case, it seems clear that the letter was included to convey a criticism of Churchill the author did not want to, or was unable to, present in his text.

11. The background to Dill's letter to Auchinleck (which took weeks to reach the Middle East) was a paper done for Dill by Kennedy entitled "Strategy in the Middle East" and printed in Bernard Fergusson, ed., *The Business of War: The War Narrative of Major-General Sir John Kennedy* (New York, 1958), 137–141. In it, Kennedy makes the point Dill would put to Auchinleck—all governments pressure field commanders, but great commanders resist the pressure. He also criticizes virtually every decision Wavell took as an example of following an unsound military course in response to political pressure. Dill's letter reflects Kennedy's critique very closely. Neither Kennedy nor Dill seems to have focused on the question of whether British failures in the desert reflected fundamental flaws in the way the British Army fought, an issue the prime minister would soon raise.

12. Ismay to Auchinleck, August 28, 1941, in Ronald Wingate, *Lord Ismay: A Biography* (London, 1970), 62. This letter, which reflects Ismay's perceptive realization that personal contact was crucial in Churchill's assessment of individuals, is in Auchinleck's papers but is not referred to by Connell. The letter reflects as well the tact, diplomacy, and sensitivity that made Ismay so successful—and so valuable to Churchill.

13. Uncertainty about the duration of Russian resistance was widespread in the summer of 1941. It affected not only Auchinleck's assessments but also those made in London, where Dill and Kennedy still thought an autumn invasion possible. Churchill's messages to Auchinleck reflect this concern as well.

14. Auchinleck to Churchill, July 4, 1941, in Connell, *Auchinleck,* 252; italics mine.

15. Note by Churchill, July 11, 1941, in Martin Gilbert, ed., *The Churchill War Papers,* vol. 3, *The Ever Widening War, 1941* (New York, 2001), 926 (hereafter *CWP3*). The whole note is worth reading as an example of the diligence and critical intelligence Churchill applied to the enormous quantity of information that came his way daily. Dill's rejoinder of July 14 is in Fergusson, *The Business of War,* 143–145. It is hard not to agree with Ismay's postwar comment to John Connell, biographer to both Wavell and Auchinleck: "If — Winston made rude remarks about the courage of the British Army . . . I either disregarded it or I laughed or I referred him to the magnificent tributes that he paid them in his various writings — Dill, on the other had, was cut to the quick that anyone should insult his beloved army." On such occasions, the CIGS "looked, and was, bitterly hurt." See Ismay to Connell, n.d., in Wingate, *Ismay,* 57. On such temperamental incompatibilities can major issues turn.

16. Winston S. Churchill, *The Grand Alliance* (Boston, 1950), 405.

17. Hastings, Baron Ismay, *The Memoirs of General Lord Ismay* (New York, 1960), 269–271. It was during this visit that Churchill gave voice to his abiding suspicion of the Indian Army when, in response to Auchinleck's observation that India had an armored

division without any equipment, he asked whether the troops could be trusted: "How do you know they wouldn't turn and fire the wrong way?" See Connell, *Auchinleck*, 274n1. Ismay's patience was clearly enormous.

18. Between 1914 and the armistice, Pope won a DSO and an MC, lost an arm, and commanded a battalion at the age of twenty-five. Ronald Lewin has written a useful brief biography, *Man of Armor* (London, 1976).

19. Major General David Belchem to Ronald Lewin, August 18, 1979, Lewin Papers, RLEW 2/13, CAC.

20. Much of the credit for the logistics of Cunningham's campaign was owed to the efforts of his quartermaster, Brigadier Sir Brian Robertson, Bt., son of the remarkable Field Marshal Sir William Robertson (CIGS from 1916 to 1918). He had done well at the staff college but then left the army for a business career; the outbreak of war found him working in South Africa. After he returned to the army, his role in the East African campaign was the first step in a brilliant career as a logistician with Monty and then under Alexander in Italy. He ended his career as General Lord Robertson of Oakridge. (His father, who had started his army career as a private soldier, had only gotten as far as a baronetcy—that is, a hereditary knighthood, signified by the "Bt." after his name.)

21. "Communication" (letter?) from Auchinleck to Correlli Barnett, n.d., quoted in the latter's *The Desert Generals* (London, 1960), 79.

22. There is no indication that Dill had a significant role in Cunningham's selection, although Auchinleck may have discussed the matter with him while he was in Britain in August. As professional head of the British Army, Dill might well have been expected to be deeply involved in what was, after all, a crucial appointment. But if he was, there seems to be no record of it. It is interesting that on October 8, Alan Brooke noted in his diary, "It is lamentable how poor we are as regards Army and Corps commanders. We ought to remove several but heaven knows where we shall find anything very much better." Reflecting on this after the war, he "came to the conclusion that it was due to the cream of our manpower having been lost in the First World War." See Alex Danchev and Daniel Todman, eds., *War Diaries, 1939–45: Field Marshal Lord Alanbrooke* (London, 2001), 188. It is, of course, impossible to test the accuracy of Brooke's judgment. (Max Hastings's observation in *Warriors* [London, 2006], 272, that "it is hard to overstate the fundamental truth of war, that most of the bravest die" might perhaps be cited in support of Brooke. Yet physical courage, though crucial, is not the only quality generals require.) A better argument is that it was not who survived that was the problem but how the army conceptualized battle. What is clear, however, is that the most powerful soldier in the British Army, soon to become CIGS, thought the talent was thin at the lieutenant general level. Auchinleck, who did not know the British Army remotely as well as Brooke, made not the best choice but perhaps the best choice he could.

23. Persia was the corridor through which aid shipments could be sent by rail from the Persian Gulf to Russia, and its government's enthusiasm for the Allied cause was limited. The nearly bloodless occupation deposed the shah and exiled him. He was replaced by his son, who would rule until 1979. The Syrian and Persian ventures marked William Slim's debut as a divisional commander.

24. The armor in the theater was, of course, entirely British, and there were two British infantry divisions. The British provided as well most of the support troops that sustained the Dominion formations. The huge administrative "tail" that so exercised the

prime minister was mostly British. But at the "sharp end," the five Dominion infantry divisions outnumbered British infantry divisions nearly two to one. Of course, the largest contributor of combat divisions to the theater was the Indian Army, something Churchill never acknowledged.

25. The Australians were replaced by the British 70th Division, originally a regular formation formed at the outbreak of the war from units already in the Middle East. A Polish brigade was also added to the Tobruk garrison.

26. *CWP3*, 1311–1313. Churchill also argued for close army-RAF cooperation, something hitherto lacking in the desert.

27. Air Chief Marshal Sir Arthur Tedder, the RAF theater commander, was unimpressed with Cunningham from the beginning. He later recalled that the Eighth Army commander gave him "the impression of feeling completely at sea in matters of armored warfare," adding a revealing anecdote—"General Cunningham remarked to me: 'I wish I knew what Rommel means to do.' This impressed me as being a strange outlook for the commander of a superior attacking force." In this remark may lie the explanation for a plan that relinquished the initiative at the outset of the battle—Cunningham was uncertain how to seize it. See Tedder, *With Prejudice* (Boston, 1966), 196. Like most senior RAF officers, Tedder was no great admirer of the army, but this observation rings true.

28. On the eve of Crusader, Rommel had 174 German tanks in the two Afrika Korps panzer divisions. The Italians had 146 but of generally inferior quality. Comparisons indicate that the Germans' numerical inferiority was by no means compensated for by any qualitative superiority.

29. Churchill, *Grand Alliance*, 556. Barnett, in *The Desert Generals,* 89, has claimed that this revelation of how much now hung upon the coming battle constituted "another tremendous anxiety." This assertion seems to take Barnett's tendency to blame Churchill whenever possible a bit far. In form from the king, the message was clearly a piece of Churchillian prose and sent to Auchinleck for his use "if, when and as" he wished. It does Cunningham little credit to claim he was such a nervous wreck that a rhetorical flourish could create "tremendous anxiety."

30. Robert Crisp, *Brazen Chariots* (New York, 1961), 31.

31. Although his name is forever linked with the Afrika Korps, Rommel actually commanded it for only a short time. By November 1941, he was commanding Panzer Group Afrika, and the Afrika Korps was commanded by Lieutenant General Cruewell.

32. The 7th Armoured Brigade reported no runners; the 22nd reported thirty. There were no reports from 4th Armoured Brigade, whose headquarters had been overrun although its tank strength was largely intact.

33. Since Godwin-Austen had been largely responsible for the initial dispersion of Norrie's armor by his insistence on close protection for his flank, his determination at a time when, as far as he knew, British tank strength had fallen almost to the vanishing point and his own accompanying tank brigade had lost a third of its strength is both curious and ironic. Carver would end his career as Field Marshal Lord Carver. His two books, *Tobruk* (London, 1964) and *Dilemmas of the Desert War* (London, 1986), are essential reading for any student of the desert war. The latter, written after he retired, is much more frank.

34. There is some confusion about who conferred with whom and where on No-

vember 23. Barnett, in *The Desert Generals,* 106–107, says Galloway, Godwin-Austen, and Carver met at XIII Corps Headquarters and Galloway took Godwin-Austen's views back to Cunningham. Carver, however, in his own study of Crusader, *Tobruk* 84–87, says it was held at Eighth Army headquarters and in Cunningham's presence. The difference may seem trivial, but Barnett's account, if correct, strengthens his picture of Galloway as the person who kept Cunningham from breaking off Crusader. Galloway provided Barnett with information but left no account of his own.

35. The Germans had begun November 23 with 162 tanks and lost 72 of them in the course of the day's fighting, nearly all the losses coming in the frontal assault the Afrika Korps launched on the 5th South African Infantry Brigade and its supporting artillery. This action proves both that headlong tank charges were not an exclusive British monopoly and that had the British used their splendid artillery in cooperation with their armor, Rommel's successes would have been fewer.

36. On the morning of November 24, Cunningham went forward to Norrie's headquarters and was there when the Afrika Korps, preceded by a flurry of British "soft-skinned" vehicles trying to get clear of it, came thundering through. His plane, hastily taking off, cleared a 3-ton truck by inches. The whole episode cannot have done anything for Cunningham's already shaken confidence.

37. The whole question of Cunningham's health and its relationship to his exercise of command is an interesting one. Correlli Barnett claims Cunningham was nearly exhausted before Crusader began and in no shape mentally to make clear decisions on difficult issues by November 23—a spent man; see Barnett, *The Desert Generals*, 108. Certainly, after Cunningham's relief, Auchinleck insisted he go into the hospital, but this may have been largely cosmetic, since medical examination—insisted upon by his brother, Admiral Sir Andrew Cunningham—found him perfectly sound. In any case, he was soon out of the hospital, and although he never again held a field command, he went on to be the last British high commissioner in Palestine (a distinctly stressful job) and live into his nineties. Instead of implying a breakdown, it might be more accurate simply to ascribe Cunningham's failure to his complete inexperience of armored warfare and a loss of nerve in the face of his heavy tank losses—the reason Auchinleck gave when reporting his action to the prime minister. Churchill was clearly uncomfortable with the pretense that Cunningham was being removed because of a physical or mental breakdown, referring to it as a "pious fraud." The statement he made in Parliament simply said that Cunningham had been found *after* his supersession to be suffering from "serious overstrain." See Churchill to David Margesson [secretary of state for war] and Dill, December 5, 1941, *CWP3*, 1565. Churchill's statement in the House is in *CWP3*, 1604.

38. G. P. B. Roberts, *From the Desert to the Baltic* (London, 1987), 59. By the war's end, Roberts was a major general commanding the 11th Armoured Division and generally regarded as the British Army's best tank commander.

39. See, for example, the rather mournful recounting by Connell, *Auchinleck*, 270–328.

40. This was particularly the case because the other British offensive action against Germany—the bombing offensive—had been shown to be largely ineffective by the "Butt Report," done in the summer of 1941 by a member of the small analysis staff that operated, under the direction of Lord Cherwell, out of the prime minister's office. If the

Russians were to see a noticeable British contribution, it would have to come from Eighth Army.

41. Brooke's account is in his diary entry for November 16, 1941, and his note of a conversation with Dill and the CIGS's speculations about his successor are in the entry for November 13; see Danchev and Todman, *War Diaries*, 198–200.

42. The Leinster Regiment was a southern Irish unit and, as such, was disbanded after 1922. Nye transferred to the Royal Warwickshire Regiment—Monty's regiment and also the regiment in which Slim began his military career.

43. Brooke's summing up of Nye is in a postwar note appended to the November 13 entry in his diary; Danchev and Todman, *War Diaries*, 198.

44. Pownall's rather dry account is in Brian Bond, ed., *Chief of Staff: The Diaries of Lieutenant-General Sir Henry Pownall*, 2 vols. (London, 1973–1974), 2:53–54.

45. Ibid., 2:54. The diary entry is for November 19.

46. Eade's notes are in *CWP3*, 1471–1472.

47. One of Brooke's first jobs was to soothe General Gordon Macready, to whom Nye had previously reported and over whose head he had suddenly vaulted. Both Pownall and Brooke told their diaries that they did not believe that Nye had intrigued for his promotion. Jock Colville, Churchill's devoted private secretary, recorded a 1945 letter of congratulations to Clement Attlee as an example of Nye's ingratitude to the man who had promoted him; see J. R. Colville, *Fringes of Power: 10 Downing Street Diaries, 1939–1945* (London, 1985), 611. Nye did not publish a memoir. He finished his career as the last British governor of Madras.

48. Danchev and Todman, *War Diaries*, 3, entry for September 28, 1939.

49. The background to the Singapore disaster is discussed in Raymond Callahan, *The Worst Disaster: The Fall of Singapore* (Newark, DE, and London, 1977). A more recent (and excellent) account is in Malcolm H. Murfett, John M. Miksic, Brian P. Farrell, and Chiang Ming Shun, *Between Two Oceans: A Military History of Singapore from the First Settlement to Final British Withdrawal* (Oxford, 1999). The papers printed in Brian Farrell and Sandy Hunter, eds., *Sixty Years On: The Fall of Singapore Revisited* (Singapore, 2002), originally read at a conference held at the National University of Singapore to mark the sixtieth anniversary of the city's fall, provide much valuable material. The most recent studies are Alan Warren, *Singapore: Britain's Greatest Defeat* (London, 2002) and Brian P. Farrell, *The Defence and Fall of Singapore, 1940–1942* (Stroud, UK, 2005).

50. Bond, *Chief of Staff*, 2:76.

51. Pownall to Churchill, December 30, 1948, Churchill Papers CHUR 4/255a, CAC. Pownall assisted Churchill during the composition of his war memoirs, drafting many of the chapters on military episodes.

52. Ismay, *Memoirs*, 247.

53. Jacob to Ismay, January 24, 1959, quoted in Callahan, *The Worst Disaster*, 60–61 and 72n37. Jacob's remark came in a letter commenting on the draft of Ismay's memoirs that included this sentence: "I had always visualized that Singapore was a self-contained fortress." After receiving Jacob's letter, this sentence was altered to the somewhat evasive phrase quoted in the text.

54. Churchill's "Most Secret" directive of April 28, 1941, is in *CWP3*, 536–537.

55. Churchill's note for the Chiefs of Staff, September 17, 1941, is in ibid., 1223.

56. It is fascinating to conjecture what impact either Paget or Pownall might have made if appointed earlier. Singapore's ultimate fate may have been the same, but the tactical handling of the army in Malaya might have been much more effective.

57. Churchill to Denis Kelly, August 7, 1950, Churchill Papers CHUR 4/255a, f. 92, CAC. Kelly was a key member of Churchill's "syndicate" of assistants, coordinating the work of the team.

58. Churchill to Ismay, December 15, 1941, *CWP3*, 1630.

59. Churchill to Wavell, December 12, 1941, ibid., 1614.

60. Churchill to Auchinleck, December 4, 1941, ibid., 1558.

61. Churchill to Auchinleck, December 25, 1941, ibid., 1681. The tanks, in the form of the 7th Armoured Brigade, never got to Singapore. Diverted to Rangoon when Singapore fell, they were essential to the success of the retreat from Burma conducted by Slim between March and May 1942.

62. Ibid, 1681–1682. Gymnast eventually became Operation Torch, launched in November 1942. In December 1941, there were no "highly trained" American formations—they were as much a fantasy as the Singapore fortress.

63. Churchill to Ismay, December 19, 1941, *CWP3*, 1648.

64. Churchill to Wavell, December 29, 1941, ibid., 1704.

65. Churchill paid a tribute to Dill's role in Washington in *Grand Alliance* (688), although it has a slightly perfunctory air.

Chapter Four. Debacles

1. There is a good description of Rommel's counterstroke in Field Marshal Lord Carver's *Dilemmas of the Desert War* (London, 1986); the quoted phrase is on 57. Briggs later commanded the 5th Indian Division in the desert and served with great distinction under Slim in Burma. After Indian independence, he retired to Cyprus and was growing lemons there when, at Slim's request, he returned to active service as director of operations in Malaya, playing a major role in the turnaround of the British counterinsurgency campaign there.

2. Shearer, who had left the army in 1929 for the business world, becoming an executive of Fortnum and Mason, once again retired from the service for business. De Guingand would go on to become Monty's chief of staff, where his tact was often sorely tried. A key role in this change was played by Eric Dorman-Smith, an increasingly influential adviser to Auchinleck. Brooke had become extremely critical of Shearer and pressed Auchinleck for his replacement, although he was also very suspicious of Dorman-Smith.

3. W. S. Churchill, *The Hinge of Fate* (Boston, 1950), 67.

4. Auchinleck to Churchill, January 30, 1942, in John Connell, *Auchinleck: A Critical Biography* (London, 1959), 446.

5. Churchill, *Hinge of Fate*, 34–35.

6. Ibid., 35.

7. Auchinleck to Churchill, January 31, 1942, in ibid., 33.

8. Brian Bond, ed., *Chief of Staff: The Diaries of Lieutenant General Sir Henry Pownall*, 2 vols. (London, 1973–1974), 2:76. Pownall's dismissive view of Percival may well have influenced the chapters on the Malayan campaign and the fall of Singapore in Chur-

chill's *Hinge of Fate*, which were, as Churchill acknowledged, drafted by Pownall. On this, see Raymond Callahan, "Churchill and Singapore," in Brian Farrell and Sandy Hunter, eds., *Sixty Years On: The Fall of Singapore Revisited* (Singapore, 2002), 165–168.

9. On this, see Brian P. Farrell, "The Dice Were Rather Heavily Loaded: Wavell and the Fall of Singapore," in Brian P. Farrell, ed., *Leadership and Responsibility in the Second World War: Essays in Honour of Robert Vogel* (Montreal, Canada, 2001), 209–246, a much-needed corrective to the picture painted by Wavell's official biographer, John Connell, in *Wavell: The Supreme Commander* (London, 1969). It is interesting that, as in the case of Neame in March 1941, Wavell made clear his lack of confidence in a field commander but stopped short of replacing him.

10. Davies to Lewin, May 15, 1974, Slim Papers 5/4, Churchill Archive Centre, Churchill College, Cambridge (hereafter CAC). Major General H. G. "Taffy" Davies served in Burma; Ronald Lewin was Slim's official biographer.

11. Brooke's diary entries from December 7 on reflect gloom about the prospects in the Far East. "I doubt whether Hong Kong will hold out a fortnight and Malaya a month," he noted on December 15. But there is no indication of any serious reflection on how Percival was conducting his battle. See A. Danchev and D. Todman, eds., *War Diaries, 1939–1945: Field Marshal Lord Alanbrooke* (London, 2001), 211.

12. Churchill to Ismay for Chiefs of Staff, November 24, 1941, in Martin Gilbert, ed., *The Churchill War Papers,* vol. 3, *The Ever Widening War, 1941* (London, 2000), 1505 (hereafter *CWP3).*

13. Churchill to Wavell, January 23, 1942, in Churchill, *Hinge of Fate*, 134.

14. Wavell to Churchill, January 16, 1942, in Connell, *Wavell,* 105, and in Churchill, *Hinge of Fate*, 48. There is an insightful discussion of Churchill and the Singapore fortress in Brian P. Farrell, *The Defence and Fall of Singapore, 1940–1942* (Stroud, UK, 2005), 283–286. Farrell's analysis deserves that overworked label "definitive."

15. Churchill prints Curtin's message of January 23 in *Hinge of Fate*, 58.

16. Ibid., 59.

17. Danchev and Todman, *War Diaries*, 222. The note follows the January 23, 1942, diary entry.

18. Churchill to Wavell, February 10, 1942, in Churchill, *Hinge of Fate*, 100. Churchill's concern about the martial qualities of British soldiers endured for some time after Singapore—perhaps until the Eighth Army's victory at El Alamein. Two days after sending this "die in the last ditch" order to Wavell, Churchill revealed his innermost fears to his close friend Lady Violet Bonham Carter, who related to Harold Nicolson that "for the first time in their long friendship she had found him depressed . . . underneath it all was a dreadful fear, she felt, that our soldiers are not as good fighters as their fathers were. 'In 1915,' said Winston, 'our men fought on even when they had only one shell left and were under a fierce barrage. Now they cannot resist dive bombers. We have so many men, in Singapore, so many men—they should have done better.'" To this, Nicolson added his own gloss: "It is the same of course in Libya. Our men cannot stand up to punishment." See Nigel Nicolson, ed., *The Diaries and Letters of Harold Nicolson,* vol. 2, *The War Years, 1939–1945* (New York, 1967), 211, entry for February 12. The fear that the casualties of World War I had weakened the fiber of the British nation haunted many, Churchill and Brooke among them. The concentration on whether the army wanted to fight tended to overshadow the question of whether its equipment, training, and leader-

ship positioned it to do so effectively. Churchill also overlooked, as he was apt to do in matters related to the Far Eastern war, the fact that most of the troops involved were actually not British at all, which rather invalidated the racial-decline interpretation. He would have a similar reaction when Tobruk fell in June.

19. Danchev and Todman, *War Diaries*, 231, entry for February 18, 1942.

20. There was a postwar epilogue to Singapore's fall. Wavell had a report compiled, using such documents and testimony as were available in India. Dated June 1, 1942, it was circulated to the War Cabinet, at Churchill's direction, in September, then embargoed for fifty years. It is a very interesting document, not least for its suggestion that the speed of the final collapse was due to desertion and indiscipline in the 8th Australian Division, a suggestion that caused outrage in Australia when the report was finally released in 1997. The allegation has been incisively examined by Brian Farrell in Malcolm Murfett, John N. Miksic, Brian P. Farrell, and Chiang Ming Shun, *Between Two Oceans: A Military History of Singapore from First Settlement to Final British Withdrawal* (Oxford, 1999), 341–364. Farrell has pointed out (in "The Dice Were Heavily Loaded") that faulting the Australians allowed Wavell to redirect blame, at least some of which he ought to have shouldered himself. Churchill took a different course. Despite having called for a royal commission to investigate Singapore's fall, he made no move to convene one, either during the war or when he returned to office in 1951. He was probably aware that Attlee's government had, on the advice of the Chiefs of Staff, decided in 1946 against any such inquiry because it would be impossible to limit it merely to the actions of the commanders in Malaya. In the relevant chapters of *Hinge of Fate*, drafted by Pownall, Churchill actually did just that. Although he never hid either his priorities or his conviction that they were correct, the focus of the account is on what the local commanders, preeminently Percival, had done or failed to do. Churchill did, however, tell his assistants that he would pick no public quarrel with the Australians. Thus, whereas Wavell privately scapegoated the Australians, Churchill's narrative focused the spotlight on Percival. The roles of Wavell, Brooke, and Churchill were somewhat obscured. History is still trying to set the record straight. Wavell's report is in the Public Record Office, PRO, CAB 119/208, which also includes the papers produced for the Attlee government in 1946. On Churchill's memoir account, see Callahan, "Churchill and Singapore," 165–168.

21. In his postwar additions to his diary (entry for February 22, 1942), Brooke argued that "the arrival of [the 7th Australian] division in Rangoon, at that time, might well have restored the situation and saved Burma"; see Danchev and Todman, *War Diaries*, 232. Since the division was spread over five convoys and would not have been completely assembled until the end of March—Rangoon fell on March 8—is it very hard to see how. The British official historians subsequently endorsed the verdict of their Australian opposite numbers about the episode: Australian troops could have made no difference to the result in Burma.

22. Churchill, *Hinge of Fate*, 166.

23. Danchev and Todman, *War Diaries*, 216, entry for December 31, 1941.

24. As with Neame and Percival, Wavell made clear his lack of confidence in a subordinate without replacing him. In all three cases, he may have been correct, but the net result in each instance was to make a weak command structure worse.

25. Danchev and Todman, *War Diaries*, 231, entry for February 19. Obviously, Brooke was inadequately informed about the state of 17th Indian Division. The decline in

quality in the Indian Army, due to excessively rapid expansion, was, like the issue of whether Singapore was a fortress, something that was getting scant attention in London.

26. Churchill, *Hinge of Fate*, 167.

27. Alexander's own recollections, *The Memoirs of Field-Marshal Earl Alexander of Tunis: 1940–1945* (London, 1962), was ghostwritten by a former member of his staff, John North, whose name appears on the title page as "editor." They tell little about Alexander or his exercise of command. Like Alex, however, the tone is amiable. Nigel Nicolson wrote the official biography, *Alex: The Life of Field Marshal Earl Alexander of Tunis* (London, 1973). It is more elegantly written than many generals' biographies, but it does not really address numerous issues about Alexander's role between 1942 and 1945. A recent entry by a devoted former staff officer, Rupert Clarke, *With Alex at War: From the Irrawaddy to the Po* (London, 2000), is a picture of a charming man but adds nothing to our understanding of the soldier. The needed analysis of Alexander the commander remains to be written.

28. A brief account of the first Burma campaign is Raymond Callahan, *Burma, 1942–45* (London, 1978). A more recent, detailed account, incorporating Japanese material, is Ian Lyall Grant and Kazuo Tamayana, *Burma, 1942: The Japanese Invasion* (Chichester, UK, 1999).

29. The brief typescript essay in which this appears is in the Slim Papers 5/2/2, CAC. During the interwar years of slow promotion, Slim moonlighted as an author to augment his pay, writing under the pen name Anthony Mills. The polished, accessible writing style he then developed, evident here, would make his account of the Burma campaign, *Defeat into Victory*, one of the most readable and attractive of all generals' memoirs.

30. The chapter in *Hinge of Fate* dealing with Burma was drafted by Pownall. Churchill's focus in the chapter is clearly the quarrel with Curtin's government over the use of Australian troops in Burma. It is nonetheless astounding that Slim is never mentioned. The chapter ends with an encomium on Alex: "He showed all those qualities of military skill, imperturbability, and wise judgement that brought him later into the first rank of allied war leaders" (171). By the time it was published, Slim was CIGS. The retreat from Burma and the collapse of the British imperium in Southeast Asia has recently been trenchantly analyzed by Christopher Bayly and Tim Harper, *Forgotten Armies: The Fall of British Asia, 1941–1945* (London, 2004). Despite the title, this is a study not of military operations but of the far-reaching and irreversible consequences of both the 1941–1942 collapse and the 1944–1945 comeback. It is indispensable to any serious student of Britain's war in Asia.

31. Danchev and Todman, *War Diaries*, 246, 249, entries for April 9 and 15. These discussions took place during a visit to London by Marshall to discuss alliance strategy for 1942.

32. Ibid., 249, postwar note added to entry for April 15, 1942.

33. Ibid., 243–244, entry for March 31, 1942. The following day, Brooke noted, "Looking back at what I wrote last night I wonder whether I was liverish!"

34. There is no question that American reservations about the shelving of a direct attack on Europe, as it transpired for two years, and the Mediterranean focus of Anglo-American strategy in 1942 and 1943 affected U.S.—and especially Marshall's—attitudes from 1942 on. Surprisingly, the American belief that British strategic choices had impe-

rial undertones still colors much American writing on the subject. The reality was that British strategy evolved out of a mix of prewar decisions and the pressures of war itself, reflecting Lord Kitchener's remark to Churchill in 1914 that nations waged war as they could, rather than as they wished. The 1942 disputes also launched another myth: that Torch foreclosed the chance for a 1943 cross-channel attack and thereby prolonged the war, to the long-term benefit of the Russians. A good example of this Cold War-influenced history is John Grigg's *1943: The Victory That Never Was* (New York, 1980). Americans who were suspicious at the time and later revisionists alike overlooked the key issue: could the British Army, with only small American and Canadian contingents, have successfully confronted the German field-force formations it was likely to face in western Europe in 1942 and 1943? In terms of numbers (and ability to replace casualties), equipment, doctrine, training, and experience, that question is difficult to answer in the affirmative. It is clear how deep the doubts of Churchill and Brooke were. It is hard to dissent from their judgment, especially in light of the difficulties experienced when Overlord was finally mounted in 1944.

35. A portion of Nye's questionnaire and Auchinleck's answers are in Compton MacKenzie, *Eastern Epic*, vol. 1, *September 1939–May 1943: Defence* (London, 1951), 538. Auchinleck had by this point decided to change the organization of British armored divisions from the tank-heavy pattern of Crusader to one resembling that of the panzer divisions. Henceforth, divisions would have only one armored brigade group, which would be balanced by an infantry brigade group. This new pattern, plus more intensive combined arms training, would doubtless have improved the performance of British armored divisions, if there had been time to give effect to it before the next round of fighting.

The whole question of an army's ability to learn and innovate during wartime has been stimulatingly addressed by Stephen Peter Rosen, *Winning the Next War: Innovation and the Modern Military* (Ithaca, NY, 1991). Rosen points out that it took the British Army some forty months "to reorient its operating concepts to make effective use of the tank" in World War I (128), a delay he ascribes to a failure to grasp exactly what the vulnerabilities of the German army on the Western Front were. In the desert war, adapting to experience was complicated by the theater's semiautonomy from the army at home and the doctrines generated there as well as by the power of the "independent action" concept so strongly embedded in theater armored doctrine. There was also a time lag, paralleling the World War I experience described by Rosen, before the British grasped that German antitank screens, not the panzers themselves, were their most lethal enemies. The British learned in the desert, not perhaps as fast as critics then and later might have wished but as quickly as they could institutionally.

36. Danchev and Todman, *War Diaries*, 224–225, 235, 259, postwar entries appended to diary entries for January 29 and March 3 and diary entry for May 19. It should be noted that when Brooke made the postwar notes reflecting his distrust of Dorman-Smith, the latter was in embittered retirement, having been one of the scapegoats for the massive British defeat between May and June. Although Dorman-Smith was very unpopular in the army, a suspicion of justifying actions taken has to cling to Brooke's postwar second thoughts on this subject.

37. I. S. O. Playfair, F. C. Flynn, C. J. C. Molony, and T. P. Gleave, *The Mediterranean and Middle East,* vol. 3 (London, 1960), 215.

38. The words are Carver's in *Dilemmas*, 141.

39. The best summary is in ibid., 62–68.

40. Lieutenant General Sir Francis Tuker, *Approach to Battle* (London, 1963), 85.

41. In the fast-moving desert battles, prisoners were often an encumbrance, consuming scarce food and water. The Germans occasionally simply turned prisoners loose rather than try to guard, transport, and provision them. Thus, of the nearly 1,000 prisoners taken from Filose's brigade, nearly 800 rejoined within a few days, having either escaped or been set free by their captors. This policy, of course, would not apply to a senior officer—if he was recognized as such.

42. The 50th Division was a Territorial formation from northern England; many of its rank and file came from chronically depressed, hardship-plagued mining and industrial regions. Their stubborn defense of this isolated box was a demonstration of the dour powers of resistance in desperate situations long characteristic of British infantry. Their virtual abandonment by Gott, Norrie, and Ritchie exemplified the sort of generalship that made such displays of die-hard courage all too frequent.

43. The inadequate 2-pounder antitank gun was finally in the process of being replaced by the much more formidable 6-pounder, but only 112 of the latter had reached the Middle East by May 1942, and they were destined for artillery units. The infantry remained dependent on the 2-pounder, and many infantry formations did not even have those.

44. In the same message to Ritchie in which he raised some questions about Aberdeen, Auchinleck told him that it was "most desireable to keep formations intact . . . one gets better results from an intact formation." He went on to add, "I visualized your using . . . 5th Indian complete as a striking force." Nonetheless, the veteran 5th Indian, Ritchie's only reserve, was broken up before the battle began. One brigade was garrisoning one of the boxes outside Tobruk. When the division was finally committed to Aberdeen, only two of its brigades were used, in hopeless circumstances, after which Briggs had to take the remnants back to Egypt to reorganize. See Carver, *Dilemmas*, 96.

45. Playfair et al., *The Mediterranean and Middle East,* 3:235.

46. Churchill, *Hinge of Fate*, 366.

47. Churchill to Auchinleck, June 11, 1942, in ibid., 366.

48. Carver, *Dilemmas*, 104. An example of what Carver meant occurred on June 12, when, Messervy having again been temporarily overrun, Norrie decided to place his tanks under Lumsden's command. He asked Lumsden at noon if he could manage this. Three and a half hours elapsed before Lumsden reported that he had done so. It is difficult to imagine Rommel displaying Norrie's patience with a dilatory subordinate at a critical moment.

49. Churchill to Auchinleck, June 14, 1942, in Churchill, *Hinge of Fate,* 369.

50. Ibid., 370.

51. Churchill to Auchinleck, June 15, 1942, in ibid., 371.

52. Auchinleck to Churchill, June 16, 1942, in ibid.

53. The use of the Indian divisions in this battle is interesting. One brigade of Tuker's 4th Indian was loaned to 2nd South African to bring it up to strength. Briggs's division was similarly broken up, one brigade being put into the El Adem box southeast of Tobruk. Major General T. W. Rees's 10th Indian handed over two brigades for boxes and lost most of one of them. It is hard to avoid the conclusion that, lacking the political

clout that kept South African, Australian, and New Zealand formations largely intact, the Indian divisions were the most readily available resource with which to execute the policy of dotting supposedly self-defending positions around the desert.

54. Carver, *Dilemmas*, 98–99.

55. Auchinleck may have been passing judgment on the fairness of Norrie's handling of Messervy when, a few days later, he named Messervy acting deputy chief of the General Staff in Cairo. Messervy later successfully commanded first a division and then a corps under Slim in Burma.

56. Klopper was actually junior to both the South African brigadiers, who were not enthusiastic about a fight to the finish. No South African officer could be unaware of what heavy casualties would mean to the already divided white community at home as well as to the balance between the ruling white minority and the black majority.

57. Churchill, *Hinge of Fate*, 382–383; Danchev and Todman, *War Diaries*, 268–269, entry for June 21 and Brooke's postwar note. Curiously, Churchill remembered it as happening in the morning, whereas Brooke placed it in the late afternoon.

58. Charles, Baron Moran, *Churchill: Taken from the Diaries of Lord Moran* (New York, 1966), 41, diary entry for June 21. The reality of Britain's war effort is illustrated by the fact that many of the troops in Tobruk were South Africans and Indians—and the Indian brigade held out after Klopper surrendered, only laying down its arms when a staff officer from Klopper's headquarters personally confirmed to Brigadier A. Anderson that the fortress had in fact been surrendered. As at Singapore, the fall of which Churchill's doctor felt had left a "scar" on the prime minister, Churchill saw the event as a sign of British martial decline without noting either the complexity of the actual situation or the true size of the British component involved, much less its composition (it included many support units).

59. Churchill, *Hinge of Fate*, 392–393.

60. Rees, a dynamic and combative man who had taken over 10th Indian Division from Slim, later became a very distinguished divisional commander in Burma. It is instructive to look at the account of this episode in Rees's papers, which are in the British Library's Oriental and India Office Collections. In a confidential letter written shortly after the event to the deputy military secretary at GHQ, Middle East, Rees explained: "What I endeavoured to point out to General Gott, in a necessarily disguised conversation over a telephone in the field, was that my Division, unsupported by adequate armour, would be unlikely to be able to hold the Solum [*sic*] position against a prolonged full-scale enemy attack. I submit we have ample evidence of this and of the fact that my appreciation of the situation was correct. Indeed, General Gott himself, less than six hours later, gave my successor instructions to evacuate the position because it was realised it was untenable"; see Rees Papers, MSS EUR F274, f. 17. The 10th Indian Division War Diary records an order from Rees at 8:15 A.M. on June 21—the day Gott relieved him: "If so ordered we would put up as stubborn a defence as any troops could, and fight until the water ran out," ibid., f. 56. Gott and Ritchie, who supported Gott but could not explain his decision to Rees, look far more rattled than Rees.

61. Churchill to Auchinleck, May 20, 1942, in Churchill, *Hinge of Fate*, 310.

62. After defeating a Russian offensive in May, taking a quarter-million prisoners, the German summer offensive began early in June and was soon making rapid progress toward the Caucasus—south of which lay Auchinleck's sparsely held northern front. In

contemplating the effect of the northern front on Auchinleck, F. W. Maitland's warning to historians ought to be borne in mind: things (in this case, Stalingrad) now safely in the past were once far in the future.

63. Churchill, *Hinge of Fate*, 368–369. Brooke felt that Ritchie had been ill used and saw that he got a second chance. He commanded a corps in the Second Army under Monty in 1944 and 1945 and ended his career a full general.

64. Playfair et al., *The Mediterranean and Middle East*, 3:287. In the discussions about the best organization for British forces, McCreery, who had been sent out by Brooke to act as Auchinleck's adviser on armor, had been consistently sidelined and ignored because, it would appear, Dorman-Smith disliked him. Here, Brooke's concern about Dorman-Smith's influence seems solidly grounded.

65. Establishing the number of British tanks at Matruh is difficult. The official history gives the total as "about 155," with fewer than 50 Grants; see Playfair et al., *The Mediterranean and Middle East,* 3:286 n. B. H. Liddell Hart, in his official history of the Royal Tank Regiment, puts it at 159, with 60 Grants; see *The Tanks: The History of the Royal Tank Regiment,* vol. 2, *1939–1945* (New York, 1959), 187. The New Zealand official history confirms these figures; see J. E. Scoullar, *The Battle for Egypt: The Summer of 1942* (Wellington, 1955), 60. If Lumsden had 60 Grants, he had quantitative and qualitative superiority over the Afrika Korps, even without his additional 100 light and medium tanks.

66. Quoted in Correlli Barnett, *The Desert Generals* (London, 1960), 184.

67. Alan Moorehead, *African Trilogy* (London, 1959), 252–253.

68. Nicolson, *Diaries and Letters of Harold Nicolson,* 226, diary entry for May 20.

69. Ibid., 228, diary entry for June 21, 1942.

70. Ibid., 229–230, diary entry for June 22, 1942.

71. R. Broad and S. Fleming, eds., *Nella Last's War: A Mother's Diary, 1939–1945* (London, 1981), 205.

72. Churchill, *Hinge of Fate*, 390.

73. Nicolson, *Diaries and Letters of Harold Nicolson,* 231, diary entry for July 1, 1942.

74. Churchill, *Hinge of Fate*, 395. It is interesting that Cripps was in touch with B. H. Liddell Hart, the military journalist who would be prominent among Churchill's postwar critics. Liddell Hart was pushing Hobart, father of the 7th Armoured Division, as Eighth Army commander. Since Hobart belonged to the "independent" school of British armored theorists, it is hard to see how he would have remedied the problems of battlefield integration of arms that had plagued the British in the desert.

75. Nicolson, *Diaries and Letters of Harold Nicolson,* 232, diary entry for July 2, 1942. Nicolson thought the best solution would be to make Wavell CIGS (!).

76. Quoted in Paul Addison, *The Road to 1945* (London, 1975), 208.

77. The Y service provided invaluable tactical intelligence derived from intercepted enemy signals, often in low-level ciphers (as opposed to the complex Enigma ciphers broken at Bletchley Park) and voice transmissions among units in forward areas.

78. According to Carver, who was on his staff, Norrie was replaced at his own request on July 8. Carver, who described Norrie as "a charmer" but "indecisive," comments: "It was a shrewd move, as he was able to present his story of what went wrong to the authorities at home before others got their word in, and he was on good personal terms with Churchill." See Carver, *Dilemmas*, 133, 145. Brooke, however, had already

noted in his diary on June 20 that Norrie "was being sent home"; see Danchev and Todman, *War Diaries*, 268. Certainly, on July 21, he was in London, where he spent an hour with Brooke; see ibid., 283. Later in the war, Norrie resurfaced, heading a military mission to the French and finally becoming the governor of South Australia.

79. Playfair et al., *The Mediterranean and Middle East*, 3:352. The authors do not, however, mention that on July 29, Auchinleck told Major General Richard McCreery, who had been sent out as major general Armoured Forces (that is, senior adviser on tank organization and tactics), that the only way to remedy the "blatant and repeated" failure of tank-infantry cooperation was to reorganize divisions so that every infantry division included an armored brigade. McCreery did not agree this was the solution, and Auchinleck fired him on the spot. See Connell, *Auchinleck,* 684. However, McCreery had been a staff officer in Alexander's division of the BEF and had been marked out for promotion by Brooke. On August 10, when Churchill signed Alexander's directive as Middle East commander-in-chief, McCreery became Alex's chief of staff. The direction in which Auchinleck wanted to move was actually the direction British armor went in the second half of the war. The proportion of infantry and artillery in armored divisions increased, and the number of such divisions dropped to make more tanks available to work with the infantry.

80. Playfair et al., *The Mediterranean and Middle East,* 3:360. This also, of course, could stand as a good example of the British habit of admiring, whenever possible, one's enemies.

81. B. H. Liddell Hart, ed., *The Rommel Papers* (New York, 1953), 260.

82. Churchill's description of Corbett is from the unpublished diary kept by Colonel Ian Jacob of Churchill's staff. The late Lieutenant General Sir Ian Jacob kindly allowed me to read the complete diary in the 1970s. Excerpts from it were used by Churchill and others, and a lengthy extract appears in Nigel Hamilton's *Monty: The Making of a General, 1887–1942* (London, 1981), 577–580. Churchill's acid remarks on Corbett are at 577–578.

83. Moran, *Churchill*, 79.

84. Churchill, *Hinge of Fate*, 458.

85. Ibid., 459.

86. Ibid.

87. Churchill reproduced this extract from Jacob's diary in *Hinge of Fate*, 468.

88. Playfair et al., *The Mediterranean and Middle East,* 3:368–369.

89. Carver, *Dilemmas*, 145.

90. Danchev and Todman, *War Diaries*, 290, postwar note added to the August 3, 1942, entry.

It is interesting to consider the fate of the officers removed in July and August 1942. Auchinleck, of course, emerged from a brief period of unemployment to once again become commander-in-chief, India—the last and possibly greatest holder of that position. Messervy commanded a division and then a corps under Slim in Burma and ended his career as the first commander-in-chief of the Pakistani army. Rees served under Slim as a very distinguished divisional commander and, at the time of the bloody partition of the Raj, as commander of the Punjab Boundary Force, a harrowingly difficult task. In short, the Indian Army officers, whose presence in the Middle East reflected the enormous Indian contribution to the theater, continued to have distinguished careers in a theater that their army dominated.

There was one exception: Corbett. He had moved to Middle East GHQ in Cairo, as Auchinleck's chief of staff. Wavell had suggested him for the corps command in Burma that ultimately went to Slim, and Brooke was willing to consider him, regarding him as a success with IV Indian Corps in Iraq. He clearly was not a great success in Cairo, but neither was he the nonentity described so pithily by Churchill. Yet he disappeared from history in a manner reminiscent of Stalin's victims vanishing from photographs. Retired in 1943 with remarkably few decorations for an officer of his rank, he later farmed in Kenya and died in 1982. The relevant volume of the official history mentions him once, in passing. Ironically, his papers ultimately came to rest in the Churchill Archive Centre at Churchill College, Cambridge. The collection includes a bitter letter to Brooke, drafted but never sent: "The principal of British justice is a fair hearing. This is one of the major causes for which we are fighting the war." Corbett to Brooke, August 15, 1942, Corbett Papers CORB 4/16, CAC. In Corbett's case, the word *purge* might come close to applying.

Of the British service officers, Norrie, as noted earlier, ended in the ornamental role of a colonial governor. Ramsden was not employed again. Dorman-Smith's subsequent career was both curious and sad. Given a brigade command in Italy, he was deemed to have failed, and his military career effectively ended there. In retirement, he became more bitter and eccentric, threatening to sue Churchill over the account of the August 1942 command changes in *Hinge of Fate* and flirting with the Irish Republican Army (IRA) (Irish by birth, he had changed his name to O'Gowan and retired to the Irish Republic). He has been the subject of a sympathetic study by Lavinia Greachen, *Chink: A Biography* (London, 1989).

When Correlli Barnett wrote his influential anti-Churchill, anti-Montgomery, pro-Auchinleck polemic, *The Desert Generals,* much of his information came from Auchinleck, Dorman-O'Gowan (as Dorman-Smith had become), Norrie, Ramsden, Corbett, Godwin-Austen, Messervy, and Creagh, together with Major Generals J. M. L. Renton and A. H. Gatehouse, who were sacked later by Montgomery. A colorful and very readable book, it therefore needs cautious handling.

91. Churchill, *Hinge of Fate*, 471.

Chapter Five. Monty and His Enemies

1. Winston S. Churchill, *The Hinge of Fate* (Boston, 1950), 603. The file in Churchill's papers (CHUR 4/284, Churchill Archive Centre, Churchill College, Cambridge [hereafter CAC]) dealing with the chapter on El Alamein indicates that the weak qualifier "it might almost be said" was added well into the process of assembling the chapter—an indication of how important Alamein had come to seem to Churchill.

2. Churchill, *Hinge of Fate*, 518. Of course, making preparations for the contingency of Rommel's reaching the delta were part of the theater commander's duties—Wavell had such plans, as did Auchinleck. Alex had them as well, which Churchill even notes (520–521). Wavell's plans enraged the prime minister when he became aware of them. Auchinleck's became part of the bill of particulars against him developed by Montgomery and accepted by Churchill. Alex, as usual, had a charmed life. The phrase *masterly exposition* was not in fact Churchill's but was suggested to him in 1950 by Lord Alanbrooke (as Brooke had become). Brooke, of course, was Monty's patron. See David

Reynolds, *In Command of History: Churchill Fighting and Writing the Second World War* (London, 2004), 308.

3. When *Hinge of Fate* was published, Auchinleck's onetime deputy chief of staff, Eric Dorman-Smith (by then retired in Ireland and known as Dorman-O'Gowan), threatened a lawsuit. Auchinleck pointedly declined to be involved, and mediation by Sir Hartley Shawcross, a former Nuremberg prosecutor and attorney general in Attlee's government, persuaded Dorman-O'Gowan to settle for the promise of a corrective footnote in future editions. On the episode, see Lavinia Greacen, *Chink: A Biography* (London, 1989), 304–310. More broadly, Churchill's memoirs and Monty's triumphalism in his own produced, almost inevitably, a backlash: Correlli Barnett's brilliant polemic *The Desert Generals* (London, 1960) is pro-Auchinleck, anti-Churchill, and very anti-Montgomery. It began a historical controversy—who really beat Rommel?—that still echoes sixty years on.

4. Churchill's political situation in 1942 is sometimes now regarded as fundamentally secure—and the concerns voiced at the time as therefore exaggerated—because there was no alternate in sight to serve as prime minister (as there had been in 1916 when Lloyd George was available as a replacement for Asquith). This assessment ignores two things. The first is that we know how the story ended, which no one could in mid-1942, and the feeling, after Singapore, Rangoon, and Tobruk, that it might end badly should be very understandable. Second and more important, Churchill was determined to remain minister of defense as well as prime minister. One more defeat might well have confronted him with an irresistible demand for a change in his methods, which, to him, would have been tantamount to dismissal. That is what those devoted to him—and surely Churchill himself—feared in the summer and autumn of 1942.

5. Churchill, *Hinge of Fate*, 603.

6. Of course, the bulk of the infantry in the theater had always been Indian Army units, which could be very freely used, as occurred with the squandering of Indian brigades in May and June 1942. But Monty was not an admirer of the Indian Army, so although Francis Tuker's 4th Indian Division had a role at Alamein and stayed with the Eighth Army for the Italian campaign, the presence of more British units gave him an important measure of latitude.

7. Invited to dine with Churchill, Montgomery, when asked what he would drink, requested water, adding that he neither smoked nor drank and was 100 percent fit. The prime minister instantly riposted that he smoked and drank and was 200 percent fit! Unlike many anecdotes clustering around Churchill, this one seems true. (Churchill died in his ninety-first year, Montgomery at eighty-nine.)

8. Churchill's account of Alam Halfa is in *Hinge of Fate*, 545–548. It was drafted, as were most of the "battle pieces" in *The Second World War*, by Lieutenant General Sir Henry Pownall. Montgomery's version is in *The Memoirs of Field Marshal Montgomery* (New York, 1958), 100–101. The stolen victory argument was advanced by Barnett in *The Desert Generals,* 243–250; see his summary of Monty's first victory: "second hand glory" (250).

9. After Montgomery published his *Memoirs*, Lieutenant General Sir Francis Tuker, an outstanding Indian Army officer whose 4th Indian Division was part of Eighth Army, wrote a note to Basil Liddell Hart about Montgomery's failure to exploit his success: "The fact of course is that Monty was too static of mind to seize an opportunity."

There is a copy of Tuker's "Further Comments on Montgomery's Memoirs," October 31, 1958, in the Lewin Papers, RLEW 2/1, CAC. In fact, Montgomery sanctioned a limited counterattack by Freyberg's New Zealanders, which failed and produced heavy casualties. "Static of mind" he may at times have been, but in early September 1942, prudence was doubtless the best course for Eighth Army.

10. Churchill, *Hinge of Fate*, 562.

11. Churchill to Alexander, September 23, 1942, in ibid., 588.

12. David French, *Raising Churchill's Army: The British Army and the War against Germany, 1919–1945* (Oxford, 2000), 210.

13. Tuker did two memos for B. H. Liddell Hart in October 1958: "Questions about Montgomery's Operations . . . " and "Further Comments on Montgomery's Memoirs." There are copies in the Lewin Papers, RLEW 2/1, CAC. Tuker's feeling that a proliferation of "special forces" indicated a belief that regular infantry units lacked the skills (and motivation?) for difficult tasks was echoed by another Indian Army officer, William Slim, in his memoir, *Defeat into Victory* (London, 1972), 546–548. It is interesting that a similar view was advanced from the other end of the chain of command. Reflecting on ten months as a platoon leader between 1944 and 1945, Sydney Jary wrote, "I now wonder if in 1940 and '41, an opportunity was not lost. Supposing, instead of forming the Commandos, our Light Infantry regiments had been returned to their original role? . . . The Light Infantry ethos was ideally suited to raiding activities, individual resourcefulness and operations requiring rapid movement"; see Jary, *18 Platoon*, 5th ed. (Winchester, UK, 2003), 107. Jary served with the Somerset Light Infantry.

14. Lieutenant General Sir Henry Pownall, in a note to Churchill accompanying his first draft of the Alamein chapter for *Hinge of Fate*, told the prime minister that "the major winning factor to my mind was the fighting of the 9th Australian Division. . . . Without it generalship and superiority of strength would not have brought the high degree of success ultimately achieved." See Pownall to Churchill, July 29, 1949, Churchill Papers CHUR 4/284, f. 65, CAC. Pownall also drew 1918 parallels (although not as censoriously as Tuker would), remarking of Montgomery's plans, "These tactics are reminiscent of many battles of the First World War" (ibid., f. 48). Churchill did not use this, but in his own summary of the battle in *Hinge of Fate*, 602–603, he compared it to "many of the battles of 1918," focusing on Montgomery's use of his artillery, whose restoration to a position of primacy on the battlefield the prime minister had called for a year earlier.

15. There is absolutely no reflection of this episode in *Hinge of Fate*. Churchill prints (505–506) a message to Alexander of October 29 that expresses unqualified support for Montgomery, something that, at least momentarily, had been far from the case. Brooke's account is in his October 29 diary entry and the postwar note glossing it; see Alex Danchev and Daniel Todman, eds., *War Diaries, 1939–45: Field Marshal Lord Alanbrooke* (London, 2001), 335–336. When comparing Churchill's account with Brooke's, it becomes easy to see why Churchill and his circle so resented the publication of Brooke's diaries by Sir Arthur Bryant.

16. The most recent and penetrating study of El Alamein—Niall Barr, *The Pendulum of War* (New York, 2005)—points out that in his initial conception of the battle, Monty had given X Corps, nominally his exploitation force, no task other than passing through the XXX Corps breach and awaiting developments. There was no current British Army

doctrine for exploiting a breakthrough—"a serious intellectual handicap," in Barr's eloquent understatement. He adds, "Montgomery's unwillingness or inability to plan for the exploitation phase demonstrated the limits of his military thinking" (259). The failures of Monty's subordinates, from the soon-to-be-dismissed Lumsden down, merely compounded this core problem.

17. Tuker's comments are in "Questions about Montgomery's Operations . . . ," October 1958, RLEW 2/1, CAC; Nigel Hamilton's are in *Monty: Master of the Battlefield* (London, 1983), 137. The literature on Alamein is vast. There are, of course, the Churchill and Montgomery versions in their respective memoirs. There are also official histories. The British volume—I. S. O. Playfair, C. J. C. Molony, F. C. Flynn, and T. P. Gleave, *The Mediterranean and Middle East,* vol. 4, *The Destruction of the Axis Forces in Africa* (London, 1966), 1–79—covers Alamein in three carefully worded chapters that nonetheless make quite clear the course of the battle was not simply the unfolding of a "master plan." Barnett's relentlessly hostile critique in *The Desert Generals* is balanced by the uncritical but massive official biography of Montgomery: Nigel Hamilton, *Monty: The Making of a General, 1887–1942* (London, 1981). One of the best attempts to assess the battle (in which he served with the 7th Armoured Division) is Michael Carver's *El Alamein* (London, 1961), as amended by Field Marshal Lord Carver's *Dilemmas of the Desert War* (London, 1986). In the latter, Carver was able to include the impact of Ultra—and exhibit a more critical view of Montgomery than in 1961, when Monty was still alive and Carver was still on active service. The sixtieth anniversary of the battle spawned a number of books. Jon Latimer's *Alamein* (London, 2002) is very readable, and Barr's *The Pendulum of War* is a first-rate analysis.

18. Playfair et al., *The Mediterranean and Middle East,* 4:232 n. Robertson's observations are dated February 14, 1943, at the end of the great pursuit. The authors of the official history provided (101–107) a vivid illustration of the logistic problems Montgomery's pursuit faced. Lumsden's X Corps, leading Eighth Army west, was made up of the New Zealand Division, 1st and 7th Armoured, and "corps troops," comprising 63,500 "mouths" from a quartermaster's perspective. The RAF, with the antiaircraft (AA) units to defend its airfields, added 11,500 more. To supply these 75,000 men and their vehicles and weapons over an ever-lengthening distance meant a steady diminution of the productivity of the General Transport (GT) Companies, whose trucks were the crucial link in the system. On November 13, the British reentered Tobruk. The railhead at the point was at Matruh, 245 miles to the east. This meant a six-day turnaround for a GT company, reducing its average daily delivery to 50 tons. A single armored division required 400 tons a day. To support the Eighth Army from Alamein 1,415 miles west to Tripoli was a herculean logistic feat, a concept that needs to be grasped in order to properly evaluate Montgomery's rate of advance. One is tempted to conclude that if Rommel had possessed a logistician of Robertson's quality—and if he had listened to him (always a big if with Rommel)—the Panzerarmee might not have found itself fighting a "battle without hope" at Alamein.

19. Denis Kelly to Ismay, June 6, 1950, Churchill Papers CHUR 4/300 C ff. 498–499, CAC. Pownall drafted the "military" chapters, into which Churchill then incorporated a careful selection of documents and some observations of his own.

20. Churchill is, of course, identified in the popular mind with the Mediterranean strategy, not least because he structured so much of his memoirs around it. The actual

evolution of British and then Allied strategy was much more ad hoc and improvisational, and in the post-Alamein months, it owed as much to Brooke as to Churchill. A good guide is Sir Michael Howard's *The Mediterranean Strategy in the Second World War* (New York, 1968). Legends, however, die very hard.

21. Danchev and Todman, *War Diaries*, 384. The quotation is from Brooke's postwar gloss on his February 22, 1943, entry. In the event, Anderson continued to command First Army until the end of the Tunisian campaign, when he returned to Britain. He was given another army command (Second Army) by Brooke but, when preparations for D day intensified, was promptly replaced by Lieutenant General Miles "Bimbo" Dempsey, a Montgomery protégé. Anderson finished the war as GOC, East Africa Command. The official historians record a favorable view of Anderson, though their summing up—"a fine soldier"—is distinctly tepid; see Playfair et al., *The Mediterranean and the Middle East,* 4:304–305, 457.

22. Churchill was notably restrained in his memoirs when discussing Kasserine, remarking only that the U.S. 1st Armored Division "was overborne, and there was much confusion"; see Churchill, *Hinge of Fate*, 731. Montgomery's waspishness about American performance was more than matched by his excoriation of British officers. He was dismissive of the senior British staff officers at Eisenhower's headquarters. One was "no good," another "not the chap." At a slightly later date, he set down a series of judgments that were relentlessly negative about Gort ("unfit to be a C-in-C in the field"), Pownall ("unfit to command anything"), Auchinleck ("suffers from an inferiority complex"), Alexander ("not clever . . . his great asset is his charm"), Anderson ("somewhat stupid . . . tactless and rude . . . small minded"), Paget ("definitely not a Commander"), and on and on in this vein. See Hamilton, *Monty: Master of the Battlefield,* 144, 377–379. Nor were his dismissive evaluations confined to his own army and his American allies. He had a low opinion of Canadian generals as well. The depth of the dislike his attitude caused was apparent enough with the Americans during the war. Only with the publication of his *Memoirs* in 1958, however (over which Auchinleck threatened legal action), and Barnett's *The Desert Generals* in 1961 did the animosity he aroused in many British officers become generally known.

23. Playfair et al., *The Mediterranean and Middle East,* 4:324, 325. Churchill, in *Hinge of Fate*, 765, had already (using Pownall's draft) highlighted this aspect of the battle: "Nothing like this example of the power of massed anti-tank artillery had yet been seen against armour."

24. Tuker's remarks are in his "Further Comments on Montgomery Memoirs"; Playfair et al., *The Mediterranean and Middle East*, 4:320–322, 331–335, 337–341. Tuker's 4th Indian Division had worked out a technique for disassembling antitank guns to allow them to be manhandled forward. This method could have gotten some antitank guns into 50th Division's bridgehead in time to meet the German counterattack. The fact that it was not utilized may explain Tuker's low opinion of the 50th Division's learning curve.

25. Playfair et al., *The Mediterranean and Middle East,* 4:343–354. There is an interesting analysis of Freyberg's role in Laurie Barber and John Tonkin-Covell, *Freyberg: Churchill's Salamander* (London, 1990), 133–184.

26. Hamilton, *Monty: Master of the Battlefield,* 214.

27. Playfair et al., *The Mediterranean and Middle East,* 4:354.

28. Alexander to Churchill, February 27, 1943, in Churchill, *Hinge of Fate*, 764.

29. Montgomery diary, quoted in Hamilton, *Monty: The Making of a General*, 269.

30. Danchev and Todman, *War Diaries*, 417, entry for June 3, 1943.

31. Carlo D'Este, *Bitter Victory: The Battle for Sicily, 1943* (New York, 1988), is a good recent analysis of the Sicilian campaign. D'Este's assessment of Montgomery is excellent—and fair.

32. Danchev and Todman, *War Diaries*, 420, 427, 429, entries for June 15 and July 7 and 14, 1943. It is clear from the postwar glosses he added to these entries that Brooke badly wanted to command in the field, and having turned down Churchill's offer of the Middle East command in August 1942, his hopes for this post were very high: "It would be a perfect climax to all my struggles" (420).

33. The case for the strategy Churchill and Brooke espoused from 1942 to 1944 was first put by Chester Wilmot, an Australian war correspondent, in his still influential *The Struggle for Europe* (New York, 1952). Hard on its heels came Churchill's own memoirs and then a somewhat distorted version of Brooke's views in Sir Arthur Bryant's *The Turn of the Tide* (New York, 1959) and *Triumph in the West* (New York, 1959), in which the author's florid prose is studded with selections from Brooke's diaries and postwar notes. This provoked an equally florid but shorter rejoinder by the Harvard historian (and author of the U.S. Navy's official history) Samuel Eliot Morison, *Strategy and Compromise* (Boston, 1958), which naturally found more merit in General Marshall's views. A more nuanced view began to emerge in Michael Howard's *The Mediterranean Strategy in the Second World War* (London, 1969). John Grigg, a British journalist and biographer of Lloyd George, argued tendentiously but very readably in *1943: The Victory That Never Was* (New York, 1980) that a successful landing in France in 1943 was possible and would have brought the war to an end much earlier and thus averted the subsequent Cold War. The passage of time has made the discussion steadily less nationalistic. Alex Danchev, no uncritical admirer of Churchill, put the case for the Italian campaign of 1943 and 1944 as an essential preliminary to Overlord in his "Great Britain: The Indirect Strategy," in David Reynolds, Warren F. Kimball, and A. O. Chubarian, eds., *Allies at War: The Soviet, American, and British Experience, 1939–1945* (New York, 1994), 1–26. Most recently, Douglas Porch, an American historian known for his work on French military history, has presented, in *The Path to Victory: The Mediterranean Theater in World War II* (New York, 2004), a massive and powerfully argued case for Brooke's original contention: Mediterranean campaigns alone could make the cross-channel assault feasible.

34. Danchev and Todman, *War Diaries*, 441–442, diary entry for August 15, 1943. In his postwar gloss on this, Alanbrooke speaks of being "swamped by a dark cloud of despair. . . . Not for one moment did [Churchill] realize what this meant to me. He offered no sympathy, no regrets . . . and dealt with the matter as if it were of minor importance." It is far from fanciful to see in this episode the point where Brooke began to feel deeply estranged from Churchill. Both the CIGS and the prime minister were tired men by this time, of course, but Brooke's sense of grievance was quite real. Might this have been one of the reasons he later allowed his diary excerpts to be published in a way sure to wound Churchill?

35. Much time at Quebec was spent on operations—or, more precisely, the lack of successful ones—in Burma. See chapter 7.

36. Winston S. Churchill, *Closing the Ring* (Boston, 1951), 85.

37. F. H. Hinsley, E. E. Thomas, C. F. G. Ransom, and R. C. Knight, *British Intelligence in the Second World War*, vol. 3, pt. 1 (London, 1984), 14–15.

38. It was an article of belief among the American leadership during the war that Churchill wanted to launch a Balkan campaign, and this and his Turkish policy were seen as attempts to somehow "vindicate" his advocacy of the 1914–1915 Gallipoli campaign (although how it would do so was never spelled out). Echoes of this lingered in much American postwar writing on Allied strategy. Churchill denied that he had ever sought major military operations in the Balkans, and the record bears him out. But it is clear that he regarded raiding forces—even quite large ones—as not constituting major operations, and it was with such forces and airpower that he hoped to support various indigenous guerrilla forces that would tie down and impose attrition on the German forces drawn into the Balkans to replace the Italian occupation forces lost in September 1943. There is an interesting and dispassionate survey of the issue in John Ehrman, *Grand Strategy*, vol. 5, *August 1943–September 1944* (London, 1956), app. 6, "The Prime Minister and the Balkans Late in 1943," 554–556.

39. Hinsley et al., *British Intelligence*, 6–7, discuss the views of the Joint Planning Staff and the Joint Intelligence Committee on Balkan possibilities and opportunities.

40. Churchill, *Closing the Ring*, 205, 114. Clive needs no gloss, and the reference to Rooke is self-explanatory, but Peterborough is long forgotten. The Earl of Peterborough was a British commander during the War of the Spanish Succession (1703–1713), with whose exploits Churchill had become familiar while writing his life of Marlborough (Marlborough had selected Peterborough to conduct a campaign that ultimately failed). Just what Churchill meant by using him as an example is unclear.

41. There is an account of the Aegean campaign in the British official history, C. J. C. Molony, F. C. Flynn, H. L. Davies, and T. P. Gleave, *The Mediterranean and Middle East* (London, 1973), 5:531–559. The summing up should be noted: "It is a commonplace of military teaching and preaching to recommend boldness, improvisation, and daring, but these qualities as a rule are commended only when they succeed" (558). Hinsley et al., *British Intelligence*, 119–133, concentrate on the intelligence that supported Churchill's decisions. There is a recent account using British and German materials by Anthony Rogers, *Churchill's Folly: Leros and the Aegean* (London, 2003). The title signals the interpretative framework.

42. Churchill, *Closing the Ring*, 220.

43. Note by WSC, November 1943, Churchill Papers CHUR 4/313A, f. 23, CAC. In the Churchill Papers, there are two thick files of material (CHUR 4/313A; 4/313B, CAC)—much more than for the Alamein chapter—on Aegean operations. Originally, the project to take Rhodes and the Leros story were each to have a chapter. Eventually, considerations of space and perhaps second thoughts about highlighting both a failure and a serious quarrel with the Americans led Churchill to have two of his assistants, Pownall and F. W. Deakin, roll the two draft chapters into one. See Denis Kelly to G. R. G. Allen, January 28, 1951, Churchill Papers CHUR 4/313B, f. 287, CAC.

44. Hinsley et al., *British Intelligence*, 129.

45. Churchill to Eden, November 21, 1943, Churchill Papers CHUR 4/313B, f. 210, CAC. The version published by Churchill, in *Closing the Ring*, 223–224, eliminates this phrase without the usual ellipsis indicating missing material.

46. Note by WSC, November 1943, Churchill Papers CHUR 4/313A, f. 24, CAC.

At one point, Churchill clearly thought of using this note in his memoirs. In the end, he did not, but a careful reading of the chapter "Island Prizes Lost" reveals that the spirit in which the note was written certainly made it into print.

47. Churchill to Wilson, October 14, 1943, in Churchill, *Closing the Ring*, 219.

48. Danchev and Todman, *War Diaries*, 464, entry for October 28, 1943. There is surprisingly little in Brooke's diary about the Aegean affair, except for a splenetic outburst on October 7—"another day of Rhodes madness" (458)—occasioned by Churchill's relentless efforts to find a way to mount Accolade. In postwar notes he added to the entries for November 1 (466) and November 20 (475–476), Brooke made it clear that he too saw merit in exploiting opportunities in the Aegean, however critical he might have been of Wilson's handling of Leros. His conclusion was: "Marshall had a holy fear of Winston's Balkans and Dardanelles ventures, and was always guarding against these dangers even when they did not exist" (476).

49. "Turkey, witnessing the extraordinary inertia of the Allies near her shores, became much less forthcoming," wrote Churchill in 1951, in *Closing the Ring*, 220. In fact, the Turks had never been very forthcoming. They certainly ignored violations of their territorial waters that made the resupply of Leros (and the escape of a few of its garrison) easier. Yet they refused the use of British-built airfields that would have allowed British fighters to intervene more effectively in the battle. Doubtless nothing but a major Allied campaign in southeastern Europe—which neither Churchill nor Brooke proposed—would have swayed the Turks, who feared not only the Germans but Britain's Russian ally as well.

50. Hamilton, *Monty: Master of the Battlefield*, 467, quoting a December 23, 1943, letter from Montgomery to Mountbatten (with whom Monty had worked closely, prior to his departure from Britain for the Middle East, on the plan that ultimately became Operation Jubilee—the August 1942 Dieppe Raid).

51. "Reflections on the Campaign in ITALY," November 23, 1943, quoted in Hamilton, *Monty: Master of the Battlefield*, 471.

Chapter Six. Alex and the Soft Underbelly

1. Churchill Papers CHUR 4/313, ff. 23–24, Churchill Archive Centre, Churchill College, Cambridge (hereafter CAC).

2. Alex Danchev and Daniel Todman, eds., *War Diaries, 1939–1945: Field Marshal Lord Alanbrooke* (London, 2001), 473, entry for November 18, 1943, and accompanying postwar note. The sense that Alex never thought much about his profession, which both Brooke and Monty gave, is almost certainly unfair. When he was a corps commander in England after Dunkirk, he was concerned enough about training issues to publish a pamphlet for his troops on infantry tactics. See Timothy Harrison Place, *Military Training in the British Army, 1940–1944: From Dunkirk to D-Day* (London, 2000), 15.

3. Montgomery note of August 22, 1943, quoted in Nigel Hamilton, *Monty: Master of the Battlefield, 1942–1944* (London, 1983), 377–378, 380.

4. John North, ed., *The Alexander Memoirs, 1940–1945* (London, 1962). North in fact wrote the book.

5. Nicolson to Lewin, March 3, 1973, Lewin Papers, RLEW 3/6, CAC.

6. Hunt also testified to Alex's abilities in his memoir, *A Don at War*, 2nd ed. (London, 1990); Hastings's judgment is in his *Warriors* (London, 2006), xvii.

7. The problem of reinforcements (and much else) is vividly illustrated in Alex Bowlby's minor classic, *The Recollections of Rifleman Bowlby* (London, 1991). Bowlby, who served with a battalion of a Greenjacket (Rifle) regiment in Italy from June 1944 until the campaign's end, has numerous references to the quality of the replacements that line units received.

8. C. J. C. Molony, F. C. Flynn, H. L. Davies, and T. P. Gleave, revised by William Jackson, *The Mediterranean and Middle East*, vol. 6, pt. 1 (London, 1984), 451 n. Many of these "nationalities," of course, such as the Basuto and Swazi, were in unarmed support units within the South African formations, but the heterogeneity of the armies Alexander commanded was nonetheless remarkable.

9. Thaddeus Holt, *The Deceivers: Allied Military Deception in the Second World War* (New York, 2004), 592–597, provides a comprehensive account. This work is an excellent general survey of an important topic.

10. Danchev and Todman, *War Diaries*, 500, 503, entry for December 15, 1943, and postwar note appended to diary entry for December 20, 1943.

11. W. S. Churchill, *Closing the Ring* (Boston, 1951), 426.

12. "Desperate for an exit from the wintry deadlock . . . Churchill championed the bold move of . . . a second amphibious landing . . . behind enemy lines at Anzio"; see David M. Kennedy, *Freedom from Fear: The American People in Depression and War, 1929–1945* (New York, 1999), 599. This Pulitzer Prize–winning volume in the Oxford History of the United States series, intended as a sophisticated new synthesis, nonetheless takes a very traditional American view of Anglo-American strategic arguments, according to which Churchill is admirable but wrong. Carlo D'Este, *Fatal Decision: Anzio and the Battle for Rome* (New York, 1991), although generally excellent, also seems eager to assign a disproportionate share of the responsibility to Churchill.

13. Churchill to Smuts, February 27, 1944, in Churchill, *Closing the Ring*, 493.

14. Danchev and Todman, *War Diaries*, 515, 517, entries for January 20 and 31, 1944.

15. Churchill to Alexander, February 10, 1944, in Churchill, *Closing the Ring*, 488–489, italics are in the original; Danchev and Todman, *War Diaries*, 519, entry for February 8, 1944.

16. Churchill to Smuts, February 27, 1944, in Churchill, *Closing the Ring*, 494.

17. Churchill to Dill, February 8, 1944, in ibid., 487.

18. Cassino has been the subject of a number of books. One of the earliest and still a very valuable work is Fred Majdalany, *Cassino: Portrait of a Battle* (Boston, 1957). The best book yet done on the Italian campaign—Dominick Graham and Shelford Bidwell, *Tug of War: The Battle for Italy: 1943–1945* (London, 1986)—has a trenchant analysis. John Ellis, *Cassino: The Hollow Victory* (London, 1984) is a quite detailed account, highly critical of Alexander and Clark. It is particularly strong on the realities of combat for infantry riflemen. The most recent account is Matthew Parker, *Monte Cassino: The Story of the Hardest Fought Battle of World War Two* (London, 2003).

Despite the importance Churchill accorded the theater and the fact that much of the fighting fell to British, Indian, and Dominion troops, there is relatively little discussion of the four separate Cassino battles in *Closing the Ring*. In part, this was due to the breakneck pace at which Churchill was working as he saw it to completion between 1950 and 1951, driven by the financial need to meet his publishers' deadlines as well as the political calendar, with a general election looming that he hoped to win. Another factor was his unwillingness to be too critical of either the Americans (with whom he hoped soon to be dealing again as prime minister) or, above all, Alex.

About the haste with which Churchill was working in 1950 and 1951 there can be no doubt. In June 1950, Denis Kelly, one of the key members of Churchill's syndicate of advisers and assistants, told Ismay, also a major adviser on the project, "Mr. Churchill is anxious to have something ready to hand before an autumn election"; see Denis Kelly to Ismay, June 6, 1950, Churchill Papers CHUR 4/300C, f. 498, CAC. And a year later in a note to Churchill himself, Kelly observed that "much of the narrative is not in accordance with your usual style"; see note by Denis Kelly, August 26, 1951, Churchill Papers CHUR 4/331, f. 32, CAC. Apart from polishing and inserting various of his contemporary telegrams, Churchill does not seem to have done much with Pownall's basic draft. To have gone into further detail would have involved some of the most controversial aspects of the Cassino operations, not least of all what Monty would have described as Alex's "grip" on his campaign.

19. Danchev and Todman, *War Diaries*, 536, entry for March 31, 1944.

20. First, 460 heavy and medium bombers dropped 1,000 tons of bombs on Cassino (about 4 tons per acre). Then, 890 guns—only slightly fewer than were employed at El Alamein—poured 195,969 rounds into the town. Although stunned and reduced in numbers, the defenders, drawn from the German 1 Parachute Division, nonetheless remained battleworthy. See Ellis, *Cassino*, 221–222.

21. Churchill to Alexander, March 20, 1944, in Churchill, *Closing the Ring*, 507–508.

22. Ibid., 509.

23. Molony et al., *The Mediterranean and Middle East*, 4, pt. 1, 10. During the long gestation of this final volume of the official history (fifteen years separated volumes 5 and 6), Brigadier Molony died and was replaced by General Sir William Jackson, who had already written a study of Alexander's generalship—*Alexander as Military Commander* (London, 1971). Perhaps as a result of this change, the general tenor of this volume is very favorable to Alex.

24. Churchill to Alexander, April 2, 1944, in Molony et al., *Mediterranean and Middle East*, 6, pt. 1, 19. Churchill did not use this telegram in his memoirs, nor did he discuss the question of the timing of Diadem.

25. Churchill to Chiefs of Staff, April 5, 1944, in ibid., 304.

26. Danchev and Todman, *War Diaries*, 539, entry for April 11, 1944. In a postwar note on this entry, Brooke admitted to being a "little unkind . . . in my remarks on Alex" but then went on to repeat the Brooke/Monty orthodoxy on him—no ideas of his own, carried by Monty and McCreery, weak without them. It is hard to avoid the conclusion that Brooke, like Monty, formed snap judgments on people that were never thereafter revisited.

27. Churchill to Alexander, May 28, 1944, in Churchill, *Closing the Ring*, 607.

28. It has been pointed out that the capture of Valmontane would not necessarily have put a large part of the Tenth Army in the bag, since much of it was retiring by other routes. This, like the aftermath of El Alamein, will continue to generate argument, but one thing is crystal clear: to reach a personal goal, Clark threw away any opportunity

there might have been to inflict further significant damage on the defeated Germans. As the British official history put it: "Clark spoiled the fulfillment of Alexander's plan in order to obtain for himself and his army the triumph of being the first to enter Rome." See Molony et al., *Mediterranean and Middle East*, 6, pt. 1, 234. Even the U.S. Army official historians admitted that Clark had never been committed to Alexander's concept for the VI Corps role in Diadem and had concealed from the army group commander his plan to drive directly on Rome until it was too late for Alex to object. Clark even evaded telling Alexander personally, leaving that to his tactful chief of staff, Major General Alfred Gruenther. See Sidney Matthews, "General Clark's Decision to Drive on Rome (1944)," in Kent Roberts Greenfield, ed., *Command Decisions* (New York, 1959), 273–284. When Matthew's essay appeared, Truscott, who had been stunned by Clark's change of plan and vainly protested against it, wrote to the U.S. Army's chief of military history to point out that his objection to Clark's order had not been noted. He received an apology, and when the relevant volume of the army official history—E. J. Fisher, *Cassino to the Alps* (Washington, DC, 1977)—was published, Truscott's dissent was duly noted. Ellis, *Cassino*, 423–427, has a very illuminating discussion of the whole episode.

29. Churchill to Alexander, May 28, 1944, in Churchill, *Closing the Ring*, 607. The next day, however, Brooke recorded: "Winston at his worst. Although Alex had brought off a master stroke, not a single word of praise for him, only threats as to what he would think of him if he did not bring off a scoop!"; see Danchev and Todman, *War Diaries*, 552, entry for May 29, 1944. Clearly, Churchill was bottling up concerns that, a few years before, would have surfaced in messages to Wavell or Auchinleck.

30. Churchill, *Closing the Ring*, 607. In a note to Churchill as the text of *Closing the Ring* was being finalized, Pownall was considerably more blunt about Clark than Churchill's ultimate text. See undated note, CHUR 4/331, f. 57, CAC. When one of his syndicate, Denis Kelly, passed on a suggestion that the chapter on Diadem would be improved by an account of the fall of Rome and Pownall supplied a draft—drawn from Clark's memoirs!—Churchill again opted for a single, factual paragraph; CHUR 4/332, f. 11, CAC, has Kelly's note and Pownall's draft.

Given the intensity of Churchill's commitment to Alexander's campaign, this bland reticence is, at first glance, rather surprising. He was, of course, working at a furious pace as he finished *Closing the Ring*, anticipating an autumn election and a return to power. If Churchill returned to Downing Street, he would again be dealing with the Americans officially, which made it not the best moment to resurrect the Anglo-American arguments over the Italian campaign.

Alex was even more bland than Churchill in his own "memoirs": "For some inexplicable reason General Clark's . . . forces never reached their objectives . . . I can only assume that the immediate lure of Rome for its publicity value persuaded him to switch the direction of his advance"; see North, *The Alexander Memoirs,* 127. Alex's aide-de-camp (ADC) and personal assistant, Rupert Clarke, perhaps reflecting what Alex really thought, later wrote of Clark's "coldly calculating act of planned disobedience" in his memoir, *With Alex at War: From the Irrawaddy to the Po* (Barnsley, UK, 2000), 149. The judgment of the British official history is given in the text; the year after its publication, the most objective analysis yet published—Graham and Bidwell's *Tug of War*—concluded that Clark "had decided to give no assistance to the Eighth Army" (336).

31. Churchill to Marshall, April 16, 1944, in Churchill, *Closing the Ring*, 513.

32. Danchev and Todman, *War Diaries*, 566, entry for July 4, 1944.

33. Molony et al., *The Mediterranean and Middle East*, 6, pt. 2, 334. This draft was not used by Churchill in his memoirs.

34. Ibid., 335. Churchill printed a version of this minute in *Triumph and Tragedy* (Boston, 1953), 691. However, it appears in the appendix, divorced from the discussion of Anvil in the text and, above all, without the last two sentences quoted earlier. After the onset of the Cold War, Churchill's concern to maintain the momentum of the Italian campaign was cast, by himself and others, in the context of his growing concerns about Soviet intentions in 1944 and 1945. It seems quite clear, however, that *at the time,* what was driving Churchill was a desperate attempt to maintain Britain's alliance parity by sustaining a British campaign, in which the most famous of British armies figured, under the direction of his favorite general. David Reynolds, *In Command of History: Churchill Fighting and Writing the Second World War* (London, 2004), incisively deconstructs the writing of *Closing the Ring* and *Triumph and Tragedy.*

35. When the British Chiefs of Staff discussed Churchill's desire to divorce a British Mediterranean theater from American interference, they noted that Alexander's operations actually depended heavily on American airpower as well as the logistic assistance of specialist American units, such as railway engineers. By 1944, a purely British operational theater was something of a fantasy. Molony et al., *Mediterranean and Middle East,* 6, pt. 1, 335.

36. Bidwell and Graham, *Tug of War*, 259–260. Graham and Bidwell take on as well the charge made by American observers that British infantrymen were not "tough" (that iconic American word) and that, though not lacking courage, they did not show sufficient determination in attack. German assessments often rated British infantry troops as superior to American troops, they point out, whereas American commanders tended to equate high casualties with tactical determination, an attitude that the British Army had been cured of on the Western Front (135–137).

37. The problem of heavy casualties and inadequate replacements reinforced caution on the part of commanders; moreover, it seems that caution was, at times, insisted upon by tired soldiers, many of whom had been overseas for long periods (Britain's war was in its fifth year). Alex Bowlby records an episode in the summer of 1944 when his company was ordered to assault a German position riding in to the attack on Sherman tanks. Knowing that a Guards unit had recently suffered very heavy casualties using exactly that tactic, Bowlby's company refused: "'Let the "Brass" sit on the tanks' they yelled." If not exactly a mutiny, it was a clear indication that the troops would attack only when the orders were changed. They were. See Bowlby, *Recollections of Rifleman Bowlby,* 45–46. His account is filled with incidents of desertion, often temporary to avoid battle—and his Greenjacket battalion was an above-average unit.

38. Bidwell and Graham, *Tug of War*, 254.

39. Molony et al., *The Mediterranean and Middle East*, 6, pt. 1, 334.

40. Ibid., 6, pt. 1, 291 n. Ellis, *Cassino*, 443, has a good analysis of the traffic problem. He estimates that some 13,000 to 14,000 vehicles were crammed into the Liri Valley at any one time.

41. Molony et al., *The Mediterranean and Middle East*, 6, pt. 1, 291.

42. Ibid., 6, pt. 1, 293–294. The phrase quoted is on 293. Ellis, *Cassino*, 338–383, pays detailed tribute to Juin's achievement.

43. Juin, the French corps commander, certainly thought so. He was particularly critical of the methodical nature of British tactics and the failure of senior commanders to think in terms of large-scale maneuver. See Ellis, *Cassino*, 272, 408–409. Of course, Juin had never met Slim.

44. Harold Macmillan, *War Diaries: Politics and War in the Mediterranean, January 1943–May 1945* (London, 1984), 153–154, entry for July 18, 1943.

45. Ibid., 374, entry for January 29, 1944.

46. On this, see the discussion in Reynolds, *In Command of History*, 363–486.

47. Danchev and Todman, *War Diaries*, 556, entry for July 4, 1944.

Chapter Seven. The Last Sepoy General

1. The Quit India rebellion (or Congress revolt) of 1942 has never, to my knowledge, been closely studied from a military point of view and is perhaps best known from Paul Scott's *Raj Quartet* novels and their subsequent adaptation for television. When it broke out, there was only one complete British field-force division in India (the 70th, training in jungle warfare under Slim's XV Corps). To be sure, a number of British battalions, mostly units considered suitable only for garrison duty, were scattered about India, but inevitably, the bulk of the troops involved—some sixty battalions, the infantry strength of six divisions—were Indian. Most of these were newly raised and incompletely trained units, in many cases drawn from groups not traditionally recruited and with Indian junior officers. The fact that there were no serious problems in the Indian Army at this critical moment speaks volumes for the toughness of its institutional structure. On the whole subject of the stability of the Indian Army during the war, see Raymond Callahan, "The Indian Army, Total War, and the Dog That Didn't Bark in the Night," in Jane Hathaway, ed., *Rebellion, Repression, Reinvention: Mutiny in Comparative Perspective* (Westport, CT, 2001), 118–128.

2. A major gap in the study of the Indian Army's last war has been filled by Daniel P. Marston's excellent *Phoenix from the Ashes: The Indian Army in the Burma Campaign* (Westport, CT, 2003), which details the rebuilding and retraining effort that ultimately produced Fourteenth Army. This chapter is heavily indebted to Marston's careful scholarship. He points out that GHQ, India, had quickly begun to try to disseminate "lessons learned" guidance from Malaya and Burma, using both "Army in India Training Memoranda" (AITM) and lectures to units by officers who had either served in Burcorps or escaped from Malaya. At least one division had set up its own jungle-warfare school by mid-1942.

Marston's work should be read in conjunction with another monograph, T. R. Moreman's *The Jungle, the Japanese and the British Commonwealth Armies at War, 1941–45: Fighting Methods, Doctrine and Training for Jungle Warfare* (London, 2005). Where Marston focuses on a cross section of Indian Army units, Moreman examines the formulation of doctrine and its translation via training into battlefield effectiveness. Together, these two monographs explain how the Indian Army turned utter defeat into resounding victory in a remarkably short time. It is instructive to compare this process with the incomplete transformation—over a longer time span—studied in another fine monograph, Timothy Harrison Place's *Military Training in the British Army, 1940–1944: From Dunkirk to D-Day* (London, 2000).

3. Wavell's paper is reproduced in John Connell, *Wavell: Supreme Commander* (London, 1969), 239–241. (Connell did not live to finish this volume of his official biography of Wavell; it was "completed and edited" by Brigadier Michael Roberts, an Indian Army officer who had worked on the official history series, *The War against Japan*, and who was a close friend of Slim's. The chapter on the first Arakan campaign, with which the book ends, is exclusively Roberts's work.) Wavell's assessment reflects not merely a blind spot of his but also a remarkable lack of information on the Imperial Japanese Army. In the late summer of 1939, it had clashed with the Red Army along the ill-defined frontiers between Inner (Japanese-dominated) and Outer (Russian-controlled) Mongolia. This brief, undeclared war, largely overlooked in the West, involved corps-sized forces on both sides. The Japanese lost both the battle and a division—but no one should have been in any doubt thereafter about the ferocity with which they would fight when on the defensive.

4. When Burcorps reached Assam, the arrangements for its reception were primitive, and Irwin, then commanding IV Corps in Assam, made matters worse by issuing an order of the day in which he implied that Burcorps had not fought hard enough. Slim protested, drawing from Irwin the immortal riposte, "I can't be rude, I'm senior."

There may well have been another reason for Irwin's attitude to Slim. As a brigade commander conducting operations on the border between the Sudan and Italian-occupied Ethiopia in November 1940, Slim, an Indian Army officer, had relieved a British battalion commander after a poor performance by his troops. The battalion concerned was from the Essex Regiment. So was Irwin. This situation exemplified the British Army "tribalism" to which Field Marshal Lord Carver referred.

5. As an example of the problems the Indian Army faced at that point, it is useful to look at the Frontier Force Regiment. Its depot at the Abbottabad provided recruits for fourteen battalions, with six different scales of arms and equipment. It is hard to resist the conclusion that those recruits were far short of being fully trained soldiers when they reached their battalions. See Moreman, *The Jungle,* 82.

6. Connell, *Wavell,* 240. See also Raymond Callahan, *Burma, 1942–45* (London, 1978), 62.

7. Brigadier Michael Roberts felt that nine was an exaggeration and that the correct number was seven. Roberts was a meticulous researcher who, it is clear, was not completely happy with Major General S. Woodburn Kirby, the head of the team that produced the official history, *The War against Japan*. But even based on Roberts's figures, Lloyd, who had started with four brigades, was trying to control far too many units. See Roberts's "Comments" on the draft of Ronald Lewin's official biography of Slim, Roberts Papers MRBS 1/4, Churchill Archive Centre, Churchill College, Cambridge (hereafter CAC).

8. Churchill to Ismay, April 8, 1943, in Winston S. Churchill, *The Hinge of Fate* (Boston, 1950), 944–945. Interestingly, Brooke was paying virtually no attention to the Arakan offensive, which produced not a single entry in his diary. Indeed, throughout the war, with the exception of the crisis months of December 1941 through June 1942, Brooke's diary shows little concern about the war in Burma.

9. Roberts, "Comments." The North-West Frontier of the Raj was Rudyard Kipling country.

10. "Report on a Visit to Maugdaw Front, 4–9 May 1943," by an unidentified XV

Corps liaison officer, Irwin Papers 2/1, Imperial War Museum, London, quoted in Callahan, *Burma,* 63.

11. The phrase is in Churchill to Ismay, July 24, 1943, in Winston S. Churchill, *Closing the Ring* (Boston, 1951), 656.

12. Wingate came from an army family and was a member of the austere fundamentalist Plymouth Brethren (Gordon of Khartoum and General Sir William Dobbie, the governor and commander-in-chief, Malta, during the darkest days of its war, also belonged to this small sect). Distantly related to T. E. Lawrence, Wingate was closely related to a pillar of the imperial establishment, General Sir Reginald "Cousin Rex" Wingate, at one time Kitchener's intelligence officer in Egypt and the Sudan, then his successor as governor-general in Khartoum, and finally British high commissioner in Cairo. Cousin Rex smoothed Orde's passage on a number of occasions early in his career, as other well-placed patrons continued to do.

The meteoric last year of his life made him perhaps the most controversial British soldier of the war (and in a war that also featured Montgomery, that was quite a feat). When he died in a plane crash in 1944, everyone—Wavell, Slim, Churchill—said the right things, but by the 1950s, second thoughts had set in. Slim's *Defeat into Victory* (London, 1956) was critical, as were the official historians, S. Woodburn Kirby, C. T. Addis, M. R. Roberts, G. T. Wards, and N. L. Desoer, *The War against Japan,* vols. 2 and 3 (London, 1958–1961). Christopher Sykes's elegant official life, *Orde Wingate: A Biography* (New York, 1959), offered an attractively written defense. But criticism continued to mount—from participants and historians. John Master's *The Road Past Mandalay* (London, 1961), Terence O'Brien's *Out of the Blue* (London, 1984), and Brigadier Shelford Bidwell's *The Chindit War* (London, 1979) provide a fair sample. One of Wingate's former officers, Brigadier Peter Mead, struck back at all the critics in *Orde Wingate and the Historians* (Braunton, Devon, UK, 1987). He was also involved in a petition to the Cabinet Office, whose Historical Section was responsible for the official histories, asking in effect for a redo of Kirby's verdict on Wingate.

Gradually, the historical consensus has come to reflect many of Slim's criticisms: Wingate drove his ideas too far, seeing them as the only way to victory, and he was a disruptive force, absorbing resources that might have been better used in other ways and seeing reasoned criticism as sabotage. Despite his charisma, he now seems a footnote (albeit a very long one) and not the central narrative of the Burma campaign. But the argument is far from over. David Rooney's *Wingate and the Chindits: Redressing the Balance* (London, 1994) is a passionate defense, reprising Mead's criticisms of Slim and Kirby, whereas Major General Julian Thompson's *The Imperial War Museum Book of War behind Enemy Lines* (London, 1998) is coolly and carefully critical.

In the interest of full disclosure, I should say that I published a study of the Burma campaign in 1978 in which I argued that Slim and Kirby were more correct than Wingate's defenders, thus incurring Brigadier Mead's wrath.

13. Neither of these concepts was original with Wingate, but his first raid into Burma did put the pieces together in actual operations for the first time.

14. Wingate had chosen as the 77th Indian Infantry Brigade's emblem the Chinthe, a mythological beast, half lion and half eagle, that guarded Burmese temples. A public relations officer turned this into the name Chindits, by which Wingate's troops are known to posterity.

15. Wingate's report on his operations in Ethiopia may have been seen by Churchill earlier—certainly, a copy was sent to Ismay.

16. Churchill to Ismay, July 24, 1943, in Churchill, *Closing the Ring*, 656.

17. Note by Ronald Lewin on a conversation with Major General H. L. "Taffy" Davies, May 18, 1973, Slim Papers 5/4, CAC.

18. Alex Danchev and Daniel Todman, eds., *War Diaries, 1939–1945: Field Marshal Lord Alanbrooke* (London, 2001), 436. Both quotations in this paragraph are from Brooke's postwar notes to his August 4, 1943, entry—that is, they were written after Wingate's death and as second thoughts about the whole Chindit enterprise were growing.

19. On the alliance politics of the war in Burma, see Callahan, *Burma,* and, in much greater detail, Christopher Thorne, *Allies of a Kind: The United States, Britain, and the War against Japan, 1941–45* (London, 1978).

20. Quoted in Julian Thompson, *War behind Enemy Lines* (London, 1998), 166.

21. Quoted in ibid., 170.

22. David Reynolds, *In Command of History: Churchill Fighting and Writing the Second World War* (London, 2004), 401.

23. Brian Bond, ed., *Chief of Staff: The Diaries of Lieutenant General Sir Henry Pownall,* vol. 2, *1940–1944* (London, 1974), 112, entry for October 17, 1943.

24. Draft chapter, "South East Asia Command," Churchill Papers CHUR 4/331, f. 131, CAC.

25. Denis Kelly to Martin Gilbert, October 11, 1988, Denis Kelly Papers DEKE 1, CAC. Kelly is referring to Wingate's decision, after a misjudgment on his part had led to the Japanese bottling up the Chindits in waterless country, to order 77th Indian Infantry Brigade to break up into small "dispersal groups," each of which would make its own way back to India. The bulk of the casualties in Chindit I were incurred during this escape-and-evasion exercise.

26. A separate theater command had, of course, been a feature of Churchill's late July suggestion on handing the war in Burma over to a Leese-Wingate combination. SEAC was a much grander version of this idea.

27. Field Marshal Viscount Slim, *Defeat into Victory*, 3rd ed. (London, 1972), 167.

28. On this, see Marston, *Phoenix from the Ashes,* especially 95–99; Moreman, *The Jungle,* 77–108.

29. Churchill to Amery, August 10, 1943, PRO, PREM 3, 232/9, quoted in Callahan, *Burma*, 96. This is a rare example of Churchill saying something positive about the Indian Army—even if it was only to contrast the long-service professionals he had seen in his youth with the poorly trained expansion units whose failure had just embarrassed him.

30. The papers of Lieutenant General Sir Reginald Savory are at the National Army Museum in London. A full study of his role has not yet been done and is needed.

31. Quoted in Connell, *Wavell,* 271.

32. Slim to Major General S. W. Kirby, December 14, 1959, Slim Papers 5/3, CAC. Slim had already expressed himself even more pungently in *Defeat into Victory*: "This cult of special forces is as sensible as to form a Royal Corps of Tree Climbers and say that no soldier, who does not wear its green hat with a bunch of oak leaves struck in it, should be expected to climb a tree" (1972 ed., 548).

33. Bond, *Chief of Staff,* 2:112, entry for October 17, 1943. Pownall went on to note

that "G. H. Q. here loathe the sight of him." One of the staff officers with whom Wingate clashed was the director of staff duties at GHQ, India, Major General Stanley Woodburn Kirby, later the chief of the team that produced the official history, *The War against Japan.*

34. Slim, *Defeat into Victory* (1972 ed.), 164.

35. The British, having understandably decided in 1940 to concentrate on fighters and bombers, were dependent for transport aircraft throughout the war on allocations from American production. There were never enough RAF transport squadrons in SEAC, but there were numerous U.S. Army Air Force (USAAF) squadrons in the theater, most dedicated to the Hump airlift to China. On several occasions, Mountbatten's ability to borrow these squadrons would be crucial to Fourteenth Army.

Wingate's first Chindit expedition is often credited with revealing the possibilities of air supply to a hidebound army headquarters in India. Like many claims for Chindit I, this is a considerable exaggeration. Air supply had been used in World War I, albeit in a primitive form. In 1931 and 1932, while a captain serving the Operations Section of Indian Army headquarters, Slim was intrigued enough by air supply's potential to propose a joint experiment to Air Headquarters, India—an initiative that earned him a "rocket" (British Army slang for a blistering rebuke) from the commander-in-chief, India, for trespassing on RAF turf. Another young officer serving with Slim in the Operations Section, W. G. H. Vickers, would, in later staff postings at GHQ, work on packaging and dropping techniques. Vickers, as a lieutenant general, became quartermaster general in India in 1942. See Ronald Lewin, *Slim: The Standardbearer* (London, 1976), 53–54. There was considerable thinking about and experimenting with air supply prior to the Burma campaign, but Slim would later tell the official historians, "It was certainly the experience gained in Arakan, not that of Special Force, which was the guide to successful air supply . . . and later developed into the standard organisation for all our air supply in Burma"; see Slim to Major General S. W. Kirby, April 24, 1959, Slim Papers 5/3, CAC. Chindit I helped in the development of techniques, but that seems the most that can be claimed for it in this respect.

36. Boxes held by infantry and guns had, of course, been a feature of the desert war, where they had been envisioned as providing "pivots of maneuver." Because of the failings of British armor, they more often wound up isolated and overrun. Slim's use of the concept as part of a carefully thought-out approach to battle was more sophisticated—and much more successful.

37. Pradeep P. Barua, *Gentlemen of the Raj: The Indian Army Officer Corps, 1817–1949* (Westport, CT, 2003), 130. This book is particularly strong on developments between the wars. The best guide to Indianization during the war is Marston, *Phoenix from the Ashes.*

38. Quoted in Marston, *Phoenix from the Ashes*, 48.

39. S. L. Menenzes, *Fidelity and Honour: The Indian Army from the Seventeenth to the Twenty First Centuries*, 2nd ed. (New Delhi, 2001), 367. The author joined Britain's Indian Army in 1942 and retired a lieutenant general in the army of the Republic of India.

40. Quoted in David Omissi, *The Sepoy and the Raj* (Basingstoke, UK, 1994), 242.

41. Brigadier Michael Roberts, "Slim Biography ch. TEN Comments. Roberts," ts., 3, Roberts Papers MRBS 1/4, CAC. Roberts commanded 114th Brigade in Messervy's 7th Indian Division. He later did much of the basic research for Slim's *Defeat into Victory*, worked on the official histories, and finished Connell's official biography of Wavell, do-

ing the Burma chapters. Like Slim, Roberts was a Gurkha Rifles officer. In many ways, he was a central, albeit forgotten, figure in the historiography of the Burma campaign.

42. Brigadier Michael Roberts, ts. note on his contacts with Slim, 1, Roberts Papers MRBS 1/4, CAC.

43. Slim's account in *Defeat into Victory*, 285–369, is highly readable. The official history—Kirby et al., *The War against Japan,* vol. 3, *The Decisive Battles*—is thorough but hard going. A good, succinct recent account is Robert Lyman, *Slim, Master of War* (London, 2004), 165–227.

44. A copy of this signal is in the Lewin Papers, RLEW 4/1, CAC.

45. Danchev and Todman, *War Diaries*, 534, entry for March 23, 1944.

46. Quoted in Sykes, *Orde Wingate*, 545. However, Brooke simply noted Wingate's death in his diary without further comment.

47. Fergusson to "My darling Mother," April 18, 1944, copy in Lewin Papers, RLEW 4/1, CAC.

48. Draft chapter, "South East Asia Command," Churchill Papers CHUR 4/311, f. 127, CAC. The Japanese, of course, needed far less logistic support than any Western army.

49. Kirby et al., *War against Japan,* 3:445–446. Of the many accounts of Chindit II, two can be singled out: John Masters, *The Road Past Mandalay* (New York, 1961) and Bernard Fergusson, *The Trumpet in the Hall* (London, 1970). Masters, a Gurkha officer, disliked Wingate; Fergusson, a British service officer, saw his faults but to the end thought him a flawed military genius. Fergusson and Masters were both born writers. The official historians' verdict on the Chindits might well be applied to the "special force" that lives on robustly to this day: the airborne units. Operation Market Garden in 1944 would clearly demonstrate what would happen when "main forces" could not reach—and rescue—the paratroopers in time.

50. Churchill, *Closing the Ring*, 566.

51. Churchill to Mountbatten, May 4, 1944, in ibid., 568.

52. Ibid., 561.

Chapter Eight. Three Victories

1. Dempsey, known as Bimbo, retired soon after the war, wrote no memoirs, and has been ignored by biographers—a serious gap in the story of the British Army at war, since he played such a crucial role from D day to VE day.

2. Max Hastings, *Overlord: D Day and the Battle of Normandy* (New York, 1984), makes this argument. The desert veterans, he contends, felt that after years overseas, they had "done their bit," and though they continued to do their job, they lacked the aggressive edge they once had had. Without denying that Hastings has put his finger on something important, it is also true that the war they faced in Normandy was markedly different from the desert war.

3. Tuker's remark is in "Further Comments on Montgomery's Memoirs," October 31, 1958, Lewin Papers, RLEW 2/1, Churchill Archive Centre, Churchill College, Cambridge (hereafter CAC).

4. Sydney Jary, *18 Platoon*, 5th ed. (Winchester, UK, 2003), 17–18. Jary's reflections

on the training he and his soldiers received (16–21) provide an important commentary on this issue.

5. Timothy Harrison Place, *Military Training in the British Army, 1940–1944: From Dunkirk to D-Day* (London, 2000), 170. This book is essential reading for any student of the British Army in World War II.

6. Ibid., 149–150. Montgomery's official biographer—Nigel Hamilton, in *Monty: The Master of the Battlefield, 1942–1944* (London, 1983)—does not discuss this episode, although he does make clear, at great length, Monty's contemptuous and dismissive attitude to Paget's Twenty-first Army Group staff. Place also documents Monty's downgrading of the importance of the training function of army group headquarters, something Hamilton passes over without comment.

7. Place, *Military Training*, 151.

8. Tuker, "Questions about Montgomery's operations in North Africa and Italy that need to be cleared up in the interests of History," October 1958, Lewin Papers, RLEW 2/1, CAC.

9. Martin Gilbert, *Winston S. Churchill,* vol. 7, *The Road to Victory, 1941–1945* (London, 1986), 744.

10. The historiography of this episode is interesting. By the time Churchill was working on *Closing the Ring,* the Montgomery version of the episode had circulated widely—which is not surprising because, his official biographer assures us, it was "one of Monty's favorite stories"; see Hamilton, *Monty,* 592. Churchill had already threatened legal action to keep the war correspondent Alan Morehead from using the story in his 1946 biography of Monty (written with the field marshal's support). Churchill, who felt "this interview has been misrepresented" and decided "to state what actually happened," admitted that he did "not remember the actual course of the conversation" but denied that there had been any confrontation or threat of resignation; see W. S. Churchill, *Closing the Ring* (Boston, 1951), 616. Monty's official biographer, writing thirty-two years later, embroidered the Montgomery version at some length without ever engaging with Churchill's denial; see Hamilton, *Monty,* 590–594. Martin Gilbert, in the relevant volume of his official biography of Churchill, published three years after Hamilton's work, in his turn ignored the Montgomery anecdote entirely, simply quoting Ismay's recollection of Churchill's concern over the teeth versus tail issue and then noting that the prime minister and Montgomery discussed it on May 19 to Churchill's satisfaction; see Gilbert, *Winston S. Churchill,* 7:772. Perhaps the best indicator that Churchill's version is closer to what happened than Monty's colorful story is the complete absence of any reference to the episode in Brooke's diary. The CIGS was Monty's patron and protector—and his own relations with the prime minister at that point were none too easy. A confrontation that led to a resignation threat by Monty and drew tears from Churchill would almost certainly have generated tremors that would have registered on Brooke's pages. There is a May 17 reference to a conversation with Churchill about the number of vehicles and support personnel scheduled to land in Normandy at an early stage but no discussion at all of Churchill's May 19 visit to Twenty-first Army Group, let alone any major blow-up during it. See Alex Danchev and Daniel Todman, eds., *War Diaries, 1939–1945: Field Marshal Lord Alanbrooke* (London, 2001), 547. The May 19 diary entry is in fact largely taken up with Diadem. It seems clear that whatever happened on

May 19 was far less dramatic than Monty later claimed. That there was, however, an edge to that exchange is perhaps best proven by the Parthian shot with which Churchill ended his account: "I still consider that the proportion of transport vehicles to fighting men in the early phase of the cross-Channel invasion was too high and that the operation suffered both in risk and execution from this fact"; see Churchill, *Closing the Ring*, 616.

11. One of the few exceptions to this is Stephen Hart's *Montgomery and "Colossal Cracks": The 21st Army Group in Northwest Europe, 1944–45* (Westport, CT, 2000), a piece of careful analysis that should be read in conjunction with the well-known narrative accounts of the campaign. Two other excellent and illuminating examinations of the Normandy fighting are Terry Copp's *Fields of Fire: The Canadians in Normandy* (Toronto, Canada, 2003) and John English, *The Canadian Army and the Normandy Campaign: A Study of Failure in High Command* (New York, 1991). Carlo D'Este's *Decision in Normandy* (New York, 1983) is also of interest, although it is now somewhat dated by later studies. A wide range of views on the fighting in Normandy is on display in Theodore A. Wilson, ed., *D-Day 1944* (Lawrence, KS, 1994).

12. There is a vivid account of a Churchillian explosion of anger at Monty in Danchev and Todman, *War Diaries*, 571–573, entry for July 19, 1944, and Brooke's postwar gloss on it. (The entry for July 6 [566–567] and Brooke's postwar note on it describe a late evening meeting at which the prime minister attacked Alex's conduct of the Cassino battles, forcing Brooke into the unusual role of defense counsel for Alexander.)

13. Sydney Jary, a platoon commander in Normandy, wrote later, "I have little doubt that had Monty succumbed to the mounting pressure . . . to take ground, he could have written off much of the British infantry by early August and probably sooner. I am profoundly grateful that he was too shrewd a commander to fall into the trap"; see Jary, *18 Platoon*, 22.

14. There is an interesting analysis of the weakness of British infantry and armor tactics in Normandy in Place, *Military Training*, 74–76, 156–167.

15. Jary, *18 Platoon*, 17.

16. G. P. B. Roberts, *From the Desert to the Baltic* (London, 1987), 209. Roberts was thirty-eight at the time and widely considered to be Britain's best armored commander.

17. Bernard Law, Viscount Montgomery, *The Memoirs of Field Marshal Montgomery* (New York, 1958), 243.

18. Ibid., 266. Brooke, in a rare criticism of his protégé, felt Monty's strategy was faulty and that clearing the approaches to Antwerp should have been given priority; see Danchev and Todman, *War Diaries,* 600, diary entry for October 5, 1944.

19. Montgomery (in ibid., 265–267) blames Eisenhower's failure to give him absolute priority, a bad choice of drop zones at Arnhem by Second Army and I Airborne Corps, the weather, and the unexpected battleworthiness of the German II SS Panzer Corps—with not a word about XXX Corps's management of the battle or any failings by the units involved.

The most recent account of Arnhem, Max Hastings's *Armageddon: The Battle for Germany, 1944–45* (London, 2004), 34–62, concludes that Eisenhower's failing was not that he refused Montgomery absolute priority but that he allowed Market Garden to happen at all. The real opportunity in September 1944, Hastings argues, was "opening Antwerp, and . . . breaking von Rundstedt's line on Bradley's front, rather than . . . the ill-conceived

British Arnhem plan" (61). Hastings also comments shrewdly that because the airborne divisions existed, they had to be used, yet "nowhere did the airborne divisions justify their cost in men and equipment by changing the outcome of a big battle which would have been lost without a drop" (59).

20. Ibid., 380.

21. Roger Parkinson, *A Day's March Nearer Home* (New York, 1974), 74.

22. Leese persuaded Alexander to shift Eighth Army back across the Apennines, a huge logistic endeavor that put the Eighth on the coastal plain of the Adriatic, where rivers—and the ridges between them—ran at right angles to its axis of advance. The difficulties thereby engendered seemed preferable to further collaboration with Clark. The link between the two armies was Kirkman's XIII Corps, serving under Fifth Army command until March 1945. Alexander (at this point still with Harding at his side) accepted this arrangement—perhaps out of sympathy with Leese's point of view, perhaps to diffuse a potentially explosive situation. In his *Memoirs*, Alex predictably said nothing about any of this.

23. The Polish commander, Lieutenant General Wladyslaw Anders, at one point threatened to drop out of the war and demand that his men be treated as POWs. In fact, it was not just Polish morale that was a concern during the last bitter winter in Italy. The lack of trained infantry replacements led, as noted, to poor-quality troops being put into line units to fill the gaps. Alex Bowlby described the result in one instance: "A private . . . told me about an unfortunate county battalion made up of 'any old shit,' as he put it, and brigaded with Indian troops. The whole Battalion had cut and run from a German tank attack. The Indians recaptured the ground. . . . The Brigadier formed both Battalions into a square, the Indians on the outside, with their weapons, the county regiment on the inside, without their weapons. He then told them what he thought of them"; see Bowlby, *Recollections of Rifleman Bowlby* (London, 1991), 230.

From a contemporaneous account, Field Marshal Lord Carver records an episode in early December 1944, just before offensive operations closed down for the winter, when a British unit was ordered into the attack one time too many: "These men had seen too many of their mates killed and wounded. They had gone through bouts of action in Tunisia . . . Salerno . . . Cassino, and . . . four months of severe battles in the Gothic Line." They refused to advance: "They said they were not going on . . . they had had it." See Carver, *The Imperial War Museum Book of the War in Italy, 1943–1945* (London, 2001), 262. A number of such episodes must have gone unrecorded. Morale cannot have been helped by the realization that their campaign was now merely a holding action in support of the great battle in northwest Europe.

24. Winston S. Churchill, *Triumph and Tragedy* (Boston, 1953), 531.

25. The monsoon pursuit was a remarkable but very costly venture conducted by XXXIII Corps, spearheaded by the 11th East African Division. Corps casualties from July through November 1944 were 50,300—only 49 of whom were killed in action. Of the 47,000 sick, over half had to be evacuated to India. Mountbatten, as avid for renown as Clark (albeit far more polished), would later claim that fighting through the monsoon was his idea. See Philip Ziegler, *Mountbatten: A Biography* (New York, 1985), 250–251. (This is the official biography of Mountbatten.) In fact, there can be little doubt that the intention was present in Slim's mind before Mountbatten's arrival. A more accurate assessment is in Robert Lyman, *Slim: Master of War* (London, 2004), 134: "The fact was that

while Mountbatten thought many of these ideas to be new, and perhaps of his own invention . . . Slim recognized them from the development of his own approach to battle over the previous two years." Slim's own official biographer, Ronald Lewin, in a letter to Mountbatten in 1975, had already maintained that "your ideas . . . many of them . . . were already present in Slim's mind"; quoted in ibid., 134.

26. Brigadier Michael Roberts to Ronald Lewin, June 11, 1976, Roberts Papers MRBS 1/4, CAC. This letter was a lengthy commentary on the galley proofs of Lewin's official biography of Slim.

27. Roberts to Slim, June 8, 1955, Slim Papers 5/1, CAC. This attitude was by no means confined to general officers. The best study of the doctrinal adaptation of the Indian Army to the needs of the war in Burma points out that "some units were unwilling to learn from their peers—particularly British units from Indian—and suffered needless loss"; see T. R. Moreman, *The Jungle, the Japanese and the British Commonwealth Armies at War, 1941–1945: Fighting Methods, Doctrine and Training for Jungle Warfare* (London, 2005), 215.

28. Christopher Bayly and Tim Harper, *Forgotten Armies: The Fall of British Asia, 1941–1945* (London, 2004), 388.

29. Raymond Callahan, *Burma 1942–45* (London, 1978), 146–147. What this meant in practice can be shown from two examples. The 8th York and Lancaster Regiment was assessed as "poor" in morale and fighting spirit in June 1944. It was understrength by 200 men (nearly 25 percent) due to casualties, repatriation, and lack of replacements. Another battalion lost 59 NCOs and 205 rank and file to repatriation.

30. Field Marshal the Viscount Slim, *Defeat into Victory*, 3rd unabridged ed. (London, 1972), 369.

31. Slim to Roberts, October 22, 1959, Slim Papers 5/3, CAC.

32. Roberts to Lewin, n.d. (but late 1974), "Comments on Chapter 12," ts, 2, Roberts Papers MRBS 1/4, CAC. It is impossible to imagine Monty making such a statement about any of his battles.

33. Ibid., 3.

34. Roberts to Lewin, May 5, 1974, Roberts Papers MRBS 1/4, CAC.

35. Dracula, the amphibious assault on Rangoon canceled for lack of resources, was revived on a limited basis as an insurance policy in case Fourteenth Army did not get to Rangoon before the monsoon. The operation was launched on May 1 with Gurkha paratroopers dropping from American planes (some with Canadian jumpmasters) and followed the next day by landings by 26th Indian Division; ironically, it was the Dracula force that actually reoccupied an undefended Rangoon.

36. Danchev and Todman, *War Diaries*,, 646, entry for January 17, 1945.

37. Churchill to Field Marshal Sir Henry Wilson, March 30, 1945, in Churchill, *Triumph and Tragedy*, 618. Wilson, Dill's successor in Washington, was the channel to Marshall.

38. Slim to Major General S. W. Kirby, January 22, 1964, Slim Papers 5/3, CAC.

39. Slim's typescript draft is in Slim Papers 2/3, CAC; Kirby to Slim, March 1, 1963, Slim Papers 5/3, CAC.

40. Ronald Lewin, *Slim: The Standard Bearer* (London, 1976), 237–246.

41. Slim later came to believe that Mountbatten was behind Leese's action. See Roberts to Lewin, February 8, 1973, Roberts Papers MRBS 1/4, CAC.

Center for the Study of War and Peace
Norwich University
158 Harmon Drive
Northfield, VT 05663
802 • 485 • 2840
http://www.norwich.edu/colby

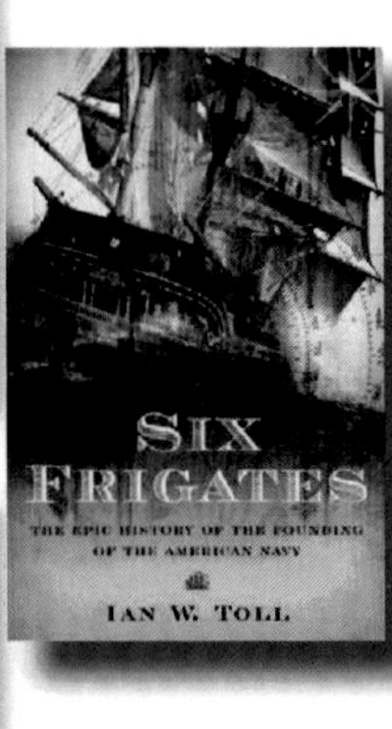

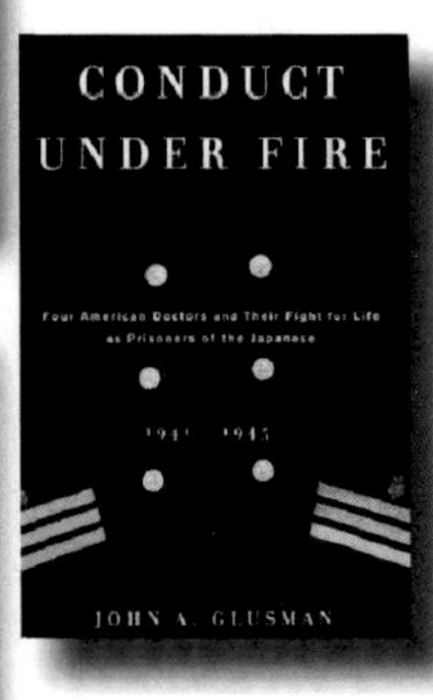

Colby Symposium

Civilians in the Path of War

April 2-3, 2007

Mountbatten was rather good at covering his tracks. As director of Combined Operations, he had been involved in planning a major cross-channel raid in 1942 (Monty, then holding South Eastern Command in Home Forces, was also deeply involved). The raid was canceled because it was believed the Germans had gotten wind of it. Monty advised against remounting it—and then left for Eighth Army. Later, it was remounted on Mountbatten's authority, without further reference to Churchill or the Chiefs of Staff, and it became the August 19 raid on Dieppe, Operation Jubilee. His "unauthorized action," as Canadian historian Brian Loring Villa has dubbed it, cost the 2nd Canadian Division nearly 70 percent of the troops embarked; see Villa, *Unauthorized Action: Mountbatten and the Dieppe Raid* (New York, 1989). When the draft chapter on Dieppe for the fourth volume of Churchill's memoirs, *The Hinge of Fate,* threatened to "out" Mountbatten's responsibility for Dieppe, Mountbatten persuaded Churchill to substitute a redraft, by Mountbatten himself, that diffused the blame very widely. See David Reynolds, *In Command of History: Churchill Fighting and Writing the Second World War* (London, 2004), 345–348.

Although no smoking gun is ever likely to surface, there are good reasons to assume Leese was doing what "Dickie" wished done—something that would not only put Slim "in his place" for ignoring ALFSEA but also remove the only rival for the limelight that victory in Burma would finally shed on SEAC—and the only possible competitor for the credit that would accrue to the commander who retook Singapore. No one in May 1945 foresaw the atomic bomb and the war's sudden end in August.

42. Slim, draft ts, 1, Slim Papers 2/3, CAC.

43. "The Life and Times of General Sir Philip Christison, Bt., G.B.E., C.B., D.S.O., M.C., B.A., D.L.: An Autobiography." This typescript memoir is in CHIE 1, CAC. Written between 1947 and 1981, it is often inaccurate on details—and very self-serving, but Christison claims to have shown his account of this episode to Leese, who agreed it was accurate.

44. Roberts to Lewin, October 7, 1972, Roberts Papers MRBS 1/4, CAC.

45. Churchill, *Triumph and Tragedy*, 621.

46. General Sir Cameron Nicolson to Ronald Lewin, November 1, 1972, Lewin Papers, RLEW 3/6, CAC.

47. Slim to Kirby, January 22, 1964, Slim Papers 5/5, CAC.

48. George MacDonald Fraser, *Quartered Safe Out Here* (London, 1992), 35–36.

49. Lyman, *Slim,* 254, 261.

50. Churchill to Curtin, January 14, 1942, Churchill Papers CHUR 4/235A, f. 128, CAC. The published version in *The Hinge of Fate* (Boston, 1950), 11, omits this sentence without ellipsis, his staff having pointed out to him that the final five words "might be read as a reflection on the Indian Army."

It is an interesting example of the durability of Churchill's view of the war that in the new Churchill Museum in London (part of the Cabinet War Rooms site), there is very little on the Burma campaign. In a section on "Commanders," Mountbatten, Wavell, Wingate, Monty, and Alex are profiled but not Slim or Auchinleck. In an exhibit of decorations, the Burma Star is absent. Only a time line acknowledges the Burma campaign took place.

There is also evidence that the views on the Indian Army noted in the attitudes of Irwin, Leese, and Monty outlived that army. Anthony Clayton's *The British Officer: Lead-*

ing the Army, 1660 to the Present (London, 2006), remarks that after 1947, a few Indian Army officers "were accepted, though not always made very welcome" in the British Army (223).

Chapter Nine. Winston and His Generals

1. Alexander was consistently undervalued and denigrated by Brooke and Montgomery, which seems to have affected subsequent writing about him. Alex was, however, a capable soldier as well as the closest thing the British Army had to an Eisenhower-style coalition commander. Diadem was every bit as impressive as Monty's better-advertised victories—and Alex never had a Market Garden.

2. Slim Papers 2/9, Churchill Archive Centre, Churchill College, Cambridge. This file is labeled "Generals," and the notes in it are not dated.

A Note on Further Reading

For a work of synthesis such as this, the product of many years of reading, a full bibliography would be excessively long. This is particularly the case given the torrent of books about World War II, which shows no sign of diminishing. Therefore, having cited in chapter notes my sources for particular statements and arguments, I have tried to indicate in this note a limited number of what seem to me "must read" titles for anyone wishing to plunge deeper into the subject.

The Minister of Defense

Churchill left a detailed record of his war in his six-volume *The Second World War* (Boston, 1948–1953), each volume of which has its own subtitle. The immense and continuing influence of these memoirs is a commonplace, and there is finally a trenchant scholarly analysis and commentary on them by David Reynolds, *In Command of History: Churchill Fighting and Writing the Second World War* (London, 2004). Churchill's reflection on World War I, the five volumes of *The World Crisis* (New York, 1923–1931), and his four-volume *Marlborough: His Life and Times* (London, 1933–1938) are also indispensable in assessing the views on war and military leadership that Churchill brought to his job in 1940. The books about him are, of course, legion, if of widely varying quality. The official biography covers the years from 1939 to 1945 in two massive volumes: Martin Gilbert, *Winston S. Churchill,* vol. 6, *Finest Hour, 1939–1941* (London, 1983), and vol. 7, *The Road to Victory, 1941–1945* (London, 1986). The "Companion Volumes" of documents that accompanied the first five volumes of the official biography have been continued as the *Churchill War Papers* (New York, 1995–). Three volumes, covering the years 1939 to 1941, have been published so far.

The quantity of information made available by Churchill and by Martin Gilbert dwarfs information and commentary from other sources. As a result, many accounts are still heavily influenced by Churchill's perspective. What is needed now is further analysis of Churchill's role rather than further narrative accounts. This has been done particularly well in two recent studies by Geoffrey Best: *Churchill: A Study in Greatness* (New York, 2001) and *Churchill and War* (New York, 2005). Richard Holmes, a distinguished military historian, has some interesting reflections in *In the Footsteps of Churchill* (New York, 2005). An assessment by Paul Addison, originally written as the entry on Churchill in the *Ox-*

ford Dictionary of National Biography, has now been expanded and separately published as *Churchill: The Unexpected Hero* (Oxford, 2005) and is an excellent introduction.

The Army

Serious scholarly research on the British Army from 1918 to 1945—as opposed to battle and campaign narratives—has only begun to appear over the last several decades. Brian Bond's *Military Policy between the Two World Wars* (Oxford, 1980) and Harold Winton's *To Change an Army: General Sir John Burdett-Stuart and British Armored Doctrine, 1927–1938* (Lawrence, KS, 1988) are excellent introductions to the very real and intractable problems the British Army faced after 1918 in absorbing the lessons of World War I and readying itself for the major European war that, until February 1939, it was officially told it would not have to fight. On the vexed issue of armored doctrine and tank developments, Basil Liddell Hart's polemics have been replaced by more nuanced views; Paul Harris, *Men, Ideas and Tanks: British Military Thought and Armoured Forces, 1903–1939* (Manchester, UK, 1995) is indispensable. Michael Carver's 1979 Lees Knowles lectures, published as *Apostles of Mobility: The Theory and Practice of Armoured Warfare* (London, 1979), is a good commentary. A comparative study by Jonathan House, *Combined Arms Warfare in the Twentieth Century* (Lawrence, KS, 2001), demonstrates that integrating armor and airpower with infantry and artillery posed issues not just for the British but also for every major army. Shelford Bidwell and Dominic Graham, in *Firepower: British Army Weapons and Theories of War, 1904–1945* (London, 1982), are particularly good on the evolution of the Royal Artillery, arguably the premier British arm in both world wars. David French, in *Raising Churchill's Army* (Oxford, 2000), has decisively moved the discussion of British military performance in World War II away from an excessive focus on personalities to the question of institutional capability (although French, like Churchill during the war, ignores the Indian Army). Timothy Harrison Place's *Military Training in the British Army, 1940–1944: From Dunkirk to D-Day* (London, 2000) is a searching examination of a neglected subject that reveals how hard it can be to change those institutional capabilities even under the pressure of national emergency. Although published too late to be used in the writing of this book, David French's *Military Identities: The Regimental System, the British Army, and the British People c. 1870–2000* (Oxford, 2006) will be indispensable to future students of the subject.

In the past, treatises on the desert war against Rommel filled library shelves, whereas the Indian Army's war against Japan was largely neglected. Two excellent monographs have changed that. Daniel Marston's *Phoenix from the Ashes: The Indian Army in the Burma Campaign* (Westport, CT, 2003) and T. R. Moreman's *The Jungle, the Japanese and the British Commonwealth Armies at War, 1941–1945* (London, 2005) together illuminate the transformation of the Indian Army that was one of the war's most remarkable stories. Montgomery has been the subject of a large number of books, many of them quite polemical. Serious analysis of his generalship has, however, been lacking. Stephen Hart's *Montgomery and "Colossal Cracks": The 21st Army Group in Northwest Europe, 1944–45* (Westport, CT, 2000) has at last begun to remedy that. The appearance of the studies mentioned thus far has left only one major British campaign substantially unexplored. Ironically, the Italian campaign, so closely identified with Churchill, has to date not gotten the scrutiny it requires, although Shelford Bidwell and Dominic Graham provide an excellent introduction in *Tug of War: The Battle for Italy, 1943–1945* (London, 1986); in addition, Douglas Porch's *The Path to Victory: The Mediterranean Theater in World War II* (New York, 2004) offers a major restatement of Brooke's argument that the vigorous prosecution of the war in that theater was an essential precondition for Overlord.

The Generals

Although the post-1945 flood of memoirs and autobiographies gives the impression that the topic of British generalship is well covered, personal accounts and biographers' assessments are only the beginning. In fact, there are relatively few accounts whose qualities match those of recent scholarship on British military leadership in World War I. The only study of Ismay is inadequate. Neither Ironside nor Dill has attracted biographers, and in the case of Dill, the materials may be lacking. Brooke was arguably ill served by Arthur Bryant's use of his diaries, which can now be read in full in Alex Danchev and Daniel Todman, eds., *War Diaries, 1939–1945: Field Marshal Lord Alanbrooke* (London, 2001). General Sir David Fraser's *Alanbrooke* (London, 1982) is very useful. J. R. Colville's *Man of Valor: Field Marshal Lord Gort, VC* (London, 1972) is an elegant effort by an eminent Churchillian to rescue Gort from historical oblivion.

The theater commanders have been very unevenly served. Wavell has fared best. John Connell's two-volume official biography, *Wavell: Soldier and Scholar* (London, 1964) and *Wavell: Supreme Commander, 1941–43* (London, 1969), found little to criticize in Wavell and much to complain of in Churchill. (Connell died in 1965, and Brigadier Michael Roberts "completed and edited" the second volume.) Ronald Lewin's *The Chief: Field Marshal Lord Wavell, Commander-in-Chief and Viceroy, 1939–1947* (New York, 1980) is more balanced. Harold Raugh, *Wavell in the Middle East: A Study in Generalship* (New York, 1993), by an American professional soldier, is very well researched but almost uncritically admiring, and by focusing on Wavell's Cairo years, it avoids his much more problematic tenure in Delhi and as ABDA commander. In addition to his work on Wavell, Connell did a biography of Auchinleck—*Auchinleck: A Critical Biography* (London, 1959), which in fact is not very critical. It prints great chunks from Auchinleck's papers but is so heavily focused on the Auk's years in Cairo that his massive contribution as commander-in-chief, India, is scanted. A new study of Auchinleck is badly needed. Correlli Barnett's *The Desert Generals*, originally published in 1960 and revised to include new material on Ultra (London, 1983), is almost certainly the most widely read book on the desert war. Still very useful, it is also strongly partisan and needs tempering by Michael Carver's work, especially *Dilemmas of the Desert War* (London, 1986).

Of course, the most famous of the desert generals was Barnett's bête noire, Montgomery. Despite Nigel Hamilton's massive and deeply admiring three-volume official life, *Monty* (London, 1981–1986), the definitive account of this strange, flawed talent has yet to be written. Until it is, an older account, Ronald Lewin's *Montgomery as Military Commander* (New York, 1971), still retains great value. Monty's onetime boss and Churchill's favorite, Harold Alexander, has been the subject of many assessments, most critical, a few highly laudatory. The official biography, Nigel Nicolson, *Alex: The Life of Field Marshal Earl Alexander of Tunis* (London, 1973), although perhaps the most elegantly written of all World War II British generals' biographies, settled nothing. As with Auchinleck, a new treatment is needed.

A Note on Further Reading

As is clear from the foregoing, most of the generals who interacted closely with Churchill, in addition to leaving memoirs, had official biographers. Reassessment, with access to archives and free of the near-compulsory piety and discretion of official biography, is overdue. One general who played a key role in 1943 and 1944 has completely escaped the historians. Henry Maitland Wilson—apart from his little-read and uninformative memoir, *Eight Years Overseas* (London, 1950)—has vanished as mysteriously as he arose. Another general, definitely not a Churchill favorite but nonetheless crucial to the sort of army Britain fielded, was the progressive and innovative adjutant general, General Sir Ronald Adam, whose tenure has been sympathetically studied by Jeremy Crang in *The British Army and the People's War, 1939–1945* (London, 2000).

The Indian Army's war, although not as heavily studied as that in the European theater, has nonetheless produced some excellent accounts. Slim's *Defeat into Victory* (London, 1956) is in a class by itself. Slim, of course, was the closest thing to a professional writer among Churchill's generals. His official biographer, Ronald Lewin, kept up the high standard in *Slim: The Standard Bearer* (London, 1976). Recently, Robert Lyman's *Slim, Master of War* (London, 2004) has thoughtfully analyzed his generalship.

The man who was Churchill's solution to the problems posed by the Burma campaign, Orde Wingate, continues to generate the attention and controversy that marked his life. Wingate's official biography, Christopher Sykes's *Orde Wingate* (New York, 1959), is very well written; Shelford Bidwell's *The Chindit War* (New York, 1979) is the better analysis. Wingate, like T. E. Lawrence (who also fascinated Churchill), seems likely to go on intriguing writers.

The View from the Sharp End

The prime minister set strategy; the generals conducted operations. But in the end, as Wellington so memorably observed, it came down to the soldier at the "sharp end." Something of the soldiers' view of the war Churchill's generals waged can be caught from the memoirs of participants referenced in the notes, themselves the tip of a very large iceberg. Robert Crisp's *Brazen Chariots* (London, 1959), John Masters's *The Road Past Mandalay* (New York, 1961), Eric Bowlby's *The Recollections of Rifleman Bowlby* (London, 1969), Sydney Jary's *18 Platoon* (Winchester, UK, 1987), and George MacDonald Fraser's *Quartered Safe out Here* (London, 1992) are among the most illuminating (the dates given are those of original publication). There is, however, one very significant gap. There are no Indian voices. The rank-and-file sepoys were, for the most part, not educated to the level where memoir writers are found, and some were illiterate. We therefore have little insight into the minds of the last generation of sepoys to serve the Raj.

Index